THE GULF SOUTH

UNIVERSITY PRESS OF FLORIDA

Florida A&M University, Tallahassee
Florida Atlantic University, Boca Raton
Florida Gulf Coast University, Ft. Myers
Florida International University, Miami
Florida State University, Tallahassee
New College of Florida, Sarasota
University of Central Florida, Orlando
University of Florida, Gainesville
University of North Florida, Jacksonville
University of South Florida, Tampa
University of West Florida, Pensacola

THE
GULF
SOUTH

An Anthology of Environmental Writing

Edited by
Tori Bush and Richard Goodman

Foreword by Bill McKibben

University Press of Florida
Gainesville · Tallahassee · Tampa · Boca Raton
Pensacola · Orlando · Miami · Jacksonville · Ft. Myers · Sarasota

26 25 24 23 22 21   6 5 4 3 2 1

Library of Congress Cataloging-in-Publication Data
Names: Bush, Tori, editor. | Goodman, Richard, 1945– editor. | McKibben,
    Bill, author of foreword.
Title: The Gulf South : an anthology of environmental writing / edited by
    Tori Bush, Richard Goodman ; foreword by Bill McKibben.
Description: Gainesville : University Press of Florida, 2021. | Includes
    bibliographical references and index.
Identifiers: LCCN 2020037904 | ISBN 9780813066790 (hardback)
Subjects: LCSH: Environmentalism—Southern States. | Environmental
    literature—Southern States. | Ecology in literature. | Nature
    conservation—Southern States.
Classification: LCC PS169.E25 G86 2021 | DDC 810.9/975—dc23
LC record available at https://lccn.loc.gov/2020037904

The University Press of Florida is the scholarly publishing agency for the State
University System of Florida, comprising Florida A&M University, Florida Atlantic
University, Florida Gulf Coast University, Florida International University, Florida State
University, New College of Florida, University of Central Florida, University of Florida,
University of North Florida, University of South Florida, and University of West Florida.

University Press of Florida
2046 NE Waldo Road
Suite 2100
Gainesville, FL 32609
http://upress.ufl.edu

CONTENTS

The Gulf South is a place of such sublime beauty—languid days, lush marsh, gators keeping a lazy watch on the wading birds—that you could fill a book with just that humid sweetness. The Gulf South is a place of such deep human drama, including some of the cruelest human oppression and some of its most joyful creativity, that one could make a volume that just commemorated and celebrated and mourned that history.

Or one could cross those books and get this one, an absolutely necessary anthology about the relations between people and the world around them in this blessed and haunted region. This book covers enormous terrain, from John Muir working out his new rhetoric of wildness as a young wanderer to Robert Bullard uncovering the nasty math of environmental racism in the trash dumps of Texas. They are both heroes, and while most readers will know of Muir, it is just as crucial to know about Bullard and other pioneers of environmental justice who have made their stand in this part of the world.

The Gulf South is contested right now like few other places on the planet. The petrochemical industry continues to build out its network of platforms and pipelines and refineries, even as scientists explain that humans simply have to stop pouring carbon into the air. Indeed, the warnings no longer need to come from scientists; a yardstick will do, as anyone who saw Hurricane Harvey set a new American rainfall record in Houston can attest. And yet the political power of the fossil fuel barons is enough to dominate legislatures, warp politics, and force valiant protesters to risk arrest in the forests and bayous.

One real value of history like this is that it equips environmental advocates to work in the present and the future. It allows us to see the blind spots even of past champions, usually around race and class, and to learn how to build movements on new lines. But it also recharges us to know that we're not the first to love and to defend these places, that a lineage proceeds us.

Sometimes I think America has decided to make the Gulf South an environmental sacrifice zone, to pile ever more polluting facilities along Cancer Alley, to run ever greater risks drilling deeper into the waters off the coast. Predictably, the poorest and most vulnerable are the first to be sacrificed, which is why they are often leading the fight against it. But this volume will remind *everyone* why they should be involved in the fight. This is one of the world's most fertile, fecund, buzzing wonderspots, a place like no other. Long may it live!

Bill McKibben

ACKNOWLEDGMENTS

This book could not have been made without the immense support of a number of people and institutions. Our thanks go to John William Nicklow, president of University of New Orleans (UNO); Kim Martin Long, dean of the College of Liberal Arts, Education, and Human Development, UNO; Mahyar A. Amouzegar, provost, UNO; Abram Himelstein, director of UNO Press; Reggie Poché, associate chair of the English Department; and Kendy Martinez, research development administrator at UNO, and her team.

We thank Rebecca Snedecker and Tulane University's Center for the Gulf South for their support through the Monroe Fellowship, without which this book would not exist. Our deep appreciation also goes to Miranda Restovic, Christopher Robert, and the Louisiana Endowment for the Humanities for their support through the Rebirth Grant. We thank the Historic New Orleans Collection, especially Bobby Ticknor, for archival assistance. We would also like to thank Baptist Community Ministries for the original grant that allowed us to begin our research.

More than one hundred writers, scientists, academics, and environmental activists and professionals responded to our original inquiry for recommendations of texts. Without their input, our original bibliography would not have been the diverse, complex collection that it was. We thank them, each and every one.

We are grateful to all the university presses, publishing houses, magazines, newspapers, and agents that allowed us to excerpt the material included here, as detailed in our source notes.

We would also like to thank Racquel Tiara Malone, Joe Kelly, and Donald Miller, graduate students who helped with research along the way.

Special thanks go to Sian Hunter, Mary Puckett, and their team at the University Press of Florida for understanding the importance of this book from the start and guiding it into reality.

We thank our families for listening to discussion about this book over many years. And finally, we greatly appreciate all the residents of the Gulf South whose stories, struggles, and achievements are the inspiration for this collection.

Editors' Introduction

In the summer of 2019, the Mississippi River, the largest river in the United States and the fourth largest in the world, had its highest water levels in modern records.[1] Looking out from the levee, the entire span of the slow-moving brown river stood almost completely level with the low-lying land. The border between land and rushing water was knife thin. The rising water originated from flooding in the Midwest, snow melt in the North, and the rainiest year on record in the United States. The waters reached their peak in the early Louisiana summer, right at the beginning of hurricane season. The river, which has been restrained for more than a century by the works of the Army Corp of Engineers, reminded residents that it is ancient and alive. If the river had risen just a few more feet or if there had been a large storm surge, the river would have drowned towns and cities in a disaster on a scale unseen since the 1927 flood, described in excerpts in this volume from Richard M. Mizelle Jr.'s *Backwater Blues* and John Barry's *Rising Tide*.

The Mississippi River is a primordial example of the ways the Gulf South's natural systems are changing quickly and profoundly. The Gulf of Mexico tidal marshes encompass the largest collection of wetlands in the United States, spanning Texas, Louisiana, Mississippi, Alabama, and Florida, and all are in ecological crisis. The rapid increase of atmospheric carbon, uncontrolled toxic emissions, and industrial development without equal concern for the people and ecology of a place, among other human follies, have led to the present moment in which the waters are high and little room is left for error.

Yet, there is hope. This anthology points to the artists and writers whose work engages the active relations between people and the Gulf South. How do stories about the land influence the way humans interact with it? How have those stories and relations changed over a century? How does language simplify or complicate the vibrant ecologies of the

Gulf? From whose or what perspectives are they told? Are they narratives that embrace an inherent relationship between humans and the Earth, or do they encourage a dominion over it? What impacts do art and literature have on political and social behavior toward the environment? This anthology seeks to rectify a gap in the collective literature and understanding. There has never been an anthology of environmental writing about the Gulf South, a region with a rich history. The question may be asked, Why publish one now?

The Gulf Coast, one could argue, is one of the front lines of climate change in the United States. Pulitzer Prize–winning writer Bob Marshall warns in a 2014 article titled "Losing Ground,"

> Scientists now say one of the greatest environmental and economic disasters in the nation's history is rushing toward a catastrophic conclusion over the next 50 years, so far unabated and largely unnoticed. At the current rates that the sea is rising and land is sinking, National Oceanic and Atmospheric Administration scientists say by 2100 the Gulf of Mexico could rise as much as 4.3 feet across this landscape, which has an average elevation of about 3 feet.

Marshall's words are confirmed through media images of flooding in Texas and ocean rise in Florida. Furthermore, the consequences of such a significant rise in the Gulf of Mexico will be dire for the entire country. More than 15 million people live along the Gulf Coast (Cohen). Many of those residents are vulnerable to potential displacement due to hurricanes or land loss. A third of the country's oil and gas supply comes from the Gulf, and the fishing industry supplies more than 40 percent of US domestic seafood. Finally, the slow loss of the diversity of culture as well as animal and plant populations along the coast would be a massive loss of historic proportions. The Gulf Coast cannot be a sacrifice zone.

This anthology looks at the impacts of climate change through the lens of regional environmental writing. By looking at the regional, one can place it in context with a planet-wide conversation, creating a dialogue that makes the scales between the vast and the small a bit more understandable and interconnected. An event as massive as climate change can be paralyzing: What can be done in the face of such enormity? Breaking down the impacts of climate change through a smaller lens can find the human-scale stories. Mike Tidwell's *Bayou Farewell* is an example; he takes an issue of mammoth proportions, the loss of the Louisiana coastline, and tells the story through people who live on the coast. Through this narrative, we can easily see the implications for the future, although how we choose to confront and address the situation is still up to us as readers, voters, and residents.

Climate change is a global fight, but the impacts on local environmental systems manifest in vastly different ways. Even within the Gulf Coast, the opportunities and issues of the Mississippi coast are notably different than those on the Texas coast. Natasha Trethewey's observation of the denuding of mangroves along the Mississippi coast tells a different story of coastal erosion than Roger Emile Stouff's contemplation of the crisscrossing oil pipelines that funnel saltwater into the wetlands around his home in Louisiana. Yet by uniting the various impacts climate change has on this region, we can gain allies and colleagues in the fight.

An important undercurrent in this anthology is that we consider the Gulf South a postcolonial space where environmental history entwines with the history of colonization. From the arrival of Spanish conquistador Juan Ponce de León in Florida in 1513, the project of colonization was predicated on the exploitation of natural resources and domination of people. Kathryn Yusoff writes, "In its brief tenure, the Anthropocene has . . . failed to do the work to properly identify its own histories of colonial earth-writing, to name the masters of broken earths, and to redress the legacy of racialized subjects that geology leaves in its wake. It has failed to grapple with the inheritance of violent dispossession of indigenous land under the auspices of a colonial geo-logic" (1). We have tried in this anthology to address the entangled nature of the environment and colonial history. Joy Harjo's poem "New Orleans" points to the ways the expansion of the United States allowed settlers to claim resources while American Indians were pushed to the edges of the swamps or forced to reservations.

An important question to consider is who has been the benefactor of the harvesting of natural resources in the Gulf South and who has not. Postcolonial scholar Dipesh Chakrabarty, referring to the Anthropocene, asks, "Who is the we in this process?" For many, violent and catastrophic ruptures to social and ecological systems have been deeply entangled. Zora Neale Hurston, in *Their Eyes Were Watching God*, reveals that environmental disaster and the disaster of Jim Crow–era policies are equally fatal. Taking our inspiration from the scholar Elizabeth DeLoughrey's definition, climate change "refers to a world-changing rupture in a social and ecological system that might be read as colonization in one context or sea-level rise in another" (7).

This collection is centered on the coastal communities of the Gulf Coast not because it is the only region affected by the changing environment but because the impacts are so clear. And this is *an* anthology of environmental writing from the Gulf South, not *the* anthology. For example, the selections focus mostly on the coastal zones, though the interior of the Gulf South is deeply implicated in this crisis as well. In order to narrow our selections, we needed to limit the focus. Though this anthology is defined by the human-made borders of Texas, Louisiana, Mississippi, Alabama, and Florida, the Gulf is not a place contained by national boundaries. The Gulf of Mexico is a system much older and grander than our national history, a scant two centuries compared to the 150 million years since its formation. Marjory Stoneman Douglas once wrote, "The men who make maps draw lines across seas and deserts and mountains and equatorial rain forests . . . but the sea and the land and the winds do not always recognize that rigidity" (15). We hope this collection considers literature not through the lens of rigid borders but through the language of the place itself.

In 2000, Nobel Prize–winner Paul Crutzen, along with a group of geologists, put forward the argument that the planet has entered into a new period. The Holocene had ended and the new Anthropocene era had begun, although the specific date and name of this period is still hotly debated. This new era is defined by how many geologically significant conditions and ecological processes have been and continue to be profoundly transformed by human activities. We are now living in the first geological era in the history of the Earth when members of a species—humans—have significantly affected ecological systems in a potentially irreparable manner. Human activities have altered ocean temperatures, changed the density of glacial ice on the planet's poles, increased carbon in the atmosphere to a level never before seen, and left a layer of plutonium within the Earth's stratosphere from nuclear testing. The ability to irrevocably alter geophysical systems has exponentially increased over the past few hundred years.

Though Svante Arrhenius made the first calculations of how burning fossil fuels changes global temperatures in 1896, much of human consciousness about climate change and global warming has developed only in the past few decades. Similarly, cultural works such as the poems and prose only began to directly grapple with climate change in recent decades. The first text in this anthology to use the term "climate change" is Mike Tidwell's 2007 book, *Bayou Farewell*. However, we included E. L. Corthell's 1897 article "The Delta of the Mississippi River" to point to the ways writers in the nineteenth century were already observing sea rise, an effect of climate change. Though writers did not have the language of climate change then, they were writing and speaking about the significant changes happening in the Gulf South in other ways, using language that described the environment and humans' relation to it.

The twentieth century has been called "the environmental century" because of a panoply of important writers, activists, scientists, and policy makers who have worked to question and consider the legacy of dominion over the Earth rather than living with it. Some of those early figures of the environmental movement are included here; John Muir, Marjory Stoneman Douglas, and John Bullard are three. They make it apparent that early on, many people in environmental movements were working, traveling, and living in or writing about the Gulf South, complicating a narrative that the South is a place with little environmental history of activism.

Here, it is important to note that this book is not a collection of texts about climate change, though almost all of the selections grapple with it specifically or tangentially. Our mission for this book is more nuanced: to explore the changing culture between humans and the Gulf South environment through the lens of narrative. Rereading these texts through a contemporary lens reveals patterns of significant cultural transformations. Many may not have used the rhetoric of climate change, but writers have been sensitive to the changing ecology of the Gulf for well over a century.

Each one of the selected texts, be it prose, poetry, or graphic story, reveals a distinct environmental history, perspective, or language for and about the Gulf South. Forty-six works speak a common language, though that language is not necessarily English, Spanish, Vietnamese, or Choctaw. Instead, they speak the shared language of a relation to place, a lexicon of style and specific words to shape the reader's sense of the region. From Jesmyn Ward's red dirt pit to Moira Crone's sunken city, each of these works builds a language specific to the natural world of the Gulf South. The result is a collection of texts that constantly questions the boundaries of what it is to live with and in the Gulf South, revealing conscious and subconscious cultural perspectives on the environment as well as the changing place itself.

Another important point to note is that the Gulf South is not one place, but a complex collection of people, cultures, natural systems, and histories. Though we frame it as a region, it is more like an amalgamation of places with distinct personalities and relations to the Gulf.

Some of the writers in this anthology are not as well known, though they deserve to be. We hope this book will rectify that. We have also tried our best to represent writers of different points of view. This hasn't always been simple, because fifty or one hundred years ago it was much easier for a white male writer to have works published than for an African American woman. But we have made rectifying this situation one of our most pressing goals.

In putting together this collection of texts, we interviewed more than sixty environmental scholars, journalists, scientists, and organizers. We asked their recommendations on what writing has moved and inspired their thinking about the Gulf South. We collected more than three hundred suggestions, read them, and selected a first round of texts with the aim of encompassing multiple genres and areas of environmental impact, diversity of authors, and span of times. Our selections should be approached as a collective in which each text informs each other, sometimes in complex and contradictory ways. The final selections included here are in no way comprehensive, yet we hope they begin to show the complexity of perspectives that interact and engage the environment.

We have suggested a few possible ways to approach this book. The first is chronological. Our hope is that readers will thus be able to track the changing relations to and rhetoric about the environment of the Gulf South. We have also included an alternate table of contents that frames the collection by themes linking diverse voices. The petrochemical industry is one of these themes; ocean rise is another. We've also arranged them by region. The problem inherent with dividing texts is that often one theme deeply involves another. For example, the slicing up of the Louisiana coastline to put in oil pipelines has been a significant contributor to ocean rise, and ocean rise has in turn affected the future of all industries in southern Louisiana. These themes are not meant to be divided, but to messily interact with and inform each other.

This anthology is a collection of "environmental writing," a term that has evolved rapidly since the 2000s. Environmental writing, once a subgenre of science or nature writing, has transcended genre and become a mode in which writers and readers respond to the era's environmental, social, and cultural crises. When Richard Powers's novel *The Overstory*, with its narrative centered around trees and their destruction, won the Pulitzer Prize in 2018, the honor confirmed that climate fiction has become a contemporary literary force. Newspapers such as the *New York Times* and the *Guardian* have developed environmental writing teams to report deeply and broadly on climate stories. The Association for the Study of Literature of the Environment doubled its conference attendance in a decade after 2009, a sign of the growing concern about climate change in the humanities. Adam Trexler has suggested that the "concept of the Anthropocene helps explain the widespread phenomenon of climate change fiction" (9). We would add that this phenomenon is not limited to specific genres; rather, it encompasses many genres and approaches. Environmental writing creates new knowledge in historicizing humans' relations to the environment and perhaps challenging notions of what *isn't* environmental literature in the era of climate change. Environmental writing has become and will continue to be for the foreseeable future an essential means to explain, lament, deconstruct, and reconstruct humans' interactions with the natural world.

Environmental writing as a literary category is a recent development. Though people have been writing about the natural environment since early history—the First Nation story Turtle Island and Noah's Ark could both be considered environmental literature—the past century has seen definitive cultural works produced that reflect the ways deforestation, urban development, toxic waste, and fossil fuels threaten the world. In order to tease out the characteristics of environmental writing here, we place it alongside a close cousin, nature writing.

Nature writing has a long tradition in the American canon, with Henry David Thoreau, Annie Dillard, and Susan Fenimore Cooper among its pillars. While some nature writing is often classified as environmental writing and vice versa, there is a significant difference between the two. Nature writing meditates on the Earth, on its beauty, its power. It is often reflective of humans, yes, but nature writing does not necessarily depend on science, politics, or cultural contexts; environmental writing does. In Bill McKibben's introduction to the anthology *American Earth,* he states, "From the beginning American writing has concerned itself with the story of people and the natural world. But 'environmental writing' is different from these [texts]. It takes as its subject the collision between people and the rest of the world and asks searching questions about that collision: Is it necessary? What are its effects? Might there be a better way?" (xxii). Much environmental writing has scientific, cultural, and political contexts as its foundations and an accessible voice meant for any reader. When a writer's singular vision and mastery of craft combine with strong science and other critical sociological elements, the best environmental writing emerges. That writing never places style above content. It places both at the same importance. Writers included in this collection like John McPhee, Edward O. Wilson, Eddy Harris, Arlie Hochschild, John Barry, and Cynthia Barnett have the rare ability to convey the most complex issues that require a deep understanding of science, history, and cultural context in a graceful, accessible manner.

One of the hallmarks of environmental writing is that the writer seeks not only to inform the reader and impress the reader with nature's beauty but to rouse the reader. It might be difficult to imagine an anthology of nature writing including a long essay about the oil companies' responsibility for Louisiana land loss. But you'd have no problem imagining that piece and others like it in an anthology of environmental writing. Put another way, environmental writing might focus on a sick or wounded planet, while nature writing most often centers around a brilliant, beautiful Earth at its most breathtaking. Nature writing often calls for a poet. Environmental writing often calls for a doctor.

Marjory Stoneman Douglas and Robert Bullard are two of the writers in this anthology whose work fundamentally changed the way people interact with the environment. Without Bullard, the environmental justice would not have had the in-depth data and community focus that has defined the movement. And Douglas's 1947 *The Everglades: River of Grass* sounded the alarm on the loss of the wetlands in Florida and helped preserve it as a national park. That is an impressive aspect of environmental writing; it is a form that has inspired action.

There is something else that distinguishes nature writing from environmental writing, though there are exceptions to this "something else," and sometimes glaring ones. That difference is pronounal. We would associate the pronoun "I" with nature writing, while we would associate the pronoun "we" (as complicated as any "we" might be) with environmental writing. Nature writing is often about the individual writer's encounter with nature and his or her reactions, often lyrical, to that encounter. Environmental writing has a collective sense to it. Indeed, it is much easier to think of movements, of people joining together to effect change, emanating more from an environmental writer's words than from a nature writer's words. The nature writer has a reverence for Earth, to be sure, but many of these texts are solitary. They often seem not to want to be with other people but to be by themselves on the ice, on the water, in the forest, on the trail, in the canyon, on top of the mountain. While the nature writer stands in solitary awe of a sunset, the environmental writer wants the reader to join him or her, to look at that sunset together, and to make sure there are others to be seen by their children and grandchildren. Of course, writers cannot be absolutely divided by style. The John Muir text included in the anthology, *A Thousand-Mile Walk to the Gulf,* has all the qualities of nature writing but is written by the founder of the Sierra Club. These distinguishing characteristics tend to be suggestive rather than definitive, and often the line between styles is quite porous.

Another close friend of environmental writing is ecocriticism. With a growing consciousness of the impact of human technology on the Earth, so too have writers of theoretical texts attempted to understand those impacts. In 1972, Joseph W. Meeker introduced the idea of "literary ecology" to the world and defined it as "the study of biological themes and relationships which appear in literary works" (9). William Rueckert coined the more common term "ecocriticism" in 1978; he defined it as the application of ecology and ecological concepts to the study of literature (107). In her introduction to the landmark 1996 book *The Ecocriticism Reader,* coeditor Cheryll Glotfelty writes, "All ecological criticism shares the fundamental premise that human culture is connected to the physical world, affecting it and affected by it. Ecocriticism takes as its subject the interconnections between nature and culture, specifically the cultural artifacts of language and literature" (xix). Glotfelty's frame is much akin to our own approach to environmental writing. Yet, while ecocriticism shares many qualities with environmental writing, there are distinctions. Ecocriticism tends to focus on the study of literature and the environment, and environmental writing focuses on narrative stories of humans in the environment. One tends to be academic in aim, the other aiming toward art. These differences are not meant as boundaries, as many texts fall firmly into both categories. Their distinction is simply meant to begin to parse out the complex, multidisciplinary ways of thinking within this expansive form. We have included a suggested reading list in the back of this book to help readers further explore these forms and themes in books outside of the Gulf South.

We began this project by looking for thoughtful, incisive writing by people from across the span of more than one hundred years who could tell stories that throw a sharp light on the changing ecology of the Gulf Coast. We hope this anthology will point to the ways writers and storytellers have constructed narratives, created language, and shared ideas about the shifting and sometimes indistinguishable boundaries between land

and sea. Great writing can shift our conceptions of the world. Stories build new realities. We hope these voices will help construct the few new realities that are desperately needed.

A Note Regarding Formatting

All texts have been reprinted in their original form, including alternate spellings and nonstandard formatting. The authors' notes are reprinted as they appear in the original texts; hence there may be some style variations in the essays' endnotes.

Works Sourced

Chakrabarty, Dipesh. "Postcolonial Studies and the Challenge of Climate Change." *New Literary History*, vol. 43, no. 1, 2012, pp. 1–18.

Cohen, Darryl T. "60 Million Live in the Path of Hurricanes." US Census Bureau, Population Division, Aug. 2018, https://www.census.gov/library/stories/2018/08/coastal-county-population-rises.html.

DeLoughrey, Elizabeth M. "The Myth of Isolates: Ecosystem Ecologies in the Nuclear Pacific." *Cultural Geographies*, vol. 20, no. 2, 2013, pp. 167–184.

Douglas, Marjory Stoneman. *The Everglades: River of Grass*. Rowman & Littlefield Publishing, 1997.

Glotfelty, Cheryll. "Introduction: Literary Studies in an Age of Environmental Crisis." *The Ecocriticism Reader: Landmarks in Literary Ecology*, edited by Cheryll Glotfelty and Harold Fromm, U of Georgia P, 1996, pp. xv–xxxvii.

Marshall, Bob, Brian Jacobs, and Al Shaw. "Losing Ground." *The Lens, ProPublica*, Aug. 28, 2014, https://projects.propublica.org/louisiana/.

McKibben, Bill. Introduction. *American Earth: Environmental Writing since Thoreau*, edited by McKibben, Literary Classics of the United States, 2008, pp. xxi–xxxi.

Meeker, Joseph. *The Comedy of Survival: Studies in Literary Ecology*. Charles Scribner & Sons, 1972.

Rueckert, William. "Literature and Ecology: An Experiment in Ecocriticism." *The Ecocriticism Reader: Landmarks in Literary Ecology*, edited by Cheryll Glotfelty and Harold Fromm, U of Georgia P, 1996, pp. 105–123.

Trexler, Adam. *Anthropocene Fictions: The Novel in the Time of Climate Change*. U of Virginia P, 2015.

Yusoff, Kathryn. *A Billion Black Anthropocenes or None*. U of Minnesota P, 2018.1.
Though the river's water levels have been recorded occasionally since the sixteenth century, high-water levels have been consistently recorded only since the Mississippi River Commission was established by Congress in 1879 (United States, 46th Congress, House, Session 1, Ch. 42, 43, June 28, 1879).

CATHERINE COLE

"Last Island"

New Orleans Daily Picayune (1888)

Catherine Cole was the pen name for Martha R. Field (1855–1898), who was the first full-time female journalist for the *New Orleans Daily Picayune*. She was a daily staff reporter and wrote a travel column that chronicled her trips criss-crossing rural Louisiana by carriage, boat, and foot. An intrepid traveler who was unafraid of choppy seas or a ten-mile walk to the next town, Cole was able to experience the environmental changes occurring as populations grew and communities carved out new ways of living throughout Louisiana.

In this selection from 1888, Cole visits the remains of Last Island (also featured in Lafcadio Hearn's *Chita* in this anthology), where the Last Island hurricane of 1856 washed away much of the island, killing approximately two hundred people. In the excerpt, nature and humans are fiercely entangled. A hundred-pound fish jumps into a canoe during a storm, and its neck breaks; a crew-member, Charlie, shoots and kills prairie chickens for lunch; a shark bites a swimmer. Though we see the Gulf Coast here teeming with life, it is also rife with death. The environment has not yet been subdued by the energy industry, nor has it begun to subside because of human control of the Mississippi River. In presenting this piece, we hope the reader can see what has already been lost in the twentieth century—Last Island no longer exists. It is now several very small islands populated mostly by pelicans.

Cole's writing offers clues to the ways women and the environment interacted at the end of the nineteenth century. Here she writes colorfully about the captain's daughter, who sails, fishes, hunts, and "can also skin, dress and prepare for shipping no less than forty birds an hour." Cole's observations about Louisiana life complicate the way women in southern history might be remembered as either stuck in the house or working the land. Cole muddies traditional gender roles throughout her adventures along the Gulf Coast.

Joan B. McLaughlin and Jack McLaughlin's book *Louisiana Voyages: The Travel Writings of Catherine Cole* would be an excellent book for anyone interested in reading more of Cole's journalism.

Work Sourced

McLaughlin, Joan B., and Jack McLaughlin. *Louisiana Voyages: The Travel Writings of Catherine Cole*, University of Mississippi Press, 2006.

"For a person to travel around and have a good time in this particular part of our state," observed a hospitable lighthouse keeper with whom I was dining the other day, "he or she must be more or less amphibious. I calculate that you are somewhat amphibious, are you not?" he questioned.

I looked down at my sun and sea-blistered wrists, at a gingham gown stiff with repeated duckings in brine and bayou, at the battered wreck of a once-beribboned palmetto woven by the deft fingers of some dark-eyed island beauty. I looked out at the lighthouse boat by which my host had just arrived on furlough, at the family lugger and the less conventional pirogue, at our own canoe—all hitched up to the front gate—out through the gaps in the rushes at the unrumpled expanse of water where our schooner was lying becalmed. I looked on all this, I say, and I felt free to admit that I was "more or less amphibious."

To have a good time in Louisiana there is no better way than for an amphibiously-inclined person to take a sloop, a catboat, a lugger or a schooner and voyage among the wonderful, desolate, but picturesque islands that fret our Gulf Coast. He will get amongst people whose total belongings are a roof-over-head of palmettos, a cast net, a pirogue, an iron pot, and an accordion. He will see grizzled old men—a hundred years old, maybe—come out of their huts in the morning barefooted, get into their pirogues and paddle away to throw a cast net and fish up a breakfast.

He will see youngsters, not able to talk plain, doing the same thing. He will hear legends of storms, and stories of sea ghosts, and of a horrid devil fish that haunts the Gulf and sometimes drags a schooner or a lugger away, away out to sea, and then down, down to the bottom of the ocean.

Once a lighthouse-keeper was on his way to Timbalier in his catboat. He was seen crossing Vine Island Pass—and never again. Perhaps a storm came up and drove him out to sea, but there are those who shrug their shoulders at this and say: "Yes, a squall indeed! Very likely! He was caught on the horns of the devil fish more likely."

Inhabitants on these islands are truly few and far between, but mosquitoes are plenty, and here the pelican and gulls are to be found, and the redfish leap in the sea, and schools of giant shrimp crumple the surface of the waters, and sharks are sometimes to be caught, with hooks half a yard long, fastened on iron chains—so that to cruise among these islands is very good sport indeed during these summer months before the islanders begin to live in fear and trembling of the storms.

The fashionable hotel, the latest cut in bathing suits, the six o'clock dinner and the Saturday night hop are all very well in their way, but to my mind they do not compare to the pleasure of the surf dashing furiously over these gray and bleak shores, to a tremendous squall with no shelter nigh, to the mad tug with which a fourteen-pound redfish runs away with one's line, to a night's sleep under the stars on a schooner's deck, to the morning surf bath and the breakfast of fried trout and salt meat and coffee by a camp fire, or on the schooner's hatch—to say nothing of the cheapness of such an outing.

A lugger that will accommodate six or eight can be hired with the services of a trusty sailor and a captain, who is a famous cook as well, for two dollars a day, and to this must only be added the expenses of provisioning the boat.

Some twelve mornings ago, when the sun was yet low in the blue and the dew still beaded on the roses, I went across the streets of the little seaport town of Morgan City to a rotting wharf at the further end of the town, where the *Julia*, a schooner that I had hired for a trip to the islands, was ready for sailing. She was a beautifully-shaped, dingy-green vessel, with gently curving breasts, floating on the water like a pelican. Her sails were tied up, a tent covered her deck, and under it were all the crew assembled waiting for me, and eyeing me reproachfully as a person who did not mind keeping a boat waiting two long hours beyond the appointed sailing hour.

Through the thoughtful courtesy of Mr. Kock of the Morgan Road, the tugboat *Cricket* was to take us to the mouth of the river and in a few moments we were lashed to her side and were on our way.

The *Julia* certainly looked provisioned for a cruise. Tubs of vegetables, piles of lemons, coops of chickens, a little green hillock of melons, and groceries stood about among the anchors, chains, ropes and piles of spare sails. It was a comforting-looking disorder, but the captain's wife and daughter were gradually getting things to rights so that by the time the *Cricket* gave us a farewell salute and her clever and entertaining Captain Smith, a hero in many sea adventures, had waved us goodbye we presented quite a ship-shape appearance, and the crew, with all sails set, had settled down to the peacefuller occupations of sorting fishing lines, mending casting nets, cleaning guns and getting dinners.

Captain Siegfried and his family live on board the schooner and during the fall and winter hunt birds, coasting among the islands for gulls, terns and pigeons, which they skin, stuff, pack in paper cornucopias and ship to France by the thousand. Last year, they shipped 5,000 birds. Miss Lena, the brave young daughter of Captain Siegfried, who can sail the *Julia*, pull a canoe, kill a shark, land a mammoth redfish, skin an otter, and kill a laughing gull on the wing, can also skin, dress and prepare for shipping no less than forty birds an hour.

It was an almost perfect day. The wide river on which not a rippled wave beat shoreward, was like a shield of quicksilver. The canopied oaks and cypress trees looked up at us from this strange mirror and out at us from the banks where a jungle of lush marsh grasses, yellow reeds and spiked fans of green palmetto grew about their roots. The sky, pale blue almost to whiteness, held not a cloud, but glittered like burnished metal, and to gaze up into it made the eyes sting and blurred and blinded one's vision.

In an hour there were no more oak trees to be seen—only here and there a straggling willow and broad, bronze-yellow and coppery reaches of marsh reeds with amber crests of feathery bloom like myriads of butterflies poised for flight. The land had dribbled down into the desolation of the salines, and already here at the mouth of the Atchafalaya we were nearing the haunts of the pelican and the blue crane and the grosbeak.

At our left was Deer Island, an irregular shape of sea marsh, with the twisted skeletons of dead oaks rising here and there, curiously like the huge antlers of deer. Within the memory of the oldest sailors these dead trees have stood on Deer Island; from their resemblance to antlers probably giving the island its name, although it is said that hereabout deer, as well as wildcat, abound.

Down in the cabin, where clothing, provisions, cooking utensils, shooting things, etc. were stored, and where the cooking-stove was, the heat was something terrific. The wind that filled our sails was hot and came in puffs. Dinner, that had been served on the hatch, was over, and we sat around, like fish out of water, gasping for breath. The sun seemed to have melted all over the heavens. Charlie, patient, brave, skillful now as he was on that first dry day of our voyage, said the sun made him grin. It was true. It shone so fiercely out of that white, molten silver sky that we all "grinned" under its glare.

We were in Four League Bay, and off in all directions a horizon was made of ragged fringes of brush, and sage-like bushes that in this luminous

atmosphere upreared like giant trees. Down in the cabin the thermom-
eter stood at 120 degrees Fahrenheit; on deck it was 105 degrees. Now and
then, the glistening sky seemed to crack and we had a flashview, too quick
for eyesight, almost too swift for thought, of some vivider brightness that
was frightful.

"What is it!" I asked Charlie, getting under the small canopy rigged over
the steersman.

"Sunshine lightning," said Charlie, and just then, off in the distance,
the low growl of thunder began. The luminous atmosphere in a moment
turned yellow—the greenish yellow of sulphur—the bay was like an olive green ink, thick, muddy, and as the sky turned from yellow to green
and from bluish black to violet, the lightning could be seen not in one
place, but everywhere. It came like harpoons of fire cast at a whale; it was
thrown, here, there, everywhere about the boat like the broken spears of
maddened warriors.

There were still no clouds, only this violet dome pressing down on us
and deepening in color every moment. Then the rain began, not as it rains
on shore, but as it rains only at sea, a white wall of water falling solidly,
shutting out the rest of the world, and so thick that from where I sat the
jib was scarcely visible. The captain, unable to see his way and fearful of
being stuck until next tide on an oyster reef, hauled the boat round and let
go an anchor.

We all huddled down in the cabin, leaving the steps in and the door
open, watching the terrific sky and the white sheets of rain. Suddenly an
enormous fish sprung far into the air and landed plump in our canoe, tied
alongside the schooner. It was a hundred pound silver fish, and in no time
at all, and before Charlie could run at the canoe with an ax, it had broken
loose the nailed seats, sent oars adrift, and filled the canoe with its own
blood.

"He's broken his neck," Charlie cried above the roar of the rain and between the poundings of the thunder, and then he climbed into the schooner again and prepared to go after the oars that were already out of sight.

"Wait a bit," said his father, and Charlie sat down, dripping, on the
cabin bench.

"It's the worst storm," bellowed the captain looking out at the emblazoned sky now written all over with the terrific autograph, but he never
finished the sentence, for there came into the cabin, seeming for a moment to cut the boat into a hundred parts, such a splendid, frightful flash
as cannot be described. It cut here and there. There was a tangle of its

fierce spearheads among the guns in their racks, and quick as the lightning, I knew we had been struck by it.

The electric shock threw Captain Siegfried on his knees, took me in the back of the head and the others also in the head and face. Momentarily, and while the crashing noise still boomed in the cabin, we were stunned and then half dazed and wholly alarmed. We sat up and began looking about, expecting to find the *Julia* a total wreck. No serious damage was done however, and with that fierce attack the backbone of the storm was broken, the lightning retired like a growling lion, and in another half hour the pale whitish blue sky, with a tender, repentant rain-drenched face, shone down upon us, and Captain Siegfried was beating about in his pirogue far astern, looking with German thrift and patience for the lost oars.

The exit from Four League Bay is through Oyster Bayou, a winding uncertain oyster-reefed lane of salt water where sea-cat and sharks and the big silver fish abound. It is only two miles long but a lugger has been known to take twenty-four hours or more in getting through it. On either side are sea marshes, a rotting, porous, fiddler-eaten crust of half earth, half sand, sown thick with a rank, coarse growth of sea rushes sharp enough to stab a murderer to the heart if daggers are scarce, hollow enough to serve a peaceable Isaac Walton with a pipe stem.

Deer are sometimes seen in these marshlands and wildcat often enough. As we drifted out, the wind, having failed almost entirely, one of these deer, a gaunt thing with mad eyes, peered out at us from the rushes and then crashed away, rustling through the brakes. Something dark blue and plumy swung overhead and dropped down in the rushes.

"It is a blue crane," Lena said.

"Where?" asked I, my untrained eyes failing to locate the bird.

"There," said the young huntress, "just beyond the grave."

The sky was darkling over for night; already silvery mists were rising out of the marshes—mists of malaria and mosquitoes and myriads of gnats and other small winged insects of the night. With only those treacherous marshes in sight, and the salt waters of the Gulf, to have Lena pointing a long forefinger at a blue crane hovering over some dead man's grave was not pleasant.

Just above the feathered tip of the rushes that grew highest near the bank, I could make out in the somber evening light a weather-beaten cross. A dead man's body had been found floating here years ago, and some fishermen had buried him in the marsh, and put a notched stick to mark his grave. It was low tide, and the black-teethed, jagged combs of the oyster reefs showed above the wimple of the bayou, or we could see a brown stretch of sand and mud that the tide had sucked dry. Some slender birds, with soft brown or gray plumage, were picking about on these sand flats, and Charlie, promising us prairie chickens for supper, took his gun and crept off in his pirogue after them.

Half a dozen times his gun was fired and the pretty things dropped one after the other. One, wounded, ran fleetly with broken, trailing wings off far into the marsh, and when our boy hunter came back and slung his three brace of birds upon the schooner's deck he only said he would "rather have not shot any than to know that one of them pretty little things was bleeding to death out there in the salt mud and a-makin' no cry."

These harvesters of the sea, what strange fruits they bring home! Charlie and his pirogue never failed us in surprises, and on this first hunting venture of his, as well as prairie chickens, tender and delicious, he tossed on board a big brown flounder, knocked in the head with a paddle, and enough salt, fine, fat oysters to make that famous mess so dear to epicures: macaroni, tomatoes, red peppers, and oysters.

The stars were out when supper was set forth on the roof of the cabin— a meal of boiled flounder and prairie chickens, tea and a crusty loaf, and as if to hearten us up still further a lusty wind came zooming up and we went flying through the crackling waves, all sail set, and Aleck up in the anchor chains making the dewless, salty July night sweet with the music of "Annie Laurie," played with many a flourish on the *Julia's* best accordion.

It was ten o'clock at night. The *Julia* flew through the waters, the spray drenching the musician tangled up in the anchor chains, when a flash of light showed off far across our bows.

"Ship Shoal light," said the captain from the tiller, the lonesomest, most man-and-God-forsaken place on the coast, twelve miles from any land, and the nearest land is that sand island with the curse upon it, that place of the great storm—Last Island. The jib came rattling down like a white sheet of rain, the topsail fell like a white pigeon wounded to the deck, the anchor chain jingled and clinked, and the *Julia* gave a lurch forward and then rode peacefully at anchor off the east shore of that fated Last Island, whose horrors are not romance to the people of the Teche country.

Here in this particular part of the state you may perhaps meet one with sad, frightened eyes, that if a storm be brewing will glare and flash like those of a wounded animal brought to bay. You may not ask with half careless, conventional courtesy if this one is afraid of storms, for someone will pluck you by the sleeve and say, "Hush, she was saved from Last Island," and here you may meet many a person of whom you will be told, "You see that one there? Well, all his family—his father, mother, all—were lost at Last Island."

At Tigerville, I think, there lives, or did live, the man who was saved by a billiard table. It floated in with this man and a Colored woman upon it, and during that terrific voyage (the storm, I am told, culminated in the daytime, not at night) the woman gave birth to a child. But these are old stories—the classics of St. Mary parish—the legends familiar to you as to the child at your knee.

That night, as we rode at anchor I lifted the flap of the tent—for we all, captain and crew and bos'n too, slept on deck on feather beds, our cheese-cloth mosquito bar rigged up on poles and ropes—and looked out at the mysterious island. A long, narrow, level stretch of sandy soil, barely rising above the sea, with only brush and bushes and rank rushes growing on it, or here and there at the edge of Village Bayou a stunted willow tree or two, with a projecting beach or shelving sand like a long underlip.

Last Island might almost, in the midnight gloom, be mistaken for the back of some dreamed of devil fish, or some fin of a giant, stealthy shark, or even what it is—the island of the curse of God—where flowers bloom not, where no clean nor honest life is, and where even the bird hunters camp with fear and trembling, because of the ghosts of those who were drowned here during the storm of '56.

Later storms have cut the island into two parts, and no one lives here save the black inhabitants of two miserable huts made of wreckage and built up in the air—like cranes standing on long legs in the rushes. There are some cattle on the island, wild, wide-horned, scraggy little beasts, fleet of foot and fierce of blood, and there are sheep—white, woolly beauties.

The Last Islanders have a dreadful name. One, it is said, stole his sheep stock from the mainland by the lugger load. We saw one of the men—a big, black-faced, black-bearded man of the sea, with shoulders like those of a huge dolphin, and a dull face. He sat low down in his lugger, well in the shadow of its bright, red sail. Presently he lifted a conch and blew three signals—three telegraphic notes of minor-toned mournful music.

Afar off from the rushes or from the waves or from the desolated sand flats of the beach, with its moving surface of black and yellow fiddlers, there came bleating back a mournful answer. Apparently it satisfied the black man in the lugger, for he turned his red sail, like a sea warrior's shield with dry blood on it, and away the small craft bounded seaward.

Like the snout of a swordfish the east end of Last Island, a long wedge or knife of yellow sand, runs out a quarter of a mile into the sea. There are no rushes here, only sand and hundreds of birds—nay, thousands have their nests here. As we came ashore and walked along, the yellow fiddlers swept away before us like a receding wave of the sea. One could not put feet down without crushing these helpless, silent, harmless little bodies moving like soldiers in retreat.

Overhead the sky was darkened by the birds—laughing gulls, terns, and pigeons. They screamed at us, the breath of their wings beat down on us, the long, scarlet scissors of their fierce beaks were close to us, their shrill cries split in our ears. Over on the sands just beyond high tide were the eggs of these birds—four together and so thick that one might have gathered a dozen barrels of them. The eggs were just hatching and one had to step carefully and look keenly to keep from crushing the sand-colored young, so closely do they resemble the sand that at a distance of three yards a young tern or gull will be invisible. The wind blew saltily off the green Gulf, the surf tumbled in superbly. The surf bathing at Last Island is said to be the finest on the continent, and before we knew what we were about, our entire crew had joined hands and we were facing and awaiting a mighty wave that came frothing and curling at us, beating us down into the sand and leveling us for the moment like so much flotsam on the shore.

During storms the waves will wash over Last Island, and few would venture to stop there without a trusty boat near at hand. There are other islands just as dreadful and desolate and insecure, but none with the curse of God on it as this one has. Only the fierce-winged gulls, the half-wild cattle feeding on salty rushes, and the half-wild inhabitants of the two little perches up in the center of the island may be said to live here.

But the redfish come in close to shore—and the man-eating sharks as well. Not long since one tore a pound of flesh from the side of a swimmer. The shore is crusted with beautiful shells—some pink as the sunset, some with shallows like silver, some like the scaly moons on the silver fish, and others brown, horny hulks crawling about with now and then a hairy claw protruding so that the beach seemed alive.

LAFCADIO HEARN

Chita: A Memory of Last Island (1889)

Lafcadio Hearn (1850–1904) was born on the Greek island of Lefkada, but due to a tumultuous family life, he lived as a child in Ireland, France, and England. Perhaps because of his island birth, he would spend the rest of his life roaming and writing about islands across the world. Hearn moved to the United States in 1869 and eventually began writing for newspapers in Cincinnati. In 1877 he moved to New Orleans, where he lived for ten years writing and editing for various newspapers. During this time, regional travel writing was at the height of popularity. Ambitious writers realized that they could make a profitable living visiting unusual places and writing about them. New Orleans provided a multicultural jumping-off point for many of Hearn's travel pieces. He began writing articles and profiles for *Harper's Weekly* in addition to books and articles about New Orleans and its culture and cuisine, especially its Creole influences.

Hearn's first novel, *Chita: A Memory of Last Island,* from which this excerpt comes, was published in 1889, the year after Catherine Cole's newspaper article about the island. *Chita* is a story of the devastating 1856 hurricane in southeastern Louisiana. The excerpt here is from the very beginning of the novel and traces a route from New Orleans through the bayous into the Gulf of Mexico. In this selection, the reader can see the deep concern for the natural world in Hearn's writing. He writes about flora and fauna of coastal Louisiana such as monarch butterflies whose populations have dwindled since then. Hearn's vision is a record of an era before some species declined in population as a consequence of massive habitat loss, climate change, and use of pesticides and herbicides. *Chita* is in many ways an exploration of the immutable forces of nature such as the migration of hundreds of millions of butterflies and the creation of islands, whose ecosystems are delicate and in danger of disappearing.

THE LEGEND OF L'ILE DERNIERE

I.

Travelling south from New Orleans to the Islands, you pass through a strange land into a strange sea, by various winding waterways. You can journey to the Gulf by lugger if you please; but the trip may be made much more rapidly and agreeably on some one of those light, narrow steamers, built especially for bayou-travel, which usually receive passengers at a point not far from the foot of old Saint-Louis Street, hard by the sugar-landing, where there is ever a pushing and flocking of steam craft—all striving for place to rest their white breasts against the levee, side by side,—like great weary swans. But the miniature steamboat on which you engage passage to the Gulf never lingers long in the Mississippi: she crosses the river, slips into some canal-mouth, labors along the artificial channel awhile, and then leaves it with a scream of joy, to puff her free way down many a league of heavily shadowed bayou. Perhaps thereafter she may bear you through the immense silence of drenched rice-fields, where the yellow-green level is broken at long intervals by the black silhouette of some irrigating machine;—but, whichever of the five different routes be pursued, you will find yourself more than once floating through sombre mazes of swamp-forest,—past assemblages of cypresses all hoary with the parasitic tillandsia, and grotesque as gatherings of fetich-gods. Ever from river or from lakelet the steamer glides again into canal or bayou,—from bayou or canal once more into lake or bay; and sometimes the swamp-forest visibly thins away from these shores into wastes of reedy morass where, even of breathless nights, the quaggy soil trembles to a sound like thunder of breakers on a coast: the storm-roar of billions of reptile voices chanting in cadence,—rhythmically surging in stupendous *crescendo* and *diminuendo*,—a monstrous and appalling chorus of frogs!....

Panting, screaming, scraping her bottom over the sand-bars—all day the little steamer strives to reach the grand blaze of blue open water below the marsh-lands; and perhaps she may be fortunate enough to enter the Gulf about the time of sunset. For the sake of passengers, she travels by day only; but there are other vessels which make the journey also by night—threading the bayou-labyrinths winter and summer: sometimes steering by the North Star,—sometimes feeling the way with poles in the white season of fogs,—sometimes, again, steering by that Star of Evening which in our sky glows like another moon, and drops over the silent lakes as she passes a quivering trail of silver fire.

Shadows lengthen; and at last the woods dwindle away behind you into thin bluish lines;—land and water alike take more luminous color;—bayous open into broad passes;—lakes link themselves with sea-bays;—and the ocean-wind bursts upon you,—keen, cool, and full of light. For the first time the vessel begins to swing—rocking to the great living pulse of the tides. And gazing from the deck around you, with no forest walls to break the view, it will seem to you that the low land must have once been rent asunder by the sea and strewn about the Gulf in fantastic tatters. . . .

Sometimes above a waste of wind-blown prairie-cane you see an oasis emerging—a ridge or hillock heavily umbraged with the rounded foliage of evergreen oaks:—a *cheniere*. And from the shining flood also kindred green knolls arise—pretty islets, each with its beach-girdle of dazzling sand and shells, yellow-white—and all radiant with semi-tropical foliage, myrtle and palmetto, orange and magnolia. Under their emerald shadows curious little villages of palmetto huts are drowsing, where dwell a swarthy population of Orientals—Malay fishermen, who speak the Spanish-Creole of the Philippines as well as their own Tagal, and perpetuate in Louisiana the Catholic traditions of the Indies. There are girls in those unfamiliar villages worthy to inspire any statuary—beautiful with the beauty of ruddy bronze—gracile as the palmettoes that sway above them. . . . Farther seaward you may also pass a Chinese settlement: some queer camp of wooden dwellings clustering around a vast platform that stands above the water upon a thousand piles;—over the miniature wharf you can scarcely fail to observe a white sign-board painted with crimson ideographs. The great platform is used for drying fish in the sun; and the fantastic characters of the sign, literally translated, mean: "*Heap—Shrimp—Plenty.*" . . . And finally all the land melts down into desolations of sea-marsh, whose stillness is seldom broken, except by the melancholy cry of long-legged birds, and in wild seasons by that sound which shakes all shores when the weird Musician of the Sea touches the bass keys of his mighty organ. . . .

II.

Beyond the sea-marshes a curious archipelago lies. If you travel by steamer to the sea-islands to-day, you are tolerably certain to enter the Gulf by Grande Pass—skirting Grande Terre, the most familiar island of all, not so much because of its proximity as because of its great crumbling fort and its graceful pharos: the stationary White-Light of Barataria. Otherwise the place is bleakly uninteresting: a wilderness of wind-swept grasses and sinewy weeds waving away from a thin beach ever speckled with drift and decaying things—worm-riddled timbers, dead porpoises.

Eastward the russet level is broken by the columnar silhouette of the light house, and again, beyond it, by some puny scrub timber, above which rises the angular ruddy mass of the old brick fort, whose ditches swarm with crabs, and whose sluiceways are half choked by obsolete cannon-shot, now thickly covered with incrustation of oyster shells. . . . Around all the gray circling of a shark-haunted sea . . .

Sometimes of autumn evenings there, when the hollow of heaven flames like the interior of a chalice, and waves and clouds are flying in one wild rout of broken gold,—you may see the tawny grasses all covered with something like husks,—wheat-colored husks,—large, flat, and disposed evenly along the lee-side of each swaying stalk, so as to present only their edges to the wind. But, if you approach, those pale husks all break open to display strange splendors of scarlet and seal-brown, with arabesque mottlings in white and black: they change into wondrous living blossoms, which detach themselves before your eyes and rise in air, and flutter away by thousands to settle down farther off, and turn into wheat-colored husks once more . . . a whirling flower-drift of sleepy butterflies!

Southwest, across the pass, gleams beautiful Grande Isle: primitively a wilderness of palmetto (*latanier*);—then drained, diked, and cultivated by Spanish sugar-planters; and now familiar chiefly as a bathing-resort. Since the war the ocean reclaimed its own—the cane-fields have degener-ated into sandy plains, over which tramways wind to the smooth beach—the plantation-residences have been converted into rustic hotels, and the negro-quarters remodelled into villages of cozy cottages for the recep-tion of guests. But with its imposing groves of oak, its golden wealth of orange-trees, its odorous lanes of oleander, its broad grazing-meadows yellow-starred with wild camomile, Grande Isle remains the prettiest is-land of the Gulf; and its loveliness is exceptional. For the bleakness of Grand Terre is reiterated by most of the other islands,—Caillou, Cas-setete, Calumet, Wine Island, the twin Timbaliers, Gull Island, and the many islets haunted by the gray pelican,—all of which are little more than sand-bars covered with wiry grasses, prairie-cane, and scrub-timber. Last Island (*L'Île Dernière*),—well worthy a long visit in other years, in spite of its remoteness, is now a ghastly desolation twenty-five miles long. Ly-ing nearly forty miles west of Grande Isle, it was nevertheless far more populated a generation ago: it was not only the most celebrated island of the group, but also the most fashionable watering-place of the aristocratic South;—today it is visited by fishermen only, at long intervals. Its admirable beach in many respects resembled that of Grande Isle to-day; the accommodations also were much similar, although finer: a charming village of cottages facing the Gulf near the western end. The hotel itself was a massive two-story construction of timber, containing many apartments, together with a large dining-room and dancing-hall. In rear of the hotel was a bayou, where passengers landed—"Village Bayou" it is still called by seamen;—but the deep channel which now cuts the island in two a little eastwardly did not exist while the village remained. The sea tore it out in one night—the same night when trees, fields, dwellings, all vanished into the Gulf, leaving no vestige of former human habitation except a few of those strong brick props and foundations upon which the frame houses and cisterns had been raised. One living creature was found there after the cataclysm—a cow! But how that solitary cow survived the fury of a storm-flood that actually rent the island in twain has ever remained a mystery . . .

III.

On the Gulf side of these islands you may observe that the trees—when there are any trees—all bend away from the sea; and, even of bright, hot days when the wind sleeps, there is something grotesquely pathetic in their look of agonized terror. A group of oaks at Grande Isle I remember as especially suggestive: five stooping silhouettes in line against the horizon, like fleeing women with streaming garments and wind-blown hair—bowing grievously and thrusting out arms desperately northward as to save themselves from falling. And they are being pursued indeed—for the sea is devouring the land. Many and many a mile of ground has yielded to the tireless charging of Ocean's cavalry: far out you can see, through a good glass, the porpoises at play where of old the sugar-cane shook out its million bannerets; and shark-fins now seam deep water above a site where pigeons used to coo. Men build dikes; but the besieging tides bring up their battering-rams—whole forests of drift—huge trunks of water-oak and weighty cypress. Forever the yellow Mississippi strives to build; forever the sea struggles to destroy—and amid their eternal strife the islands and the promontories change shape, more slowly, but not less fantastically, than the clouds of heaven.

And worthy of study are those wan battle-grounds where the woods made their last brave stand against the irresistible invasion—usually at some long point of sea-marsh, widely fringed with billowing sand. Just where the waves curl beyond such a point you may discern a multitude of blackened, snaggy shapes protruding above the water—some high enough to resemble ruined chimneys, others bearing a startling likeness to enormous skeleton-feet and skeleton-hands,—with crustaceous white growths clinging to them here and there like remnants of integument. These are bodies and limbs of drowned oaks—so long drowned that the shell-scurf is inch-thick upon parts of them. Farther in upon the beach immense trunks lie overthrown. Some look like vast broken columns; some suggest colossal torsos imbedded, and seem to reach out mutilated stumps in despair from their deepening graves;—and beside these are others which have kept their feet with astounding obstinacy, although the barbarian tides have been charging them for twenty years, and gradually torn away the soil above and beneath their roots. The sand around,—soft beneath and thinly crusted upon the surface,—is everywhere pierced with holes made by a beautifully mottled and semi-diaphanous crab, with hairy legs, big staring eyes, and milk-white claws;—while in the green sedges beyond there is a perpetual rustling, as of some strong wind beating among reeds: a marvelous creeping of "fiddlers," which the inexperienced visitor might at first mistake for so many peculiar beetles, as they run about sideways, each with his huge single claw folded upon his body like a wing-case. Year by year that rustling strip of green land grows narrower; the sand spreads and sinks, shuddering and wrinkling like a living brown skin; and the last standing corpses of the oaks, ever clinging with naked, dead feet to the sliding beach, lean more and more out of the perpendicular. As the sands subside, the stumps appear to creep; their intertwisted masses of snakish roots seem to crawl, to writhe—like the reaching arms of cephalopods. . . .

Grande Terre is going: the sea mines her fort and will before many years carry the ramparts by storm. Grande Isle is going—slowly but surely: the Gulf has eaten three miles into her meadowed land. Last Island has gone! How it went I first heard from the lips of a veteran pilot, while we sat one evening together on the trunk of a drifted cypress which some high tide had pressed deeply into the Grande Isle beach. The day had been tropically warm; we had sought the shore for a breath of living air. Sunset came, and with it the ponderous heat lifted—a sudden breeze blew—lightnings flickered in the darkening horizon—wind and water began to strive together—and soon all the low coast boomed. Then my companion began his story; perhaps the coming of the storm inspired him to speak! And as I listened to him, listening also to the clamoring of the coast, there flashed back to me recollection of a singular Breton fancy: that the Voice of the Sea is never one voice, but a tumult of many voices—of drowned men,—the muttering of multitudinous dead,—the moaning of innumerable ghosts, all rising, to rage against the living, at the great Witch call of storms. . . .

E. L. CORTHELL

"The Delta of the Mississippi River"

National Geographic, 1897

Elmer Corthell (1840–1916) was not a writer by profession, yet in this article from *National Geographic*, he writes poignantly about subsidence, the sinking of land, as well as the lack of sedimentation being brought down the Mississippi River. This was in 1897, well before many recognized that these were symptoms of land loss.

Corthell was a civil engineer who worked with James Buchanan Eads, the man who designed the jetty system that has, in part, held the lower Mississippi River in place for the past century (Barry, 1997). The two men were tasked by the US War Department (yes, the War Department) with engineering a way to control the river and clear out the sand and sediment that hindered the commercial traffic. Eads and Corthell, along with their team, built long wooden projections called jetties that force water to move rapidly out of the mouth of the river. This jetty system maintains a deep riverbed because sediment is rushed far out into the Gulf of Mexico instead of settling along the coastline. It has made the Port of New Orleans the sixth busiest in the country.

What is significant about this article is that it shows that before the turn of the twentieth century, the public was aware that the process of engineering the river was stopping land-building sediment from going to the wetlands, in part leading to the coastal land loss Louisiana struggles with today. Corthell describes the subsidence of the land through the image of an old colonial Spanish fort, which was at the very mouth of the Mississippi River, sinking slowly into the water. This piece was selected because it is important to note that although engineers were writing about coastal land loss since the 1890s, it took more than a century, until 2007, to rally officials to produce the first state plan for large-scale restoration and protection of the Louisiana coast.

Works Sourced

Barry, John. *Rising Tide: The Great Mississippi Flood of 1927 and How It Changed America.* Simon & Schuster, 1997.

Comprehensive Master Plan for a Sustainable Coast. Louisiana Coastal Protection and Restoration Authority, 2007. http://sonris-www.dnr.state.la.us/dnrservices/redirectUrl.jsp?dID =4063376.

The Mississippi delta proper extends over 100 miles by the course of the river above the city of New Orleans. The materials composing this great mass of sedimentary deposit have been partly disclosed by numerous artisan wells which have from time to time been driven for the purpose of obtaining, if possible, potable water. The most notable instance, and where probably the most careful observations were made, is the artesian well at Lafayette square, New Orleans. At a depth of 1,042 feet the tool was broken and the work ended, but driftwood was pumped up at the last foot.

Many interesting facts bearing upon the question of the geological formation of the Mississippi delta were brought to attention two years ago through the investigations and discussions connected with an engineering question which arose between the executors of the late Mr. James B. Eads and the War Department as to what is the legal plane of reference for ascertaining the depths and widths of channel which Mr. Eads was required by law of the federal congress to maintain between the deep water of the South Pass of the Mississippi River and the Gulf of Mexico.

On Belize Bayou, which leads out to the Gulf from one of the now unused passes of the river, stands an old Spanish magazine, built over 200 years ago. At the time of building the jetties at the mouth of South Pass this magazine was in a fair state of preservation. The exterior was intact and there were no cracks which would indicate settlement, the building standing perfectly level, but with the surface of the water stretching across the arch which crowned the entrance door, the sill of which must have been at least two feet below the water. This was in the year 1877. Nineteen years later a part of the structure had been removed, but enough of the roof and arches remained to show that the subsidence had continued steadily during that period of nineteen years at about the same rate as during the preceding two hundred years. It may be stated that this rate, both from this instance and from other information, is, at the mouth of the Mississippi about one-half of one-tenth of a foot per annum. Numerous illustrations going to prove the general subsidence of the delta lands might be stated. Not only are these lands unstable in a vertical direction, but they are often found to be so in a lateral direction. It is an interesting engineering as well as physical fact that an accurately measured baseline exactly seven hundred feet in length was found, after a lapse of five years to be seven hundred and twelve feet in length. . . .

It is a fact well known to people living in the delta of the Mississippi that large tracts of land were long ago abandoned in consequence of over-flow by Gulf waters due to the sinking of the lands.

The conditions are very different now from those existing prior to the existence of levees. There are at present no annual accretions of sedimentary matters from the periodical overflows of the river. These accretions formerly were a little more than equal to the annual subsidence of the lands.

The geology of the delta of the Mississippi is an interesting local study. The effect of the withholding by the levees from the great areas of the delta of the annual contributions of sedimentary matters, and the steady, though slow, subsidence of these areas, is one which should be taken into account in deciding the important question of how to protect the people from the flood waters of the river. No doubt the great benefit to the present and two or three following generations accruing from a complete system of absolutely protective levees, excluding the flood waters entirely from the lower delta country, far outweighs the disadvantages to future generations from the subsidence of the Gulf delta lands below the level of the sea and their gradual abandonment due to this cause. While it would be generally conceded that the present generation should not be selfish yet is safe to say that the development of the delta country during the twentieth century by a fully protective levee system, at whatever cost to the riparian states and the federal government will be so remarkable that people of the whole United States can well afford, when the time comes, to build a protective levee against the Gulf waters, as the City of New Orleans has done on a small scale against the sea waters of Lake Pontchartrain and as Holland has done for centuries.

JOHN MUIR

A Thousand-Mile Walk to the Gulf (1916)

John Muir (1838–1914) has been thought of as the quintessential American environmentalist. A prominent nature writer, explorer, and founder of the Sierra Club, his influence on American thinking about the environment is lasting. Muir was born in Scotland in 1838, and his family immigrated to Wisconsin in 1849. He attended the University of Wisconsin, and although he didn't graduate, he was first exposed to botany classes there. Muir's writing was deeply influenced by British Romanticism and by American Transcendentalism, which can be seen over and over again in his preference for the nonhuman world. His sympathies lay more with nature, as he expresses in the excerpt when he speculates on conflict between humans and wild creatures: "I would be tempted to sympathize with the bears."

In 1867, after a workplace accident in a factory that nearly blinded him, Muir set out to walk from Kentucky to Florida and kept a journal of his trek that was posthumously published as *A Thousand-Mile Walk to the Gulf*, excerpted here. Walking through the American South shortly after the end of the Civil War, Muir clearly recognized the way the natural environment had been ravaged by the violence. Eventually he reached Cedar Key, about 135 miles north of Tampa on the west coast of Florida, where he worked for a time in a sawmill, most likely processing, among other trees, the longleaf pines that have vanished across the Gulf. Muir encountered Florida's combination of natural beauty and inhospitable environment. He experienced the mosquitoes firsthand, and in this excerpt he gives a terrifying description of succumbing to malaria and nearly dying.

In 1868 Muir first explored what is today Yosemite National Park, and he championed preservation of that wilderness. In 1892 he and some like-minded individuals founded the Sierra Club, which immediately became a leading American environmental advocacy group. Muir in many ways led the twentieth-century charge for American environmentalism, though he also solidified many of the problems inherent in it, notably a preponderance of white, middle- to upper-class activists who could not foresee the intersectional issues that would dominate the end of the twentieth century in the environmental justice movement.

Works Sourced

Cauthen, Sudye. "Muir, John: (1838–1914) Naturalist, Environmentalist, Explorer, Writer." *The New Encyclopedia of Southern Culture*, volume 8: *Environment*, volume editor Martin Melosi, general editor Charles Reagan Wilson, University of North Carolina Press, 2007, pp. 243–245.
Scott, Rebecca R. "Love." *Veer Ecology: A Companion for Environmental Thinking*, edited by Jeffrey Jerome Cohen and Lowell Duckert, U of Minnesota P, 2017, pp. 377–391.

CHAPTER V: THROUGH FLORIDA SWAMPS AND FORESTS

October 20. Swamp very dense during this day's journey. Almost one continuous sheet of water covered with aquatic trees and vines. No stream that I crossed to-day appeared to have the least idea where it was going. Saw an alligator plash into the sedgy brown water by the roadside from an old log.

Arrived at night at the house of Captain Simmons, one of the very few scholarly, intelligent men that I have met in Florida. He had been an officer in the Confederate army in the war and was, of course, prejudiced against the North, but polite and kind to me, nevertheless. Our conversation, as we sat by the light of the fire, was on the one great question, slavery and its concomitants. I managed, however, to switch off to something more congenial occasionally—the birds of the neighborhood, the animals, the climate, and what spring, summer, and winter are like in these parts.

About the climate, I could not get much information, as he had always lived in the South and, of course, saw nothing extraordinary in weather to which he had always been accustomed. But in speaking of animals, he at once became enthusiastic and told many stories of hairbreadth escapes, in the woods about his house, from bears, hungry alligators, wounded deer, etc. "And now," said he, forgetting in his kindness that I was from the hated North, "you must stay with me a few days. Deer are abundant. I will lend you a rifle and we'll go hunting. I hunt whenever I wish venison, and I can get it about as easily from the woods near by as a shepherd can get mutton out of his flock. And perhaps we will see a bear, for they are far from scarce here, and there are some big gray wolves, too."

I expressed a wish to see some large alligators. "Oh, well," said he, "I can take you where you will see plenty of those fellows, but they are not much to look at. I once got a good look at an alligator that was lying at the bottom of still, transparent water, and I think that his eyes were the most impressively cold and cruel of any animal I have seen. Many alligators go out to sea among the keys. These sea alligators are the largest and most ferocious, and sometimes attack people by trying to strike them with their tails when they are out fishing in boats.

"Another thing I wish you to see," he continued, "is a palmetto grove on a rich hummock a few miles from here. The grove is about seven miles in length by three in breadth. The ground is covered with long grass, uninterrupted with bushes or other trees. It is the finest grove of palmettos I have ever seen and I have oftentimes thought that it would make a fine subject for an artist."

I concluded to stop—more to see this wonderful palmetto hummock than to hunt. Besides, I was weary and the prospect of getting a little rest was a tempting consideration after so many restless nights and long, hard walks by day.

October 21. Having outlived the sanguinary hunters tales of my loquacious host, and breakfasted sumptuously on fresh venison and "caller" fish from the sea, I set out for the grand palm grove. I had seen these dazzling sun-children in every day of my walk through Florida, but they were usually standing solitary, or in groups of three or four; but to-day I was to see them by the mile. The captain led me a short distance through his corn field and showed me a trail which would conduct me to the palmy hummock. He pointed out the general direction, which I noted upon my compass.

"Now," said he, "at the other side of my farthest field you will come to a jungle of cat-briers, but will be able to pass them if you manage to keep the trail. You will find that the way is not by any means well marked, for in passing through a broad swamp, the trail makes a good many abrupt turns to avoid deep water, fallen trees, or impenetrable thickets. You will have to wade a good deal, and in passing the water-covered places you will have to watch for the point where the trail comes out on the opposite side."

I made my way through the briers, which in strength and ferocity equaled those of Tennessee, followed the path through all of its dim waverings, waded the many opposing pools, and, emerging suddenly from the leafy darkness of the swamp forest, at last stood free and unshaded on the border of the sun-drenched palm garden. It was a level area of grasses and sedges, smooth as a prairie, well starred with flowers, and bounded like a clearing by a wall of vine-laden trees.

The palms had full possession and appeared to enjoy their sunny home. There was no jostling, no apparent effort to outgrow each other. Abundance of sunlight was there for every crown, and plenty to fall between.

I walked enchanted in their midst. What a landscape! Only palms as far as the eye could reach! Smooth pillars rising from the grass, each capped with a sphere of leaves, shining in the sun as bright as a star. The silence and calm were as deep as ever I found in the dark, solemn pine woods of Canada, and that contentment which is an attribute of the best of God's plant people was as impressively felt in this alligator wilderness as in the homes of the happy, healthy people of the North.

The admirable Linnæus calls palms "the princes of the vegetable world." I know that there is grandeur and nobility in their character, and that there are palms nobler far than these. But in rank they appear to me to stand below both the oak and the pine. The motions of the palms, their gestures, are not very graceful. They appear to best advantage when perfectly motionless in the noontide calm and intensity of light. But they rustle and rock in the evening wind. I have seen grasses waving with far more dignity. And when our northern pines are waving and bowing in sign of worship with the winter storm-winds, where is the prince of palms that could have the conscience to demand their homage!

Members of this palm congregation were of all sizes with respect to their stems; but their glorious crowns were all alike. In development there is only the terminal bud to consider. The young palm of this species emerges from the ground in full strength, one cluster of leaves arched every way, making a sphere about ten or twelve feet in diameter. The outside lower leaves gradually become yellow, wither, and break off, the petiole snapping squarely across, a few inches from the stem. New leaves develop with wonderful rapidity. They stand erect at first, but gradually arch outward as they expand their blades and lengthen their petioles.

New leaves arise constantly from the center of the grand bud, while old ones break away from the outside. The splendid crowns are thus kept about the same size, perhaps a little larger than in youth while they are yet on the ground. As the development of the central axis goes on, the crown is gradually raised on a stem of about six to twelve inches in diameter. This stem is of equal thickness at the top and at the bottom and when young is roughened with the broken petioles. But these petiole-stumps fall off and disappear as they become old, and the trunk becomes smooth as if turned in a lathe.

After some hours in this charming forest I started on the return journey before night, on account of the difficulties of the swamp and the brier patch. On leaving the palmettos and entering the vine-tangled, half-submerged forest I sought long and carefully, but in vain, for the trail, for I had drifted about too incautiously in search of plants. But, recollecting the direction that I had followed in the morning, I took a compass bearing and started to penetrate the swamp in a direct line.

Of course I had a sore weary time, pushing through the tanglement of falling, standing, and half-fallen trees and bushes, to say nothing of knotted vines as remarkable for their efficient army of interlocking and lancing prickers as for their length and the number of their blossoms. But these were not my greatest obstacles, nor yet the pools and lagoons full of dead leaves and alligators. It was the army of cat-briers that I most dreaded. I knew that I would have to find the narrow slit of a lane before dark or spend the night with mosquitoes and alligators, without food or fire. The entire distance was not great, but a traveler in open woods can form no idea of the crooked and strange difficulties of pathless locomotion in these thorny, watery Southern tangles, especially in pitch darkness. I struggled hard and kept my course, leaving the general direction only when drawn aside by a plant of extraordinary promise, that I wanted for a specimen, or when I had to make the half-circuit of a pile of trees, or of a deep lagoon or pond.

In wading I never attempted to keep my clothes dry, because the water was too deep, and the necessary care would consume too much time. Had the water that I was forced to wade been transparent it would have lost much of its difficulty. But as it was, I constantly expected to plant my feet on an alligator, and therefore proceeded with strained caution. The opacity of the water caused uneasiness also on account of my inability to determine its depth. In many places I was compelled to turn back, after wading forty or fifty yards, and to try again a score of times before I succeeded in getting across a single lagoon.

At length, after miles of wading and wallowing, I arrived at the grand cat-brier encampment which guarded the whole forest in solid phalanx, unmeasured miles up and down across my way. Alas! the trail by which I had crossed in the morning was not to be found, and night was near. In vain I scrambled back and forth in search of an opening. There was not even a strip of dry ground on which to rest. Everywhere the long briers arched over to the vines and bushes of the watery swamp, leaving no standing-ground between them. I began to think of building some sort of a scaffold in a tree to rest on through the night, but concluded to make one more desperate effort to find the narrow track.

After calm, concentrated recollection of my course, I made a long exploration toward the left down the brier line, and after scrambling a mile or so, perspiring and bleeding, I discovered the blessed trail and escaped to dry land and the light. Reached the captain at sundown. Dined on milk and johnny-cake and fresh venison. Was congratulated on my singular good fortune and woodcraft, and soon after supper was sleeping the deep sleep of the weary and the safe.

October 22. This morning I was easily prevailed upon by the captain and an ex-judge, who was rusticating here, to join in a deer hunt. Had a delightful ramble in the long grass and flowery barrens. Started one deer but did not draw a single shot. The captain, the judge, and myself stood at different stations where the deer was expected to pass, while a brother of the captain entered the woods to arouse the game from cover. The one deer that he started took a direction different from any which this particular old buck had ever been known to take in times past, and in so doing was cordially cursed as being the "d—dest deer that ever ran unshot." To me it appeared as "d—dest" work to slaughter God's cattle for sport. "They were made for us," say these self-approving preachers; "for our food, our recreation, or other uses not yet discovered." As truthfully we might say on behalf of a bear, when he deals successfully with an unfortunate hunter, "Men and other bipeds were made for bears, and thanks be to God for claws and teeth so long."

Let a Christian hunter go to the Lord's woods and kill his well-kept beasts, or wild Indians, and it is well; but let an enterprising specimen of these proper, predestined victims go to houses and fields and kill the most worthless person of the vertical godlike killers,—oh! that is horribly unorthodox, and on the part of the Indians atrocious murder! Well, I have precious little sympathy for the selfish propriety of civilized man, and if a war of races should occur between the wild beasts and Lord Man, I would be tempted to sympathize with the bears.

CHAPTER VI: CEDAR KEYS

October 23. Today I reached the sea. While I was yet many miles back in the palmy woods, I caught the scent of the salt sea breeze which, although I had so many years lived far from sea breezes, suddenly conjured up Dunbar, its rocky coast, winds and waves; and my whole childhood, that seemed to have utterly vanished in the New World, was now restored amid the Florida woods by that one breath from the sea. Forgotten were the palms and magnolias and the thousand flowers that enclosed me. I could see only dulse and tangle, long-winged gulls, the Bass Rock in the Firth of Forth, and the old castle, schools, churches, and long country rambles in search of birds nests. I do not wonder that the weary camels coming from the scorching African deserts should be able to scent the Nile.

How imperishable are all the impressions that ever vibrate one's life! We cannot forget anything. Memories may escape the action of will, may sleep a long time, but when stirred by the right influence, though that influence be light as a shadow, they flash into full stature and life with everything in place. For nineteen years my vision was bounded by forests, but to-day, emerging from a multitude of tropical plants, I beheld the Gulf of Mexico stretching away unbounded, except by the sky. What dreams and speculative matter for thought arose as I stood on the strand, gazing out on the burnished, treeless plain!

But now at the seaside I was in difficulty. I had reached a point that I could not ford, and Cedar Keys had an empty harbor. Would I proceed down the peninsula to Tampa and Key West, where I would be sure to find a vessel for Cuba, or would I wait here, like Crusoe, and pray for a ship. Full of these thoughts, I stepped into a little store which had a considerable trade in quinine and alligator and rattlesnake skins, and inquired about shipping, means of travel, etc.

The proprietor informed me that one of several sawmills near the village was running, and that a schooner chartered to carry a load of lumber to Galveston, Texas, was expected at the mills for a load. This mill was situated on a tongue of land a few miles along the coast from Cedar Keys, and I determined to see Mr. Hodgson, the owner, to find out particulars about the expected schooner, the time she would take to load, whether I would be likely to obtain passage on her, etc.

Found Mr. Hodgson at his mill. Stated my case, and was kindly furnished the desired information. I determined to wait the two weeks likely to elapse before she sailed, and go on her to the flowery plains of Texas, from any of whose ports, I fancied, I could easily find passage to the West Indies. I agreed to work for Mr. Hodgson in the mill until I sailed, as I had but little money. He invited me to his spacious house, which occupied a shell hillock and commanded a fine view of the Gulf and many gems of palmy islets, called "keys," that fringe the shore like huge bouquets—not too big, however, for the spacious waters. Mr. Hodgson's family welcomed me with that open, unconstrained cordiality which is characteristic of the better class of Southern people.

At the sawmill a new cover had been put on the main driving pulley, which, made of rough plank, had to be turned off and smoothed. He asked me if I was able to do this job and I told him that I could. Fixing a rest and making a tool out of an old file, I directed the engineer to start the engine and run slow. After turning down the pulley and getting it true, I put a keen edge on a common carpenter's plane, quickly finished the job, and was assigned a bunk in one of the employees lodging-houses.

The next day I felt a strange dullness and headache while I was botanizing along the coast. Thinking that a bath in the salt water might refresh me, I plunged in and swam a little distance, but this seemed only to make me feel worse. I felt anxious for something sour, and walked back to the village to buy lemons.

Thus and here my long walk was interrupted. I thought that a few days sail would land me among the famous flower-beds of Texas. But the expected ship came and went while I was helpless with fever. The very day after reaching the sea I began to be weighed down by inexorable leaden numbness, which I resisted and tried to shake off for three days, by bathing in the Gulf, by dragging myself about among the palms, plants, and strange shells of the shore, and by doing a little mill work. I did not fear any serious illness, for I never was sick before, and was unwilling to pay attention to my feelings.

But yet heavier and more remorselessly pressed the growing fever, rapidly gaining on my strength. On the third day after my arrival I could not take any nourishment, but craved acid. Cedar Keys was only a mile or two distant, and I managed to walk there to buy lemons. On returning, about the middle of the afternoon, the fever broke on me like a storm, and before I had staggered halfway to the mill I fell down unconscious on the narrow trail among dwarf palmettos.

When I awoke from the hot fever sleep, the stars were shining, and I was at a loss to know which end of the trail to take, but fortunately, as it afterwards proved, I guessed right. Subsequently, as I fell again and again after walking only a hundred yards or so, I was careful to lie with my head in the direction in which I thought the mill was. I rose, staggered, and fell, I know not how many times, in delirious bewilderment, gasping and throbbing with only moments of consciousness. Thus passed the hours till after midnight, when I reached the mill lodging-house.

The watchman on his rounds found me lying on a heap of sawdust at the foot of the stairs. I asked him to assist me up the steps to bed, but he thought my difficulty was only intoxication and refused to help me. The mill hands, especially on Saturday nights, often returned from the village drunk. This was the cause of the watchman's refusal. Feeling that I must get to bed, I made out to reach it on hands and knees, tumbled in after a desperate struggle, and immediately became oblivious to everything.

I awoke at a strange hour on a strange day to hear Mr. Hodgson ask a watcher beside me whether I had yet spoken, and when he replied that I had not, he said: "Well, you must keep on pouring in quinine. That's all we can do." How long I lay unconscious I never found out, but it must have been many days. Some time or other I was moved on a horse from the mill quarters to Mr. Hodgson's house, where I was nursed about three months with unfailing kindness, and to the skill and care of Mr. and Mrs. Hodgson I doubtless owe my life. Through quinine and calomel—in sorry abundance—with other milder medicines, my malarial fever became typhoid. I had night sweats, and my legs became like posts of the temper and consistency of clay on account of dropsy. So on until January, a weary time.

As soon as I was able to get out of bed, I crept away to the edge of the wood, and sat day after day beneath a moss-draped live-oak, watching birds feeding on the shore when the tide was out. Later, as I gathered some strength, I sailed in a little skiff from one key to another. Nearly all the shrubs and trees here are evergreen, and a few of the smaller plants are in flower all winter. The principal trees on this Cedar Key are the juniper, long-leafed pine, and live-oak. All of the latter, living and dead, are heavily draped with tillandsia, like those of Bonaventure. The leaf is oval, about two inches long, three fourths of an inch wide, glossy and dark green above, pale beneath. The trunk is usually much divided, and is extremely unwedgeable. The specimen on the opposite page [in Muir's journal] is growing in the dooryard of Mr. Hodgson's house. It is a grand old king, whose crown gleamed in the bright sky long ere the Spanish shipbuilders felled a single tree of this noble species.

The live-oaks of these keys divide empire with the long-leafed pine and palmetto, but in many places on the mainland there are large tracts exclusively occupied by them. Like the Bonaventure oaks they have the upper side of their main spreading branches thickly planted with ferns, grasses, small saw palmettos, etc. There is also a dwarf oak here, which forms dense thickets. The oaks of this key are not, like those of the Wisconsin openings, growing on grassy slopes, but stand, sunk to the shoulders, in flowering magnolias, heathworts, etc.

During my long sojourn here as a convalescent I used to lie on my back for whole days beneath the ample arms of these great trees, listening to the winds and the birds. There is an extensive shallow on the coast, close by, which the receding tide exposes daily. This is the feeding-ground of thousands of waders of all sizes, plumage, and language, and they make a lively picture and noise when they gather at the great family board to eat their daily bread, so bountifully provided for them.

Their leisure in time of high tide they spend in various ways and places. Some go in large flocks to reedy margins about the islands and wade and stand about quarrelling or making sport, occasionally finding a stray mouthful to eat. Some stand on the mangroves of the solitary shore, now and then plunging into the water after a fish. Some go long journeys inland, up creeks and inlets. A few lonely old herons of solemn look and wing retire to favorite oaks. It was my delight to watch those old white sages of immaculate feather as they stood erect drowsing away the dull hours between tides, curtained by long skeins of tillandsia. White-bearded hermits gazing dreamily from dark caves could not appear more solemn or more becomingly shrouded from the rest of their fellow beings.

One of the characteristic plants of these keys is the Spanish bayonet, a species of yucca, about eight or ten feet in height, and with a trunk three or four inches in diameter when full grown. It belongs to the lily family and develops palmlike from terminal buds. The stout leaves are very rigid, sharp-pointed and bayonet-like. By one of these leaves a man might be as seriously stabbed as by an army bayonet, and woe to the luckless wanderer who dares to urge his way through these armed gardens after dark. Vegetable cats of many species will rob him of his clothes and claw his flesh, while dwarf palmettos will saw his bones, and the bayonets will glide to his joints and marrow without the smallest consideration for Lord Man.

The climate of these precious islets is simply warm summer and warmer summer, corresponding in time with winter and summer in the North. The weather goes smoothly over the points of union betwixt the twin summers. Few of the storms are very loud or variable. The average temperature during the day, in December, was about sixty-five degrees in the shade, but on one day a little damp snow fell.

Cedar Key is two and one half or three miles in diameter and its highest point is forty-four feet above mean tide-water. It is surrounded by scores of other keys, many of them looking like a clump of palms, arranged like a tasteful bouquet, and placed in the sea to be kept fresh. Others have quite a sprinkling of oaks and junipers, beautifully united with vines. Still others consist of shells, with a few grasses and mangroves, circled with a rim of rushes. Those which have sedgy margins furnish a favorite retreat for countless waders and divers, especially for the pelicans that frequently whiten the shore like a ring of foam.

It is delightful to observe the assembling of these feathered people from the woods and reedy isles; herons white as wave-tops, or blue as the sky, winnowing the warm air on wide quiet wing; pelicans coming with baskets to fill, and the multitude of smaller sailors of the air, swift as swallows, gracefully taking their places at Nature's family table for their daily bread. Happy birds!

The mockingbird is graceful in form and a fine singer, plainly dressed, rather familiar in habits, frequently coming like robins to door-sills for crumbs—a noble fellow, beloved by everybody. Wild geese are abundant in winter, associated with brant, some species of which I have never seen in the North. Also great flocks of robins, mourning doves, bluebirds, and the delightful brown thrashers. A large number of the smaller birds are fine singers. Crows, too, are here, some of them cawing with a foreign accent. The common bob-white quail I observed as far south as middle Georgia.

Lime Key, sketched on the opposite page, is a fair specimen of the Florida keys on this part of the coast. A fragment of cactus, *Opuntia*, sketched on another page, is from the above-named key, and is abundant there. The fruit, an inch in length, is gathered, and made into a sauce, of which some people are fond. This species forms thorny, impenetrable thickets. One joint that I measured was fifteen inches long.

The mainland of Florida is less salubrious than the islands, but no portion of this coast, nor of the flat border which sweeps from Maryland to Texas, is quite free from malaria. All the inhabitants of this region, whether black or white, are liable to be prostrated by the ever-present fever and ague, to say nothing of the plagues of cholera and yellow fever that come and go suddenly like storms, prostrating the population and cutting gaps in it like hurricanes in woods.

The world, we are told, was made especially for man—a presumption not supported by all the facts. A numerous class of men are painfully astonished whenever they find anything, living or dead, in all God's universe, which they cannot eat or render in some way what they call useful to themselves. They have precise dogmatic insight of the intentions of the Creator, and it is hardly possible to be guilty of irreverence in speaking of *their* God any more than of heathen idols. He is regarded as a civilized, law-abiding gentleman in favor either of a republican form of government or of a limited monarchy; believes in the literature and language of England; is a warm supporter of the English constitution and Sunday schools and missionary societies; and is as purely a manufactured article as any puppet of a half-penny theater.

With such views of the Creator it is, of course, not surprising that erroneous views should be entertained of the creation. To such properly trimmed people, the sheep, for example, is an easy problem—food and clothing "for us," eating grass and daisies white by divine appointment for this predestined purpose, on perceiving the demand for wool that would be occasioned by the eating of the apple in the Garden of Eden.

In the same pleasant plan, whales are store houses of oil for us, to help out the stars in lighting our dark ways until the discovery of the Pennsylvania oil wells. Among plants, hemp, to say nothing of the cereals, is a case of evident destination for ships rigging, wrapping packages, and hanging the wicked. Cotton is another plain case of clothing. Iron was made for hammers and ploughs, and lead for bullets; all intended for us. And so of other small handfuls of insignificant things.

But if we should ask these profound expositors of God's intentions, How about those man-eating animals—lions, tigers, alligators—which smack their lips over raw man? Or about those myriads of noxious insects that destroy labor and drink his blood? Doubtless man was intended for food and drink for all these? Oh, no! Not at all! These are unresolvable difficulties connected with Eden's apple and the Devil. Why does water drown its lord? Why do so many minerals poison him? Why are so many plants and fishes deadly enemies? Why is the lord of creation subjected to the same laws of life as his subjects? Oh, all these things are satanic, or in some way connected with the first garden.

Now, it never seems to occur to these farseeing teachers that Nature's object in making animals and plants might possibly be first of all the happiness of each one of them, not the creation of all for the happiness of one. Why should man value himself as more than a small part of the one great unit of creation? And what creature of all that the Lord has taken the pains to make is not essential to the completeness of that unit—the cosmos? The universe would be incomplete without man; but it would also be incomplete without the smallest transmicroscopic creature that dwells beyond our conceitful eyes and knowledge.

From the dust of the earth, from the common elementary fund, the Creator has made *Homo sapiens*. From the same material he has made every other creature, however noxious and insignificant to us. They are earth-born companions and our fellow mortals. The fearfully good, the orthodox, of this laborious patchwork of modern civilization cry "Heresy" on everyone whose sympathies reach a single hair's breadth beyond the boundary epidermis of our own species. Not content with taking all of earth, they also claim the celestial country as the only ones who possess the kind of souls for which that imponderable empire was planned.

This star, our own good earth, made many a successful journey around the heavens ere man was made, and whole kingdoms of creatures enjoyed existence and returned to dust ere man appeared to claim them. After human beings have also played their part in Creation's plan, they too may disappear without any general burning or extraordinary commotion whatever.

Plants are credited with but dim and uncertain sensation, and minerals with positively none at all. But why may not even a mineral arrangement of matter be endowed with sensation of a kind that we in our blind exclusive perfection can have no manner of communication with?

But I have wandered from my object. I stated a page or two back that man claimed the earth was made for him, and I was going to say that venomous beasts, thorny plants, and deadly diseases of certain parts of the earth prove that the whole world was not made for him. When an animal from a tropical climate is taken to high latitudes, it may perish of cold, and we say that such an animal was never intended for so severe a climate. But when man betakes himself to sickly parts of the tropics and perishes, he cannot see that he was never intended for such deadly climates. No, he will rather accuse the first mother of the cause of the difficulty, though she may never have seen a fever district; or will consider it a providential chastisement for some self-invented form of sin.

Furthermore, all uneatable and uncivilizable animals, and all plants which carry prickles, are deplorable evils which, according to closet researches of clergy, require the cleansing chemistry of universal planetary combustion. But more than aught else mankind requires burning, as being in great part wicked, and if that transmundane furnace can be so applied and regulated as to smelt and purify us into conformity with the rest of the terrestrial creation, then the tophetization of the erratic genus Homo were a consummation devoutly to be prayed for. But, glad to leave these ecclesiastical fires and blunders, I joyfully return to the immortal truth and immortal beauty of Nature.

JOVITA GONZÁLEZ

"El Cenizo," "The Mocking Bird," and "The Guadalupana Vine"

Texas and Southwestern Lore, 1927

Jovita González (1904–1983) was a novelist, folklorist, and educator who lived in Texas her entire life. In these short folktales excerpted here, González documented the indigenous knowledge and stories of the natural world in southern Texas at the beginning of the twentieth century as massive changes to the Rio Grande Valley were taking place politically, culturally, and environmentally. González witnessed the evolution of Texas family ranching into industrial agriculture, the influx of people to the border after the Mexican Revolution ended in 1920, and the complex cultural spaces that developed between indigenous, Mexican, and American peoples in the Rio Grande Valley.

Priscilla Solis Ybarra, a professor of Chicana/o literature and ecocriticism, writes that González's works "represent a hitherto-unrecognized source of environmental writing . . . although at first glance these tales may seem soft and lighthearted, they prove to be intricately disguised critiques" (177). Questions of gender and race and the complexities of language are major themes in these stories. Using traditional Native forms of storytelling, González pokes holes in the ideas of western medicine, patriarchy, and Jim Crow–era racism, pointing instead to the natural world as a source of knowledge, culture, and healing. In "The Mocking Bird" she writes, "There was a time when all the creatures of Nature talked a common language." Though she continues on to say that language was Spanish, the passage could also be read that there is a shared way of communicating with the environment that should never be lost.

Endnotes included are from the original text.

Work Sourced

Ybarra, Priscilla Solis. "Borderlands as Bioregion: Jovita González, Gloria Anzaldúa, and the Twentieth-Century Ecological Revolution in the Rio Grande Valley." *MELUS*, vol. 34, no. 2, 2009, pp. 175–189.

El Cenizo

It had been an unusually hard winter, cold and dry. But then coyotes had in the fall announced it would be so, for their fur had been heavy and thick, and they had stayed close to the ranches, not daring to go to the hills. All vegetation had been killed by *el hielo prieto* (the black frost), and even the cactus, the always reliable food for the cattle, had wilted.

Spring came, and with it new hope. But whatever young, green things sprang up died for need of water. The mesquites were mere ghosts; the huisaches, shameful of not bearing their sweet-smelling velvety blooms, hid their leaves. All the waterholes had dried up, and death and starvation ruled the prairie. The buzzard was lord of the plains, and as it flew over the trees was a constant reminder of death. The cattle, once so plentiful and fat, had diminished to a few, and those that remained looked at the world with sad, death-like eyes.

"*Por qué no llueve, Dios mío?*" ("Why do you not make it rain, my Lord?") the vaquero said, looking up at the sky. And with a sigh of resignation he added, "*Así es la suerte.*" ("That's luck.")

There was just one possible way of salvation, and that was prayer, prayer to the Virgin. The cowmen gathered together and reverently knelt on the plain to beg for help. As the last prayer of the rosary was said, a soft breeze,[1] a *lagueño* blew from the east. Soon drops began to fall; all night the rain fell like a benediction.

Filled with new hope, the people rose early the next day to see the blessing that had fallen over the land. And indeed it was a beautiful blessing. For as far as the eye could see, the plain was covered with silvery shrubs, sparkling with rain-drops and covered with flowers, pink, lavender, and white.

It was a gift of the Virgin, and because the day was Ash Wednesday the shrub was called *el cenizo*.[2] The interpretation given by the vaquero is charming, to say the least; the gray of the leaves signifies the Passion of Christ; the white flowers, the purity of the mother; and the pink, the new dawn for the cowmen and the resurrection of life.

The Mocking Bird

An equally interesting story tells how the mocking bird got the white feathers of its wings. There was a time when all the creatures of Nature talked a common language. This language was Spanish. *El sensontle*, the mocking bird, had the sweetest voice of all. The other birds stopped their flight to listen to him; the Indian lover ceased his words of love; even the talkative *arroyo* hushed. He foretold the spring, and when the days grew short and his song was no longer heard, the north winds came. Although he was not a foolish bird, *el zenzontle* was getting conceited.

"I am great, indeed," he said to his mate. "All Nature obeys me. When I sing, the blossoms hid in the trees come forth; the prairie flowers put on their gayest garments at my call and the birds begin to mate; even man, the all wise, heeds my voice and dances with joy, for the happy season draws near."

"Hush, you are foolish and conceited like all men," replied his wife. "They listen and wait for the voice of God, and when He calls, even you sing."

He did not answer his wife, for you must remember he was not so foolish after all, but in his heart he knew that he was right.

That night after kissing his wife goodnight, he said to her, "Tomorrow I will give a concert to the flowers, and you shall see them sway and dance when they hear me."

"*Con el favor de Dios*," she replied. ("If God wills it.") "Whether God wills it or not I shall sing," he replied angrily. "Have I not told you that the flowers obey me and not God?"

Early next morning *el zenzontle* could be seen perched on the highest limb of a huisache. He cleared his throat, coughed, and opened his bill to sing, but no sound came. For down with the force of a cyclone swooped a hawk and grabbed with his steel-like claws the slender body of the singer.

"*Con el favor de Dios, con el favor de Dios*," he cried in distress, while he thought of his wise little wife. As he was being carried up in the air, he realized his foolishness and repented of it, and said, "O God, it is you who make the flowers bloom and the birds sing, not I." As he thought thus, he felt himself slipping and falling, falling, falling. He fell on a ploughed field, and what a fall it was. A white dove who had her nest nearby picked him up and comforted him.

"My wings," he mourned, looking at them, "how tattered and torn they look! Whatever shall I tell my wife?" The dove took pity on him, and plucking three of her white feathers, mended his wings.

As a reminder of his foolish pride, the mocking bird to this day has the white feathers of the dove. And it is said by those who know that he never begins to sing without saying, "*con el favor de Dios*."

THE GUADALUPANA VINE

In south Texas there is a vine used for medicinal purposes known as the Guadalupana vine. It bears small gourd-like fruit. The seeds have a bright red covering, which on being removed show the image of our Lady of Guadalupe. Everybody is acquainted with the story of the apparition of our Lady of Guadalupe in Mexico. The story of the vine in itself is equally as interesting.

Two vaqueros were going to the nearest town for provisions. One of them was riding a very spirited *potro*. On coming to a creek the horse was frightened, and in spite of all that the rider could do the bronco threw him on the rocky banks. The other, terrified by the accident, did not know how to help his companion, who was slowly bleeding to death. As he sat there, a lovely lady came to him. She was dressed in blue, and he noticed that her mantle was sprinkled with stars. What astonished him more was to see that she floated, her feet not touching the ground. But he attributed this phenomenon to his bewildered condition. She approached, holding a small red fruit in her hand.

"Try this, my son," the lady said; "dip it in mescal and put it on the wound."

"But it will burn," stammered the surprised vaquero. The lovely lady smiled, shook her head, and whispered, "*No arde, no arde.*" ("It will not burn.")

The vaquero did as he was told, and, strange as it may seem, his companion was cured immediately. The vaqueros consider this a miracle of the Virgin, and to verify this story they point to the fact that the Virgin left her image engraved on all the seed.[3]

NOTES

1. Breeze from the Gulf.

2. Ceniza means ashes. The shrub is common all over Southwest Texas and is known to country people of that section only by the Mexican name, ceniso or coniza (pronounced conisa), a name probably derived from the ashen color of the leaves. The botanical term is Laeophlluma tesaum. Nurseries are popularizing it as a shrub for landscape planting-and it certainly has a great deal more character than the ligustrum! In the more arid parts of Texas it blooms after every summer rain; it is evergreen-or, more accurately, ever ashen. Mexicans make a medicinal tea of it.

3. On the border, the Mexican housewife puts up jars of the Guadalupana fruit in mescal. The people use no other remedy for cuts and wounds.

ZORA NEALE HURSTON

Their Eyes Were Watching God (1937)

In her lifetime, Zora Neale Hurston (1891/1901–1960) published four novels, two collections of folklore, an autobiography, and nine plays; she won two Guggenheim fellowships and was a seminal figure of the Harlem Renaissance. (Hurston's date of birth is much debated; Adno's essay has further information.) Yet, she died in relative obscurity, and her books vanished from print in the 1970s. Alice Walker, another formative American author of the South, tracked down the lost grave of Hurston in 1975 and wrote about it in a *Ms* magazine article, "In Search of Zora Neale Hurston." That work, in part, sparked a national return to Hurston's works, including to her most popular novel, *Their Eyes Were Watching God*, from which this excerpt comes.

Hurston's body of work reveals the ways African American culture, especially oral narratives from the southern United States, were made invisible in American literature. Her stories observe not just the structural systems that treated black and brown bodies as disposable but also the way those same systems made the environment disposable as well. The excerpt included here begins with the main character, Janie Crawford, and her lover, Tea Cake, on Lake Okeechobee in the Florida Everglades. They have been harvesting beans in "the muck" and made friends with workers from the Bahamas who play musical saws each night around a fire. Though Janie has observed animals fleeing and a tribe of Seminole Indians headed inland, Tea Cake says, "You ain't seen de bossman go up." He explains that since the white people haven't left, it must be safe. However, it is the bossman's desire for money that lets the workers endanger themselves in the same way that the same greed allows the environmental landscape of the Everglades to be exploited. Environment and workers are both jeopardized because of long-standing patterns of subjugation.

It is important to note that the storm Hurston wrote about was a historical one rather than fictional; the Great Okeechobee hurricane of September 17, 1928, killed thousands in Florida, many of whom were the migrant farmworkers from across the Caribbean whom Hurston depicts here. *Their Eyes Were Watching God* is already an essential novel in the canon of southern literature, yet it is also an early exploration of the way systems of oppression against people of color are deeply entangled with and inextricable from the environment of the Gulf South in the twentieth century.

Works Sourced

Adno, Michael. "The Sum of Life: Zora Neale Hurston." *The Bitter Southerner*, bittersoutherner.com/the-sum-of-life-zora-neale-hurston.

Rieger, Christopher. "Connecting Inner and Outer Nature: Zora Neale Hurston's Personal Pastoral." *Clear-Cutting Eden: Ecology and the Pastoral in Southern Literature*. University of Alabama Press, 2009, pp. 92–134.

Walker, Alice. "In Search of Zora Neale Hurston." *Ms*, vol. 3, Mar. 1975, pp. 74–89.

Since Tea Cake and Janie had friended with the Bahaman workers in the 'Glades, they, the "Saws," had been gradually drawn into the American crowd. They quit hiding out to hold their dances when they found that their American friends didn't laugh at them as they feared. Many of the Americans learned to jump and liked it as much as the "Saws." So they began to hold dances night after night in the quarters, usually behind Tea Cake's house. Often now, Tea Cake and Janie stayed up so late at the fire dances that Tea Cake would not let her go with him to the field. He wanted her to get her rest.

So she was home by herself one afternoon when she saw a band of Seminoles passing by. The men walking in front and the laden, stolid women following them like burros. She had seen Indians several times in the 'Glades, in twos and threes, but this was a large party. They were headed towards the Palm Beach road and kept moving steadily. About an hour later another party appeared and went the same way. Then another just before sundown. This time she asked where they were all going and at last one of the men answered her.

"Going to high ground. Saw-grass bloom. Hurricane coming."

Everybody was talking about it that night. But nobody was worried. The fire dance kept up till nearly dawn. The next day, more Indians moved east, unhurried but steady. Still a blue sky and fair weather. Beans running fine and prices good, so the Indians could be, must be, wrong. You couldn't have a hurricane when you're making seven and eight dollars a day picking beans. Indians are dumb anyhow, always were. Another night of Stew Beef making dynamic subtleties with his drum and living, sculptural, grotesques in the dance. Next day, no Indians passed at all. It was hot and sultry and Janie left the field and went home.

Morning came without motion. The winds, to the tiniest, lisping baby breath had left the earth. Even before the sun gave light, dead day was creeping from bush to bush watching man.

Some rabbits scurried through the quarters going east. Some possums slunk by and their route was definite. One or two at a time, then more. By the time the people left the fields the procession was constant. Snakes, rattlesnakes began to cross the quarters. The men killed a few, but they could not be missed from the crawling horde. People stayed indoors until daylight. Several times during the night Janie heard the snort of big animals like deer. Once the muted voice of a panther. Going east and east. That night the palm and banana trees began that long distance talk with rain. Several people took fright and picked up and went in to Palm Beach anyway. A thousand buzzards held a flying meet and then went above the clouds and stayed.

One of the Bahaman boys stopped by Tea Cake's house in a car and hollered. Tea Cake came out throwin' laughter over his shoulder into the house.

"Hello Tea Cake."

"Hello 'Lias. You leavin', Ah see."

"Yeah man. You and Janie wanta go? Ah wouldn't give nobody else uh chawnce at uh seat till Ah found out if you all had anyway tuh go."

"Thank yuh ever so much, Lias. But we 'bout decided stay."

"De crow gahn up, man."

"Dat ain't nothin'. You ain't seen de bossman go up, is yuh: Well all right now. Man, de money's too good on the muck. It liable tuh fair off by tuh-morrer. Ah wouldn't leave if Ah wuz you."

"Mah uncle come for me. He say hurricane warning out in Palm Beach. Not so bad dere, but man, dis muck is too low and dat big lake is liable tuh bust."

"Ah naw, man. Some boys in dere now talkin' 'bout it. Some of 'em been in de 'Glades fuh years. 'Tain't nothin' but uh blow. You'll lose de whole day tuhmorrer tryin' tuh git back out heah."

"De Indians gahn east, man. It's dangerous."

"Dey don't always know. Indians don't know much uh nothin', tuh tell de truth. Else dey'd own dis country still. De white folks ain't gone nowhere. Dey oughta know if it's dangerous. You better stay heah, man. Big jumpin' dance tuhnight right heah, when it fair off."

Lias hesitated and started to climb out, but his uncle wouldn't let him. "Dis time tuhmorrer you gointuh wish you follow crow," he snorted and drove off. Lias waved back to them gaily.

"If Ah never see you no mo' on earth, Ah'll meet you in Africa."

Others hurried east like the Indians and rabbits and snakes and coons. But the majority sat around laughing and waiting for the sun to get friendly again.

Several men collected at Tea Cake's house and sat around stuffing courage into each other's ears. Janie baked a big pan of beans and something she called sweet biscuits and they all managed to be happy enough.

Most of the great flame-throwers were there and naturally, handling Big John de Conquer and his works. How he had done everything big on earth, then went up tuh heben without dying atall. Went up there picking a guitar and got all de angels doing the ring-shout round and round de throne. Then everybody but God and Old Peter flew off on a flying race to Jericho and back and John de Conquer won the race; went on down to hell, beat the old devil and passed out ice water to everybody down there. Somebody tried to say that it was a mouth organ harp that John was playing, but the rest of them would not hear that. Don't care how good anybody could play a harp, God would rather to hear a guitar. That brought them back to Tea Cake. How come he couldn't hit that box a lick or two? Well, all right now, make us know it.

When it got good to everybody, Muck-Boy woke up and began to chant with the rhythm and everybody bore down on the last word of the line:

Yo' mama don't wear no *Draws*
Ah seen her when she took 'em *Off*
She soaked 'em in alco*Hol*
She sold 'em tuh de Santy *Claus*
He told her 'twas aginst de *Law*
To wear dem dirty *Draws*

Then Muck-Boy went crazy through the feet and danced himself and everybody else crazy. When he finished he sat back down on the floor and went to sleep again. Then they got to playing Florida flip and coon-can. Then it was dice. Not for money. This was a show-off game. Everybody posing his fancy shots. As always it broiled down to Tea Cake and Motor Boat. Tea Cake with his shy grin and Motor Boat with his face like a little black cherubim just from a church tower doing amazing things with anybody's dice. The others forgot the work and the weather watching them throw. It was art. A thousand dollars a throw in Madison Square Garden wouldn't have gotten any more breathless suspense. It would have just been more people holding in.

After a while somebody looked out and said, "It ain't girting no fairer out dere. B'lieve Ah'll git on over tuh mah shack." Motor Boat and Tea Cake were still playing so everybody left them at it.

Sometime that night the winds came back. Everything in the world had a strong rattle, sharp and short like Stew Beef vibrating the drum head near the edge with his fingers. By morning Gabriel was playing the deep tones in the center of the drum. So when Janie looked out of her door she saw the drifting mists gathered in the west—that cloud field of the sky—to arm themselves with thunders and march forth against the world. Louder and higher and lower and wider the sound and motion spread, mounting, sinking, darking.

It woke up old Okechobee and the monster began to roll in his bed. Began to roll and complain like a peevish world on a grumble. The folks in the quarters and the people in the big houses further around the shore heard the big lake and wondered. The people felt uncomfortable but safe because there were the seawalls to chain the senseless monster in his bed. The folks let the people do the thinking. If the castles thought themselves secure, the cabins needn't worry. Their decision was already made as always. Chink up your cracks, shiver in your wet beds and wait on the mercy of the Lord. The bossman might have the thing stopped before morning anyway. It is so easy to be hopeful in the day time when you can see the things you wish on. But it was night, it stayed night. Night was striding across nothingness with the whole round world in his hands.

A big burst of thunder and lightning that trampled over the roof of the house. So Tea Cake and Motor stopped playing. Motor looked up in his angel-looking way and said, "Big Massa draw him chair upstairs."

"Ah'm glad y'all stop dat crap-shootin' even if it wasn't for money," Janie said. "Ole Massa is doin' His work now. Us oughta keep quiet."

They huddled closer and stared at the door. They just didn't use another part of their bodies, and they didn't look at anything but the door. The time was past for asking the white folks what to look for through that door. Six eyes were questioning God.

Through the screaming wind they heard things crashing and things hurtling and dashing with unbelievable velocity. A baby rabbit, terror ridden, squirmed through a hole in the floor and squatted off there in the shadows against the wall, seeming to know that nobody wanted its flesh at such a time. And the lake got madder and madder with only its dikes between them and him.

In a little wind-lull, Tea Cake touched Janie and said, "Ah reckon you wish now you had of stayed in yo' big house 'way from such as dis, don't yuh?"

"Naw."

"Naw?"

"Yeah, naw. People don't die till dey time come nohow, don't keer where you at. Ah'm wid mah husband in uh storm, dat's all."

"Thanky, Ma'am. But 'sposing you wuz tuh die, now. You wouldn't git mad at me for draggin' yuh heah?"

"Naw. We been tuhgether round two years. If you kin see de light at daybreak, you don't keer if you die at dusk. It's so many people never seen de light at all. Ah wuz fumblin' round and God opened de door."

He dropped to the floor and put his head in her lap. "Well then, Janie, you meant whut you didn't say, 'cause Ah never knowed you wuz so satisfied wid me lak dat. Ah kinda thought—"

The wind came back with triple fury, and put out the light for the last time. They sat in company with the others in other shanties, their eyes straining against crude walls and their souls asking if He meant to measure their puny might against His. They seemed to be staring at the dark, but their eyes were watching God.

As soon as Tea Cake went out pushing wind in front of him, he saw that the wind and water had given life to lots of things that folks think of as dead and given death to so much that had been living things. Water everywhere. Stray fish swimming in the yard. Three inches more and the water would be in the house. Already in some. He decided to try to find a car to take them out of the 'Glades before worse things happened. He turned back to tell Janie about it so she could be ready to go.

"Git our insurance papers tuhgether, Janie. Ah'll tote mah box mahself and things lak dat."

"You got all de money out de dresser drawer, already?"

"Naw, git it quick and cut up piece off de table-cloth tuh wrap it up in. Us liable tuh git wet tuh our necks. Cut uh piece uh dat oilcloth quick fuh our papers. We got tuh go, ifit ain't too late. De dish can't bear it out no longer."

He snatched the oilcloth off the table and took out his knife. Janie held it straight while he slashed off a strip.

"But Tea Cake, it's too awful out dere. Maybe it's better tuh stay heah in de wet than it is tuh try tuh—"

He stunned the argument with half a word. "Fix," he said and fought his way outside. He had seen more than Janie had.

Janie took a big needle and ran up a longish sack. Found some news-paper and wrapped up the paper money and papers and thrust them in and whipped over the open end with her needle. Before she could get it thoroughly hidden in the pocket of her overalls, Tea Cake burst in again.

"'Tain't no cars, Janie."

"Ah thought not! Whut we gointuh do now?"

"We got tuh walk."

"In all dis weather, Tea Cake? Ah don't b'lieve Ah could make it out de quarters."

"Oh yeah you kin. Me and you and Motor Boat kin all lock arms and hold one 'nother down. Eh, Motor?"

"He's sleep on de bed in yonder," Janie said. Tea Cake called without moving.

"Motor Boat! You better git up from dere! Hell done broke loose in Georgy. Dis minute! How kin you sleep at uh time lak dis? Water knee deep in de yard."

They stepped out in water almost to their buttocks and managed to turn east. Tea Cake had to throw his box away, and Janie saw how it hurt him. Dodging flying missiles, floating dangers, avoiding stepping in holes and warmed on the wind now at their backs until they gained compara-tively dry land. They had to fight to keep from being pushed the wrong way and to hold together. They saw other people like themselves strug-gling along. A house down, here and there, frightened cattle. But above all the drive of the wind and the water. And the lake. Under its multiplied roar could be heard a mighty sound of grinding rock and timber and a wail. They looked back. Saw people trying to run in raging waters and screaming when they found they couldn't. A huge barrier of the makings of the dike to which the cabins had been added was rolling and tumbling forward. Ten feet higher and as far as they could see the muttering wall advanced before the braced-up waters like a road crusher on a cosmic scale. The monstro-polous beast had left his bed. The two hundred miles an hour wind had loosed his chains. He seized hold of his dikes and ran forward until he met the quarters; uprooted them like grass and rushed on after his supposed-to-be conquerors, rolling the dikes, rolling the houses, rolling the people in the houses along with other timbers. The sea was walking the earth with a heavy heel.

"De lake is comin'!" Tea Cake gasped.

"De lake!" In amazed horror from Motor Boat, "De lake!"

"It's comin' behind us!" Janie shuddered. "Us can't fly."

"But we still kin run," Tea Cake shouted and they ran. The gushing water ran faster. The great body was held back, but rivers spouted through fissures in the rolling wall and broke like day. The three fugitives ran past another line of shanties that topped a slight rise and gained a little. They cried out as best they could,

"De lake is comin'!" and barred doors flew open and others joined them in flight crying the same as they went. "De lake is comin'!" and the pursuing waters growled and shouted ahead, "Yes, Ah'm comin'!," and those who could fled on.

They made it to a tall house on a hump of ground and Janie said, "Less stop heah. Ah can't make it no further. Ah'm done give out."

"All of us is done give out," Tea Cake corrected. "We'se goin' inside out dis weather, kill or cure." He knocked with the handle of his knife, while they leaned their faces and shoulders against the wall. He knocked once more then he and Motor Boat went round to the back and forced a door. Nobody there.

"Dese people had mo' sense than Ah did," Tea Cake said as they dropped to the floor and lay there panting. "Us oughta went on wid 'Lias lak he ast me."

"You didn't know," Janie contended. "And when yuh don't know, yuh just don't know. De storms might not of come sho nuff."

They went to sleep promptly but Janie woke up first. She heard the sound of rushing water and sat up.

"Tea Cake! Motor Boat! De lake is comin'!"

The lake was coming on. Slower and wider, but coming. It had trampled on most of its supporting wall and lowered its front by spreading. But it came muttering and grumbling onward like a tired mammoth just the same.

"Dis is uh high tall house. Maybe it won't reach heah at all," Janie counseled. "And if it do, maybe it won't reach tuh de upstairs part."

"Janie, Lake Okechobee is forty miles wide and sixty miles long. Dat's uh whole heap uh water. If dis wind is shovin' dat whole lake disa way, dis house ain't nothin' tuh swaller. Us better go. Motor Boat!"

"Whut you want, man?"

"De lake is comin'!"

"Aw, naw it 'tain't."

"Yes, it is so comin'! Listen! You kin hear it way off."

"It kin jus' come on. Ah'll wait right here."

"Aw, get up, Motor Boat! Less make it tuh de Palm Beach road. Dat's on uh fill. We'se pretty safe dere."

"Ah'm safe here, man. Go ahead if yuh wants to. Ah'm sleepy."

"Whut you gointuh do if de lake reach heah?"

"Go upstairs."

"S'posing it come up dere?"

"Swim, man. Dat's all."

"Well, uh, Good bye, Motor Boat. Everything is pretty bad, yuh know. Us might git missed of one 'nother. You sho is a grand friend fuh uh man tuh have."

"Good bye, Tea Cake. Y'all oughta stay here and sleep, man. No use in goin' off and leavin' me lak dis."

"We don't wanta. Come on wid us. It might be night time when de water hem you up in heah. Dat's how come Ah won't stay. Come on, man."

"Tea Cake, Ah got tuh have mah sleep. Definitely."

"Good bye, then, Motor. Ah wish you all de luck. Goin' over tuh Nassau fuh dat visit widja when all dis is over."

"Definitely, Tea Cake. Mah mama's house is yours."

Tea Cake and Janie were some distance from the house before they struck serious water. Then they had to swim a distance, and Janie could not hold up more than a few strokes at a time, so Tea Cake bore her up till finally they hit a ridge that led on towards the fill. It seemed to him the wind was weakening a little so he kept looking for a place to rest and catch his breath. His wind was gone. Janie was tired and limping, but she had not had to do that hard swimming in the turbulent waters, so Tea Cake was much worse off. But they couldn't stop. Gaining the fill was something but it was no guarantee. The lake was coming. They had to reach the six-mile bridge. It was high and safe perhaps.

Everybody was walking the fill. Hurrying, dragging, falling, crying, calling out names hopefully and hopelessly. Wind and rain beating on old folks and beating on babies. Tea Cake stumbled once or twice in his weariness and Janie held him up. So they reached the bridge at Six Mile Bend and thought to rest.

But it was crowded. White people had preempted that point of elevation and there was no more room. They could climb up one of its high sides and down the other that was all. Miles further on, still no rest.

They passed a dead man in a sitting position on a hummock, entirely surrounded by wild animals and snakes. Common danger made common friends. Nothing sought a conquest over the other.

Another man clung to a cypress tree on a tiny island. A tin roof of a building hung from the branches by electric wires and the wind swung it back and forth like a mighty ax. The man dared not move a step to his right lest this crushing blade split him open. He dared not step left for a large rattlesnake was stretched full length with his head in the wind. There was a strip of water between the island and the fill, and the man clung to the tree and cried for help.

"De snake won't bite yuh," Tea Cake yelled to him. "He skeered tuh go intuh uh coil. Skeered he'll be blowed away. Step round dat side and swim off."

Soon after that Tea Cake felt he couldn't walk anymore. Not right away. So he stretched long side of the road to rest. Janie spread herself between him and the wind and he closed his eyes and let the tiredness seep out of his limbs. On each side of the fill was a great expanse of water like lakes-water full of things living and dead. Things that didn't belong in water. As far as the eye could reach, water and wind playing upon it in fury; A large piece of tar-paper roofing sailed through the air and scudded along the fill until it hung against a tree. Janie saw it with joy. That was the very thing to cover Tea Cake with. She could lean against it and hold it down. The wind wasn't quite so bad as it was anyway. The very thing. Poor Tea Cake!

She crept on hands and knees to the piece of roofing and caught hold of it by either side. Immediately the wind lifted both of them and she saw herself sailing off the fill to the right, out and out over the lashing water. She screamed terribly and released the roofing which sailed away as she plunged downward into the water.

"Tea Cake!" He heard her and sprang up. Janie was trying to swim but fighting water too hard. He saw a cow swimming slowly towards the fill in an oblique line. A massive built dog was sitting on her shoulders and shivering and growling. The cow was approaching Janie. A few strokes would bring her there.

"Make it tuh de cow and grab hold of her tail! Don't use yo' feet. Jus' yo' hands is enough. Dat's right, come on!"

Janie achieved the tail of the cow and lifted her head up along the cow's rump, as far as she could above water. The cow sunk a little with the added load and thrashed a moment in terror. Thought she was being pulled down by a gator. Then she continued on. The dog stood up and growled like a lion, stiff standing hackles, stiff muscles, teeth uncovered as he lashed up his fury for the charge. Tea Cake split the water like an otter, opening his knife as he dived. The dog raced down the backbone of the cow to the attack and Janie screamed and slipped far back on the tail of the cow, just out of reach of the dog's angry jaws. He wanted to plunge in after her but dreaded the water, somehow. Tea Cake rose out of the water at the cow's rump and seized the dog by the neck. But he was a powerful dog and Tea Cake was over-tired. So he didn't kill the dog with one stroke as he had intended. But the dog couldn't free himself either. They fought and somehow he managed to bite Tea Cake high up on his cheek-bone once. Then Tea Cake finished him and sent him to the bottom to stay there. The cow relieved of a great weight was landing on the fill with Janie before Tea Cake stroked in and crawled weakly upon the fill again.

Janie began to fuss around his face where the dog had bitten him but he said it didn't amount to anything. "He'd uh raised hell though if he had uh grabbed me uh inch higher and bit me in mah eye. Yuh can't buy eyes in de store, yuh know." He flopped to the edge of the fill as if the storm wasn't going on at all. "Lemme rest awhile, then us got tuh make it on intuh town somehow."

It was next day by the sun and the clock when they reached Palm Beach. It was years later by their bodies. Winters and winters of hardship and suffering. The wheel kept turning round and round. Hope, hopelessness and despair. But the storm blew itself out as they approached the city of refuge.

Havoc was there with her mouth wide open. Back in the Everglades the wind had romped among lakes and trees. In the city it had raged among houses and men. Tea Cake and Janie stood on the edge of things and looked over the desolation.

"How kin Ah find uh doctor fuh yo' face in all dis mess?" Janie wailed.

"Ain't got de damn doctor tuh study 'bout. Us needs uh place tuh rest."

A great deal of their money and perseverance and they found a place to sleep. It was just that. No place to live at all. Just sleep. Tea Cake looked all around and sat heavily on the side of the bed.

"Well," he said humbly, "reckon you never 'spected tuh come tuh dis when you took up wid me, didja?"

"Once upon uh time, Ah never 'spected nothin', Tea Cake, but bein' dead from the standin' still and tryin' tuh laugh. But you come 'long and made somethin' outa me. So Ah'm thankful fuh anything we come through together."

"Thanky, Ma'am."

"You was twice noble tuh save me from dat dawg. Tea Cake, Ah don't speck you seen his eyes lak Ah did. He didn't aim tuh jus' bite me, Tea

Cake. He aimed tuh kill pie stone dead. Ah'm never tuh fuhgit dem eyes. He wuzn't nothin' all over but pure hate. Wonder where he come from?"

"Yeah, Ah did see 'im too. It wuz frightenin'. Ah didn't mean tuh take his hate neither. He had tuh die uh me one. Mah switch blade said it wuz him."

"Po' me, he'd tore me tuh pieces, if it wuzn't fuh you, honey."

"You don't have tuh say, if it wuzn't fuh me, baby, cause Ah'm *heah*, and then Ah want yuh tuh know it's uh man heah."

MARJORIE KINNAN RAWLINGS

The Yearling (1938)

Marjorie Kinnan Rawlings (1896–1953) bought seventy-four acres of orange groves in Cross Creek, Florida, in 1928, before the population boom in the mid-twentieth century. It was here that Rawlings wrote stories of hardworking hunters, adventurous children, and the land, lakes, and rivers surrounding them. Rawlings wrote prolifically. Her oeuvre is made up of four novels, two novellas, two works of nonfiction, and many short stories, yet for many years after her death she was remembered as a regional writer. Perhaps because she was a woman, perhaps because she wrote often of children, her work was overlooked for many years. Since the 2000s, there has been a resurgence of scholarly interest in her writing due to the subtle descriptions and lyrical quality of her writing about the natural environment of Florida.

In Rawlings's Pulitzer Prize–winning novel, *The Yearling* (1938), from which this excerpt is taken, she tells the story of a young boy, Jody, and how he grows to understand the natural world around him. The story begins with Jody unable to sleep because he is overwhelmed by the beauty of the world. He is still innocent to violence and treachery. By the end of the book, Jody's worldview has drastically changed. He is forced to shoot his pet deer, who has eaten the family crops. His mother, who takes the first shot, only wounds the yearling. Jody kills the deer out of mercy but also because his family's needs come before the animal. Though this book can be read as an affirmation of human primacy, Jody's sensitivity and joy in the natural world reveal time and time again the way all life is interconnected.

In this selection, Rawlings's delight in the natural world is evident in the way she describes how Jody and his father, Penny, come upon a flock of whooping cranes. Her descriptions of the cranes as "cotillion dancers" is exemplary of the way Rawlings conceptualized the natural world, as equal in sophisticated social systems to humankind. Humans are simply a part of a network of relations that share her Florida landscape.

Work Sourced

Rieger, Christopher. "Cross Creek Culture: Marjorie Kinnan Rawlings's Wilderness Pastoral." *Clear-Cutting Eden: Ecology and the Pastoral in Southern Literature.* University of Alabama Press, 2009, pp. 53-91.

The moon was now wrong. It was no longer feed-time. The fish were not striking. Suddenly he heard his father whistle like a quail. It was the signal they used together in squirrel hunting. Jody laid down his pole and looked back to make sure he could identify the tuft of grass where he had covered his bass from the rays of the sun. He walked cautiously to where his father beckoned.

Penny whispered, "Foller me. We'll ease up clost as we dare."

He pointed. "The whoopin' cranes is dancin'."

Jody saw the great white birds in the distance. His father's eye, he thought, was like an eagle's. They crouched on all fours and crept forward slowly. Now and then Penny dropped flat on his stomach and Jody dropped behind him. They reached a clump of high saw-grass and Penny motioned for concealment behind it. The birds were so close that it seemed to Jody he might touch them with his long fishing pole. Penny squatted on his haunches and Jody followed. His eyes were wide. He made a count of the whooping cranes. There were sixteen.

The cranes were dancing a cotillion as surely as it was danced at Volusia. Two stood apart, erect and white, making a strange music that was part cry and part singing. The rhythm was irregular, like the dance. The other birds were in a circle. In the heart of the circle, several moved counter-clock-wise. The musicians made their music. The dancers raised their wings and lifted their feet, first one and then the other. They sank their heads deep in their snowy breasts, lifted them and sank them again. They moved soundlessly, part awkwardness, part grace. The dance was solemn. Wings fluttered, rising and falling like out-stretched arms. The outer circle shuffled around and around. The group in the center attained a slow frenzy.

Suddenly all motion ceased. Jody thought the dance was over, or that the intruders had been discovered. Then the two musicians joined the circle. Two others took their places. There was a pause. The dance was resumed. The birds were reflected in the clear marsh water. Sixteen white shadows reflected the motions. The evening breeze moved across the saw-grass. It bowed and fluttered. The water rippled. The setting sun lay rosy on the white bodies. Magic birds were dancing in a mystic marsh. The grass swayed with them, and the shallow waters, and the earth fluttered under them. The earth was dancing with the cranes, and the low sun, and the wind and sky.

Jody found his own arms lifting and falling with his breath, as the cranes' wings lifted. The sun was sinking into the saw-grass. The marsh was golden. The whooping cranes were washed with gold. The far hammocks were black. Darkness came to the lily pads, and the water blackened. The cranes were whiter than any clouds, or any white bloom of oleander or of lily. Without warning, they took flight. Whether the hour-long dance was, simply, done, or whether the long nose of an alligator had lifted above the water to alarm them, Jody could not tell, but they were gone. They made a great circle against the sunset, whooping their strange rusty cry that sounded only in their flight. Then they flew in a long line into the west, and vanished.

Penny and Jody straightened and stood up. They were cramped from the long crouching. Dusk lay over the saw-grass, so that the ponds were scarcely visible. The world was shadow, melting into shadow. They turned to the north. Jody found his bass. They cut to the east, to leave the marsh behind them, then north again. The trail was dim in the growing darkness. It joined the scrub road and they turned once more east, continuing now in a certainty, for the dense growth of the scrub bordered the road like walls. The scrub was black and the road was a dark gray strip of carpet, sandy and soundless. Small creatures darted across in front of them and scurried in the bushes. In the distance, a panther screamed. Bull-bats shot low over their heads. They walked in silence.

At the house, bread was baked and waiting, and hot fat was in the iron skillet. Penny lighted a fat-wood torch and went to the lot to do his chores. Jody scaled and dressed the fish at the back stoop, where a ray of light glimmered from the fire on the hearth. Ma Baxter dipped the pieces in meal and fried them crisp and golden. The family ate without speaking.

She said, "What ails you fellers?"

They did not answer. They had no thought for what they ate nor for the woman. They were no more than conscious that she spoke to them. They had seen a thing that was unearthly. They were in a trance from the strong spell of its beauty.

WILLIAM FAULKNER

"Old Man"

The Wild Palms (1939)

William Faulkner (1897–1962) is seldom considered an environmental writer; instead, he is known as *the* southern writer in American literary history. Yet, Faulkner's devotion to place, both the fictional Yoknapatawpha County and the US South, led him to observe and record the ways that the region's relation to the environment were implicated in the same social structures that determined systems of race and economy. Faulkner was born and raised in Mississippi, and even in his first novel, *Soldier's Pay* (1926), which takes place in Georgia, his attention is focused on the South as a region, particularly in respect to its diction and cadence of speech. Faulkner was a prodigious writer. He wrote thirteen novels, many short stories, two books of poetry, and five screenplays for Hollywood. He won the Pulitzer Prize twice, the National Book Award, and the Nobel prize.

The excerpt we have included here is from the story "Old Man," which was first published in *The Wild Palms* (1939), later retitled *If I Forget Thee, Jerusalem*, and now usually referred to by both names. This story opens with twenty-two prisoners being transported by truck to the flooding banks of the Mississippi River where they witness a montage of horrific images. The prisoners pass a black family scrambling to get onto the rooftop and away from the rising river; the mother screams at the passing truck until the prisoners can no longer hear her. They pass a burning plantation and towns that look as if they are floating away. Faulkner presents here the terror of the Mississippi Flood of 1927 through images of the immensity and power of the river. Toward the end of the excerpt, a prisoner who is only referred to as "the taller convict" looks out across the river and sees only a hair-thin levee. He imagines himself from the other side and feels his own precarity. Later, the convict sees a barn that had floated away in the flood and has come to rest on the levee. Men, like "a swarm of ants" strip the lost building down to its frame. Faulkner's almost hallucinogenic depictions of the flood reveal the trope of man versus nature, yet in this story, man is clearly losing. Faulkner's story speaks to the tradition of human against nature rather than the human in nature, a perspective that continues in this generations continued control of the river through levees, dams, and floodplains with not enough thought to ecological long-term health.

Work Sourced

Hoefer, Anthony Dyer. "'They're Trying to Wash Us Away': Revisiting Faulkner's *If I Forget Thee, Jerusalem* [*The Wild Palms*] and Wright's 'Down by the Riverside' after the Flood." *Mississippi Quarterly*, vol. 63, no. 3/4, Summer/Fall 2010, pp. 537–554.

When the belated and streaming dawn broke the two convicts, along with twenty others, were in a truck. A trusty drove, two armed guards sat in the cab with him. Inside the high, stall-like topless body the convicts stood, packed like matches in an upright box or like the pencil-shaped ranks of cordite in a shell, shackled by the ankles to a single chain which wove among the motionless feet and swaying legs and a clutter of picks and shovels among which they stood, and was riveted by both ends to the steel body of the truck.

Then and without warning they saw the flood about which the plump convict had been reading and they listening for two weeks or more. The road ran south. It was built on a raised levee, known locally as a dump, about eight feet above the flat surrounding land, bordered on both sides by the barrow pits from which the earth of the levee had been excavated. These barrow pits had held water all winter from the fall rains, not to speak of the rain of yesterday, but now they saw that the pit on either side of the road had vanished and instead there lay a flat still sheet of brown water which extended into the fields beyond the pits, raveled out into long motionless shreds in the bottom of the plow furrows and gleaming faintly in the gray light like the bars of a prone and enormous grating. And then (the truck was moving at good speed) as they watched quietly (they had not been talking much anyway but now they were all silent and quite grave, shifting and craning as one to look soberly off to the west side of the road) the crests of the furrows vanished too and they now looked at a single perfectly flat and motionless steel-colored sheet in which the telephone poles and the straight hedgerows which marked section lines seemed to be fixed and rigid as though set in concrete.

It was perfectly motionless, perfectly flat. It looked, not innocent, but bland. It looked almost demure. It looked as if you could walk on it. It looked so still that they did not realize it possessed motion until they came to the first bridge. There was a ditch under the bridge, a small stream, but ditch and stream were both invisible now, indicated only by the rows of cypress and bramble which marked its course. Here they both saw and heard movement—the slow profound eastward and upstream ("It's running backward," one convict said quietly.) set of the still rigid surface, from beneath which came a deep faint subaquean rumble which (though none in the truck could have made the comparison) sounded like a subway train passing far beneath the street and which inferred a terrific and secret speed. It was as if the water itself were in three strata, separate and distinct, the bland and unhurried surface bearing a frothy scum and a miniature flotsam of twigs and screening as though by vicious calculation the rush and fury of the flood itself, and beneath this in turn the original stream, trickle, murmuring along in the opposite direction, following undisturbed and unaware its appointed course and serving its Lilliputian end, like a thread of ants between the rails on which an express train passes, they (the ants) as unaware of the power and fury as if it were a cyclone crossing Saturn.

Now there was water on both sides of the road and now, as if once they had become aware of movement in the water the water seemed to have given over deception and concealment, they seemed to be able to watch it rising up the flanks of the dump; trees which a few miles back had stood on tall trunks above the water now seemed to burst from the surface at the level of the lower branches like decorative shrubs on barbered lawns. The truck passed a negro cabin. The water was up to the window ledges. A woman clutching two children squatted on the ridgepole, a man and a halfgrown youth, standing waist-deep, were hoisting a squealing pig onto the slanting roof of a barn, on the ridgepole of which sat a row of chickens and a turkey. Near the barn was a haystack on which a cow stood tied by a rope to the center pole and bawling steadily; a yelling negro boy on a saddleless mule which he flogged steadily, his legs clutching the mule's barrel and his body leaned to the drag of a rope attached to a second mule, approached the haystack, splashing and floundering. The woman on the housetop began to shriek at the passing truck, her voice carrying faint and melodious across the brown water, becoming fainter and fainter as the truck passed and went on, ceasing at last, whether because of distance or because she had stopped screaming those in the truck did not know.

Then the road vanished. There was no perceptible slant to it yet it had slipped abruptly beneath the brown surface with no ripple, no ridgy demarcation, like a flat thin blade slipped obliquely into flesh by a delicate hand, annealed into the water without disturbance, as if it had existed so for years, had been built that way. The truck stopped. The trusty descended from the cab and came back and dragged two shovels from among their feet, the blades clashing against the serpentining of the chain about their ankles. "What is it?" one said. "What are you fixing to do?" The trusty didn't answer. He returned to the cab, from which one of the guards had descended, without his shotgun. He and the trusty, both in hip boots and each carrying a shovel, advanced into the water, gingerly, probing and feeling ahead with the shovel handles. The same convict spoke again. He was a middle-aged man with a wild thatch of iron-gray hair and a slightly mad face. "What the hell are they doing?" he said. Again nobody answered him. The truck moved, on into the water, behind the guard and the trusty, beginning to push ahead of itself a thick slow viscid ridge of chocolate water. Then the gray-haired convict began to scream. "God damn it, unlock the chain!" He began to struggle, thrashing violently about him, striking at the men nearest him until he reached the cab, the roof of which he now hammered on with his fists, screaming. "God damn it, unlock us! Unlock us! Son of a bitch!" he screamed, addressing no one. "They're going to drown us! Unlock the chain!" But for all the answer he got the men within radius of his voice might have been dead. The truck crawled on, the guard and the trusty feeling out the road ahead with the reversed shovels, the second guard at the wheel, the twenty-two convicts packed like sardines into the truck bed and padlocked by the ankles to the body of the truck itself. They crossed another bridge—two delicate and paradoxical iron railings slanting out of the water, travelling parallel to it for a distance, then slanting down into it again with an outrageous quality almost significant yet apparently meaningless like something in a dream not quite nightmare. The truck crawled on.

Along toward noon they came to a town, their destination. The streets were paved; now the wheels of the truck made a sound like tearing silk. Moving faster now, the guard and the trusty in the cab again, the truck even had a slight bone in its teeth, its bow-wave spreading beyond the submerged sidewalks and across the adjacent lawns, lapping against the stoops and porches of houses where people stood among piles of furniture. They passed through the business district; a man in hip boots emerged knee-deep in water from a store, dragging a flat-bottomed skiff containing a steel safe.

At last they reached the railroad. It crossed the street at right angles, cutting the town in two. It was on a dump, a levee, also, eight or ten feet above the town itself; the street ran blankly into it and turned at right angles beside a cotton compress and a loading platform on stilts at the level of a freight car door. On this platform was a khaki army tent and a uniformed National Guard sentry with a rifle and bandolier.

The truck turned and crawled out of the water and up the ramp which cotton wagons used and where trucks and private cars filled with household goods came and unloaded onto the platform. They were unlocked from the chain in the truck and shackled ankle to ankle in pairs they mounted the platform and into an apparently inextricable jumble of beds and trunks, gas and electric stoves, radios and tables and chairs and framed pictures which a chain of negroes under the eye of an unshaven white man in muddy corduroy and hip boots carried piece by piece into the compress, at the door of which another guardsman stood with his rifle, they (the convicts) not stopping here but herded on by the two guards with their shotguns, into the dim and cavernous building where among the piled heterogeneous furniture the ends of cotton bales and the mirrors on dressers and sideboards gleamed with an identical mute and unreflecting concentration of pallid light.

They passed on through, onto the loading platform where the army tent and the first sentry were. They waited here. Nobody told them for what nor why. While the two guards talked with the sentry before the tent the convicts sat in a line along the edge of the platform like buzzards on a fence, their shackled feet dangling above the brown motionless flood out of which the railroad embankment rose, pristine and intact, in a kind of paradoxical denial and repudiation of change and portent, not talking, just looking quietly across the track to where the other half of the amputated town seemed to float, house shrub and tree, ordered and pageant-like and without motion, upon the limitless liquid plain beneath the thick gray sky.

After a while the other four trucks from the Farm arrived. They came up, bunched closely, radiator to tail light, with their four separate sounds of tearing silk and vanished beyond the compress. Presently the ones on the platform heard the feet, the mute clashing of the shackles, the first truckload emerged from the compress, the second, the third; there were more than a hundred of them now in their bed-ticking overalls and jumpers and fifteen or twenty guards with rifles and shotguns. The first lot rose and they mingled, paired, twinned by their clanking and clashing umbilicals; then it began to rain, a slow steady gray drizzle like November instead of May. Yet not one of them made any move toward the open door of the compress. They did not even look toward it, with longing or hope or without it. If they thought at all, they doubtless knew that the available space in it would be needed for furniture, even if it were not already filled. Or perhaps they knew that, even if there were room in it, it would not be for them, not that the guards would wish them to get wet but that the guards would not think about getting them out of the rain. So they just stopped talking and with their jumper collars turned up and shackled in braces like dogs at a field trial they stood, immobile, patient, almost ruminant, their backs turned to the rain as sheep and cattle do.

After another while they became aware that the number of soldiers had increased to a dozen or more, warm and dry beneath rubberised ponchos, there was an officer with a pistol at his belt, then and without making any move toward it, they began to smell food and, turning to look, saw an army field kitchen set up just inside the compress door. But they made no move, they waited until they were herded into line, they inched forward, their heads lowered and patient in the rain, and received each a bowl of stew, a mug of coffee, two slices of bread. They ate this in the rain. They did not sit down because the platform was wet, they squatted on their heels as country men do, hunching forward trying to shield the bowls and mugs into which nevertheless the rain splashed steadily as into miniature ponds and soaked, invisible and soundless, into the bread.

After they had stood on the platform for three hours, a train came for them. Those nearest the edge saw it, watched it—a passenger coach apparently running under its own power and trailing a cloud of smoke from no visible stack, a cloud which did not rise but instead shifted slowly and heavily aside and lay upon the surface of the aqueous earth with a quality at once weightless and completely spent. It came up and stopped, a single old fashioned open-ended wooden car coupled to the nose of a pushing switch engine considerably smaller. They were herded into it, crowding forward to the other end where there was a small cast iron stove. There was no fire in it, nevertheless they crowded about it—the cold and voiceless lump of iron stained with fading tobacco and hovered about by the ghosts of a thousand Sunday excursions to Memphis or Moorhead and return—the peanuts, the bananas, the soiled garments of infants—huddling, shoving for places near it. "Come on, come on," one of the guards shouted. "Sit down, now." At last three of the guards, laying aside their guns, came among them and broke up the huddle, driving them back and into seats.

There were not enough seats for all. The others stood in the aisle, they stood braced, they heard the air hiss out of the released brakes, the engine whistled four blasts, the car came into motion with a snapping jerk;

the platform, the compress fled violently as the train seemed to transpose from immobility to full speed with that same quality of unreality with which it had appeared, running backward now though with the engine in front where before it had moved forward but with the engine behind.

When the railroad in its turn ran beneath the surface of the water, the convicts did not even know it. They felt the train stop, they heard the engine blow a long blast which wailed away unechoed across the waste, wild and forlorn, and they were not even curious; they sat or stood behind the rainstreaming windows as the train crawled on again, feeling its way as the truck had while the brown water swirled between the trucks and among the spokes of the driving wheels and lapped in cloudy steam against the dragging fire-filled belly of the engine; again it blew four short harsh blasts filled with the wild triumph and defiance yet also with repudiation and even farewell, as if the articulated steel itself knew it did not dare stop and would not be able to return. Two hours later in the twilight they saw through the streaming windows a burning plantation house. Juxtaposed to nowhere and neighbored by nothing it stood, a clear steady pyre-like flame rigidly fleeing its own reflection, burning in the dusk above the watery desolation with a quality paradoxical, outrageous and bizarre.

Sometime after dark the train stopped. The convicts did not know where they were. They did not ask. They would no more have thought of asking where they were than they would have asked why and what for. They couldn't even see, since the car was unlighted and the windows fogged on the outside by rain and on the inside by the engendered heat of the packed bodies. All they could see was a milky and sourceless flick and glare of flashlights. They could hear shouts and commands, then the guards inside the car began to shout; they were herded to their feet and toward the exit, the ankle chains clashing and clanking. They descended into a fierce hissing of steam, through ragged wisps of it blowing past the car. Laid-to alongside the train and resembling a train itself was a thick blunt motor launch to which was attached a string of skiffs and flat boats. There were more soldiers; the flashlights played on the rifle barrels and bandolier buckles and flicked and glinted on the ankle chains of the convicts as they stepped gingerly down into knee-deep water and entered the boats; now car and engine both vanished completely in steam as the crew began dumping the fire from the firebox.

After another hour they began to see lights ahead—a faint wavering row of red pin-pricks extending along the horizon and apparently hanging low in the sky. But it took almost another hour to reach them while the convicts squatted in the skiffs, huddled into the soaked garments (they no longer felt the rain anymore at all as separate drops) and watched the lights draw nearer and nearer until at last the crest of the levee defined itself; now they could discern a row of army tents stretching along it and people squatting about the fires, the wavering reflections from which, stretching across the water, revealed an involved mass of other skiffs tied against the flank of the levee which now stood high and dark overhead. Flashlights glared and winked along the base, among the tethered skiffs; the launch, silent now, drifted in.

When they reached the top of the levee they could see the long line of khaki tents, interspersed with fires about which people—men, women and children, negroes and white—crouched or stood among shapeless bales of clothing, their heads turning, their eyeballs glinting in the firelight as they looked quietly at the striped garments and the chains; further down the levee, huddled together too though untethered, was a drove of mules and two or three cows. Then the taller convict became conscious of another sound. He did not begin to hear it all at once, he suddenly became aware that he had been hearing it all the time, a sound so much beyond all his experience and his powers of assimilation that up to this point he had been as oblivious of it as an ant or a flea might be of the sound of the avalanche on which it rides; he had been travelling upon water since early afternoon and for seven years now he had run his plow and harrow and planter within the very shadow of the levee on which he now stood, but this profound deep whisper which came from the further side of it he did not at once recognize. He stopped. The line of convicts behind jolted into him like a line of freight cars stopping, with an iron clashing like cars. "Get on!" a guard shouted.

"What's that?" the convict said. A negro man squatting before the nearest fire answered him:

"Dat's him. Dat's de Ole Man."

"The old man?" the convict said.

"Get on! Get on up there!" the guard shouted. They went on; they passed another huddle of mules, the eyeballs rolling too, the long morose faces turning into and out of the firelight; they passed them and reached a section of empty tents, the light pup tents of a military campaign, made to hold two men. The guards herded the convicts into them, three brace of shackled men to each tent.

They crawled in on all fours, like dogs into cramped kennels, and settled down. Presently the tent became warm from their bodies. Then they became quiet and then all of them could hear it, they lay listening to the bass whisper deep, strong and powerful. "The old man?" the train-robber convict said.

"Yah," another said. "He don't have to brag."

At dawn the guards waked them by kicking the soles of the projecting feet. Opposite the muddy landing and the huddle of skiffs an army field kitchen was set up, already they could smell the coffee. But the taller convict at least, even though he had had but one meal yesterday and that at noon in the rain, did not move at once toward the food. Instead and for the first time he looked at the River within whose shadow he had spent the last seven years of his life but had never seen before; he stood in quiet and amazed surmise and looked at the rigid steel-colored surface not broken into waves but merely slightly undulant. It stretched from the levee on which he stood, further than he could see—a slowly and heavily roiling chocolate—frothy expanse broken only by a thin line a mile away as fragile in appearance as a single hair, which after a moment he recognized. *It's another levee* he thought quietly. *That's what we look like from there. That's what I am standing on looks like from there.* He was prodded from the rear; a guard's voice carried forward: "Go on! Go on! You'll have plenty of time to look at that!"

They received the same stew and coffee and bread as the day before, they squatted again with their bowls and mugs as yesterday, though it was not raining yet. During the night an intact wooden barn had floated up. It now lay jammed by the current against the levee while a crowd of negroes swarmed over it, ripping off the shingles and planks and carrying them up the bank; eating steadily and without haste, the taller convict watched the barn dissolve rapidly down to the very waterline exactly as a dead fly vanished beneath the moiling industry of a swarm of ants.

MARJORY STONEMAN DOUGLAS

The Everglades: River of Grass (1947)

Marjory Stoneman Douglas (1890–1998) and the Florida Everglades are forever intertwined, the one preserving the other through time. Douglas was a journalist, author, women's suffragist, and conservationist who helped to preserve the Florida Everglades from being drained and reclaimed as land for development during the housing boom of the early twentieth century. Through her journalism at *The Miami Herald*, organizing work, and advocating for the complex and interconnected nature of the Everglades, she helped to make the tropical wilderness a federally protected site. Douglas's seminal work, *The Everglades: River of Grass*, was published in 1947, the same year the Florida Everglades were dedicated as a national park by President Harry Truman.

Douglas was also a strong women's rights supporter. She is a clear example of the many women in the South who were forerunners of the environmental movement of the twentieth century when Americans organized to counter the unprecedented exploitation and pollution in Florida and across the Gulf South. The creation of Everglades National Park was seen as a sign of an American turn toward an early mainstream environmental movement in the United States. Douglas outlines these changing attitudes toward the Everglades from a "vast, miasmic swamp" to her own vision of a "vast glittering openness." This excerpt reveals how Douglas's precise and poetic language redefined how Americans understood the Everglades, not as worthless swamp to be drained but as essential to the delicate ecology of the area.

Work Sourced

Davis, Jack E. *An Everglades Providence: Marjory Stoneman Douglas and the American Environmental Century.* University of Georgia Press, 2009.

I. THE NAME

There are no other Everglades in the world.

They are, they have always been, one of the unique regions of the earth, remote, never wholly known. Nothing anywhere else is like them: their vast glittering openness, wider than the enormous visible round of the horizon, the racing free saltness and sweetness of their massive winds, under the dazzling blue heights of space. They are unique also in the simplicity, the diversity, the related harmony of the forms of life they enclose. The miracle of the light pours over the green and brown expanse of saw grass and of water, shining and slow-moving below, the grass and water that is the meaning and the central fact of the Everglades of Florida. It is a river of grass. The great pointed paw of the state of Florida, familiar as the map of North America itself, of which it is the most noticeable appendage, thrusts south, farther south than any other part of the mainland of the United States. Between the shining aquamarine waters of the Gulf of Mexico and the roaring deep-blue waters of the north-surging Gulf Stream, the shaped land points toward Cuba and the Caribbean. It points toward and touches within one degree of the tropics.

More than halfway down that thrusting sea-bound peninsula nearly everyone knows the lake that is like a great hole in that pawing shape, Lake Okeechobee, the second largest body of fresh water, it is always said, "within the confines of the United States." Below that lie the Everglades.

They have been called "the mysterious Everglades" so long that the phrase is a meaningless platitude. For four hundred years after the discovery they seemed more like a fantasy than a simple geographic and historic fact. Even the men who in the later years saw them more clearly could hardly make up their minds what the Everglades were or how they could be described, or what use could be made of them. They were mysterious then. They are mysterious still to everyone by whom their fundamental nature is not understood.

Off and on for those four hundred years the region now called "The Everglades" was described as a series of vast, miasmic swamps, poisonous lagoons, huge dismal marshes without outlet, a rotting, shallow, inland sea, or labyrinths of dark trees hung and looped about with snakes and dripping mosses, malignant with tropical fevers and malarias, evil to the white man.

Even the name, "The Everglades," was given them and printed on a map of Florida within the past hundred years. It is variously interpreted. There were one or two other names we know, which were given them before that, but what sounds the first men had for them, seeing first, centuries and centuries before the discovering white men, those sun-blazing solitudes, we shall never know.

The shores that surround the Everglades were the first on this continent known to white men. The interior was almost the last. They have not yet been entirely mapped.

Spanish mapmakers who never saw them, printed over the unknown blank space where they lay on those early maps the words "El Laguna del Espiritu Santo." To the early Spanish they were truly mysterious, fabulous with a wealth they were never able to prove.

The English from the Bahamas, charting the Florida coasts in the early seventeen hundreds, had no very clear idea of them. Gerard de Brahm, the surveyor, may have gone up some of the east-coast rivers and stared out on that endless, watery bright expanse, for on his map he called them "River Glades." But on the later English maps "River" becomes "Ever," so it is hard to tell what he intended.

The present name came into general use only after the acquisition of Florida from Spain in 1819 by the United States. The Turner map of 1823 was the first to use the word "Everglades." The fine Ives map of 1856 prints the words separately, "Ever Glades." In the text of the memorial that accompanied the map they were used without capitals, as "ever glades."

The word "glade" is of the oldest English origin. It comes from the Anglo-Saxon "glaed," with the "ae" diphthong, shortened to "glad." It meant "shining" or "bright," perhaps as of water. The same word was used in the Scandinavian languages for "a clear place in the sky, a bright streak or patch of light," as Webster's International Dictionary gives it. It might even first have referred to the great openness of the sky over it, and not to the land at all.

In English for over a thousand years the word "glaed" or "glyde" or "glade" has meant an open green grassy place in the forest. And in America of the English colonies the use was continued to mean stretches of natural pasture, naturally grassy.

But most dictionaries nowadays end a definition of them with the qualifying phrase, "as of the Florida Everglades." So that they have thus become unique in being their own, and only, best definition.

Yet the Indians, who have known the Glades longer and better than any dictionary-making white men, gave them their perfect, and poetic name, which is also true. They called them "Pa-hay-okee," which is the Indian word for "Glassy Water." Today Everglades is one word and yet plural. They are the only Everglades in the world.

Men crossed and recrossed them leaving no trace, so that no one knew men had been there. The few books or pamphlets written about them by Spaniards or surveyors or sportsmen or botanists have not been generally read. Actually, the first accurate studies of Everglades geology, soil, archaeology, even history, are only just now being completed.

The question was at once, where do you begin? Because, when you think of it, history, the recorded time of the earth and of man, is in itself something like a river. To try to present it whole is to find oneself lost in the sense of continuing change. The source can be only the beginning in time and space, and the end is the future and the unknown. What we can know lies somewhere between. The course along which for a little way one proceeds, the changing life, the varying light, must somehow be fixed in a moment clearly, from which one may look before and after and try to comprehend wholeness.

So it is with the Everglades, which have that quality of long existence in their own nature. They were changeless. They are changed.

They were complete before man came to them, and for centuries afterward, when he was only one of those forms which shared, in a finely balanced harmony, the forces and the ancient nature of the place.

Then, when the Everglades were most truly themselves, is the time to begin with them.

II. THE GRASS

The Everglades begin at Lake Okeechobee.

That is the name later Indians gave the lake, a name almost as recent as the word "Everglades." It means "Big Water." Everybody knows it.

Yet few have any idea of those pale, seemingly illimitable waters. Over the shallows, often less than a foot deep but seven hundred fifty or so square miles in actual area, the winds in one gray swift moment can shatter the reflections of sky and cloud whiteness standing still in that shining, polished, shimmering expanse. A boat can push for hours in a day of white sun through the short, crisp lake waves and there will be nothing to be seen anywhere but the brightness where the color of the water and the color of the sky become one. Men out of sight of land can stand in it up to their armpits and slowly "walk in" their long nets to the waiting boats. An everglade kite and his mate, questing in great solitary circles, rising and dipping and rising again on the wind currents, can look down all day long at the water faintly green with floating water lettuce or marked by thin standing lines of reeds, utter their sharp goat cries, and be seen and heard by no one at all.

There are great shallow islands, all brown reeds or shrubby trees thick in the water. There are masses of water weeds and hyacinths and flags rooted so long they seem solid earth, yet there is nothing but lake bottom to stand on. There the egret and the white ibis and the glossy ibis and the little blue herons in their thousands nested and circled and fed.

A long northeast wind, a "norther," can lash all that still surface to dirty vicious gray and white, over which the rain mists shut down like stained rolls of wool, so that from the eastern sand rim under dripping cypresses or the west ridge with its live oaks, no one would guess that all that waste of empty water stretched there but for the long monotonous wash of waves on unseen marshy shores.

Saw grass reaches up both sides of that lake in great enclosing arms, so that it is correct to say that the Everglades are there also. But south, southeast and southwest, where the lake water slopped and seeped and ran over and under the rock and soil, the greatest mass of the saw grass begins. It stretches as it always has stretched, in one thick enormous curving river of grass, to the very end. This is the Everglades.

It reaches one hundred miles from Lake Okeechobee to the Gulf of Mexico, fifty, sixty, even seventy miles wide. No one has ever fought his way along its full length. Few have ever crossed the northern wilderness of nothing but grass. Down that almost invisible slope the water moves. The grass stands. Where the grass and the water are there is the heart, the current, the meaning of the Everglades.

The grass and the water together make the river as simple as it is unique. There is no other river like it. Yet within that simplicity, enclosed within the river and bordering and intruding on it from each side, there is subtlety and diversity, a crowd of changing forms, of thrusting teeming life. And all that becomes the region of the Everglades.

The truth of the river is the grass. They call it saw grass. Yet in the botanical sense it is not grass at all so much as a fierce, ancient, cutting sedge. It is one of the oldest of the green growing forms in this world.

There are many places in the South where this saw grass with its sharp central fold and edges set with fine saw teeth like points of glass, this sedge called *Cladium jamaicensis* exists. But this is the greatest concentration of saw grass in the world. It grows fiercely in the fresh water creeping down below it. When the original saw grass thrust up its spears into the sun, the fierce sun, lord and power and first cause over the Everglades as of all the green world, then the Everglades began. They lie wherever the saw grass extends: 3,500 square miles, hundreds and thousands and millions, of acres, water and saw grass.

The first saw grass, exactly as it grows today, sprang up and lived in the sweet water and the pouring sunlight, and died in it, and from its own dried and decaying tissues and tough fibers bright with silica sprang up more fiercely again. Year after year it grew and was fed by its own brown rotting, taller and denser in the dark soil of its own death. Year after year after year, hundreds after hundreds of years, not so long as any geologic age but long in botanic time, far longer than anyone can be sure of, the saw grass grew. Four thousand years, they say, it must at least have grown like that, six feet, ten feet, twelve feet, even fifteen in places of deepest water. The edged and folded swords bristled around the delicate straight tube of pith that burst into brown flowering. The brown seed, tight enclosed after the manner of sedges, ripened in dense brownness. The seed was dropped and worked down in the water and its own ropelike mat of roots. All that decay of leaves and seed covers and roots was packed deeper year after year by the elbowing upthrust of its own life. Year after year it laid down new layers of virgin muck under the living water.

There are places now where the depth of the muck is equal to the height of the saw grass. When it is uncovered and brought into the sunlight, its stringy and grainy dullness glitters with the myriad unrotted silica points, like glass dust.

At the edges of the Glades, and toward those southern and southwestern most reaches where the great estuary or delta of the Glades river takes another form entirely, the saw grass is shorter and more sparse, and the springy, porous muck deposit under it is shallower and thinner. But where the saw grass grows tallest in the deepest muck, there goes the channel of the Glades.

The water winks and flashes here and there among the sawgrass roots, as the clouds are blown across the sun. To try to make one's way among these impenetrable tufts is to be cut off from all air, to be beaten down by the sun and ripped by the grassy saw-toothed edges as one sinks in mud and water over the roots. The dried yellow stuff holds no weight. There is no earthly way to get through the mud or the standing, keen edged blades that crowd these interminable miles.

Or in the times of high water in the old days, the flood would rise until the highest tops of that sharp grass were like a thin lawn standing out of water as blue as the sky, rippling and wrinkling, linking the pools and spreading and flowing on its true course southward.

A man standing in the center of it, if he could get there, would be as lost in saw grass, as out of sight of anything but saw grass as a man drowning in the middle of Okeechobee—or the Atlantic Ocean, for that matter—would be out of sight of land.

The water moves. The saw grass, pale green to deep-brown ripeness, stands rigid. It is moved only in sluggish rollings by the vast push of the winds across it. Over its endless acres here and there the shadows of the dazzling clouds quicken and slide, purple-brown, plum-brown, mauve-brown, rust-brown, bronze. The bristling, blossoming tops do not bend easily like standing grain. They do not even in their own growth curve all one way but stand in edged clumps, curving against each other, all the massed curving blades making millions of fine arching lines that at a little distance merge to a huge expanse of brown wires or bristles or, farther beyond, to deep-piled plush. At the horizon they become velvet. The line they make is an edge of velvet against the infinite blue, the blue-and-white, the clear fine primrose yellow, the burning brass and crimson, the molten silver, the deepening hyacinth sky.

The clear burning light of the sun pours daylong into the saw grass and is lost there, soaked up, never given back. Only the water flashes and glints. The grass yields nothing.

Nothing less than the smashing power of some hurricane can beat it down. Then one can see, from high up in a plane, where the towering weight and velocity of the hurricane was the strongest and where along the edges of its whorl it turned less and less savagely and left the saw grass standing. Even so, the grass is not flattened in a continuous swath but only here and here and over there, as if the storm bounced or lifted and smashed down again in great hammering strokes or enormous cat-licks.

Only one force can conquer it completely and that is fire. Deep in the layers of muck there are layers of ashes, marks of old fires set by lightning or the early Indians. But in the early days the water always came back and there were long slow years in which the saw grass grew and died, laying down again its tough resilient decay. This is the saw grass, then, which seems to move as the water moved, in a great thick arc south and south-westward from Okeechobee to the Gulf. There at the last imperceptible incline of the land the saw grass goes along the headwaters of many of those wide, slow, mangrove-bordered fresh-water rivers, like a delta or an estuary into which the salt tides flow and draw back and flow again.

The mangrove becomes a solid barrier there, which by its strong, arched and labyrinthine roots collects the sweepage of the fresh water and the salt and holds back the parent sea. The supple branches, the oily green leaves, set up a barrier against the winds, although the hurricanes prevail easily against them. There the fresh water meets the incoming salt and is lost.

It may be that the mystery of the Everglades is the saw grass, so simple, so enduring, so hostile. It was the saw grass and the water which divided east coast from west coast and made the central solitudes that held in them the secrets of time, which has moved here so long unmarked.

III: THE WATER

In the Everglades one is most aware of the superb monotony of saw grass under the world of air. But below that and before it, enclosing and causing it, is the water.

It is poured into Lake Okeechobee from the north and west, from that fine chain of lakes which scatter up and down the center of Florida, like bright beads from a string. They overflow southward. The water is gathered from the northwest through a wide area of open savannas and prairies. It swells the greatest contributing streams, the Kissimmee River, and the Taylor River and Fisheating Creek, and dozens of other smaller named and unnamed creeks or rivulets, and through them moves down into the great lake's tideless blue-misted expanse.

The water comes from the rains. The northern lakes and streams, Okeechobee itself, are only channels and reservoirs and conduits for a surface flow of rain water, fresh from the clouds. A few springs may feed them, but no melting snow water, no mountain freshets, no upgushing from caverns in ancient rock. Here the rain is everything.

Here the rain falls more powerfully and logically than anywhere else upon the temperate mainland of the United States. There are not four sharply marked seasons, as in the North. Here winter and spring and summer and fall blend into each other subtly, with nothing like such extremes of heat and cold. Here, actually, there are only two seasons, the wet and the dry, as there are in the tropics. The rains thunder over all this long land in their appointed season from the low clouds blowing in from the sea or pour from clouds gathered all morning from the condensation of the wet below. Then for months it will not rain at all, or very little, and the high sun glares over the drying saw grass and the river seems to stand still.

This land, by the maps, is in the temperate zone. But the laws of the rain and of the seasons here are tropic laws.

The men who make maps draw lines across seas and deserts and mountains and equatorial rain forests to show where the Temperate Zone is cut off sharply from the middle equatorial belt. But the sea and the land and the winds do not always recognize that rigidity. Nor do southern Florida and the Everglades.

To the west the map shows the Gulf of Mexico, that warm land-sheltered, almost inland ocean; and from it, moved by the power of the turning world itself, the Gulf Stream pours its warm deep indigo and white-flecked waters north of Cuba and ever northeastward. "The Stream" is a huge swift-running river of warm salt water forced between the Florida coast, which it has shaped, and the Bahama banks, until high up on the blue globe of ocean it swings far across into the gray latitudes, toward frozen seas.

With all that surrounding warm sea water and not forgetting Okeechobee's over seven hundred shallow watery square miles, east forty miles from the sea, and from the Gulf eighty, the whole southern part of Florida might as well be an island. All summer long the trade winds, or winds blowing so steadily nightlong and daylong from the southeast that it makes no difference if weather men quarrel about their being called the true trades, pour across the land their cool stiff tides of ten miles an hour.

Summer and winter its climate is more equable than that of the mainland regions to the north. And because of its average sixty-five inches a year of rainfall on the east coast and sixty-three in the interior of the Everglades, this region actually resembles certain warm and rainy but not too hot tropic lands more than it does those other dry and mountainous countries which lie exactly on the equator. It is a question of the ratio between the temperature and the rainfall and the evaporation. There is an arc at the very tip of Florida, up the lower west coast to Gordon Pass and up the east coast to the Miami and New rivers, which is the only place on the mainland of the United States where tropical and West Indian plants will grow native, because of that warmth and rainfall.

The northern Glades, and Lake Okeechobee, would seem to be in the South Temperate Zone, but the rainfall is subtropic here too.

The rains begin in the spring, in April or even late in May. There may be a few days of stuffy wet heat and brassy sunlight and a great piling up and movement of clouds by the heavy fretful southeast winds. There may be a continuous bumping of thunder far off. The winds that change their compass positions, east to south to west to north to east again, never on the east and south coasts, in any other way but clockwise, are thrashing and uncertain. Then in a sudden chill the rain may shut down in one long slashing burst in which even hailstones may bounce like popcorn against all that darkening land. Then the rain has moved away and the sun flashes again.

Somewhere thereafter it rains over the Glades or the lake for an hour or two every day in switching long bright lines through which the hot sun glistens. Then the marching wet will start again the next day or so, hissing and leaping down in narrow sharply defined paths as the clouds are pushed about here and there in the bright sky. Sometimes the rains may last only a few weeks in May. After that the summer is a long blazing drying time of brilliant sun and trade winds all night under the steady wheeling of the stars. The great piles of vapor from the Gulf Stream, amazing cumulus clouds that soar higher than tropic mountains from their even bases four thousand feet above the horizon, stand in ranked and glistening splendor in those summer nights; twenty thousand feet or more they tower tremendous, cool-pearl, frosty heights, blue-shadowed in the blue-blazing days.

On summer mornings over the Glades the sky is only faintly hazed. The moisture is being drawn up from the sheen among the saw grass. By noon, the first ranks of the clouds will lie at the same height across the world, cottony and growing. The moisture lifts the whipped and glistening heights. The bases darken, grow purple, grow brown. The sun is almost gone. The highest clouds loose their moisture, which is condensed into cloud again before it can reach the earth. Then they grow more heavy. The winds slash before them and the rains roar down, making all the saw grass somber.

Sometimes the rainy season goes on all summer, casually raining here and there so that the green things never quite dry out while salt-water mosquitoes from the brackish pools about the coasts blow on the west wind in thin screaming hordes. When high water in the Glades flows south, the mosquitoes do not breed in it.

But in late August, or perhaps in September, the rainy season sets in in earnest. White-heaped Gulf clouds, colored by afterglows in some tremendous summer sunsets stand like Alps of pure rose and violet and ice-gray against the ultimate blue until they are harried by the more ir-regular winds. White streamers are blown from their tops, veils from their sides, and they themselves are pushed and scuffled and beaten down into long moving snowy sheets or rolls of gray, yellowish-gray, lavender-gray, greenish-gray-until they smash down in long marching, continuous, rever-berating downfalls.

You can see it raining darkly and fiercely far off over there at the horizon across the scorched saw grass. The sky will be a boiling panorama of high and low cloud shapes, cumulus, strato-cumulus, alto-cumulus, dazzling and blue and dun. Sometimes far up, far away, between all that panoply, there will be a glimpse of outer space as green as ice.

Then the lion-colored light shuts down as the rain does, or the clouds fill with their steely haze every outline of the visible world and water falls solid, in sheets, in cascades. When the clouds lift, the long straight rainy lines blow and curve from the sagging underbelly of the sky in steely wires or long trailing veils of wet that glitter in some sudden shaft of light from the forgotten sun.

There will be the smack of cool, almost chilling hard air and the rising sound of long drumming as if the grassy places were hard and dry, or the earth hollow. You hear the tearing swish of the rain on the stiff saw grass as it comes over and beats and goes by slashing its steely whips. There may be short bursts of thunder and veins of lightning cracking the whole sky. They are dwarfed by the power of the rain and the wind.

Below all that the glistening water will be rising, shining like beaten pewter, and the light will lift as if itself relieved of all that weight of the rain. It will change from pewter to silver to pure brightness everywhere. The brownness that has been dullness will be bright tawniness and the reaches and changing forms of the sky will lift higher and higher, lifting the heart. Suddenly all those thousands and thousands of acres of saw grass that have been so lightless and somber will burst into a million million flashes from as many gleaming and trembling drops of wet, flashing back their red and emerald and diamond lights to the revealed glory of the sun in splendor.

Inches of water will have fallen in an hour and still far off the rain will trample below the horizon, undiminished.

In the course of a single day so much rain will fall, as much sometimes as ten or twelve inches, that the glitter of rising water will be everywhere. The blue of the sky is caught down there among the grass stems, in pools stretching and spreading. In a few days of rain, acre after acre of new water will flash in sheets under the sun. Then, as the rain clouds go over every day, the currents will be gathering their small visible courses, streaming and swirling past every grass blade, moving south and again south and by west. Places of open currents have been measured to show a steady running four miles an hour, in the old days, in watercourses and wandering streams among the straight bristle of the saw grass. Sometimes more than half the year's average will have fallen in less than two months.

Meanwhile the rain has been falling far to the northward. Over Okeechobee it has been moved here and there as the steady drive of the trades is changed to fitful inland airs. Thunderstorms roll and reverberate over the surface and lightning marbles the clouds as storms seem to come together from every direction while the greenish and grayish world blinks with acid radiance. The lake may be blotted out by white falling water that sings with a rising note as the surface brims and is beaten. The curtains of rain, the rain fogs, move off or hang and sway in a dirty gray half-light as the descending water smacks on the pitted and broken waves. The world is all water, is drowned in water, chill and pale and clean.

North, still farther up that chain of lakes, the rains fall and brim the fine green-ringed cups. The waters begin again their southward flow. The Kissimmee River is swollen and strongly swirling between its wet marshy banks, but still the water does not move off fast enough. The banks are overflowing and the spongy ground between it and Fisheating Creek is all one swamp. The rains fling their solid shafts of water down the streaming green land, and Okeechobee swells and stirs and creeps south down the unseen tilt of the Glades.

The grass, like all the other growing things after the long terrible dry seasons, begins in the flooding wet its strong sunward push again, from its ropy roots. The spears prick upward tender green, glass green, bright green, darker green, to spread the blossoms and the fine seeds like brown lace. The grass stays. The fresh river flows.

But even from earliest times, when in the creeping spread of water the grass turned up its swords and made the Everglades, there was too much water in the great lake to carry itself off through the Glades southward. There was nothing but the east and west sandy ridges to hold back the water. To the east from Okeechobee it seeped and was not carried off and stood along an old wandering watercourse soon filled not only with saw grass but reeds and sedges and purple arrowy lilies and floating masses of grass and small trees. That is still called the Loxahatchee Slough. "Hatchee" means "river" in that same Indian tongue which named the lake. "Slough," in south Florida, means any open swampy place which may once have been a tongue of the sea or a river of fresh water, green, watery, flowery country, a place of herons and small fish and dragonflies and blue sky flashing from among the lily pads.

Loxahatchee is pitted with innumerable pools held in by the coastal rock. South of that, from the overflow of the Glades basin itself, the rivers of the east coast run, St. Lucie and the Hillsborough, the New River and Little River and the Miami River, spilling over the rock rim to the tides.

In the, same way, west of Lake Okeechobee, at least twice as far from the Gulf, the water spilled and crept out over soggy level lands, half lakes, half swamps, and so into the Caloosahatchee, the left shoulder of the Glades region.

The Caloosahatchee never rose directly in Okeechobee, but in a wide rain-filled funnel of shallow, grassy lakes between Hicpochee and Lake Flirt. Often they dried up and were not there.

West of Lake Flirt, the Caloosahatchee began in earnest, a river so remote, so lonely that even in the days when it was best known it must have been like a dream. It was a river wandering among half-moon banks hung with green dripping trees and enshrouding grapevines, green misted, silent, always meandering. It has that quality of dreaming still, neglected and changed as it is, to this very day.

But in the days of full flood, Caloosahatchee rose and overflowed the flat country for miles, north and south. The water crept and flowed and stood bright under the high water oaks and the cabbage palms, so that a light boat could go anywhere under them. In the clear water all the light under the wet trees was green. Lower down, the more tropic green stood in solid jungles to the reflecting water. The rain water went east and west of the lake, but most strongly along the great course of the Everglades.

Often the rainy season finds its terrible climax in September or October, in the crashing impact of a hurricane, the true cyclonic storm of the tropics. July is not too early to expect hurricanes. In the West Indies they have occurred in June. The old jingle that fishermen recite along these coasts tells the story: "June—too soon. July—stand by. August—look out you must. September—remember. October—all over." Officially in Florida the fifteenth of November closes the hurricane season but farther south these storms occur in November and even in December.

The hurricanes make up, although no man has yet seen the actual beginning of one, as far east as the Azores, where the hot air rises all along the line of the equator as the Northern Hemisphere cools toward winter.

Their enormous high-spinning funnels, moving always counterclockwise this north side of the tropic belt, are begun when the rising hot air is flung into circular motion by the immeasurable spinning power of the world. The velocity of that spin around their hollow centers has been recorded as moving as fast as two hundred miles. But generally the recording instruments are blown away before that, so no one knows their greatest speed. Laterally, they creep westward more slowly, ten to forty miles an hour. They enter the Caribbean at some airy rift between those island mountains rising from the sea, which are often engulfed by them. They may turn northward and eastward through the Mona or the Windward Passage, or across the Cuban coast or through the Bahamas, to drive on southern Florida. They may go howling up these coasts and north along, to show the Temperate Zone what the roused raging power of the tropics can be like.

Smaller but intense and dangerous hurricanes spring up sometimes in the late fall in the Yucatan channel and thrash the Gulf of Mexico and harry the Texas or Florida coast. They attack the Glades from there. Later still, they become more freakish and unpredictable, like maelstroms of wind gone wild.

But as the northern winter creeps downward, the hurricane season is slowly conquered. The towering clouds of summer are leveled to mild sheets and rolls of gleaming stuff, widespread, dappled and mackereled, or with the great silvery brushings of mares'-tails. Often there are no clouds at all toward the zenith, which has lost its summer intensity of violet and burns now with the bright crisp blue of northern autumns. Then the air is fresh and sweet.

This is the dry season. Officially, no rain should fall. Yet there have been wet, chill winters in which the rains have come down on the edge of a northern cold front while the east winds go around south and west and north, and stand there for three days of cold, or die utterly so that the frost drifts into the low places and at first sun the hoar-rimmed leaves grow black.

In the winter dry season, there takes place here another and gentler phenomenon of the equatorial tropics. In a windless dawn, in some light winter ground fogs, in mists that stand over the Everglades watercourses, the dew creeps like heavy rain down the shining heavy leaves, drips from the saw-grass edges, and stands among the coarse blossoming sedges and the tall ferns. Under the tree branches it is a steady soft drop, drop and drip, all night long. In the first sunlight the dew, a miracle of freshness, stands on every leaf and wall and petal, in the finest of tiny patterns, in bold patterns of wide-strung cobwebs; like pearls in a silvery melting frostwork. The slant yellow sun of winter dries it up in the next hour but all the secret roots are nourished by it in the dry ground.

Then toward what the North would call spring, dryness creeps again over the land, with the high-standing sun. Between one day and the next the winds grow new and powerful. In the Glades the water shrinks below the grass roots. In open muddy places far south the surface dries and cracks like the cracks in old china, and where some alligator has hitched his slow armored length from one drying water hole to another the pattern of his sharp toes and heavy dragging belly in the marl is baked hard.

The saw grass stands drying to old gold and rustling faintly, ready, if there is a spark anywhere, to burst into those boiling red flames which crackle even at a great distance like a vast frying pan, giving off rolling clouds of heavy cream-colored smoke, shadowed with mauve by day and by night mile-high pillars of roily tangerine and orange light. The fires move crackling outward as the winds blow them, black widening rings where slow embers burn and smolder down into the fibrous masses of the thousand-year-old peat.

Then the spring rains put out the fires with their light moving tread, like the tread of the running deer, and the year of rainy season and of dry season has made its round again.

"Look where the sun draws up water," people say of those long shafts of brightness between clouds. The saw grass and all those acres of green growing things draw up the water within their cells and use it and breathe it out again, invisibly. Transpiration and evaporation, it is called; an unending usage of all the water that has fallen and that flows. Sixty per cent of it, over half of all those tons and tons of water which fall in any rainy season, is taken up again. Dried up. The air is fresh with it, or humid, if it is warm. But in the middle of the Glades in the full heat of summer the condensation is so great that the air is cooled and the temperature lowered half a degree with every two miles or so inland. It is not so much the cool movement of wind as standing coolness, freshness without salt, wetness that is sweet with the breath of hidden tiny blossoming things luminous in the darkness under the height and white magnificence of the stars. Such coolness is a secret that the deep Glades hold.

On the west coast there are land breezes and sea breezes. West-flowing winds often sweep out of those cooling Glades down the slow mangrove rivers and out to the islands on the coasts, rivers of coolness among warm and standing airs.

With all this, it is the subtle ratio between rainfall and evaporation that is the final secret of water in the Glades. We must know a great deal more about that ratio and its effect on temperature in all this region to understand its influence on the weather, on frosts and winds and storms.

All this has been caused by other cycles dictated by remote and terrible occurrences beyond this infinitesimal world, the cyclones of heat and shadow that pass across the utter fire of the sun. Or other laws of a universe only half guessed at. Those majestic affairs reach here in long cycles of alternating wet and dry. There have been years after years of long rainy seasons when the Glades indeed were a running river, more water than grass. Or, more recently, cycles of drought, when there is never enough rain to equal the evaporation and transpiration and the runoff.

Because of all this, the high rate of water usage as against the natural runoff, it is clear that rainfall alone could not have maintained the persistent fine balance between wet and dry that has created and kept the Everglades, the long heart of this long land. If Okeechobee and the lakes and marshes north that contribute to it, if rivers and swamps and ponds had not existed to hoard all that excess water in a great series of reservoirs by which the flow was constantly checked and regulated, there would have been no Everglades. The whole system was like a set of scales on which the forces of the seasons, of the sun and the rains, the winds, the hurricanes, and the dewfalls, were balanced so that the life of the vast grass and all its encompassed and neighbor forms were kept secure.

THEODORE ROSENGARTEN

All God's Dangers: The Life of Nate Shaw (1974)

Theodore Rosengarten's book *All God's Dangers: The Life of Nate Shaw*, an account of a black sharecropper from southern Alabama, was published in 1974. The book is a compilation of interviews that Rosengarten, while a graduate student at Harvard in the late 1960s, had with Nate Shaw, Ned Cobb's pseudonym. Cobb was a sharecropper who had farmed the same land his entire life (1885–1973). In many ways, this book calls to mind the Federal Writers Projects of the 1930s that hired writers to document the lives of Americans. Yet, it is worth noting that this book is not an oral history, nor it is exactly nonfiction, but a co-created work of art that reveals all the complexities of collaboration. Rosengarten was an outsider to Alabama, with every privilege possible in 1970s America. He recorded interviews, transcribed them, and put them together into a narrative of the life of Cobb. As the interviewee, Cobb narrated his life skillfully and with great technique, yet because Rosengarten is interpreting it, the story is not only his own. There inevitably are aspects that Rosengarten could not understand or misunderstood about Cobb's life. This short excerpt from that book concerns Shaw's discovery that a creek he and his friend Josie fished has been polluted by a cotton mill. He speaks about the laxness of environmental laws that might keep companies from polluting the waterways and foodways of the Gulf South.

Work Sourced

Trower, Shelley. "Auto/Biographical Oral Histories, from 'Oral Memoirs' to the Life of Nate Shaw (1948–1974)." *Oral History: The Journal of the Oral History Society*, vol. 45, no. 1, 2017, pp. 43–54.

Everybody knowed Josie was a workin woman. And she's a woman likes sports—especially fishin. And she was fishin right there. They was livin close to Sitimachas Creek when they stayed up there by Apafalya; the creek was just back up north of their home. And her and another colored woman, they stayed on the creek; soon as she'd be got done with her work, she'd take up her fishin pole and hit it to the creek. Josie would rather go fishin today than eat when she's hungry. She goes fishin now every chance she gets. Somebody come along and goin fishin that she knows, well, she gone. Fishin on the backwaters between here and Beaufort.

I never did care nothin much bout fishin with a hook and line. I always when I stayed close to Sitimachas Creek, soon as I got big enough to have me a basket in the creek—I was born just across Sitimachas on top of a hill. Not no more than a quarter mile from the creek. And I fished the creek with baskets all durin of my boyhood life. And after I married, good God—there's a cotton mill up there at Opelika, they just poured dye in the creek, poison, and killed out the catfish in Sitimachas. You could see the signs of it way down in here, the color of the water—killed them catfish a goin and a comin. It's a pity to kill what people love, it's a pity to kill it out. Well, the government, I think, made a racket behind em. That didn't help, they bummed the creek on the sly. People goin up and down Sitimachas to fish and just find the top of the water covered with nice catfish, poisoned. They ought to put em in the penitentiary about poisonin the earth and the air and the waters, killin the fish in the rivers and the water coasts and all like that. The devil is just loose on earth and the laws is not hard enough on em.

FLORIDA TRIBE OF EASTERN CREEK INDIANS

"Petition for Recognition" (1978)

The United States government recognizes 566 tribal governments within the United States, meaning that a tribe is treated as a nation within a nation, able to set up its own government, legal system, taxes, and fees. However, for many American Indian tribes of the Gulf South, a space that was the center of the Indian Removal Act of 1830, the petition for federal recognition has been a difficult and painful process. American Indians of the Gulf South, because of the legacy of genocide and forced removal to other states such as Kansas and Oklahoma, have few historical documents that could verify a tribe's history. Some of the tribes from the Gulf South still awaiting federal recognition include the Muscogee Nation of Florida; the United Houma Nation of Louisiana; the Biloxi, Chitimacha Confederation of Muskogees of Louisiana; and the Pointe-au-Chien Indian Tribe. The text included here is from the Muscogee Nation of Florida's petition to the Bureau of Indian Affairs for recognition. It was written in 1978. Their petition has still not been approved.

The Gulf South is a place defined by many languages, and to understand how narratives have constructed a relation to place, it is important to step outside the English language. Here, a message from Hesaketamese, the giver of life and breath, advises the Creek people on how to live on the land. In imagining the future in the Gulf South, it is essential to have other models for connecting to and living in the natural world. This text offers one of many.

This text's translation and footnotes come from the original letter and was approved by tribal leadership.

Works Sourced

Hobson, Geary, and Janet McAdams, *The People Who Stayed: Southeastern Indian Writing after Removal.* University of Oklahoma Press, 2010.

Usner, Daniel H. *American Indians in the Lower Mississippi Valley: Social and Economic Histories.* University of Nebraska Press, 1999.

Our legendary origin, like that of all Creek people, was in a land to the west whence our earliest forefathers crossed a great river in their passage to the southeastern area of the North American continent, there to congregate in various groups—Cussetahs, Kawetas, and others[1]—and to evolve a loose political structure based on kinship, clan organization, and etalwas (tribal towns).[2] Early in historic times the Creek domain extended through most of Alabama, Georgia, and parts of Mississippi, southward to the Gulf of Mexico, including parts of peninsula Florida as well as the whole area of present west Florida.[3] In this area these aboriginal inhabitants came to be known as the Creek Nation, and were treated as such both by the Indians and by other governments. The Creek Indians accepted into their numbers other peoples—e.g., the Uchees, Natchez, and Yemassees. The great majority of larger and more permanent Creek etalwas (tribal towns) were concentrated about such river systems as the Alabama, the Coosa, the Chatahootchee, the Appalachicola, and the Flint.[4] Other sites of varying degrees of permanence, trading trails, gathering places, and of course the all-important hunting grounds, involved the whole Creek domain. The lands southward to the Gulf from the Alabama River eastward to and including much of peninsula Florida,[5] were mostly hunting grounds with the scattered permanent and semi-permanent sites normal to the life of Indian people. Streams and rivers along the Gulf have long furnished access to the coast where fish and shellfish were easy to obtain.

Gulf of Mexico rivers frequented by the Creeks, included the Escambia, the Yellow, the Choctahatchee, the Chipola, and the Apalachicola.[6] Many places names—Indian Crossing, Chumuckla, Ucheeala, et al.—are living reminders of this, in the counties of present northwest Florida. A legend of Florida region handed down from the hofenalke (Creek forefathers) tells the Creeks to come here, take good care of this place, and make this our home—It is a message from Hesaketamese (God, the Giver of Life and Breath):

Yv kvnyoksvn os
Yvmv estofis rvfot ocefes
momis eto pvkpvkeu
oketcken cenmakvkakes . . .

This place is kun-yoksau
Here is never any winter
but the trees and blossoms
to tell you the seasons . . .

Govern yourselves by my laws
and it will be so forever
My children
live here in peace
I shall always be with you
in this land . . . [7]

Notes

1. Albert S. Gatschet, *A Migration Legend of the Creek Indians*, Vol. I (1884).

2. John R. Swanton, *Social Organization and Social Usages of the Creek Indian Confederacy*, (Forty-Second Annual Report, Bureau of American Ethnology, 1928).

3. Indian Claims Commission, No. 21, *Creek Nation v. United States, Brief of the Creek Nation*, pp. 1–2.

4. Swanton, op. cit.

5. Louis DeVorsey Jr., *The Indian Boundary in the 1763–1775*, UNC Press. pp. 230–234.

6. Cf. discussions infra.

7. Kun-yoksau (Florida) adopted from the version in M. L. King Jr., History of Santa Rosa County, (Individually published, 1972), p. 12. In Santa Rosa County Public Library, Milton, Florida.

JOY HARJO

"New Orleans"

She Had Some Horses (1983)

Joy Harjo (b. 1951) became the first American Indian Poet Laureate of the United States in 2019. Born in Tulsa, Oklahoma, Harjo is an enrolled member of the Mvskoke/Creek Nation. Throughout her numerous books of poetry as well as published plays and a memoir, Harjo's work examines the tangled histories of the origins of the United States and the environment, with particular attention to the American Indian and white cultures from which she is descended. Harjo has received numerous awards for her writing, including the William Carlos Williams Award from the Poetry Society of America, the American Indian Distinguished Achievement in the Arts Award, the PEN Open Book Award, and two fellowships from the National Endowment for the Arts, among others.

The poem included here, "New Orleans," is from her book of poetry *She Had Some Horses* (1983). Harjo interrogates the history of the Mississippi River and the city of New Orleans within the context of the Trail of Tears, the forced removals of American Indians from their ancestral homelands in the southeastern United States starting in 1831. Looking beneath the waters of the Mississippi River, Harjo finds the ghosts of European colonists, de Soto in particular, whose hunger for gold and natural resources brought them to her ancestors' land along the Gulf South. Harjo's poetry searches for the ways that the past still leaves traces on the environment, haunting it but also reminding the reader that those ghosts still live on in the language in which she composes her work, the culture of the United States, and the land itself.

This is the south. I look for evidence
of other Creeks, for remnants of voices,
or for tobacco brown bones to come wandering
down Conti Street, Royale, or Decatur.
Near the French Market I see a blue horse
caught frozen in stone in the middle of

a square. Brought in by the Spanish on
an endless ocean voyage he became mad
and crazy. They caught him in blue
rock, said
                Don't talk.

I know it wasn't just a horse
                    that went crazy.

Nearby is a shop with ivory and knives.
There are red rocks. The man behind the
counter has no idea that he is inside
magic stones. He should find out before
they destroy him. These things
have memory,
                you know.

I have a memory.
                It swims deep in blood,
a delta in the skin. It swims out of Oklahoma,
deep the Mississippi River. It carries my
feet to these places: the French Quarter,
stale rooms, the sun behind thick and moist
clouds, and I hear boats hauling themselves up
and down the river

My spirit comes here to drink.
My spirit comes here to drink.
Blood is the undercurrent.

There are voices buried in the Mississippi
mud. There are ancestors and future children
buried beneath the currents stirred up by
pleasure boats going up and down.
There are stories here made of memory.

I remember DeSoto. He is buried somewhere in
this river, his bones sunk like the golden
treasure he traveled half the earth to find,
came looking for gold cities, for shining streets
of beaten gold to dance with silk ladies.

He should have stayed home.

(Creeks knew of him for miles
before he came to town.
Dreamed of silver blades
and crosses.)
And knew he was one of the ones who yearned
for something his heart wasn't big enough
to handle.
(And DeSoto thought it was gold.)

The Creeks lived in earth towns,
not gold,
spun children, not gold.
That's not what DeSoto thought he wanted to see.
The Creeks knew it, and drowned him in
the Mississippi River
so he wouldn't have to drown himself.

Maybe his body is what I am looking for
As evidence. To know in another way
that my memory is alive.
But he must have gotten away, somehow,
because I have seen New Orleans,
the lace and silk buildings,
trolley cars on beaten silver paths,
graves that rise up out of the soft earth in the rain,
shops that sell black mammy dolls
holding white babies.

And I know I have seen DeSoto,
having a drink on Bourbon Street,
mad and crazy,
dancing with a woman as gold
as the river bottom.

EDDY HARRIS

Mississippi Solo (1988)

Eddy L. Harris (b. 1956) has joined that list of Americans such as Mark Twain who have journeyed down the Mississippi River and written about that experience memorably. Harris, who lives in St. Louis, Missouri, is a nonfiction author of four books, many of which are travelogues of his experiences through certain parts of the world. In his book *Mississippi Solo: A River Quest* (1988), Harris begins a long canoe journey from the headwaters of the Mississippi River in Lake Itasca, Minnesota, and follows it all the way to the Gulf of Mexico, aiming "to be somehow part of the river." A way of getting intimate with nature is in a canoe, and the except from Harris's book gives a sense of the Mississippi River as a "comfortable buddy sharing a lazy day," as he puts it. However, in other moments, Harris notes that the industrialization of the river has made it very difficult for an individual to navigate the river alone. *Mississippi Solo* presents the joys and difficulties of simply being at one with the river. In this excerpt, a lulling enchantment is suddenly disrupted by a storm. Harris experiences an important quality that many often forget and shouldn't in the face of a river—humility.

Too many marvelous days in a row and you begin to get used to it, to think that's the way it's supposed to be. Too many good days, too many bad days—you need some break in the monotony of one to appreciate the other. If you only get sunshine, someone said, you end up in a desert.

I guess I'd had enough hard days to last me for a while, enough scary times to be able to appreciate the peaceful, easy, glorious days. On the way to Natchez, I had another one and I took full advantage of it to do absolutely nothing. No singing, no thinking, no talking to myself. Just feeling. Watching the river, noticing the changes in color, seeing the way it rises and falls depending on the wind and on what lay on the river bed. Each change had something to say, and I listened to the river. The river was talking to me, changing colors from puce to brown to thick murky green. Saying nothing. The idle chatter you get when you walk with your favorite niece or nephew going no place in particular with nothing special on your minds and the little kid just jabbers away because it's comfortable and he feels like it. The river was like that to me. A comfortable buddy sharing a lazy day.

Nothing else mattered then. Going someplace or not. Arriving in New Orleans or shooting past and landing in Brazil. I didn't care about anything. The river kept me company and kept me satisfied. Nothing else mattered.

Then the river whispered, "Get ready. Get ready."

The day turned grey and strange. Clouds rolled overhead in wild swirls like batter in a bowl. I could see the rain storm forming off in the distance but swirling rapidly toward me like a dark grey avalanche. I felt the river dip down and up—a shallow dale in the water. I passed from the cool moisture surrounding me and into a pocket of thin air hot and dry. It was as though a gap had opened in the clouds and the sun streamed through to boil the water and heat up this isolated patch of river a scant thirty yards long. My first thought was to shed a shirt and stay cool, but when I passed through the far curtain of the insulated air, I knew I had better do just the opposite. I drifted and donned my yellow rain suit and hood. The sky above grew serious and advanced in my direction with the speed of a hurricane. Looking for a place to land I scanned the shore. There was no shore. Only trees. Because of the heavy rains and the high water, the shore had disappeared and the new shoreline of solid earth had been pushed back through the trees and beyond the woods. How far beyond, I couldn't tell. I looked across to the other side of the river half a mile away. No way could I have made it over there. Halfway across and the wind would have kicked up and trapped me in the middle.

The leading edge of the storm came and the first sprinkles passed over like army scouts. The wooded area lasted only another hundred yards or so and I thought I could easily get there before the rains arrived. I could then turn left and find ground to pull out and wait out the storm. But the voice of the river came out and spoke to me teasingly but with a chill of seriousness down my spine. I could have ignored it, but as if reading my thoughts and not wanting me to fight it, the river grabbed the end of the canoe and turned me toward the trees. I thought I was looking for land. I wasn't. I was looking for shelter.

The urge to get into the trees came on me quite suddenly and really without thought or effort on my part. Almost an instinct.

No sooner had I ducked into the trees than the sky split open with a loud crash and a splintery crackle of lightning. I was not going to make it through the trees. The wind came in at hurricane strength. The tips of the trees bent way over and aimed toward the ground, like fishing rods hooked on a big one. Water flooded like the tide rushing upstream. The trees swooshed loudly as the leaves and branches brushed hard together. Branches fell. Rains came and poured down buckets-full.

The trees were tall and no more than three feet around. I maneuvered the canoe as best I could in the wind and rushing water, turned it to face upstream and kept my back to the rain which slanted in at a sharp angle. I reached out for the sturdiest tree I could get my arms around and I held on.

Water everywhere. The river sloshed over the side and into the canoe. I tried to keep the stem pointed right into the flow so the canoe could ride the waves, but it didn't work. The canoe was twisted about and water poured over the side. The rain was heavier than any I had ever been in or seen before. It really was more like a tropical storm. The heavy winds, the amount of water, the warmth of the air and the cold rain. Only my neck was exposed to the rain. When the rain hit my neck, it ran under the suit and very cold down my back.

The wind shifted as the storm came directly overhead. Water streamed straight down. I was drenched and the canoe was filling up quickly. Anything in the canoe that could float was floating. If the rain continued for long or if the wind kept up strong and rain kept spilling into the canoe, I would sink. But I was not worried, hardly more than concerned. In fact I enjoyed the feeling of the water all around me and on me, enveloping me like a cocoon, and despite the drama I felt no real threat. I was more amazed than anything, trying to analyze the voice I had heard or whatever instinct or intuition it was that urged me to park in these trees. It had been something so very definite that I could feel it and yet so ethereal that I could not put my finger on it. So I stopped trying and just sat there patiently waiting and hugging my tree. I was one with this river and nothing could happen to me.

The storm slid forward and the rain slanted in on my face. Then it moved on farther up river to drench someone else. It was gone as suddenly as it had arisen. Only the trailing edge was left, a light rain that lasted almost until I reached Natchez.

The sky remained grey but lightened and I paddled from my rainforest and down river to Natchez. My little boat lumbered through the water. The canoe carried six inches of water and was heavy and I could find no speed. But I didn't need any. I was relaxed and floating in the mist as thick as the mysteries of the river. It was evening when I reached Natchez.

JOHN MCPHEE

"Atchafalaya"

The Control of Nature (1989)

The author of more than thirty books and still counting, John McPhee
(b. 1931) is one of America's most celebrated and versatile writers of nonfiction. His subjects have an almost unlimited range, taking him where his seemingly insatiable curiosity leads him. A fixture of the pages of *The New Yorker*
magazine since 1963, he has written on subjects as diverse as canoes, cooking, tennis, geology, the New Jersey Pine Barrens, oranges, lacrosse, doctors,
farmers markets, private schools, and most recently, writing. For years, he has
taught writing at Princeton University.

The Control of Nature was published in 1989. One of the texts in the book,
"Atchafalaya," is excerpted here in its complete form. It concerns human de-
signs to try to control the Mississippi River in Louisiana, an effort that has
gone on in various incarnations seriously for 150 years with debatable success. (The excerpt from John Barry's *Rising Tide* has more on the subject.)
McPhee explains in simple terms that the Mississippi River created much of
the Gulf Coast, and it would not have done so if it had been locked in the
same course for thousands of years. Now, more than ever, the effort to keep
the river within one channel has revealed its effects of land subsidence and
rising sea levels, all exacerbated by climate change.

Three hundred miles up the Mississippi River from its mouth—many parishes above New Orleans and well north of Baton Rouge—a navigation
lock in the Mississippi's right bank allows ships to drop out of the river.
In evident defiance of nature, they descend as much as thirty-three feet,
then go off to the west or south. This, to say the least, bespeaks a rare relationship between a river and adjacent terrain—any river, anywhere, let
alone the third-ranking river on earth. The adjacent terrain is Cajun country, in a geographical sense the apex of the French Acadian world, which
forms a triangle in southern Louisiana, with its base the Gulf Coast from
the mouth of the Mississippi almost to Texas, its two sides converging up
here near the lock—and including neither New Orleans nor Baton Rouge.

The people of the local parishes (Pointe Coupee Parish, Avoyelles Parish) would call this the apex of Cajun country in every possible sense—no one more emphatically than the lockmaster, on whose face one day I noticed a spreading astonishment as he watched me remove from my pocket a red bandanna.

"You are a coonass with that red handkerchief," he said.

A coonass being a Cajun, I threw him an appreciative smile. I told him that I always have a bandanna in my pocket, wherever I happen to be—in New York as in Maine or Louisiana, not to mention New Jersey (my home)—and sometimes the color is blue. He said, "Blue is the sign of a Yankee. But that red handkerchief—with that, you are pure coonass." The lockmaster wore a white hard hat above his creased and deeply tanned face, his full but not overloaded frame. The nameplate on his desk said *Rabalais*.

The navigation lock is not a formal place. When I first met Rabalais, six months before, he was sitting with his staff at 10 a.m. eating homemade bread, macaroni and cheese, and a mound of rice that was concealed beneath what he called "smoked old-chicken gravy." He said, "Get yourself a plate of that." As I went somewhat heavily for the old chicken, Rabalais said to the others, "He's pure coonass. I knew it."

If I was pure coonass, I would like to know what that made Rabalais—Norris F. Rabalais, born and raised on a farm near Simmesport, in Avoyelles Parish, Louisiana. When Rabalais was a child, there was no navigation lock to lower ships from the Mississippi. The water just poured out—boats with it—and flowed on into a distributary waterscape known as Atchafalaya. In each decade since about 1860, the Atchafalaya River had drawn off more water from the Mississippi than it had in the decade before. By the late nineteen-forties, when Rabalais was in his teens, the volume approached one-third. As the Atchafalaya widened and deepened, eroding headward, offering the Mississippi an increasingly attractive alternative, it was preparing for nothing less than an absolute capture: before long, it would take all of the Mississippi, and itself become the master stream. Rabalais said, "They used to teach us in high school that one day there was going to be structures up here to control the flow of that water, but I never dreamed I was going to be on one. Somebody way back yonder—which is dead and gone now—visualized it. We had some pretty sharp teachers."

The Mississippi River, with its sand and silt, has created most of Louisiana, and it could not have done so by remaining in one channel. If it had, southern Louisiana would be a long narrow peninsula reaching into the

Gulf of Mexico. Southern Louisiana exists in its present form because the Mississippi River has jumped here and there within an arc about two hundred miles wide, like a pianist playing with one hand—frequently and radically changing course, surging over the left or the right bank to go off in utterly new directions. Always it is the river's purpose to get to the Gulf by the shortest and steepest gradient. As the mouth advances southward and the river lengthens, the gradient declines, the current slows, and sediment builds up the bed. Eventually, it builds up so much that the river spills to one side. Major shifts of that nature have tended to occur roughly once a millennium. The Mississippi's main channel of three thousand years ago is now the quiet water of Bayou Teche, which mimics the shape of the Mississippi. Along Bayou Teche, on the high ground of ancient natural levees, are Jeanerette, Breaux Bridge, Broussard, Olivier—arcuate strings of Cajun towns. Eight hundred years before the birth of Christ, the channel was captured from the east. It shifted abruptly and flowed in that direction for about a thousand years. In the second century A.D., it was captured again, and taken south, by the now unprepossessing Bayou Lafourche, which, by the year 1000, was losing its hegemony to the river's present course, through the region that would be known as Plaquemines. By the nineteen-fifties, the Mississippi River had advanced so far past New Orleans and out into the Gulf that it was about to shift again, and its offspring Atchafalaya was ready to receive it. By the route of the Atchafalaya, the distance across the delta plain was a hundred and forty-five miles—well under half the length of the route of the master stream.

For the Mississippi to make such a change was completely natural, but in the interval since the last shift Europeans had settled beside the river, a nation had developed, and the nation could not afford nature. The consequences of the Atchafalaya's conquest of the Mississippi would include but not be limited to the demise of Baton Rouge and the virtual destruction of New Orleans. With its fresh water gone, its harbor a silt bar, its economy disconnected from inland commerce, New Orleans would turn into New Gomorrah. Moreover, there were so many big industries between the two cities that at night they made the river glow like a worm. As a result of settlement patterns, this reach of the Mississippi had long been known as "the German coast," and now, with B. F. Goodrich, E. I. du Pont, Union Carbide, Reynolds Metals, Shell, Mobil, Texaco, Exxon, Monsanto, Uniroyal, Georgia-Pacific, Hydrocarbon Industries, Vulcan Materials, Nalco Chemical, Freeport Chemical, Dow Chemical, Allied Chemical, Stauffer Chemical, Hooker Chemicals, Rubicon Chemicals, American Petrofina—with an infrastructural concentration equaled in few other places—it was often called "the American Ruhr." The industries were there because of the river. They had come for its navigational convenience and its fresh water. They would not, and could not, linger beside a tidal creek. For nature to take its course was simply unthinkable. The Sixth World War would do less damage to southern Louisiana. Nature, in this place, had become an enemy of the state.

Rabalais works for the U.S. Army Corps of Engineers. Some years ago, the Corps made a film that showed the navigation lock and a complex of associated structures built in an effort to prevent the capture of the Mississippi. The narrator said, "This nation has a large and powerful adversary. Our opponent could cause the United States to lose nearly all her seaborne commerce, to lose her standing as first among trading nations. . . . We are fighting Mother Nature. . . . It's a battle we have to fight day by day, year by year; the health of our economy depends on victory."

Rabalais was in on the action from the beginning, working as a construction inspector. Here by the site of the navigation lock was where the battle had begun. An old meander bend of the Mississippi was the conduit through which water had been escaping into the Atchafalaya. Complicating the scene, the old meander bend had also served as the mouth of the Red River. Coming in from the northwest, from Texas via Shreveport, the Red River had been a tributary of the Mississippi for a couple of thousand years—until the nineteen-forties, when the Atchafalaya captured it and drew it away. The capture of the Red increased the Atchafalaya's power as it cut down the country beside the Mississippi. On a map, these entangling watercourses had come to look like the letter "H." The Mississippi was the right-hand side. The Atchafalaya and the captured Red were the left-hand side. The crosspiece, scarcely seven miles long, was the former meander bend, which the people of the parish had long since named Old River. Sometimes enough water would pour out of the Mississippi and through Old River to quintuple the falls at Niagara. It was at Old River that the United States was going to lose its status among the world's trading nations. It was at Old River that New Orleans would be lost, Baton Rouge would be lost. At Old River, we would lose the American Ruhr. The Army's name for its operation there was Old River Control.

Rabalais gestured across the lock toward what seemed to be a pair of placid lakes separated by a trapezoidal earth dam a hundred feet high. It weighed five million tons, and it had stopped Old River. It had cut Old River in two. The severed ends were sitting there filling up with weeds.

Where the Atchafalaya had entrapped the Mississippi, bigmouth bass were now in charge. The navigation lock had been dug beside this monument. The big dam, like the lock, was fitted into the mainline levee of the Mississippi. In Rabalais's pickup, we drove on the top of the dam, and drifted as well through Old River country. On this day, he said, the water on the Mississippi side was eighteen feet above sea level, while the water on the Atchafalaya side was five feet above sea level. Cattle were grazing on the slopes of the levees, and white horses with white colts, in deep-green grass. Behind the levees, the fields were flat and reached to rows of distant trees. Very early in the morning, a low fog had covered the fields. The sun, just above the horizon, was large and ruddy in the mist, rising slowly, like a hot-air balloon. This was a countryside of corn and soybeans, of grain-fed-catfish ponds, of feed stores and Kingdom Halls in crossroad towns. There were small neat cemeteries with ranks of white sarcophagi raised a foot or two aboveground, notwithstanding the protection of the levees. There were tarpapered cabins on concrete pylons, and low brick houses under planted pines. Pickups under the pines. If this was a form of battlefield, it was not unlike a great many battlefields—landscapes so quiet they belie their story. Most battlefields, though, are places where something happened once. Here it would happen indefinitely.

We went out to the Mississippi. Still indistinct in mist, it looked like a piece of the sea. Rabalais said, "That's a wide booger, right there." In the spring high water of vintage years—1927, 1937, 1973—more than two million cubic feet of water had gone by this place in every second. Sixty-five kilotons per second. By the mouth of the inflow channel leading to the lock were rock jetties, articulated concrete mattress revetments, and other heavy defenses. Rabalais observed that this particular site was no more vulnerable than almost any other point in this reach of river that ran so close to the Atchafalaya plain. There were countless places where a breakout might occur: "It has a tendency to go through just anywheres you can call for."

Why, then, had the Mississippi not jumped the bank and long since diverted to the Atchafalaya?

"Because they're watching it close," said Rabalais. "It's under close surveillance."

After the Corps dammed Old River, in 1963, the engineers could not just walk away, like roofers who had fixed a leak. In the early planning stages, they had considered doing that, but there were certain effects they could not overlook. The Atchafalaya, after all, was a distributary of the Mississippi—the major one, and, as it happened, the only one worth mentioning that the Corps had not already plugged. In time of thundering flood, the Atchafalaya was used as a safety valve, to relieve a good deal of pressure and help keep New Orleans from ending up in Yucatán. The Atchafalaya was also the source of the water in the swamps and bayous of the Cajun world. It was the water supply of small cities and countless towns. Its upper reaches were surrounded by farms. The Corps was not in a political or moral position to kill the Atchafalaya. It had to feed it water. By the principles of nature, the more the Atchafalaya was given, the more it would want to take, because it was the steeper stream. The more it was given, the deeper it would make its bed. The difference in level between the Atchafalaya and the Mississippi would continue to increase, magnifying the conditions for capture. The Corps would have to deal with that. The Corps would have to build something that could give the Atchafalaya a portion of the Mississippi and at the same time prevent it from taking all. In effect, the Corps would have to build a Fort Laramie: a place where the natives could buy flour and firearms but where the gates could be closed if they attacked.

Ten miles upriver from the navigation lock, where the collective sediments were thought to be more firm, they dug into a piece of dry ground and built what appeared for a time to be an incongruous, waterless bridge. Five hundred and sixty-six feet long, it stood parallel to the Mississippi and about a thousand yards back from the water. Between its abutments were ten piers, framing eleven gates that could be lifted or dropped, opened or shut, like windows. To this structure, and through it, there soon came a new Old River—an excavated channel leading in from the Mississippi and out seven miles to the Red-Atchafalaya. The Corps was not intending to accommodate nature. Its engineers were intending to control it in space and arrest it in time. In 1950, shortly before the project began, the Atchafalaya was taking thirty per cent of the water that came down from the north to Old River. This water was known as the latitude flow, and it consisted of a little in the Red, a lot in the Mississippi. The United States Congress, in its deliberations, decided that "the distribution of flow and sediment in the Mississippi and Atchafalaya Rivers is now in desirable proportions and should be so maintained." The Corps was thereby ordered to preserve 1950. In perpetuity, at Old River, thirty per cent of the latitude flow was to pass to the Atchafalaya.

The device that resembled a ten-pier bridge was technically a sill, or weir, and it was put on line in 1963, in an orchestrated sequence of events that flourished the art of civil engineering. The old Old River was closed. The new Old River was opened. The water, as it crossed the sill from the Mississippi's level to the Atchafalaya's, tore to white shreds in the deafening turbulence of a great new falls, from lip to basin the construction of the Corps. More or less simultaneously, the navigation lock opened its chamber. Now everything had changed and nothing had changed. Boats could still drop away from the river. The ratio of waters continued as before—this for the American Ruhr, that for the ecosystems of the Cajun swamps. Withal, there was a change of command, as the Army replaced nature.

In time, people would come to suggest that there was about these enterprises an element of hauteur. A professor of law at Tulane University, for example, would assign it third place in the annals of arrogance. His name was Oliver Houck. "The greatest arrogance was the stealing of the sun," he said. "The second-greatest arrogance is running rivers backward. The third-greatest arrogance is trying to hold the Mississippi in place. The ancient channels of the river go almost to Texas. Human beings have tried to restrict the river to one course—that's where the arrogance began." The Corps listens closely to things like that and files them in its archives. Houck had a point. Bold it was indeed to dig a fresh conduit in the very ground where one river had prepared to trap another, bolder yet to build a structure there meant to be in charge of what might happen.

Some people went further than Houck, and said that they thought the structure would fail. In 1980, for example, a study published by the Water Resources Research Institute, at Louisiana State University, described Old River as "the scene of a direct confrontation between the United States Government and the Mississippi River," and—all constructions of the Corps notwithstanding—awarded the victory to the Mississippi River. "Just when this will occur cannot be predicted," the report concluded. "It could happen next year, during the next decade, or sometime in the next thirty or forty years. But the final outcome is simply a matter of time and it is only prudent to prepare for it."

The Corps thought differently, saying, "We can't let that happen. We are charged by Congress not to let that happen." Its promotional film referred to Old River Control as "a good soldier." Old River Control was, moreover, "the keystone of the comprehensive flood-protection project for the lower Mississippi Valley," and nothing was going to remove the keystone. People arriving at New Orleans District Headquarters, U.S. Army Corps of Engineers, were confronted at the door by a muralled collage of maps and pictures and bold letters unequivocally declaring, "The Old River Control Structures, located about two hundred miles above New Orleans on the Mississippi River, prevent the Mississippi from changing course by controlling flows diverted into the Atchafalaya Basin."

No one's opinions were based on more intimate knowledge than those of LeRoy Dugas, Rabalais's upstream counterpart—the manager of the apparatus that controlled the flow at Old River. Like Rabalais, he was Acadian and of the country. Dugie—as he is universally called—had worked at Old River Control since 1963, when the water started flowing. In years to follow, colonels and generals would seek his counsel. "Those professors at L.S.U. say that whatever we do we're going to lose the system," he remarked one day at Old River, and, after a pause, added, "Maybe they're right." His voice had the sound of water over rock. In pitch, it was lower than a helicon tuba. Better to hear him indoors, in his operations office, away from the structure's competing thunders. "Maybe they're right," he repeated. "We feel that we can hold the river. We're going to try. Whenever you try to control nature, you've got one strike against you."

Dugie's face, weathered and deeply tanned, was saved from looking weary by the alertness and the humor in his eyes. He wore a large, lettered belt buckle that said *to help control the Mississippi*. "I was originally born in Morganza," he told me. "Thirty miles down the road. I have lived in Pointe Coupee Parish all my life. Once, I even closed my domicile and went to work in Texas for the Corps—but you always come back." (Rabalais also—as he puts it—"left out of here one time," but not for long.) All through Dugie's youth, of course, the Mississippi had spilled out freely to feed the Atchafalaya. He took the vagaries of the waters for granted, not to mention the supremacy of their force in flood. He was a naval gunner on Liberty ships in the South Pacific during the Second World War, and within a year or two of his return was astonished to hear that the Corps of Engineers was planning to restrain Old River. "They were going to try to control the flow," he said. "I thought they had lost their marbles."

Outside, on the roadway that crosses the five-hundred-and-sixty-six-foot structure, one could readily understand where the marbles might have gone. Even at this time of modest normal flow, we looked down into a rage of water. It was running at about twelve miles an hour—significantly faster than the Yukon after breakup—and it was pounding into the so-called stilling basin on the downstream side, the least still place you would ever see. The No. 10 rapids of the Grand Canyon, which cannot be run without risk of life, resemble the Old River stilling basin, but the rapids of the canyon are a fifth as wide. The Susitna River is sometimes more like it—melted glacier ice from the Alaska Range. Huge trucks full of hardwood logs kept coming from the north to cross the structure, on their way to a chipping mill at Simmesport. One could scarcely hear them as they went by.

There was a high sill next to this one—a separate weir, two-thirds of a mile long and set two feet above the local flood stage, its purpose being to help regulate the flow of extremely high waters. The low sill, as the one we stood on was frequently called, was the prime valve at Old River, and dealt with the water every day. The fate of the project had depended on the low sill, and it was what people meant when, as they often did, they simply said "the structure." The structure and the high sill—like the navigation lock downstream—were filled into the Mississippi's mainline levee. Beyond the sound of the water, the broad low country around these structures was quiet and truly still. Here and again in the fields, pump jacks bobbed for oil. In the river batcher—the silt-swept no man's land between waterline and levee—lone egrets sat in trees, waiting for the next cow.

Dugie remarked that he would soon retire, that he felt old and worn down from fighting the river.

I said to him, "All you need is a good flood."

And he said, "Oh, no. Don't talk like that, man. You talk vulgar."

It was odd to look out toward the main-stem Mississippi, scarcely half a mile away, and see its contents spilling sideways, like cornmeal pouring from a hole in a burlap bag. Dugie said that so much water coming out of the Mississippi created a powerful and deceptive draw, something like a vacuum, that could suck in boats of any size. He had seen some big ones up against the structure. In the mid-sixties, a man alone had come down from Wisconsin in a small double-ended vessel with curling ends and tumblehome—a craft that would not have been unfamiliar to the Algonquians, who named the Mississippi. Dugie called this boat "a pirogue." Whatever it was, the man had paddled it all the way from Wisconsin, intent on reaching New Orleans. When he had nearly conquered the Mississippi, however, he was captured by the Atchafalaya. Old River caught him, pulled him off the Mississippi, and shot him through the structure. "He was in shock, but he lived," Dugie said. "We put him in the hospital in Natchez."

After a moment, I said, "This is an exciting place."

And Dugie said, "You've heard of Murphy—'What can happen will happen'? This is where Murphy lives."

A towboat coming up the Atchafalaya may be running from Corpus Christi to Vicksburg with a cargo of gasoline, or from Houston to St. Paul with ethylene glycol. Occasionally, Rabalais sees a sailboat, more rarely a canoe. One time, a cottonwood-log dugout with a high Viking bow went past Old River. A ship carrying Leif Eriksson himself, however, would be less likely to arrest the undivided attention of the lockmaster than a certain red-trimmed cream-hulled vessel called Mississippi, bearing Major General Thomas Sands.

Each year, in late summer or early fall, the Mississippi comes down its eponymous river and noses into the lock. This is the Low-Water Inspection Trip, when the General makes a journey from St. Louis and into the Atchafalaya, stopping along the way at river towns, picking up visitors, listening to complaints. In external configuration, the Mississippi is a regular towboat—two hundred and seventeen feet long, fifty feet wide, its horsepower approaching four thousand. The term "towboat" is a misnomer, for the river towboats all push their assembled barges and are therefore designed with broad flat bows. Their unpleasant profiles seem precarious, as if they were the rear halves of ships that have been cut in two. The Mississippi triumphs over these disadvantages. Intended as a carrier of influenceable people, it makes up in luxury what it suffers in form. Only its red trim is martial. Its over-all bright cream suggests globules that have risen to the top. Its broad flat front is a wall of picture windows, of riverine panoramas, faced with cream-colored couches among coffee tables and standing lamps. A river towboat will push as many as fifty barges at one time. What this boat pushes is the program of the Corps.

The Mississippi, on its fall trip, is the site of on-board hearings at Cape Girardeau, Memphis, Vicksburg, and, ultimately, Morgan City. Customarily, it arrives at Old River early in the morning. Before the boat goes through the lock, people with names like Broussard, Brignac, Begnaud, Blanchard, Juneau, Gautreau, Caillouet, and Smith get on—people from the Atchafalaya Basin Levee Board, the East Jefferson Levee Board, the Pontchartrain Levee Board, the Louisiana Office of Public Works, the United States Fish and Wildlife Service, the Teche-Vermilion Fresh Water District. Oliver Houck, the Tulane professor, gets on, and nine people—seven civilians and two colonels—from the New Orleans District of the Corps of Engineers. "This is the ultimate in communications," says the enthusiastic General Sands as he greets his colleagues and guests. The gates close behind the Mississippi. The mooring bits inside the lock wail like coyotes as the water and the boat go down.

The pilothouse of the Mississippi is a wide handsome room directly above the lounge and similarly fronted with a wall of windows. It has map-and-chart tables, consoles of electronic equipment, redundant radars. The pilots stand front and center, as trim and trig as pilots of the air—John Dugger, from Collierville, Tennessee (the ship's home port is Memphis), and Jorge Cano, a local "contact pilot," who is here to help the regular pilots sense the shoals of the Atchafalaya. Among the mutating profiles of the river, their work is complicated. Mark Twain wrote of river pilots, "Two things seemed pretty apparent to me. One was, that in order to be a pilot a man had got to learn more than any one man ought to be allowed to know; and the other was, that he must learn it all over again in a different way every twenty-four hours. . . . Your true pilot cares nothing about anything on earth but the river, and his pride in his occupation surpasses the pride of kings." Cano, for his part, is somewhat less flattering on the subject of Twain. He says it baffles him that Twain has "such a big reputation for someone who spent so little time on the river." Today, the Atchafalaya waters are twelve feet lower than the Mississippi's. Cano says that the difference is often as much as twenty. Now the gates slowly open, revealing the outflow channel that leads into old Old River and soon to the Atchafalaya.

The Mississippi River Commission, which is part civilian and part military, with General Sands as president, is required by statute to make these trips—to inspect the flood-control and navigation systems from Illinois to the Gulf, and to hold the hearings. Accordingly, there are two major generals and one brigadier aboard, several colonels, various majors—in all, a military concentration that is actually untypical of the U.S. Army Corps of Engineers. The Corps consists essentially of civilians, with a veneer of military people at and near the top. For example, Sands has with him his chief executive assistant, his chief engineer, his chief planner, his chief of operations, and his chief of programming. All these chiefs are civilians. Sands is commander of the Corps' Lower Mississippi Valley Division, which the New Orleans District, which includes Old River, is a part. The New Orleans District, U.S. Army Corps of Engineers, consists of something like ten Army officers and fourteen hundred civilians.

Just why the Army should be involved at all with levee systems, navigation locks, rock jetties, concrete revetments, and the austere realities of deltaic geomorphology is a question that attracts no obvious answer. The Corps is here because it is here. Its presence is an expression not of contemporary military strategy but of pure evolutionary tradition, its depth of origin about a century and three-quarters. The Corps is here specifically to safeguard the nation against any repetition of the War of 1812. When that unusual year was in its thirty-sixth month, the British Army landed on the Gulf Coast and marched against New Orleans. The war had been promoted, not to say provoked, by territorially aggressive American Midwesterners who were known around the country as hawks. It had so far produced some invigorating American moments ("We have met the enemy and they are ours"), including significant naval victories by ships like the Hornet and the Wasp. By and large, though, the triumphs had been British. The British had repelled numerous assaults on Canada. They had established a base in Maine. In Washington, they had burned the Capitol and the White House, and with their rutilant rockets and airburst ballistics they tried to destroy Baltimore. New Orleans was not unaware of these events, and very much dreaded invasion. When it came, militarily untrained American backwoods sharpshooters, standing behind things like cotton bales, picked off two thousand soldiers of the King while losing seventy-one of their own. Nonetheless, the city's fear of invasion long outlasted the war.

Despite the Treaty of Ghent, there was a widespread assumption that the British would attack again and, if so, would surely attack where they had attacked before. One did not have to go to the War College to learn that lightning enjoys a second chance. Fortifications were therefore required in the environs of New Orleans. That this was an assignment for the Army Corps of Engineers was obvious in more than a military sense. There was—and for another decade would be—only one school of engineering in America. This was the United States Military Academy, at West Point, New York. The academy had been founded in 1802. The beginnings of the Army Corps of Engineers actually date to the American Revolution. General Washington, finding among his aroused colonists few engineers worthy of the word, hired engineers from Louis XVI, and the first Corps was for the most part French.

The Army engineers chose half a dozen sites near New Orleans and, setting a pattern, signed up a civilian contractor to build the fortifications. Congress also instructed the Army to survey the Mississippi and its tributaries with an eye to assuring and improving inland navigation. Thus the Corps spread northward from its military fortifications into civil works along the rivers. In the eighteen-forties and fifties, many of these projects were advanced under the supervision of Pierre Gustave Toutant Beauregard, West Point '38, a native of St. Bernard Parish, and ranking military engineer in the district. Late in 1860, Beauregard was named superintendent of the United States Military Academy. He served five days, resigned to become a Confederate general, and opened the Civil War by directing the bombardment of Fort Sumter.

So much for why there are military officers on the towboat Mississippi inspecting the flood controls of Louisiana's delta plain. Thomas Sands with his two stars, his warm smile, his intuitive sense of people, and his knowledge of hydrology—is Pierre Gustave Toutant Beauregard's apostolic successor. Sands is trim, athletic, and, in appearance, youthful. Only in his Vietnam ribbons does he show the effects of his assignments as a combat engineer. One of his thumbs is larger and less straight than the other, but that is nothing more than an orthopedic reference to the rigors of plebe lacrosse—West Point '58. He grew up near Nashville, and has an advanced degree in hydrology from Texas A. & M. and a law degree he earned at night while working in the Pentagon. As a colonel, he spent three years in charge of the New Orleans District. As a brigadier general, he was commander of the Corps' North Atlantic Division, covering military and civil works from Maine to Virginia. Now, from his division headquarters, in Vicksburg, he is in charge of the Mississippi Valley from Missouri to the Gulf. On a wall of his private office is a board of green slate. One day when I was interviewing him there, he spent much of the time making and erasing chalk diagrams. "Man against nature. That's what life's all about," he said as he sketched the concatenating forces at Old River and the controls the Corps had applied. He used only the middle third of the slate. The rest had been preempted. The words *be innovative, be responsive, and operate with a touch of class* were chalked across the bottom. "Old River is a true representation of a confrontation with nature," he went on. "Folks recognized that Mother Nature, being what she is—having changed course many times—would do it again. Today, Mother Nature is working within a constrained environment in the lower Mississippi. Old River is the key element. Every facet of law below there relates to what goes on in this little out-of-the-way point that most folks have never heard about." Chalked across the upper third of the state were the words *do what's right, and be prepared to fight as infantry when required!!!*"

Now, aboard the towboat Mississippi, the General is saying, "In terms of hydrology, what we've done here at Old River is stop time. We have, in effect, stopped time in terms of the distribution of flows. Man is directing the maturing process of the Atchafalaya and the lower Mississippi." There is nothing formal about these remarks. The General says that this journey downriver is meant to be "a floating convention." Listening to him is not a requirement. From the pilothouse to the fantail, people wander where they please, stopping here and again to converse in small groups.

Two floatplanes appear above the trees, descend, flare, and land side by side behind the Mississippi. The towboat reduces power, and the airplanes taxi into its wake. They carry four passengers from Morgan City—latecomers to the floating convention. They climb aboard, and the airplanes fly away. These four, making such effort to advance their special interests, are four among two million nine hundred thousand people whose livelihoods, safety, health, and quality of life are directly influenced by the Corps' controls at Old River. In years gone by, when there were no control structures, naturally there were no complaints. The water went where it pleased. People took it as it came. The delta was in a state of nature. But now that Old River is valved and metered there are two million nine hundred thousand potential complainers, very few of whom are reluctant to present a grievance to the Corps. When farmers want less water, for example, fishermen want more, and they all complain to the Corps. In General Sands' words, "We're always walkin' around with, by and large, the black hat on. There's no place in the U.S. where there are so many competing interests relating to one water resource."

Aboard the Mississippi, this is the primary theme. Oliver Houck, professor of ecoprudence, is heard to mutter, "What the Corps does with the water decides everything." And General Sands cheerfully remarks that every time he makes one of these trips he gets "beaten on the head and shoulders." He continues, "In most water-resources stories, you can identify two sides. Here there are many more. The crawfisherman and the shrimper come up within five minutes asking for opposite things. The crawfishermen say, 'Put more water in, the water is low.' Shrimpers don't want more water. They are benefitted by low water. Navigation interests say, 'The water is too low, don't take more away or you'll have to dredge.' Municipal interests say, 'Keep the water high or you'll increase saltwater intrusion.' In the high-water season, everybody is interested in less water. As the water starts dropping, upstream farmers say, 'Get the water off of us quicker.' But folks downstream don't want it quicker. As water levels go up, we divert some fresh water into marshes, because the marshes need it for the nutrients and the sedimentation, but oyster fishermen complain. They all complain except the ones who have seed-oyster beds, which are destroyed by excessive salinity. The variety of competing influences is phenomenal."

In southern Louisiana, the bed of the Mississippi River is so far below sea level that a flow of at least a hundred and twenty thousand cubic feet per second is needed to hold back salt water and keep it below New Orleans, which drinks the river. Along the ragged edges of the Gulf, whole ecosystems depend on the relationship of fresh to salt water, which is in large part controlled by the Corps. Shrimp people want water to be brackish, waterfowl people want it fresh—a situation that causes National Marine Fisheries to do battle with United States Fish and Wildlife while both simultaneously attack the Corps. The industrial interests of the American Ruhr beseech the Corps to maintain their supply of fresh water. Agricultural pumping stations demand more fresh water for their rice but nervily ask the Corps to keep the sediment. Morgan City needs water to get oil boats and barges to rigs offshore, but if Morgan City gets too much water it's the end of Morgan City. Port authorities present special needs, and the owners of grain elevators, and the owners of coal elevators, barge interests, flood-control districts, levee boards. As General Sands says, finishing the list, "A guy who wants to put a new dock in has to come to us." People suspect the Corps of favoring other people. In addition to all the things the Corps actually does and does not do, there are infinite actions it is imagined to do, infinite actions it is imagined not to do, and infinite actions it is imagined to be capable of doing, because the Corps has been conceded the almighty role of God.

The towboat enters the Atchafalaya at an unprepossessing T in a jungle of phreatophytic trees. Atchafalaya. The "a"s are broad, the word rhymes with "jambalaya," and the accents are on the second and fourth syllables. Among navigable rivers, the Atchafalaya is widely described as one of the most treacherous in the world, but it just lies there quiet and smooth. It lies there like a big alligator in a low slough, with time on its side, waiting—waiting to outwit the Corps of Engineers—and hunkering down ever lower in its bed and presenting a sort of maw to the Mississippi, into which the river could fall. In the pilothouse, standing behind Jorge Cano and John Dugger as they swing the ship to port and head south, I find myself remembering an exchange between Cano and Rabalais a couple of days ago, when Cano was speculating about the Atchafalaya's chances of capturing the Mississippi someday despite all efforts to prevent it from doing so. "Mother Nature is patient," he said. "Mother Nature has more time than we do."

Rabalais said, "She has nothing but time."

Frederic Chatry happens to be in the pilothouse, too, as does Fred Bayley. Both are civilians: Chatry, chief engineer of the New Orleans District; Bayley, chief engineer of the Lower Mississippi Valley Division. Chatry is short and slender, a courtly and formal man, his uniform a bow tie. He is saying that before the control structures were built water used to flow in either direction through Old River. It would flow into the Mississippi if the Red happened to be higher. This was known as a reversal, and the last reversal occurred in 1945. The enlarging Atchafalaya was by then so powerful in its draw that it took all of the Red and kept it. "The more water the Atchafalaya takes, the bigger it gets; the bigger it gets, the more water it takes. The only thing that interrupts it is Old River Control. If we had not interrupted it, the main river would now be the Atchafalaya, below this point. If you left it to its own devices, the end result had to be that it would become the master stream. If that were to happen, below Old River the Mississippi reach would be unstable. Salt would fill it in. The Corps could not cope with it. Old River to Baton Rouge would fill in. River traffic from the north would stop. Everything would go to pot in the delta. We couldn't cope. It would be plugged."

I ask to what extent they ever contemplate that the structures at Old River might fail.

Bayley is quick to answer—Fred Bayley, a handsome sandy-haired man in a regimental tie and a cool tan suit, with the contemplative manner of an academic and none of the defenses of a challenged engineer. "Anything can fail," he says. "In most of our projects, we try to train natural effects instead of taking them head on. I never approach anything we do with the idea that it can't fail. That is sticking your head in the sand."

We are making twelve knots on a two-and-a-half-knot current under bright sun and cottony bits of cloud—flying along between the Atchafalaya levees, between the river-batcher trees. We are running down the reach above Simmesport, but only a distant bridge attests to that fact. From the river you cannot see the country. From the country you cannot see the river. I once looked down at this country from the air, in a light plane, and although it is called a floodway—this segment of it the West Atchafalaya Floodway—it is full of agriculture, in plowed geometries of brown, green, and tan. The Atchafalaya from above looks like the Connecticut winding past New Hampshire floodplain farms. If you look up, you do not see Mt. Washington. You see artificial ponds, now and again, as far as the horizon—square ponds, dotted with the cages of crawfish. You see dark-green pastureland, rail fences, cows with short fat shadows.

The unexpected happens—unthinkable, unfortunate, but not unimaginable. At first with a modest lurch, and then with a more pronounced lurch, and then with a profound structural shudder, the Mississippi is captured by the Atchafalaya. The mid-American flagship of the U.S. Army Corps of Engineers has run aground.

After going on line, in 1963, the control structures at Old River had to wait ten years to prove what they could do. The nineteen-fifties and nineteen-sixties were secure in the Mississippi Valley. In human terms, a generation passed with no disastrous floods. The Mississippi River and Tributaries Project—the Corps' total repertory of defenses from Cairo, Illinois, southward—seemed to have met its design purpose: to confine and conduct the run of the river, to see it safely into the Gulf. The Corps looked upon this accomplishment with understandable pride and, without intended diminution of respect for its enemy, issued a statement of victory: "We harnessed it, straightened it, regularized it, shackled it."

Then, in the fall of 1972, the winter of 1973, river stages were higher than normal, reducing the system's tolerance for what might come in spring. In the upper valley, snows were unusually heavy. In the South came a season of exceptional rains. During the uneventful era that was about to end, the Mississippi's main channel, in its relative lethargy, had given up a lot of volume to accumulations of sediment. High water, therefore, would flow that much higher. As the spring runoff came down the tributaries, collected, and approached, computers gave warning that the mainline levees were not sufficient to contain it. Eight hundred miles of frantically filled sandbags were added to the levees. Bulldozers added potato ridges—barriers of uncompacted dirt. While this was going on, more rain was falling. In the southern part of the valley, twenty inches fell in a day and a half.

At Old River Control on an ordinary day, when the stilling basin sounds like Victoria Falls but otherwise the country is calm and dry—when sandy spaces and stands of trees fill up the view between the structure and the Mississippi—an almost academic effort is required to visualize a slab of water six stories high, spread to the ends of perspective. That is how it was in 1973. During the sustained spring high water—week after week after week—the gathered drainage of Middle America came to Old River in units exceeding two million cubic feet a second. Twenty-five per cent of that left the Mississippi channel and went to the Atchafalaya. In aerial view, trees and fields were no longer visible, and the gated stronghold of the Corps seemed vulnerable in the extreme—a narrow causeway, a thin fragile line across a brown sea.

The Corps had built Old River Control to control just about as much as was passing through it. In mid-March, when the volume began to approach that amount, curiosity got the best of Raphael G. Kazmann, author of a book called "Modern Hydrology" and professor of civil engineering at Louisiana State University. Kazmann got into his car, crossed the Mississippi on the high bridge at Baton Rouge, and made his way north to Old River. He parked, got out, and began to walk the structure. An extremely low percentage of its five hundred and sixty-six feet eradicated his curiosity. "That whole miserable structure was vibrating," he recalled in 1986, adding that he had felt as if he were standing on a platform at a small rural train station when "a fully loaded freight goes through." Kazmann opted not to wait for the caboose. "I thought, This thing weighs two hundred thousand tons. When two hundred thousand tons vibrates like this, this is no place for R. G. Kazmann. I got into my car, turned around, and got the hell out of there. I was just a professor—and, thank God, not responsible."

Kazmann says that the Tennessee River and the Missouri River were "the two main culprits" in the 1973 flood. In one high water and another, the big contributors vary around the watershed. An ultimate deluge might possibly involve them all. After Kazmann went home from Old River that time in 1973, he did his potamology indoors for a while, assembling daily figures. In some of the numbers he felt severe vibrations. In his words, "I watched the Ohio like a hawk, because if that had come up, I thought, Katie, bar the door!"

The water was plenty high as it was, and continuously raged through the structure. Nowhere in the Mississippi Valley were velocities greater than in this one place, where the waters made their hydraulic jump, plunging over what Kazmann describes as "concrete falls" into the regime of the Atchafalaya. The structure and its stilling basin had been configured to dissipate energy—but not nearly so much energy. The excess force was attacking the environment of the structure. A large eddy had formed. Unbeknownst to anyone, its swirling power was excavating sediments by the inflow apron of the structure. Even larger holes had formed under the apron itself. Unfortunately, the main force of the Mississippi was crashing against the south side of the inflow channel, producing unplanned turbulence. The control structure had been set up near the outside of a bend of the river, and closer to the Mississippi than many engineers thought wise.

On the outflow side—where the water fell to the level of the Atchafalaya—a hole had developed that was larger and deeper than a football stadium, and with much the same shape. It was hidden, of course, far beneath the chop of wild water. The Corps had long since been compelled to leave all eleven gates wide open, in order to reduce to the greatest extent possible the force that was shaking the structure, and so there was no alternative to aggravating the effects on the bed of the channel. In addition to the structure's weight, what was holding it in place was a millipede of stilts— steel H-beams that reached down at various angles, as pilings, ninety feet through sands and silts, through clayey peats and organic mucks. There never was a question of anchoring such a fortress in rock. The shallowest rock was seven thousand feet straight down. In three places below the structure, sheet steel went into the substrate like fins; but the integrity of the structure depended essentially on the H-beams, and vehicular traffic continued to cross it en route to San Luis Rey.

Then, as now, LeRoy Dugas was the person whose hand controlled Old River Control—a thought that makes him smile. "We couldn't afford to close any of the gates," he remarked to me one day at Old River. "Too much water was passing through the structure. Water picked up riprap off the bottom in front, and rammed it through to the tail bed." The riprap included derrick stones, and each stone weighed seven tons. On the level of the road deck, the vibrations increased. The operator of a moving crane let the crane move without him and waited for it at the end of the structure. Dugie continued, "You could get on the structure with your automobile and open the door and it would close the door." The crisis recalled the magnitude of "the '27 high water," when Dugie was a baby. Up the valley somewhere, during the '27 high water, was a railroad bridge with a train sitting on it loaded with coal. The train had been put there because its weight might help keep the bridge in place, but the bridge, vibrating in the floodwater, produced so much friction that the coal in the gondolas caught fire. Soon the bridge, the train, and the glowing coal fell into the water.

One April evening in 1973—at the height of the flood—a fisherman walked onto the structure. There is, after all, order in the universe, and some things take precedence over impending disasters. On the inflow side, facing the Mississippi, the structure was bracketed by a pair of guide walls that reached out like curving arms to bring in the water. Close by the guide wall at the south end was the swirling eddy, which by now had become a whirlpool. There was other motion as well—or so it seemed. The fisherman went to find Dugas, in his command post at the north end of the structure, and told him the guide wall had moved. Dugie told the fisherman he was seeing things. The fisherman nodded affirmatively.

When Dugie himself went to look at the guide wall, he looked at it for the last time. "It was slipping into the river, into the inflow channel." Slowly it dipped, sank, broke. Its foundations were gone. There was nothing below it but water. Professor Kazmann likes to say that this was when the Corps became "scared green." Whatever the engineers may have felt, as soon as the water began to recede they set about learning the dimensions of the damage. The structure was obviously undermined, but how much so, and where? What was solid, what was not? What was directly below the gates and the roadway? With a diamond drill, in a central position, they bored the first of many holes in the structure. When they had penetrated to basal levels, they lowered a television camera into the hole. They saw fish.

This was scarcely the first time that an attempt to control the Mississippi had failed. Old River, 1973, was merely the most emblematic place and moment where, in the course of three centuries, failure had occurred. From the beginnings of settlement, failure was the par expectation with respect to the river—a fact generally masked by the powerful fabric of ambition that impelled people to build towns and cities where almost any camper would be loath to pitch a tent.

If you travel by canoe through the river swamps of Louisiana, you may very well grow uneasy as the sun is going down. You look around for a site—a place to sleep, a place to cook. There is no terra firma. Nothing is solider than duckweed, resting on the water like green burlap. Quietly, you slide through the forest, breaking out now and again into acreages of open lake. You study the dusk for some dark cap of uncovered ground. Seeing one at last, you occupy it, limited though it may be. Your tent site may be smaller than your tent, but in this amphibious milieu you have found yourself terrain. You have established yourself in much the same manner that the French established New Orleans. So what does it matter if your leg spends the night in the water.

The water is from the state of New York, the state of Idaho, the province of Alberta, and everywhere below that frame. Far above Old River are places where the floodplain is more than a hundred miles wide. Spaniards in the sixteenth century came upon it at the wrong time, saw an ocean moving south, and may have been discouraged. Where the delta began, at Old River, the water spread out even more—through a palimpsest of bayous and distributary streams in forested paludal basins—but this did not dissuade the French. For military and commercial purposes, they wanted a city in such country. They laid it out in 1718, only months before a great flood. Even as New Orleans was rising, its foundations filled with water. The message in the landscape could not have been more clear: like the aboriginal people, you could fish and forage and move on, but you could not build there—you could not create a city, or even a cluster of modest steadings—without declaring war on nature. You did not have to be Dutch to understand this, or French to ignore it. The people of southern Louisiana have often been compared unfavorably with farmers of the pre-Aswan Nile, who lived on high ground, farmed low ground, and permitted floods to come and go according to the rhythms of nature. There were differences in Louisiana, though. There was no high ground worth mentioning, and planters had to live on their plantations. The waters of the Nile were warm; the Mississippi brought cold northern floods that sometimes stood for months, defeating agriculture for the year. If people were to farm successfully in the rich loams of the natural levees—or anywhere nearby—they could not allow the Mississippi to continue in its natural state. Herbert Kassner, the division's public-relations director, once remarked to me, "This river used to meander all over its floodplain. People would move their tepees, and that was that. You can't move Vicksburg."

When rivers go over their banks, the spreading water immediately slows up, dropping the heavier sediments. The finer the silt, the farther it is scattered, but so much falls close to the river that natural levees rise through time. The first houses of New Orleans were built on the natural levees, overlooking the river. In the face of disaster, there was no better place to go. If there was to be a New Orleans, the levees themselves would have to be raised, and the owners of the houses were ordered to do the raising. This law (1724) was about as effective as the ordinances that compel homeowners and shopkeepers in the North to shovel snow off their sidewalks. Odd as it seems now, those early levees were only three feet high, and they were rife with imperfections. To the extent that they were effective at all, they owed a great deal to the country across the river, where there were no artificial levees, and waters that went over the bank flowed to the horizon. In 1727, the French colonial governor declared the New Orleans levee complete, adding that within a year it would be extended a number of miles up and down the river, making the community floodproof. The governor's name was Perrier. If words could stop water, Perrier had found them—initiating a durable genre.

In 1735, New Orleans went under—and again in 1785. The intervals—like those between earthquakes in San Francisco—were generally long enough to allow the people to build up a false sense of security. In response to the major floods, they extended and raised the levees. A levee appeared across the river from New Orleans, and by 1812 the west bank was leveed to the vicinity of Old River, a couple of hundred miles upstream. At that time, the east bank was leveed as far as Baton Rouge. Neither of the levees was continuous. Both protected plantation land. Where the country remained as the Choctaws had known it, floodwaters poured to the side, reducing the threat elsewhere. Land was not cheap—forty acres cost three thousand dollars—but so great was the demand for riverfront plantations that by 1828 the levees in southern Louisiana were continuous, the river artificially confined. Just in case the levees should fail, some plantation houses—among their fields of sugarcane, their long bright rows of oranges—were built on Indian burial mounds. In 1828, Bayou Manchac was closed. In the whole of the Mississippi's delta plain, Bayou Manchac happened to have been the only distributary that went east. It was dammed at the source. Its discharge would no longer ease the pressures of the master stream.

By this time, Henry Shreve had appeared on the scene—in various ways to change it forever. He was the consummate riverman: boatman, pilot, entrepreneur, empirical naval architect. He is noted as the creator of the flat-hulled layer-cake stern-wheel Mississippi steamboat, its shallow draft the result of moving the machinery up from below to occupy its own deck. The Mississippi steamboat was not invented, however. It evolved. And Shreve's contribution was less in its configuration than its power. A steamboat built and piloted by Henry Shreve travelled north against the current as far as Louisville. He demonstrated that commerce could go both ways. Navigation was inconvenienced, though, by hazards in the river—the worst of which were huge trees that had drifted south over the years and become stuck in various ways. One kind was rigid in the riverbed and stood up like a spear. It was called a planter. Another, known as a sawyer sawed up and down with the vagaries of the current, and was likely to rise suddenly in the path of a boat and destroy it. In the Yukon River, such logs—eternally bowing—are known as preachers. In the Mississippi, whatever the arrested logs were called individually, they were all "snags," and after the Army engineers had made Shreve, a civilian, their Superintendent of Western River Improvements he went around like a dentist yanking snags. The multihulled snag boats were devices of his invention. In the Red River, he undertook to disassemble a "raft"—uprooted trees by the tens of thousands that were stopping navigation for a hundred and sixty miles. Shreve cleared eighty miles in one year. Meanwhile, at 31 degrees north latitude (about halfway between Vicksburg and Baton Rouge) he made a bold move on the Mississippi. In the sinusoidal path of the river, any meander tended to grow until its loop was so large it would cut itself off. At 31 degrees north latitude was a west-bending loop that was eighteen miles around and had so nearly doubled back upon itself that Shreve decided to help it out. He adapted one of his snag boats as a dredge, and after two weeks of digging across the narrow neck he had a good swift current flowing. The Mississippi quickly took over. The width of Shreve's new channel doubled in two days. A few days more and it had become the main channel of the river.

The great loop at 31 degrees north happened to be where the Red-Atchafalaya conjoined the Mississippi, like a pair of parentheses back to back. Steamboats had had difficulty there in the colliding waters. Shreve's purpose in cutting off the loop was to give the boats a smoother shorter way to go, and, as an incidental, to speed up the Mississippi, lowering, however slightly, its crests in flood. One effect of the cutoff was to increase the flow of water out of the Mississippi and into the Atchafalaya, advancing the date of ultimate capture. Where the flow departed from the Mississippi now, it followed an arm of the cutoff meander. This short body of water soon became known as Old River. In less than a fortnight, it had been removed as a segment of the main-stem Mississippi and restyled as a form of surgical drain.

In city and country, riverfront owners became sensitive about the fact that the levees they were obliged to build were protecting not only their properties but also the properties behind them. Levee districts were established—administered by levee boards—to spread the cost. The more the levees confined the river, the more destructive it became when they failed. A place where water broke through was known as a crevasse—a source of terror no less effective than a bursting dam—and the big ones were memorialized, like other great disasters, in a series of proper names: the Macarty Crevasse (1816), the Sauvé Crevasse (1849). Levee inspectors were given power to call out male slaves—aged fifteen to sixty—whose owners lived within seven miles of trouble. With the approach of mid-century, the levees were averaging six feet—twice their original height—and calculations indicated that the flow line would rise. Most levee districts were not populous enough to cover the multiplying costs, so the United States Congress, in 1850, wrote the Swamp and Overflow Land Act. It is possible that no friend of Peter had ever been so generous in handing over his money to Paul. The federal government deeded millions of acres of swampland to states along the river, and the states sold the acreage to pay for the levees. The Swamp Act gave eight and a half million acres of river swamps and marshes to Louisiana alone. Other states, in aggregate, got twenty million more. Since time immemorial, these river swamps had been the natural reservoirs where floodwaters were taken in and held, and gradually released as the flood went down. Where there was timber (including virgin cypress), the swampland was sold for seventy-five cents an acre, twelve and a half cents where there were no trees. The new owners were for the most part absentee. An absentee was a Yankee. The new owners drained much of the swampland, turned it into farmland, and demanded the protection of new and larger levees. At this point, Congress might have asked itself which was the act and which was the swamp.

River stages, in their wide variations, became generally higher through time, as the water was presented with fewer outlets. People began to wonder if the levees could ever be high enough and strong enough to make the river safe. Possibly a system of dams and reservoirs in the tributaries of the upper valley could hold water back and release it in the drier months, and possibly a system of spillways and floodways could be fashioned in the lower valley to distribute water when big floods arrived. Beginning in the eighteen-fifties, these notions were the subject of virulent debate among civilian and military engineers. Four major floods in ten years and thirty-two disastrous crevasses in a single spring were not enough to suggest to the Corps that levees alone might never be equal to the job. The Corps, as things stood, was not yet in charge. District by district, state by state, the levee system was still a patchwork effort. There was no high command in the fight against the water. In one of the Corps' official histories, the situation is expressed in this rather preoccupied sentence: "By 1860, it had become increasingly obvious that a successful war over such an immense battleground could be waged only by a consolidated army under one authority." While the Civil War came and went, the posture of the river did not change. Vicksburg fell but did not move. In the floods of 1862, 1866, and 1867, levees failed. Catastrophes notwithstanding, Bayou Plaquemine—a major distributary of the Mississippi and a natural escape for large percentages of spring high water—was closed in 1868, its junction with the Mississippi sealed by an earthen dam. Even at normal stages, the Mississippi was beginning to stand up like a large vein on the back of a hand. The river of the eighteen-seventies ran higher than it ever had before.

In 1879, Congress at last created the Mississippi River Commission, which included civilians but granted hegemony to the Corps. The president of the commission would always be an Army engineer, and all decisions were subject to veto by the commandant of the Corps. Imperiously, Congress ordered the commission to "prevent destructive floods," and left it to the Corps to say how. The Corps remained committed to the argument that tributary dams and reservoirs and downstream spillways would create more problems than they would solve. "Hold by levees" was the way to do the job.

The national importance of the commission is perhaps illuminated by the fact that one of its first civilian members was Benjamin Harrison. Another was James B. Eads, probably the most brilliant engineer who has ever addressed his attention to the Mississippi River. As a young man, he had walked around on its bottom under a device of his own invention that he called a submarine. As a naval architect in the Civil War, he had designed the first American ironclads. Later, at St. Louis, he had built the first permanent bridge across the main stem of the river south of the Missouri. More recently, in defiance of the cumulative wisdom of nearly everyone in his profession, he had solved a primal question in anadromous navigation: how to get into the river. The mouth was defended by a mud-lump blockade—impenetrable masses of sediment dumped by the river as it reached the still waters of the Gulf. Dredging was hopeless. What would make a channel deep enough for ships? The government wouldn't finance him, so Eads bet his own considerable fortune on an elegant idea: he built parallel jetties in the river's mouth. They pinched the currents. The accelerated water dug out and maintained a navigable channel.

To the Corps' belief that a river confined by levees would similarly look after itself the success of the jetties gave considerable reinforcement. And Eads added words that spoke louder than his actions. "If the profession of an engineer were not based upon exact science," he said, "I might tremble for the result, in view of the immensity of the interests dependent on my success. But every atom that moves onward in the river, from the moment it leaves its home among the crystal springs or mountain snows, throughout the fifteen hundred leagues of its devious pathway, until it is finally lost in the vast waters of the Gulf, is controlled by laws as fixed and certain as those which direct the majestic march of the heavenly spheres. Every phenomenon and apparent eccentricity of the river—its scouring and depositing action, its caving banks, the formation of the bars at its mouth, the effect of the waves and tides of the sea upon its currents and deposits—is controlled by law as immutable as the Creator, and the engineer need only to be insured that he does not ignore the existence of any of these laws, to feel positively certain of the results he aims at."

When the commission was created, Mark Twain was forty-three. A book he happened to be working on was "Life on the Mississippi." Through a character called Uncle Mumford, he remarked that "four years at West Point, and plenty of books and schooling, will learn a man a good deal, I reckon, but it won't learn him the river." Twain also wrote, "One who knows the Mississippi will promptly aver—not aloud but to himself—that ten thousand River Commissions, with the mines of the world at their back, cannot tame that lawless stream, cannot curb it or confine it, cannot say to it, 'Go here,' or 'Go there,' and make it obey; cannot save a shore which it has sentenced; cannot bar its path with an obstruction which it will not tear down, dance over, and laugh at. But a discreet man will not put these things into spoken words; for the West Point engineers have not their superiors anywhere; they know all that can be known of their abstruse science; and so, since they conceive that they can fetter and handcuff that river and boss him, it is but wisdom for the unscientific man to keep still, lie low, and wait till they do it. Captain Eads, with his jetties, has done a work at the mouth of the Mississippi which seemed clearly impossible; so we do not feel full confidence now to prophesy against like impossibilities. Otherwise one would pipe out and say the Commission might as well bully the comets in their courses and undertake to make them behave, as try to bully the Mississippi into right and reasonable conduct."

In 1882 came the most destructive flood of the nineteenth century. After breaking the levees in two hundred and eighty-four crevasses, the water spread out as much as seventy miles. In the fertile lands on the two sides of Old River, plantations were deeply submerged, and livestock survived in flatboats. A floating journalist who reported these scenes in the March 29th New Orleans *Times-Democrat* said, "The current running down the Atchafalaya was very swift, the Mississippi showing a predilection in that direction, which needs only to be seen to enforce the opinion of that river's desperate endeavors to find a short way to the Gulf." The capture of the Mississippi, in other words, was already obvious enough to be noticed by a journalist. Seventy-eight years earlier—just after the Louisiana Purchase—the Army officer who went to take possession of the new country observed the Atchafalaya "completely obstructed by logs and other material" and said in his report, "Were it not for these obstructions, the probability is that the Mississippi would soon find a much nearer way to the Gulf than at present, particularly as it manifests a constant inclination to vary its course." The head of the Atchafalaya was plugged with logs for thirty miles. The raft was so compact that El Camino Real, the Spanish trail coming in from Texas, crossed the Atchafalaya near its head, and cattle being driven toward the Mississippi walked across the logs. The log-jam was Old River Control Structure No. 0. Gradually, it was disassembled, freeing the Atchafalaya to lower its plain. Snag boats worked on it, and an attempt was made to clear it with fire. The flood of 1863 apparently broke it open, and at once the Atchafalaya began to widen and deepen, increasing its draw on the Mississippi. Shreve's clearing of the Red River had also increased the flow of the Atchafalaya. The interventional skill of human engineers, which would be called upon in the twentieth century to stop the great shift at Old River, did much in the nineteenth to hurry it up.

For forty-eight years, the Mississippi River Commission and the Corps of Engineers adhered strictly to the "hold by levees" policy—levees, and levees only. It was important that no water be allowed to escape the river, because its full power would be most effective in scouring the bed, deepening the channel, increasing velocity, lowering stages, and preventing destructive floods. This was the hydraulic and hydrological philosophy not only of the U.S. Army Corps of Engineers but also of the great seventeenth-century savant Domenico Guglielmini, whose insights, ultimately, were to prove so ineffective in the valley of the Po. In 1885, one of General Sands' predecessors said, "The commission is distinctly committed to the idea of closing all outlets. . . . It has consistently opposed the fallacy known as the 'Outlet System.'"

Slaves with wheelbarrows started the levees. Immigrants with wheelbarrows replaced the slaves. Mule-drawn scrapers replaced the wheelbarrows, but not until the twentieth century. Fifteen hundred miles of earthen walls—roughly six, then nine, then twelve feet high, and a hundred feet from side to side—were built by men with shovels. They wove huge mats of willow poles and laid them down in cutbanks as revetments. When floods came, they went out to defend their defenses, and, in the words of a Corps publication, the effort was comparable to "the rigors of the battlefield." Nature was not always the only enemy. Anywhere along the river, people were safer if the levee failed across the way. If you lived on the east side, you might not be sad if water flooded west. You were also safer if the levee broke on your own side downstream. Armed patrols went up and down the levees. They watched for sand boils—signs of seepage that could open a crevasse from within. And they watched for private commandos, landing in the dark with dynamite.

Bayou Lafourche, a major distributary, was dammed in 1904. In something like twenty years, the increased confinement of the river had elevated floodwaters in Memphis by an average of about eight feet. The Corps remained loyal to the teachings of Guglielmini, and pronouncements were still forthcoming that the river was at last under control and destructive floods would not occur again. Declarations of that sort had been made in the quiet times before the great floods of 1884, 1890, 1891, 1897, 1898, and 1903, and they would be made again before 1912, 1913, 1922, and 1927.

The '27 high water tore the valley apart. On both sides of the river, levees crevassed from Cairo to the Gulf, and in the same thousand miles the flood destroyed every bridge. It killed hundreds of people, thousands of animals. Overbank, it covered twenty-six thousand square miles. It stayed on the land as much as three months. New Orleans was saved by blowing up a levee downstream. Yet the total volume of the 1927 high water was nowhere near a record. It was not a hundred-year flood. It was a form of explosion, achieved by the confining levees.

The levees of the nineteen-twenties were about six times as high as their earliest predecessors, but really no more effective. In a sense, they had been an empirical experiment—in aggregate, fifteen hundred miles of trial and error. They could be—and they would be—raised even higher. But in 1927 the results of the experiment at last came clear. The levees were helping to aggravate the problem they were meant to solve. With walls alone, one could only build an absurdly elevated aqueduct. Resistance times the resistance distance amplified the force of nature. Every phenomenon and apparent eccentricity of the river might be subject to laws as fixed and certain as those which direct the majestic march of the heavenly spheres, but, if so, the laws were inexactly understood. The Corps had attacked Antaeus without quite knowing who he was.

Congress appropriated three hundred million dollars to find out. This was more money in one bill—the hopefully titled Flood Control Act (1928)—than had been spent on Mississippi levees in all of Colonial and American history. These were the start-up funds for the Mississippi River and Tributaries Project, the coordinated defenses that would still be incomplete in the nineteen-eighties and would ultimately cost about seven billion dollars. The project would raise levees and build new ones, pave cutbanks, sever loops to align the current, and hold back large volumes of water with substantial dams in tributary streams. Dredges known as dustpans would take up sediment by the millions of tons. Stone dikes would appear in strategic places, forcing the water to go around them, preventing the channel from spreading out. Most significantly, though, the project would acknowledge the superiority of the force with which it was meant to deal. It would give back to the river some measure of the freedom lost as the delta's distributaries one by one were sealed. It would go into the levees in certain places and build gates that could be opened in times of extraordinary flood. The water coming out of such spillways would enter new systems of levees guiding it down floodways to the Gulf. But how many spillways? How many floodways? How many tributary dams? Calculating maximum storms, frequency of storms, maximum snowmelts, sustained saturation of the upper valley, coincident storms in scattered parts of the watershed, the Corps reached for the figure that would float Noah. The round number was three million—that is, three million cubic feet per second coming past Old River. This was twenty-five per cent above the 1927 high. The expanded control system, with its variety of devices, would have to be designed to process that. Various names were given to this blue-moon superflow, this concatenation of recorded moments written in the future unknown. It was called the Design Flood. Alternatively, it was called the Project Flood.

Bonnet Carre was the first spillway—completed in 1931, roughly thirty miles upriver from New Orleans. The water was meant to spill into Lake Pontchartrain and go on into the Gulf, dispersing eight and a half per cent of the Project Flood. Bonnet Carre (locally pronounced "Bonny Carey") would replace dynamite in the defense of New Orleans. When the great crest of 1937 came down the river—setting an all-time record at Natchez—enough of the new improvements were in place to see it through in relative safety, with the final and supreme test presented at Bonnet Carre, where the gates were opened for the first time. At the high point, more than two hundred thousand feet per second were diverted into Lake Pontchartrain, and the flow that went on by New Orleans left the city low and dry.

For the Corps of Engineers, not to mention the people of the southern parishes, the triumph of 1937 brought fresh courage, renewed confidence—a sense once again that the river could be controlled. Major General Harley B. Ferguson, the division commander, became a regional military hero. It was he who had advocated the project's many cutoffs, all made in the decade since 1927, which shortened the river by more than a hundred miles, reducing the amount of friction working against the water. The more distance, the more friction. Friction slows the river and raises its level. The mainline levees were rebuilt, extended, reinforced—and their height was almost doubled, reaching thirty feet. There was now a Great Wall of China running up each side of the river, with the difference that while the levees were each about as long as the Great Wall they were in many places higher and in cross-section ten times as large. Work continued on the floodways. There was one in Missouri that let water out of the river and put it back into the river a few miles downstream. But the principal conduit of release—without which Bonnet Carre would be about as useful as a bailing can—was the route of the Atchafalaya. Since the lower part of it was the largest river swamp in North America, it was, by nature, ready for the storage of water. The Corps built guide levees about seventeen miles apart to shape the discharge toward Atchafalaya Bay, incidentally establishing a framework for the swamp. In the northern Atchafalaya, near Old River, they built a three-chambered system of floodways involving so many intersecting levees that the country soon resembled a cranberry farm developed on an epic scale. The West Atchafalaya Floodway had so many people in it, and so many soybeans, that its levees were to be breached only by explosives in extreme emergency—maybe once in a hundred years. The Morganza Floodway, completed in the nineteen-fifties, contained farmlands but no permanent buildings. A couple of towns and the odd refinery were surrounded by levees in the form of rings. But the plane geometry of the floodways was primarily intended to take the water from the Mississippi and get it to the swamp.

The flood-control design of 1928 had left Old River open—the only distributary of the Mississippi to continue in its natural state. The Army was aware of the threat from the Atchafalaya. Colonel Charles Potter, president of the Mississippi River Commission, told Congress in 1928 that the Mississippi was "just itching to go that way." In the new master plan, however, nothing resulted from his testimony. The Corps, in making its flow diagrams, planned that the Atchafalaya would take nearly half the Mississippi during the Design Flood. It was not in the design that the Atchafalaya take it all.

The Atchafalaya, continuing to grow, had become, by volume of discharge, the second-largest river in the United States. Compared with the Mississippi, it had a three-to-one advantage in slope. Around 1950, geologists predicted that by 1975 the shift would be unstoppable. The Mississippi River and Tributaries Project would be in large part invalidated, the entire levee system of southern Louisiana would have to be rebuilt, communities like Morgan City in the Atchafalaya Basin would be a good deal less preserved than Pompeii, and the new mouth of the Mississippi would be a hundred and twenty miles from the old. Old River Control was authorized in 1954.

The levees were raised again. What had been adequate in 1937 was problematical in the nineteen-fifties. New grades were set. New dollars were spent to meet the grades. So often compared with the Great Wall of China, the levees had more in common with the Maginot Line. Taken together, they were a retroactive redoubt, more than adequate to wage a bygone war but below the requirements of the war to come. The levee grades of the nineteen-fifties would prove inadequate in the nineteen-seventies. Every shopping center, every drainage improvement, every square foot of new pavement in nearly half the United States was accelerating runoff toward Louisiana. Streams were being channelized to drain swamps. Meanders were cut off to speed up flow. The valley's natural storage capacities were everywhere reduced. As contributing factors grew, the river delivered more flood for less rain. The precipitation that produced the great flood of 1973 was only about twenty per cent above normal. Yet the crest at St. Louis was the highest ever recorded there. The flood proved that control of the Mississippi was as much a hope for the future as control of the Mississippi had ever been. The 1973 high water did not come close to being a Project Flood. It merely came close to wiping out the project.

While the control structure at Old River was shaking, more than a third of the Mississippi was going down the Atchafalaya. If the structure had toppled, the flow would have risen to seventy per cent. It was enough to scare not only a Louisiana State University professor but the division commander himself. At the time, this was Major General Charles Noble. He walked the bridge, looked down into the exploding water, and later wrote these words: "The south training wall on the Mississippi River side of the structure failed very early in the flood, causing violent eddy patterns and extreme turbulence. The toppled training wall monoliths worsened the situation. The integrity of the structure at this point was greatly in doubt.

It was frightening to stand above the gate bays and experience the punishing vibrations caused by the violently turbulent, massive flood waters."

If the General had known what was below him, he might have sounded retreat. The Old River Control Structure—this two-hundred-thousand-ton keystone of the comprehensive flood-protection project for the lower Mississippi Valley—was teetering on steel pilings above extensive cavities full of water. The gates of the Morganza Floodway, thirty miles downstream, had never been opened. The soybean farmers of Morganza were begging the Corps not to open them now. The Corps thought it over for a few days while the Old River Control Structure, absorbing shock of the sort that could bring down a skyscraper, continued to shake. Relieving some of the pressure, the Corps opened Morganza.

The damage at Old River was increased but not initiated by the 1973 flood. The invasive scouring of the channel bed and the undermining of the control structure may actually have begun in 1963, as soon as the structure opened. In years that followed, loose barges now and again slammed against the gates, stuck there for months, blocked the flow, enhanced the hydraulic jump, and no doubt contributed to the scouring. Scour holes formed on both sides of the control structure, and expanded steadily. If they had met in 1973, they might have brought the structure down.

After the waters quieted and the concrete had been penetrated by exploratory diamond drills, Old River Control at once became, and has since remained, the civil-works project of highest national priority for the U.S. Army Corps of Engineers. Through the surface of Louisiana 15, the road that traverses the structure, more holes were drilled, with diameters the size of dinner plates, and grout was inserted in the cavities below, like fillings in a row of molars. The grout was cement and bentonite. The drilling and filling went on for months. There was no alternative to leaving gates open and giving up control. Stress on the structure was lowest with the gates open. Turbulence in the channel was commensurately higher. The greater turbulence allowed the water on the Atchafalaya side to dig deeper and increase its advantage over the Mississippi side. As the Corps has reported, "The percentage of Mississippi River flow being diverted through the structure in the absence of control was steadily increasing." That could not be helped.

After three and a half years, control was to some extent restored, but the extent was limited. In the words of the Corps, "The partial foundation undermining which occurred in 1973 inflicted permanent damage to the foundation of the low sill control structure. Emergency foundation repair, in the form of rock riprap and cement grout, was performed to safeguard the structure from a potential total failure. The foundation under approximately fifty per cent of the structure was drastically and irrevocably changed." The structure had been built to function with a maximum difference of thirty-seven feet between the Mississippi and Atchafalaya sides. That maximum now had to be lowered to twenty-two feet—a diminution that brought forth the humor in the phrase "Old River Control." Robert Fairless, a New Orleans District engineer who has long been a part of the Old River story, once told me that "things were touch and go for some months in 1973" and the situation was precarious still. "At a head greater than twenty-two feet, there's danger of losing the whole thing," he said. "If loose barges were to be pulled into the front of the structure where they would block the flow, the head would build up, and there'd be nothing we could do about it."

A sign appeared on one of the three remaining wing walls:

"fishing and shad dipping off this wing wall is prohibited."

A survey boat, Navy-gray and very powerful and much resembling PT-109, began to make runs toward the sill upstream through the roiling brown rapids. Year after year—at least five times a week—this has continued. The survey boat drives itself to a standstill in the whaleback waves a few yards shy of the structure. Two men in life vests, who stand on the swaying deck in spray that curls like smoke, let go a fifty-pound ball that drops on a cable from a big stainless reel. The ball sinks to the bottom. The crewmen note the depth. They are not looking for mark twain. For example, in 1974 they found three holes so deep that it took a hundred and eighty-five thousand tons of rock to fill them in.

The 1973 flood shook the control structure a whole lot more than it shook the confidence of the Corps. When a legislative committee seemed worried, a Corps general reassured them, saying, "The Corps of Engineers can make the Mississippi River go anywhere the Corps directs it to go." On display in division headquarters in Vicksburg is a large aerial photograph of a school bus moving along a dry road beside a levee while a Galilee on the other side laps at the levee crown. This picture alone is a triumph for the Corps. Herbert Kassner, the public-relations director and a master of his craft, says of the picture, "Of course, I tell people the school bus may have been loaded with workers going to fix a break in the levee, but it looks good." And of course, after 1973, the flow lines were recomputed and the levees had to be raised. When the river would pool against the stratosphere was only a question of time.

The Washington Post, in an editorial in November of 1980, called attention to the Corps' efforts to prevent the great shift at Old River, and concluded with this paragraph:

> Who will win as this slow-motion confrontation between humankind and nature goes on? No one really knows. But after watching Mt. St. Helens and listening to the guesses about its performance, if we had to bet, we would bet on the river.

The Corps had already seen that bet, and was about to bump it, too. Even before the muds were dry from the 1973 flood, Corps engineers had begun building a model of Old River at their Waterways Experiment Station, in Vicksburg. The model was to cover an acre and a half. A model of that size was modest for the Corps. Not far away, it had a fifteen-acre model of the Mississippi drainage, where water flowing in from the dendritic tips could get itself together and attack Louisiana. The scale was one human stride to the mile. In the time it took to say "one Mississippi," if fourteen gallons went past Arkansas City that was a Project Flood. Something like eight and a half gallon was "a high-water event." "It's the ultimate sandbox—these guys have made a profession of the sandbox," Tulane's Oliver Houck has said, with concealed admiration. "They've put the whole river in a sandbox." The Old River model not only helped with repairs, it also showed a need for supplementary fortification. Since the first control structure was irreparably damaged, a second one, nearby, with its own inflow channel from the Mississippi, should establish full control at Old River and take pressure off the original structure in times of high stress.

To refine the engineering of the auxiliary structure, several additional models, with movable beds, were built on a distorted scale. Making the vertical scale larger than the horizontal was believed to eliminate surface-tension problems in simulating the turbulence of a real river. The channel beds were covered with crushed coal—which has half the specific gravity of sand—or with walnut shells, which were thought to be better replicas of channel-protecting rock but had an unfortunate tendency to decay, releasing gas bubbles. In one model, the stilling basin below the new structure was filled with driveway-size limestone gravel, each piece meant to represent a derrick stone six feet thick. After enough water had churned through these models to satisfy the designers, ground was broken at Old River, about a third of a mile from the crippled sill, for the Old River Control Auxiliary Structure, the most advanced weapon ever developed to prevent the capture of a river—a handsome gift to the American Ruhr, worth three hundred million dollars. In Vicksburg, Robert Fletcher—a sturdily built, footballish sort of engineer, who had explained to me about the nutshells, the coal, and the gravel—said of the new structure, "I hope it works."

The Old River Control Auxiliary Structure is a rank of seven towers, each buff with a white crown. They are vertical on the upstream side, and they slope toward the Atchafalaya. Therefore, they resemble flying buttresses facing the Mississippi. The towers are separated by six arciform gates, convex to the Mississippi, and hinged in trunnion blocks secured with steel to carom the force of the river into the core of the structure. Lifted by cables, these tainter gates, as they are called, are about as light and graceful as anything could be that has a composite weight of twenty-six hundred tons. Each of them is sixty-two feet wide. They are the strongest the Corps has ever designed and built. A work of engineering such as a Maillart bridge or a bridge by Christian Menn can outdo some other works of art, because it is not only a gift to the imagination but also structural in the matrix of the world. The auxiliary structure at Old River contains too many working components to be classed with such a bridge, but in grandeur and in profile it would not shame a pharaoh.

The original Old River Control project, going on line in 1963, cost eighty-six million dollars. The works of repair and supplement have extended the full cost of the battle to five hundred million. The disproportion in these figures does, of course, reflect inflation, but to a much greater extent it reflects the price of lessons learned. It reflects the fact that no one is stretching words who says that in 1973 the control structure failed. The new one is not only bigger and better and more costly; also, no doubt, there are redundancies in its engineering in memory of '73.

In 1983 came the third-greatest flood of the twentieth century—a narrow but decisive victory for the Corps. The Old River Control Auxiliary Structure was nothing much by then but a foundation that had recently been poured in dry ground. The grout in the old structure kept Old River stuck together. Across the Mississippi, a few miles downstream, the water rose to a threatening level at Louisiana's maximum-security prison. The prison was protected not only by the mainline levee but also by a ring levee of its own. Nonetheless, as things appeared for a while the water was going to pour into the prison. The state would have to move the prisoners, taking them in buses out into the road system, risking Lord knows what. The state went on its knees before the Corps: Do something. The Corps evaluated the situation and decided to bet the rehabilitation of the control structure against the rehabilitation of the prisoners. By letting more water through the control structure, the Corps caused the water at the prison to go down.

Viewed from five or six thousand feet in the air, the structures at Old River inspire less confidence than they do up close. They seem temporary, fragile, vastly outmatched by the natural world—a lesion in the side of the Mississippi butterflied with surgical tape. Under construction nearby is a large hydropower plant that will take advantage of the head between the two rivers and light the city of Vidalia. The channel cut to serve it raises to three the number of artificial outlets opened locally in the side of the Mississippi River, making Old River a complex of canals and artificial islands, and giving it the appearance of a marina. The Corps is officially confident that all this will stay in place, and supports its claim with a good deal more than walnuts. The amount of limestone that has been imported from Kentucky is enough to confuse a geologist. As Fred Chatry once said, "The Corps of Engineers is convinced that the Mississippi River can be convinced to remain where it is."

I once asked Fred Smith, a geologist who works for the Corps at New Orleans District Headquarters, if he thought Old River Control would eventually be overwhelmed. He said, "Capture doesn't have to happen at the control structures. It could happen somewhere else. The river is close to it a little to the north. That whole area is suspect. The Mississippi wants to go west. Nineteen-seventy-three was a forty-year flood. The big one lies out there somewhere—when the structures can't release all the floodwaters and the levee is going to have to give way. That is when the river's going to jump its banks and try to break through."

Geologists in general have declared the capture inevitable, but, of course, they would. They know that in 1852 the Yellow River shifted its course away from the Yellow Sea, establishing a new mouth four hundred miles from the old. They know the story of catastrophic shifts by the Mekong, the Indus, the Po, the Volga, the Tigris and the Euphrates. The Rosetta branch of the Nile was the main stem of the river three thousand years ago.

Raphael Kazmann, the hydrologic engineer, who is now emeritus at Louisiana State, sat me down in his study in Baton Rouge, instructed me to turn on a tape recorder, and, with reference to Old River Control, said, "I have no fight with the Corps of Engineers. I may be a critic, but I'm not mad at anybody. It's a good design. Don't get me wrong. These guys are the best. If it doesn't work for them, nobody can do it."

A tape recorder was not a necessity for gathering the impression that nobody could do it. "More and more energy is being dissipated there," Kazmann said. "Floods are more frequent. There will be a bigger and bigger differential head as time goes on. It almost went out in '73. Sooner or later, it will be undermined or bypassed—give way. I have a lot of respect for Mother . . . for this alluvial river of ours. I don't want to be around here when it happens."

The Corps would say he won't be.

"Nobody knows where the hundred-year flood is," Kazmann continued. "Perspective should be a minimum of a hundred years. This is an extremely complicated river system altered by works of man. A fifty-year prediction is not reliable. The data have lost their pristine character. It's a mixture of hydrologic events and human events. Floods across the century are getting higher, low stages lower. The Corps of Engineers—they're scared as hell. They don't know what's going to happen. This is planned chaos. The more planning they do, the more chaotic it is. Nobody knows exactly where it's going to end."

ROBERT BULLARD

"Houston's Northwood Manor Neighborhood"

Dumping in Dixie: Race, Class,
and Environmental Quality (1990)

Robert Bullard's (b. 1946) book *Dumping in Dixie: Race, Class, and Environmental Quality* (1990) is a seminal work on environmental justice in the South and widely regarded as the first to fully articulate the concept of environmental justice. Bullard, who is a distinguished professor of urban planning and environmental policy at Texas Southern University, is often described as the father of environmental justice.

In *Dumping in Dixie*, he chronicles the efforts of five African American communities in the South and their fight to address systemic pollution and racism. In the excerpt included here, Bullard highlights his early findings of patterns of environmental pollution in Houston, Texas. Bullard was a young sociologist in the 1970s when his wife, the attorney Linda McKeever Bullard, needed information for a lawsuit on the spatial locations of municipal solid waste disposal facilities in Houston. Robert Bullard found that 100 percent of all the city-owned landfills in Houston were in black neighborhoods and with them, the incinerators, transfer stations, and other infrastructure relegating the neighborhoods as "the dumping grounds for the city's household garbage." The Bullards' work confirmed that environmental quality is fundamentally linked to power, class, and race.

Robert Bullard's writing reveals the work of a compelling scientist; facts and figures are as important to him as prose. He is equally an academic and an activist. Along with his many books on environmental justice, he helped plan the first National People of Color Environmental Leadership Summit in 1991 and encouraged the establishment of the Environmental Protection Agency's Office of Environmental Equity. Bullard is a seminal figure in the American environmental movement.

Work Sourced

Bullard, Robert D. "Phylon: Vol. 49, No. 3, 4, 2001 Environmental Justice in the 21st Century: Race Still Matters." *Phylon*, vol. 52, no. 1, 2015, pp. 72–94.

In the 1970s, Houston was dubbed the "golden buckle" of the Sunbelt and the "petrochemical capital" of the world. The city experienced unparalleled economic expansion and population growth during the 1970s. By 1982, Houston emerged as the nation's fourth largest city with a population of 1.7 million persons spread over more than 585 square miles. In 1980, the city's black community was made up of nearly a half million residents, or 28 percent of the city's total population. Black Houston, however, remained residentially segregated from the larger community. More than 81 percent of the city's blacks lived in mostly black areas with major concentrations in northeast and southeast sections of the city.

Houston is the only major city in the United States that does not have zoning. The city's landscape has been shaped by haphazard and irrational land-use planning, a pattern characterized by excessive infrastructure chaos. In the absence of zoning, developers have used renewable deed restrictions as a means of land-use control within subdivisions. Lower-income, minority, and older neighborhoods have had difficulty enforcing and renewing deed restrictions. Deed restrictions in these areas are often allowed to lapse because individuals may be preoccupied with making a living and may not have the time, energy, or faith in government to get the needed signatures of neighborhood residents to keep their deed restrictions in force. Moreover, the high occupancy turnover and large renter population in many inner-city neighborhoods further weaken the efficacy of deed restrictions as a protectionist device.

Ineffective land-use regulations have created a nightmare for many of Houston's neighborhoods—especially the ones that are ill equipped to fend off industrial encroachment. Black Houston, for example, has had to contend with a disproportionately large share of garbage dumps, landfills, salvage yards, automobile "chop" shops, and a host of other locally unwanted land uses. The siting of nonresidential facilities has heightened animosities between the black community and the local government. This is especially true in the case of solid-waste disposal siting.

Public officials learn fast that solid-waste management can become a volatile political issue. Generally, controversy centers around charges that disposal sites are not equitably spread in quadrants of the city; equitable siting would distribute the burden and lessen the opposition. Finding suitable sites for sanitary landfills has become a critical problem mainly because no one wants to have a waste facility as a neighbor. Who wants to live next to a place where household waste—some of which is highly toxic—is legally dumped and where hazardous wastes may be illegally dumped?

The burden of having a municipal landfill, incinerator, transfer station, or some other type of waste disposal facility near one's home has not been equally borne by Houston's neighborhoods. Black Houston has become the dumping grounds for the city's household garbage. Over the past fifty years, the city has used two basic methods of disposing of its solid waste: incineration and landfill. Thirteen disposal facilities were operated by the city from the late 1920s to the mid-1970s. The city operated eight garbage incinerators (five large units and three mini-units), six of which were located in mostly black neighborhoods, one in a Hispanic neighborhood, and one in a mostly white area.

All five of the large garbage incinerators were located in minority neighborhoods—four black and one Hispanic. All five of the city-owned landfills were found in black neighborhoods. Although black neighborhoods composed just over one-fourth of the city's population, more than three-fourths of Houston's solid-waste facilities were found in these neighborhoods. Moreover, lower-income areas, or "pockets of poverty," have a large share—twelve out of thirteen—of the city-owned garbage dumps and incinerators.

These environmental stressors compound the myriad of social ills (e.g., crowding, crime, poverty, drugs, unemployment, congestion, infrastructure deterioration, etc.) that exist in Houston's Community Development Block Grant (CDBG) target area neighborhoods.

The Texas Department of Health (TDH) is the state agency that grants permits for standard sanitary landfills. From 1970 to 1978, TDH issued four sanitary landfill permits for the disposal of Houston's solid waste. The data illustrates that siting of privately owned sanitary landfills in Houston followed the pattern established by the city. That is, disposal sites were located in mostly black areas of the city. Three of the four privately owned landfill sites are located in black neighborhoods. Controversy surrounding landfill siting peaked in the late 1970s with the proposal to build the Whispering Pines landfill in Houston's Northwood Manor neighborhood. In 1980, the suburban neighborhood had a population of 8,449 residents, of whom 82.4 percent were black. The subdivision consists primarily of single-family home owners. It also sits in the midst of the predominately black North Forest Independent School District—one of the poorest suburban districts in the Houston area.

Northwood Manor residents thought they were getting a shopping center or new homes in their subdivision when construction on the landfill site commenced. When they learned the truth, they began to organize their efforts to stop the dump. It is ironic than many of the residents who were fighting the construction of the waste facility had moved to Northwood Manor in an effort to escape landfills in their former Houston neighborhoods.

Local residents formed the Northeast Community Action Group (NECAG)—a spinoff organization from the local neighborhood civic association—to halt the construction of the facility. They later filed a lawsuit in federal court to stop the siting of the landfill in their neighborhood. The residents and their black attorney, Linda McKeever Bullard, charged the Texas Department of Health and the private disposal company (Browning Ferris Industries) with racial discrimination in the selection of the Whispering Pines landfill site.[1] Residents were upset because the proposed site was not only near their homes but within 1,400 feet of their high school. Smiley High School was not equipped with air conditioning—not an insignificant point in the hot and humid Houston climate. Windows are usually left open while school is in session. Moreover, seven North Forest Schools—also without air conditioning—can be found in Northwood Manor and contiguous neighborhoods.

The lawsuit that was filed in 1979 finally went to trial in 1984. The federal district judge in Houston ruled against the residents and the landfill was built. The class-action lawsuit, however, did produce some changes in the way environmental issues were dealt with in the city's black community. First, the Houston city council, acting under intense political pressure from local residents, passed a resolution in 1980 that prohibited city-owned trucks carrying solid waste from dumping at the controversial landfill. Second, the Houston city council passed an ordinance restricting the construction of solid-waste sites near public facilities such as schools. This action was nothing less than a form of zoning. Third, the Texas Department of Health updated its requirements of landfill permit applicants to include detailed land-use, economic, and socio-demographic data on areas where they proposed to site standard sanitary landfills. Fourth, and probably most important, black residents sent a clear signal to the Texas Department of Health, city government, and private disposal companies that they would fight any future attempts to place waste disposal facilities in their neighborhoods. The landfill question appears to have galvanized and politicized a part of the Houston community, the black community, which for years had been inactive on environmental issues.

NOTE

1. For a detailed account of this dispute, see Bullard, *Invisible Houston,* Chapter 6, *Houston Chronicle,* November 8, 11, 15, 22, 1979, December 15, 22, 1979, June 19, 1980; *Houston Post,* December 15, 1981.

JOHN BARRY

*Rising Tide: The Great Mississippi Flood of 1927 and
How It Changed America* (1997)

Perhaps no living writer is as conversant with the history and current status of
the southeastern Louisiana environment, as well as the influence of the Mississippi River on that environment, as John Barry (b. 1947). The author of *Rising
Tide: The Great Mississippi Flood of 1927 and How It Changed America*, Barry is
also an influential advocate for the river. After Hurricane Katrina, John Barry
sat on the board overseeing levee districts in metropolitan New Orleans and
on the Louisiana Coastal Protection and Restoration Authority. Not one to shy
from confrontation, he sued oil companies that had cut canals into Louisiana's
swamps to transport their oil, demanding that they restore the land they had
marred, per their agreements. This suit, in all its labyrinthine disappointments,
is chronicled in an extensive *New York Times* article, "The Most Ambitious Environmental Lawsuit Ever."

 In the selection included here from *Rising Tide*, Barry writes about the
extraordinary nineteenth-century inventor and engineer James Eads. As a
young man, Eads designed a diving suit and boat that allowed him to search
for underwater salvage of wrecked ships throughout the Mississippi River;
in this way he gained detailed knowledge of the river and how to navigate
it. In response to the Mississippi River's tendency to accumulate silt near the
Gulf of Mexico and thus make navigation for some ships difficult, Eads proposed a series of jetties, underwater wooden walls, to narrow and deepen
the river. (For another text on this jetty, read E. L. Corthell's "The Delta of
the Mississippi River" included in this anthology.) His plan, however, was
in heated debate with Andrew A. Humphries, head of the Army Corps of
Engineers at that time. Humphries, along with the military engineer Henry
Larcom Abbot, wrote the monumental 500-page *Report on the Physics and
Hydraulics of the Mississippi River*, in which they argue that continuous levees built back from the river would concentrate its flow. Another civil engineer, Charles S. Ellet Jr., was also involved in the debate and is named in this
excerpt. Although Eads achieved success in building a jetty at the mouth
of the Mississippi, his efforts helped usher in a new era of control of the
river that continues today. In the end, both Eads and Humphries believed

human intervention in the river, for the benefit of business, was just. Today, in this excerpt, it is clear they were early contributors to the ongoing land loss along the Gulf Coast.

Work Sourced

Rich, Nathaniel. "The Most Ambitious Environmental Lawsuit Ever." *The New York Times Magazine*, October 2, 2014.

A year before Eads' victory dinner, in the spring of 1874, the Mississippi River had overflowed from Illinois south. It had devastated the lower Mississippi region and focused the nation's attention fully on the great river. In response, the government had created the U.S. Levee Commission to decide upon a river control policy to prevent future floods.

G. K. Warren, the Humphreys loyalist who had tried to destroy Eads' bridge, chaired it; other members included Henry Abbot, coauthor with Humphreys of Physics and Hydraulics, and Paul Hebert, the former Louisiana governor who was then lobbying against the jetties. Despite the importance of its charge, this commission conducted no fieldwork, made no measurements, visited no sites. Its sole source of information was the Humphreys and Abbot report; it did not even review any observations or measurements made by others. Unsurprisingly, its conclusions conformed to Humphreys' earlier ones.

As Humphreys had, it rejected reservoirs, cutoffs, and the engineering theory associated with the levees-only policy, saying, "The idea that the river would scour its bed deeper if confined . . . [is] erroneous." As Humphreys had, it emphasized the importance of keeping all natural outlets open, and it was "forced unwillingly to" reject artificial outlets because of the cost. As Humphreys had, it stated flatly, "The alluvial regions of the Mississippi can only be reclaimed by levees."

The report appeared in January 1875. The 1874 flood and this report had not entered directly into the debate over the jetties, and until his jetty contract was secure, Eads refrained from comment on it. But then he attacked. Dismissing the entire report and its recommendations, he urged, in effect, the use of jetties on the entire river. His reasoning superficially resembled the theory that levees would increase current velocity and scour out the bottom. But there was an immense difference. Levees were built back from the river's natural banks, sometimes more than a mile back. The river had to overflow its banks before the levees could begin to confine it;

as a result, any force generated by this confinement was dissipated over an area far greater than the river's natural channel. Also, levees only confined the river during floods. Thus, levees could increase current velocity for only a few weeks each year—and not necessarily every year.

This was a crucial point. Neither Humphreys nor Ellet had ever disputed the fact that a faster current increased scouring of the bottom. The question was, how much? The river in flood carried several orders of magnitude more volume than when it was at low water. Levees did confine floods, and did increase scour, but could levees cause enough increased current and scour to accommodate a flood?

Humphreys, Ellet, and Eads all agreed that levees could *not* do so. But Eads proposed to concentrate the river's force constantly, year-round. He planned to invade the river, to build not levees back from the banks but jetties in the river's channel. These would constrict the water year-round, even at low water, and apply a constant scouring of the bottom. He also called for cutoffs to create a far straighter and faster river. All this, he was certain, would significantly deepen the river.

He declared: "By such correction the flood . . . can be permanently lowered, and in this way the entire alluvial basin, from Vicksburg to Cairo, can be lifted as it were above all overflow, and levees in that part of the river rendered [superfluous]. . . . *There can be no question of this fact, and it is well for those most deeply interested to ponder it carefully before rejecting it; for the increased value given to the territory thus reclaimed can scarcely be estimated.*"

Eads was directly contradicting Humphreys, the U.S. Levee Commission, and the entire Corps of Engineers. If the jetties in South Pass succeeded, Eads would clearly try to apply his theory to the length of the river, and make the Corps irrelevant.

In early May 1875, Eads arrived in New Orleans. He had delayed starting work until the end of the flood season, and the city that had earlier fought him now waited anxiously. Upon his arrival he was entertained at the Canal Street mansion of Dr. William Mercer, who used the same gold service for Eads that he had used for the Grand Duke Alexis of Russia during Mardi Gras three years earlier. The city council formally applauded Eads' "grand enterprise," while the Chamber of Commerce, the Cotton Exchange, the Merchant Exchange, the Ship and Steamship Association, and others of prominence hosted a reception at the St. Charles Hotel, which called itself the most elegant in the country. There, under the chandeliers sat Creoles and Americans, carpetbaggers and Confederates, fanning themselves with the printed menus commemorating the occasion. One thing brought them together—money.

In a toast simultaneously blunt and gracious, General Cyrus Bussey announced: "Captain Eads has fought his way with an address and vigor and courage which deserve unqualified admiration. Against the most persistent misrepresentations that ever beset any human endeavor, against ignorance, angry and false witness, he has at last brought his efforts to a successful termination. That he has the sympathy of the community in this hour of his triumph, and at the outset of the enterprise, is eminently fit and proper. That he did not have it when it was most sorely needed, Captain Eads can afford to forget. The struggle is over."

The struggle was not over.

Eads had always loved the river and knew it more intimately than he had ever known any man or woman. He knew it in private ways that would never be known by any river captain, by any fisherman, by any levee contractor, by any engineer. He had buried his hands in the rich silt of its bottom, wandered blind in its depths, and come as close to breathing it as a man could do and live. The river had taken him from his family and wrapped itself around him. Now, finally, in his great pride, he had determined that he would command it, the great, great river, the Mississippi itself.

But Humphreys had said: *Anyone who knows me intimately knows I had more of the soldier than a man of science in me. . . . We must get ready for a combat. . . . The contest must be sharp and merciless.*

The morning after the reception and Bussey's toast, Eads, his contractor James Andrews, a determined and bold man who had worked with him on the bridge, and two other engineers left behind the city's elegance and proceeded downriver aboard a small steamer.

Below New Orleans the river resembles a 100-mile-long arm crooked at the elbow, narrowing gradually, to Head of Passes. There the river divides into three main channels, Southwest Pass, Pass a l'Outre, and South Pass, each extending like a long thin finger—the land separating the passes from the sea is as narrow as a few hundred yards—out into the Gulf.

At Head of Passes the party crossed over a shoal and entered the finger that was South Pass. It ran in an almost perfectly straight line 700 feet wide for 12.9 miles. Along its banks were dense, impenetrable reeds, 10 to 12 feet high, interrupted by an occasional copse of willow trees in the upper reaches. This was, geologically, truly the river's delta, created as the Mississippi River deposited its immense sediment load. It was the newest land in North America, a mixture of water and earth so soft that, except for the banks immediately adjacent to the pass, it could not support a man's weight. The animal life was primitive; muskrats and minks, herons and gulls and ducks, and snakes. The closer to the Gulf, the more desolate and solitary the marsh became, the grayer the reeds and grasses.

Upon reaching the sea, they anchored, rowed to shore, and walked on the beach. The Gulf surf lapped gently, but the jetties would have to withstand the most violent hurricanes. In the already steamy heat, clouds of mosquitoes, gnats, and sand flies began to swarm around them. Then they climbed the lighthouse.

It was the only elevation for 100 miles. From it they could see the whole country. River, land, and sea were barely differentiated. Every inch of land within view could be overflowed by tides or the river. Out in the Gulf, beyond the pass, the sandbars and mud lumps were in the process of becoming land. For miles beyond the bars, out into the sea, the Mississippi continued to have an identity. Half a century earlier a European visitor had described the scene: "The first indication of our approach to land was the appearance of this mighty river pouring forth its muddy mass of waters and mingling with the deep blue of the Mexican Gulf. I never beheld a scene so utterly desolate as this entrance of the Mississippi. Had Dante seen it, he might have drawn images of another Bolgia from its horrors."

South Pass was dying, becoming land, shoaling at its entrance and exit. Eads needed to produce a channel with a continuous depth of 30 feet. For a distance of 12,000 feet, more than 2 miles, the depth was less than that. At high tide, the deepest water over the bar itself was 9 feet, and the bar was 3,000 feet thick.

But after three days of study the Eads party left more confident than ever. Light, silty sand made up the bar; Eads was certain a strong current could easily cut through it. Equally important, deep water lay beyond the bar, and a strong coastal current ran across it, so sediment flushed out by the jetties would either sink or be swept away. Any unspoken concern in Eads' heart about the formation of a new bar beyond the jetties vanished.

Upon their return to New Orleans, Eads was so confident that he wrote his New Orleans attorney, Henry Leavy, whose clients included Jefferson Davis, about plans for a railroad to the mouth of the river: "[T]ransfers of cargoes of grains from barges into ships can be made quite as cheaply as by elevator in the City and with an important saving in port charges. . . .

I believe the stock of the [rail]road would become quite valuable. I am willing to make some arrangement, mutually beneficial, by which I received stock in exchange for land at Port Eads, as I own ten miles front on each side of the pass with the riparian right out to sea on both sides of the channel."

He also promised a channel deep enough to use by July 4, 1876, thirteen months away. An assistant told the *Picayune,* "Assurance of success is absolute."

Regardless of his engineering, however, if Eads could not raise capital, or if he had to pay too high a premium to attract it, he would fail. This was his weakness, and here Humphreys aimed his attack.

To raise money, Eads organized the South Pass Jetty Company. Investors in it would be paid only if the jetties succeeded. But then they would receive double their investment plus 10 percent interest. He capitalized the company at $750,000 but planned to raise only what was needed to keep work going until the first government payment. Raising the money was not easy. He exhausted his own contacts, then urged Elmer Corthell, a young Brown University graduate still in New England who would become resident engineer at the jetties, to make "any 'bloated bondholder' or 'money aristocrat' wish he had a hand in" by telling anyone who had $100,000 to invest that Eads would negotiate a private, even more lucrative deal.

Andrews & Company, of which Eads was a minority owner, agreed to supply all equipment—pile drivers, barges, steamers, housing, office space, materials, and labor—and build and place all piling, plus 450,000 cubic yards of stone and wood fillers, for $2.5 million. Eads believed this would be enough to get a 26-foot-deep channel.

Eads would pay Andrews & Company nothing until 60,000 cubic yards of material were in place, at which point Andrews would get $300,000. The company was guaranteed one-half of all subsequent government payments until it was paid.

Like Eads himself, the company's majority owner, James Andrews, moved quickly. Andrews had first seen the bar in late May 1875. On June 12 he left New Orleans with several dozen men and a steam tug pulling a pile driver and three flatboats, one for boarding workers and two loaded with material to build housing. They arrived in a steaming marsh, and were promptly tormented by small gray motile clouds of biting insects.

One of Andrews' first acts was to establish direct communication by telegraph with New Orleans, and soon equipment and supplies began arriving at what ultimately became Port Eads, a small town complete with hotel, offices, and boardinghouses for 850 men. For now the men lived on the boarding boat; no liquor was allowed. There was no relief from the insects and heat, not even in the water; water moccasins kept the men from swimming.

Only five days after Andrews arrived at the river's mouth, on June 17, he drove the first piles into the floor of the ocean. The work went quickly. In one day they could drive 176 piles. Lumber came from Mississippi and New Orleans; crushed stone, discharged from ships as ballast, came from New Orleans; limestone carried in fleets of twelve to twenty barges at a time came from 1,400 miles upriver, quarried from the blue and gray limestone bluffs of the Ohio River at Rose Clare, Indiana.

By September 9 the guide piling for the east jetty was finished and extended in a lonely curve of wood two and one-third miles into the Gulf. The job was executed with extraordinary precision; the piles farthest from land's end were located within a few inches of their planned site. Work on the west jetty had already begun. Next came the heart of the jetty: the fascine mattresses. These were made of willow tree trunks, which were thin, flexible, and straight. The trunks were to be linked, secured to the guide piling, and sunk. Eads expected the river to deposit sediment upon them and eventually make them impermeable. Then they would do their work.

Harvesting the willows was the worst work. The trees came from 6,000 acres of land 30 miles upriver and formed only 40 years earlier, when fishermen, seeking a quicker route to the Gulf, had cut a canal there. The river had quickly overwhelmed the lock, and forced an opening 1,400 feet wide and initially 80 feet deep. This opening became known as "the Jump," but after the first surge of water the river had begun depositing sediment and making land. The trees had grown rapidly on it.

To get to the area the men traveled on a barge where they slept stacked in bunks. Ventilation was as good as Eads could design, but in the near-tropical heat and with swarming mosquitoes, nights were awful. Days were worse. The men, half-naked, without shade, chopped down trees and dragged them, at every step sinking—sometimes shoulder-deep—into the soft mud, 200 yards to waiting barges. Moccasins and leeches made the water and marsh frightening.

Once the barges were full, tugs towed them to the sandbar. There, on an inclined, 100-yard-long platform, men constructed the mattresses of willow trees.

Upon this construction depended Eads' success. The river would rip apart an improperly built mattress. And in the construction process itself lay Eads' profit.

The board of engineers had anticipated his using willow mattresses but had estimated the cost based on techniques developed by the Dutch, who intertwined the willows, virtually weaving them together.

Eads and Andrews designed a different process, and later patented it. They first laid out strips of yellow pine 20 to 40 feet long, 6 inches wide, and 2.5 inches thick. These strips were bolted together, and the willow trees were laid within them. Other layers, each one at a right angle to the proceeding one, were added, then more strips of yellow pine were bolted on top, and the whole thing was lashed together. The resulting mattress was 100 feet long, 35 to 60 feet wide (depending upon where it would be placed), and 2 feet thick.

Workers could make and launch it in two hours. The Dutch method required two days to do the same. It was this innovation that had allowed Eads to offer to build the jetties at Southwest Pass at one-half the board's estimate.

A tug towed the barge to the guide pilings. The men then launched the mattresses, covered them with stone, and sank them in layers—as many as sixteen layers.

In less than a year Andrews drove all the guide piles and laid much of the mattressing. The jetties were incomplete walls of willows, not yet filled in with sediment and consolidated. But already they were succeeding. They were compressing the current, increasing its force, and deepening the channel.

Yet Eads had received no payments and his initial capital was running out. To attract more, he hired the luxurious steamer *Grand Republic* for her maiden voyage, May 2, 1876, to carry investors and the press to the jetties. Traveling amid the glamour of the grand steamer, dining on exquisite preparations of oysters, shrimp, and beef, he sensed only goodwill and excitement on the trip from New Orleans.

Meanwhile, Charles Howell, whom Humphreys had recently promoted to major, was 30 miles away dredging Southwest Pass, still trying to achieve 18 feet of water there. Howell certainly knew of the *Grand Republic*'s visit and its purpose. He had no role in inspecting the jetties, and an official inspection mandated by Eads' contract and to be conducted by a visiting team of surveyors was scheduled in only a few days. Yet Howell dispatched an assistant in a steam launch who, in full view of Eads' guests, took repeated soundings at the South Pass. This assistant, instead of returning to Howell, disembarked at Port Eads. A few hours later the *Grand Republic* also stopped at Port Eads. Howell's man, carrying charts, boarded her. During the long trip back to New Orleans, feigning reluctance, he stood in the saloon allowing reporters to pry his findings from him.

Eads claimed South Pass was 16 feet deep at high tide. The soundings, official measurements by Army engineers, showed 12 feet. More important, they also showed a new sandbar forming 1,000 feet beyond the jetties. If the soundings were correct, they proved Humphreys right and doomed the jetties to failure.

The news shot northward up the Mississippi valley. Stock in the jetty company collapsed. Howell pressed his attack in the New Orleans papers, accusing Eads of bilking investors. Suddenly, for the first time since his wife died, Eads was desperate.

He tried to negotiate a loan. Without it the project could collapse. But to get it, he needed the findings of the official inspection to refute Howell. The Army engineer who sounded the pass refused to give Eads the results, insisting he could only give them to General C. B. Comstock, who had come to Port Eads from Detroit expressly for the survey. Eads asked Comstock for them. Comstock too refused, saying he "had no authority to divulge my report."

Eads immediately wired Secretary of War Alphonso Taft, "Please instruct General Comstock, now at Port Eads, to sound channel between jetties with me . . . and furnish results promptly. Major Howell has published a misstatement affecting public confidence in my work, and this information is required in justice to myself, and the public."

Taft did not reply. Comstock left. Eads appealed to the superintendent of the Coastal Survey for results of separate soundings it had conducted—using Eads' own launch for them. He was refused. He appealed to the secretary of the treasury and was informed, "General Comstock will give all information required by law."

The law required Comstock's report to go to Humphreys, then to the secretary of war, then to Congress, and only then to the public. The results would not appear for months.

Eads' loan negotiations collapsed. By the time the official results were scheduled to become public, there might be no jetty company left.

Eads had one last chance at a rebuttal. On May 12, 1876, the oceangoing steamer *Hudson* was due at the mouth of the river. She was 280 feet long and 1,182 tons, and drawing 14 feet, 7 inches.

E. V. Gager was her captain, and Eads' friend. He had once said he hoped to captain the first oceangoing ship through the jetties. Never would there be a better time. When she arrived, Eads, the pilot, and a few reporters boarded her outside the bar. The pilot reported that his earlier soundings had indicated sufficient water in the jetties for her to use them, but the tide had turned since then and was falling fast. He could not recommend the attempt.

Every moment the water was growing shallower. Gager did not hesitate, waved the pilot away, and ordered, "Head her for the jetties."

The pilot obeyed.

Three hundred men understood what was happening, and its significance. Everywhere, on the barges sinking willows, on the shore at Port Eads, on the launches, on the Hudson herself, men ceased what they were doing and watched silently. In a calm sea, with swells barely whitening against the jetties, all was still. Only the ship moved.

"Shall we run in slow?" the pilot asked.

"No!" Gager snapped. "Let her go at full speed."

The engines churned. She seemed almost to leap forward. At full ahead, Corthell later wrote, "on she came like a thing of life."

Her speed increased still further. If Howell's soundings were correct, she could destroy herself, rip a great gouge out of her bottom. Faster she went, the great white bow wave climbing higher up her hull, her wake swamping the Gulf's swells, steaming onward, racing the falling tide down through the two-and-one-third-mile-long channel. As Corthell recalled, "As long as she carried that 'white bone in her teeth,' the great wave that her proud bows pushed ahead of her as she sped onward—we knew that she had found more than Major Howell's twelve feet."

Then she was through! On the *Hudson*, on the barges, at Port Eads, the men erupted in cheers, and kept cheering, and kept cheering, and kept cheering. She stopped at Port Eads for a brief celebration. The reporters wired their stories the length and breadth of the country. The channel was open!

"No event in the whole history of the jetties gave us such intense pleasure and satisfaction as the successful passage of this beautiful ship through the jetties," Corthell said. "It is not too much to say that Capt. Gager, who took the risk and responsibility of this trial trip, greatly assisted the enterprise in one of its darkest hours; for the stubborn facts brought out by his brave action could not be gainsaid. They restored confidence in the jetties, and the much-needed loan was soon afterward secured for the further prosecution of the work."

Meanwhile, Eads was pressing Congress for help. It passed a resolution demanding the release of the official survey. The secretary of the treasury obeyed.

The survey showed 16 feet of water in the channel, and no bar forming beyond the jetties.

Yet Eads' financial squeeze and his problems with the government continued. Despite his achieving the required depths, several times the government delayed payment until the cabinet debated the question. One such debate lasted three days, ending only when the attorney general informed the cabinet that the government had to pay.

At one point, out of money, Eads wired Corthell, "Discharge the whole force except those necessary to protect property, unless they are willing to work on certificates, payable on receipt of 22 foot payment." Seventy-four of seventy-six men agreed.

Only the work went well. The South Pass had been surveyed for 150 years; no prior survey had ever found more than 9 feet of water over the bar. Eads officially achieved a 20-foot-deep channel October 4, 1876. Oceangoing ships began routinely using his still unfinished channel.

Eads then built a new series of dikes, which increased the slope of the river from .24 foot per mile to .505 foot per mile, producing, according to the Army report, "a marked scour in the channel." On March 7, 1877, Comstock reported 23.9 feet of water there.

The law stipulated that Howell's dredging at Southwest Pass must end whenever the jetties achieved an 18-foot channel. Howell continued dredging in violation of the law. But on August 22, 1877, his appropriations ran out. There would be no more. The dredging ended.

Even then, financial pressure on Eads continued. Ultimately, he lobbied Congress to accelerate the payment schedule, and added to his usual lobbyists Grant's former secretary Porter, the Union general who had captured Jefferson Davis, and P.G.T. Beauregard, the Confederate general who fired on Fort Sumter to begin the Civil War, whom he paid $5,000. Congress finally pushed forward payment.

Now Eads turned his attention to Humphreys.

Eads wanted a civilian commission independent of the Corps of Engineers to govern the Mississippi River. Although civil engineers and their supporters had called for one for years, it was now being spoken of as "the Eads commission."

In response, Humphreys lashed out with blind enmity, insisting in a letter to Congress, despite all data, that a new sandbar was forming beyond the jetties: "*The results actually attained at the South Pass disprove the views advanced by Mr. Eads, and confirms those of the Engineer Department. Hence, any claim that he shall be intrusted with the control of the Mississippi River, in so far as it rests upon the results thus far achieved by him, has no proper basis.*"

Eads had had enough. He wrote an article for *Van Nostrand's Engineering Magazine*, had it reprinted as a pamphlet, and distributed it to congressmen, reporters, and engineers across the country. It was entitled, "Review of the Humphreys and Abbot Report."

It was a crushing article. Eads derisively subtitled sections, "The Laws of Gravity Ignored"; "How the Wonderful Discovery Was Made"; "No Relation Between Cause and Effect!" He used Humphreys' own data to deliver blow after blow, describing Humphreys' calculations as "totally wrong," "mathematically . . . a blunder that would disgrace a boy in High School," and, finally, "The mistake made by Humphreys and Abbot is one unpardonable in the merest tyro in the science of dynamics."

Two years earlier a Prussian engineer had written an article in the same magazine also attacking Humphreys and Abbot's original report. The two men had written a forty-three-page rebuttal. But now Abbot warned against replying to Eads at all, arguing, "a reply might advantage him. . . . [M]ake an end of it."

At Humphreys' insistence, Abbot did finally write a rebuttal. It was ignored by all except Humphreys' most loyal supporters.

In the midst of these exchanges, Humphreys received more blows. The National Academy of Sciences urged the creation of the U.S. Geological Survey to survey the West—work formerly done by the Corps of Engineers. Humphreys, an original founder of the academy, resigned from it. As he had before, he fought the proposal in Congress. But no longer did he have the power to ward off passage of the legislation.

Then on June 28, 1879, Congress created the Mississippi River Commission, a mix of Army and civilian engineers, to control the entire river. Both private individuals and state governments would have to obey it. Upon the bill's passage, Humphreys resigned as chief of engineers and retired from the Army, effective June 30.

Exactly one week later, U.S. Army Captain Micah Brown certified that the South Pass channel had reached the final goal, a depth of 30 feet.

On July 11, the *New Orleans Daily Times* announced: "The work is done. Human patience and courage and industry, backed by an indomitable and untiring will, and informed and directed by human skill, have applied the forces of nature to the accomplishment of an end too vast for mere artificial agencies. Man has used the tremendous river which uncontrolled has been its own oppressor and imprisoner, and has now become its own liberator and saviour. There is no achievement of mechanical genius which compares with it in the splendor of its economies or in the magnitude of its results. There is no parallel instance of man's employment of the prodigious energies of nature in the realization of his aims. It stands alone in these respects as in the almost incalculable possibilities which it has brought within our reach."

In 1875, when Eads began work on the jetties, 6,857 tons of goods were shipped from St. Louis through New Orleans to Europe. In 1880, the year after he finished, 453,681 tons were shipped by that route. New Orleans rose from the ninth-largest port in the United States to the second-largest, trailing only New York. (In 1995, by volume of cargo greater New Orleans ranked as the world's largest port.)[1]

Yet the impact of the jetties on the Mississippi River far exceeded that of anything else that had happened at the river's mouth. That impact would be felt through the Mississippi River Commission.

It never became, formally or informally, "the Eads Commission." Though Humphreys and the War Department could not prevent the establishment of the commission, they did succeed in having Congress stipulate that Army officers outnumber civilians on it by three to two, that an Army officer serve as president, and that this officer report to his military superior, the chief of engineers. Eads was named to the commission, but he could not dominate it. In 1882 he resigned to protest its compromises.

Science, he knew, does not compromise. Instead, science forces ideas to compete in a dynamic process. This competition refines or replaces old hypotheses, gradually approaching a more perfect representation of the truth, although one can reach truth no more than one can reach infinity.

But the Mississippi River Commission never became a scientific enterprise. It was a bureaucracy. The natural process of a bureaucracy, by contrast, tends to compromise competing ideas. The bureaucracy then adopts the compromise as truth and incorporates it into its being. The military hierarchy in the river commission exacerbated these bureaucratic tendencies. Over time, as Army engineers staffed nearly all key posts, the commission lost any real independence from the Corps of Engineers. And with rare exceptions, the Army controlled even civilian appointments.

The commission took positions, and the positions became increasingly petrified and rigid. Unfortunately, these positions combined the worst, not the best, of the ideas of Eads, Ellet, and Humphreys.

Both Eads and Humphreys opposed outlets. Ellet proposed them. Ellet was right. But the commission opposed outlets.

Both Eads and Humphreys opposed building reservoirs. Ellet had proposed them. Ellet was right. But the commission opposed reservoirs.

Eads wanted to build cutoffs, believing they had enormous impact on floods. Humphreys and Ellet opposed cutoffs. Eads was right. The commission followed Humphreys and Ellet.

Yet the greatest and most dangerous mistake of the Mississippi River Commission still lay elsewhere—in its position on the levees-only policy. Almost inconceivably, the commission arrived at a position that Eads, Humphreys, and Ellet had all violently rejected. It did so by compromising and mushing together its analysis over time. It embraced Humphreys' levees-only idea and justified the decision by citing *Physics and Hydraulics*. But, as years passed, commission engineers ignored his reasoning and espoused the theory that levees would cause the river to scour out the channel enough to accommodate floods. Ellet had called this idea "a delusive hope, and most dangerous to indulge." Humphreys had proved the theory "untenable." Eads too had rejected it, distinguishing between the scouring effects of "contraction works" built into the river channel and levees far back from the banks.

On this one point, Eads, Humphreys, and Ellet all concurred. Nonetheless, the levees rose, confining the river while failing to increase velocity enough to deepen the channel. No reservoirs were built, as Ellet had wanted. No outlets were built, as Ellet had also wanted, and as even Humphreys would likely have accepted, as the cost-benefit equation changed with development. No cutoffs were built, as Eads had wanted. Only levees were built.

So the water rose higher. In turn, the levees rose higher; as more lands were reclaimed and water was cut off from it, the water also rose, and so on, and so on. At College Point, Louisiana, 40 miles above New Orleans, a levee 1.5 feet high had held the flood of 1850, a flood Humphreys investigated in detail; by the mid-1920s the levee exceeded 20 feet. At Morganza, Louisiana, a levee 7.5 feet high had held the flood of 1850; by the mid-1920s it towered 38 feet, nearly the height of a four-story building.

By the 1920s, the commission went further. To increase the volume of the Mississippi River, without building the contraction works Eads had demanded, it began closing all natural outlets. This policy, Humphreys had warned, "would, if executed, entail disastrous consequences."

The Mississippi River is wild and random. High water magnifies its wildness. It also magnifies its power. At its head, as Army engineer D. O. Elliot said, the river "is held in place . . . by the gorge in the Commerce hills. Its mouth in the Gulf of Mexico is fixed by the works of man. Between these points it writhes like an imprisoned snake constantly seeking to establish and maintain a state of equilibrium, between its length; its slope; and the volume and velocity of its discharge."

In the century of the engineers the study of this writhing river began as a scientific enterprise. The resulting policy became a corruption of science. Indeed, the policy was scientific only in that it began an immense, if unintended, experiment with the forces of the river.

For thousands of centuries the river had roamed over its alluvial valley, its vast natural floodplain. The Mississippi River Commission, certain of its theories, constrained the river within levees, believing that the levees alone, without any other means to release the tension of the river, could hold within narrow banks this force immense enough to have spread its waters over tens of thousands of square miles, where millions of people would settle.

The Mississippi River Commission promised protection to this great valley, a valley filled with the richest earth in the world. It was earth rich enough that men would risk everything for it. Given just the promise of protection, large men willed that the valley would hum with money, and culture, and industry. And they waited to discover whether the great unintended experiment of the levees-only policy would prove a success or a failure.

NOTE

1. The Corps soon took credit for the jetties, saying as early as 1886, "The present successful results might have been obtained years before Mr. Eads took hold of the work if Congress had not handicapped the Corps. It is certainly unjust to blame the Engineer Corps because its recommendations were not followed." In 1924 the chief of engineers officially informed the secretary of war: "The Army Engineers did not oppose the jetties. As a matter of fact, the plan for the construction of the jetties was originated by the Corps of Engineers, and Captain Eads merely carried out plans which had been previously discussed." It also soon became clear that, as Eads had predicted, South Pass was too small to accommodate heavy shipping traffic and that the larger Southwest Pass had to be opened. In 1893, Eads' former assistant Corthell offered to do the work on the same terms as had Eads: he would receive nothing unless successful. This time the Corps outmaneuvered Corthell and was given the task, but twenty-one years later the channel was still only 27 feet deep. "The plan did not prove to be successful," conceded Major General Lansing Beach, chief of engineers.

SUSAN ORLEAN

The Orchid Thief: A True Story of Beauty and Obsession
(1998)

Susan Orlean (b. 1955) is an author and staff writer for *The New Yorker* whose 1998 book, *The Orchid Thief,* follows the story of orchid collector John Laroche. He extracts the rare ghost orchid from the protected Florida Everglades by using Seminole Indians—who he claimed had the right to do so—as labor. Laroche is caught, tried, and found guilty, though larger questions of justice for the tribal community's right to sovereignty evade the courtroom. Throughout the story, Orlean explores the vast wilderness within the Everglades in hopes of catching a glimpse of an elusive orchid. Part journalism, part travel writing, part botanical history, *The Orchid Thief* weaves multiple genres together. The multifaceted nature of the book is why it was the inspiration for the film *Adaptation.*

In this excerpt, Orlean searches the depths of the Fakahatchee Strand in the Everglades for the white mystery of the ghost orchid; she does not find it there. This reading would be paired well with Marjory Stoneman Douglas's *The Everglades: River of Grass.*

You would have to want something very badly to go looking for it in the Fakahatchee Strand. The Fakahatchee is a preserve of sixty-three thousand coastal lowland acres in the southwestern corner of Florida, about twenty-five miles south of Naples, in that part of Collier County where satiny lawns and golf courses give way to an ocean of saw grass with edges as sharp as scythes. Part of the Fakahatchee is deep swamp, part is cypress stands, part is wet woods, part is estuarine tidal marsh, and part is parched prairie.

The limestone underneath it is six million years old and is capped with hard rock and sand, silt and shell marls, and a grayish-greenish clay. Overall, the Fakahatchee is as flat as a cracker. Ditches and dents fill up fast with oozing groundwater. The woods are dense and lightless. In the open stretches the land unrolls like a smooth grass mat and even small bumps and wrinkles are easy to see. Most of the land is at an elevation of only five or ten feet, and it slopes millimeter by millimeter until it is dead even with the sea. The Fakahatchee has a particular strange and exceptional beauty. The grass prairies in sunlight look like yards of raw silk. The tall, straight palm trunks and the tall, straight cypress trunks shoot up out of the flat land like geysers. It is beautiful the way a Persian carpet is beautiful— thick, intricate, lush, almost monotonous in its richness.

People live in the Fakahatchee and around it, but it is an unmistakably inhospitable place. In 1872 a surveyor made this entry in his field notes: "A pond, surrounded by bay and cypress swamp, impracticable. Pond full of monstrous alligators. Counted fifty and stopped." In fact, the hours I spent in the Fakahatchee retracing Laroche's footsteps were probably the most miserable I have spent in my entire life. The swampy part of the Fak-ahatchee is hot and wet and buggy and full of cottonmouth snakes and diamondback rattlers and alligators and snapping turtles and poisonous plants and wild hogs and things that stick into you and on you and fly into your nose and eyes. Crossing the swamp is a battle. You can walk through about as easily as you could walk through a car wash. The sinkholes are filled with as much as seven feet of standing water, and around them the air has the slack, drapey weight of wet velvet. Sides of trees look sweaty. Leaves are slick from the humidity. The mud sucks your feet and tries to keep ahold of them; if it fails it will settle for your shoes. The water in the swamp is stained black with tannin from the bark of cypress trees that is so corrosive it can cure leather. Whatever isn't wet in the Fakahatchee is blasted. The sun pounds the treeless prairies. The grass gets so dry that the friction from a car can set it on fire, and the burning grass can engulf the car in flames. The Fakahatchee used to be littered with burned-up cars that had been abandoned by panfried adventurers—a botanist who traveled through in the 1940s recalled in an interview that he was most impressed by the area's variety of squirrels and the number of charred Model T's. The swamp's stillness and darkness and thickness can rattle your nerves. In 1885 a sailor on a plume-collecting expedition wrote in his diary: "The place looked wild and lonely. About three o'clock it seemed to get on Hen-ry's nerves and we saw him crying, he could not tell us why, he was just plain scared."

Spooky places are usually full of death, but the Fakahatchee is crazy with living things. Birders used to come from as far away as Cuba and leave with enough plumes to decorate thousands of ladies' hats; in the 1800s one group of birders also took home eight tons of birds' eggs. One turn-of-the-century traveler wrote that on his journey he found the swamp's abundance marvelous—he caught two hundred pounds of lobsters, which he ate for breakfasts, and stumbled across a rookery where he gathered "quite a supply of cormorant and blue heron eggs, with which I intend to make omelets." That night he had a dinner of a fried blue heron and a cabbage-palm heart. In the Fakahatchee there used to be a carpet of lubber grasshoppers so deep that it made driving hazardous and so many orchids that visitors described their heavy sweet smell as nauseating. On my first walk in the swamp I saw strap lilies and water willows and sumac and bladderwort, and resurrection ferns springing out of a fallen dead tree; I saw oaks and pines and cypress and pop ash and beauty-berry and elderberry and yellow-eyed grass and camphor weed. When I walked in, an owl gave me a lordly look, and when I walked out three tiny alligators skittered across my path. I wandered into a nook in the swamp that was girdled with tall cypress. The rangers call this nook the Cathedral. I closed my eyes and stood in the stillness for a moment hardly breathing, and when I opened my eyes and looked up I saw dozens of bromeliad plants roosting in the branches of almost every tree I could see. The bromeliads were bright red and green and shaped like fright wigs. Some were spider-sized and some were as big as me. The sun shooting through the swamp canopy glanced off their sheeny leaves. Hanging up there on the branches the bromeliads looked not quite like plants. They looked more like a crowd of animals, watching everything that passed their way.

I had decided to go to the Fakahatchee after the hearing because I wanted to see what Laroche had wanted. I asked him to go with me, but because the judge had banned him from the swamp until the case was over I had to look around for someone else. I suppose I could have gone alone, but I had heard the Fakahatchee was a hard place and even a few brave-seeming botanists I'd talked to told me they didn't like to go in by themselves. At last, I was introduced to a park ranger named Tony who said he would go in with me. I then spent the next several days talking myself into being unafraid. A few days before we were supposed to go Tony called and asked if I was really sure I wanted to make the trip. I said I was. I'm actually pretty tough. I've run a marathon and traveled by myself to weird places and engaged in conversations with a lot of strangers, and when my toughness runs out I can rely on a certain willful obliviousness to keep me going. On the other hand, my single most unfavorite thing in life so far has been to touch the mushy bottom of the lake during swimming lessons at summer camp and feel the weedy slime squeeze between my clenched toes, so the idea of walking through the swamp was a little bit extra-horrible to me. The next day Tony called and asked again if I was really ready for the Fakahatchee. At that point I gave up trying to be tough and let every moment in the lake at Camp Cardinal ooze back into my memory, and when I finally met Tony at the ranger station I almost started to cry.

But I was determined to see orchids, so Tony and I went deep into the Fakahatchee to try to find them. We walked from morning until late in the afternoon with little luck. The light was hot and the air was airless. My legs ached and my head ached and I couldn't stand the sticky feel of my own skin. I began having the frantic, furtive thoughts of a deserter and started wondering what Tony would do if I suddenly sat down and refused to keep walking. He was a car-length ahead of me; from what I could tell he felt terrific. I muttered to myself and caught up. As we marched along Tony told me about his life and mentioned that he was an orchid collector himself and that he had a little home orchid lab, where he was trying to produce a hybrid that would have the wraparound lip of an *Encyclia* but would be the color of a certain *Cattleya* that is maroon with small lime-green details. He said that he would find out if he had succeeded in seven or eight years, when the hybrid seedlings would bloom. I said nothing for the next mile or so. When we stopped to rest and Tony tried to figure out what was wrong with his compass, I asked him what he thought it was about orchids that seduced humans so completely that they were compelled to steal them and worship them and try to breed new and specific kinds of them and then be willing to wait for nearly a decade for one of them to flower.

"Oh, mystery, beauty, unknowability, I suppose," he said, shrugging. "Besides, I think the real reason is that life has no meaning. I mean, no *obvious* meaning. You wake up, you go to work, you do stuff. I think everybody's always looking for something a little unusual that can preoccupy them and help pass the time."

The orchid I really wanted to see was *Polyrrhiza lindenii*, the ghost orchid. Laroche had taken more of other orchid and bromeliad species when he went poaching, but he told me that the ghost orchids were the ones he had wanted the most. *Polyrrhiza lindenii* is the only really pretty orchid in the Fakahatchee. Technically it is an orchid of the Vandaneae tribe, Sarcanthinae subtribe; *Polyrrhiza* is its genus (the genus is sometimes also called *Polyradicion*). The ghost is a leafless species named in honor of the Belgian plantsman Jean-Jules Linden, who first discovered it in Cuba in 1844. It was seen for the first time in the United States in 1880 in Collier County. The ghost orchid usually grows around the trunks of pop ash and pond apple and custard apple trees. It blooms once a year. It has no foliage—it is nothing but roots, a tangle of flat green roots about the width of linguine, wrapped around a tree. The roots are chlorophyllus; that is, they serve as both roots and leaves. The flower is a lovely papery white. It has the intricate lip that is characteristic of all orchids, but its lip is especially pronounced and pouty, and each corner tapers into a long, fluttery tail. In pictures the flower looks like the face of a man with a Fu Manchu mustache. These tails are so delicate that they tremble in a light breeze. The whiteness of the flower is as startling as a spotlight in the grayness and greenness of a swamp. Because the plant has no foliage and its roots are almost invisible against tree bark, the flower looks magically suspended in midair. People say a ghost orchid in bloom looks like a flying white frog—an ethereal and beautiful flying white frog. Carlyle Luer, the author of *The Native Orchids of Florida*, once wrote of the ghost orchid: "Should one be lucky enough to see a flower, all else will seem eclipsed."

Near a large sinkhole Tony pointed out some little green straps on a young tree and said they were ghost orchids that were done blooming for the year. We walked for another hour, and he pointed out more green ghost-orchid roots on more trees. The light was flattening out and I was muddy and scratched and scorched. Finally we turned around and walked five thousand miles or so back to Tony's Jeep. It had been a hard day and I hadn't seen what I'd come to see. I kept my mind busy as we walked out by wondering if the hard-to-find, briefly seen, irresistibly beautiful, impossible-to-cultivate ghost orchid was just a fable and not a real flower at all. Maybe it really was a ghost. There are certainly ghosts in the Fakahatchee—ghosts of rangers who were murdered years ago by illegal plume hunters, and of loggers who were cut to pieces in fights and then left to cool and crumble into dirt, and for years there has been an apparition wandering the swamp, the Swamp Ape, which is said to be seven feet tall and weigh seven hundred pounds and have the physique of a human, the posture of an ape, the body odor of a skunk, and an appetite for lima beans. There is also an anonymous, ghostly human being whom the Fakahatchee rangers call the Ghost Grader, who brings real—not imaginary—construction equipment into the swamp every once in a while and clears off the vine-covered roads.

If the ghost orchid was really only a phantom it was still such a bewitching one that it could seduce people to pursue it year after year and mile after miserable mile. If it was a real flower I wanted to keep coming back to Florida until I could see one. The reason was not that I love orchids. I don't even especially like orchids. What I wanted was to see this thing that people were drawn to in such a singular and powerful way. Everyone I was meeting connected to the orchid poaching had circled their lives around some great desire. Laroche had his crazy inspirations and orchid lovers had their intense devotion to their flowers and the Seminoles had their burning dedication to their history and culture—a desire that then answered questions for them about how to spend their time and their money and who their friends would be and where they would travel and what they did when they got there. It was religion. I *wanted* to want something as much as people wanted these plants, but it isn't part of my constitution. I think people my age are embarrassed by too much enthusiasm and believe that too much passion about anything is naive. I suppose I do have one unembarrassing passion—I want to know what it feels like to care about something passionately. That night I called Laroche and told him that I had come back from looking for ghost orchids in the Fakahatchee but that I had seen nothing but bare roots. I said that I was wondering whether I had missed this year's flowers or where perhaps the only place the ghost orchid bloomed was in the imagination of people who'd walked too long in the swamp. What I didn't say was that strong feelings always make me skeptical at first. What else I didn't say was that his life seemed to be filled with things that were just like the ghost orchid—wonderful to imagine and easy to fall in love with but a little fantastic and fleeting and out of reach.

I could hear a soft puckery gulp as he inhaled cigarette smoke. Then he said, "Jesus Christ, of course there are ghost orchids out there! I've *stolen* them for Chrissake! I know exactly where they are." The phone was silent for a moment, and then he cleared his throat and said, "You *should* have gone with me."

ROGER EMILE STOUFF

"The Back End of the Canal" (2003)

Roger Emile Stouff (b. 1964) is the managing editor of the *St. Mary and Franklin Banner-Tribune* and a member of the Chitimacha Tribe of Louisiana. Stouff, who has lived in St. Mary Parish, Louisiana, his whole life, writes a regular column about local culture and politics. His columns muse on fly-fishing, the habits of the Atchafalaya waters, and his father, chief of the Chitimacha, among other topics. Stouff's writing, at times funny, at times angry, maintains a singular curmudgeonly yet wise voice that reminds his readers how much the natural world has changed.

Stouff's article "The Back End of the Canal" floats through the waters of Louisiana like a dream, revealing the stories of his tribespeople, who have inhabited the Gulf Coast for thousands of years. Stouff finds traces of the past in the waters, the memories and stories left behind that mark the changing peoples as much as the changing land around him.

Chasing bream across the north shore of Grande Avoille Cove, to little avail, the boat drifted upon a wide but short canal cut into the bank. The loggers likely left it there, before 1930, when nearly all the old growth cypress in Louisiana was felled. Grande Avoille Cove was a pivotal point for the deforestation of St. Mary Parish, and the many thousands of logs which were floated out of that small bay of Grand Lake staggers the imagination.

It was late in the day, and the sun was over my left shoulder as the boat brought me to the mouth of that canal, probably used to stash logs awaiting transport to the mills which once dotted the parish from one end to the other. It was covered by a thick canopy of new-growth cypress along with European and Asian invaders. Though I knew the canal was no more than fifty yards deep, I could see only darkness in its depths. I made a few half-hearted casts into the mouth of the canal with my four-weight, but the size eight black wooly bugger went unmolested. The boat touched stem to a sunken log and waited there for me to push it free.

But the darkness at the end of that canal held my attention. Late in the day like this, when skies are clear, the Atchafalaya River basin turns golden and green, quiet, breezeless and still. Here and there, egrets rest on ancient, worm-ridden logs, peck at bugs in rotting stumps. A water moccasin coils within a patch of irises, and far, far behind me, I hear the splash of a largemouth. Down there, at the end of that dark canal, another world exists. A world of twilight, where the margins of the present and past, the dividers separating this world from the next and that which has come before, are feeble, thin. When this was a giant system of interconnected lakes, before the levee was built, and farther back still when there was no one here but Chitimacha, this was a metropolis. White clamshell, evidence of a thriving culture from which I am descended, peeks unblinkingly like disturbed bones from layers of fallen cypress needles. Down at the end of that short canal, in the blackness, I can almost see the way it was. Lodged there against a log, the bow of the boat held firm, I can almost see all my relations since before there was time.

It looks like a tunnel, a cave, a passage. With a push of my paddle, the boat is freed, and I negotiate around the log, then point the bow into the canal. With the deft accuracy of a man searching for erudition, I fade from the sunlit world into the darkness of the ages. I can still see in here, and above me, the canopy of mingling limbs are like lovers, locked in death's embrace. Not a peek of light comes from above, but the glow of the cove is behind me now. The boat drifts a moment then settles quietly, almost in reverence. That part of me which stubbornly insists upon being a twenty-first century man removes the woolly bugger from the leader of my line, replacing it with a black rubber spider. The part of me that exists in the here-and-now plays out a little slack and carefully sends a roll cast to the back corner of that dim canal's termination.

It saddens me that people who lived their lives in the light of day, who frolicked and played and worked and hunted or fished under the full face of the sun now lurk in shadows at the back end of shallow canals. That people who touched Creation by keeping an eternal flame burning not far from here should be cloaked in darkness after the end of their days. Most of all that I should drift into a world of distant forebears and feel I should roll cast to a corner of their resting-place to make sense of the world.

I glance behind me, and the waters of the cove are bright. Ahead of me, the foam spider is motionless, neglected. Past the end of the little canal, I peer into darkness and a shadow, a patch of darkness blacker than the rest, darts away behind the thicket. I think of *Neka sama*, the "new devil," which moved across these swamps from west to east each year, whistling and making a sound as if pounding on a hollow log with a tree branch. Does *Neka sama* still haunt the darkness at the end of that canal, afraid of the light and illumination of disbelief? A beast once so feared children were huddled close to the breast when the whistling and pounding was heard far off. Now a prisoner. It may lurk in here, looking out at the bright cove beyond, hear and watch the speeding, noisy boats, recoiling from the noxious fumes of two-cycle engines. It may snarl softly at fishermen who pass by it, casting into the canal's mouth, uncertain why they are suddenly so uneasy and quicken their trolling motors to pass.

When a people fade into the darkness at the back end of shallow canals, they take their monsters with them.

I move the spider to the opposite corner with a careful twitch sideways. The ripples of its fall expand outward, touching darkness. There are no fish here. The darkness is all I may catch, and the soft, fluid motions within it, final breaths drawn from behind curtains, like fingers tapping on a drum which once resounded over swamps and marshes, grassy prairies and cypress forests. I draw in the line and back the boat out slowly. The shadows recede from me, and the sunlight basks over the stern of the boat first, moves amidships and finally floods me with warmth.

No breeze could penetrate the thicket behind that canal from the northwest. No wind could find its way through the dense growth. But it came nonetheless, pushing the boat just a little more, fondling my hair, tugging at my clothes. Then I was back on Grande Avoille Cove, and the air was still, that exhalation from the back end of the canal abbreviated and done. There were whispers on the breeze, inaudible but my perceptions were keen to them.

Perhaps that's why the black back ends of shallow canals on Grande Avoille Cove fascinate me so. I am no oracle, no seer. Just a wayward son who came home in the nick of time. Perhaps there's no one left who desires to see.

It is nearing sunset. I start the engine and idle out of Grande Avoille Cove slowly, the prop kicking up mud from the shallow bottom. Instead of turning east for home, I guide the boat west, down the rest of the borrow pit that was dug to build the levee. Less than a tenth of a mile and the pit opens up into Lake Fausse Point, *Sheti*, Lake of the Chitimachas. The surface is smooth as crystal, holding silent secrets. I throttle up a bit, not too fast, but circle the lake once, breathing in the dusk. I let the oranges and greens and saturated silvers sink deep within me. The depth finder shows me that I am moving through barely two feet of water; this lake once ran half a dozen feet deep in its shallow spots. But the levee has changed all that, filled it up with sediment, like darkness under a cypress canopy. I dare not slow down or I'll be idling out of the lake as well. On the other side of that levee is Grand Lake, and once all that separated it from Lake Fausse Point were two islands, Big Pass and Little Pass. The levee linked and absorbed these. Round Island lies to the north, across the levee, as does Buffalo Cove, perhaps the most beautiful spot in all the river basin.

My circumference of the lake complete, I return to the borrow pit channel and make my way home. I pass by Grande Avoille Cove on my way, and it seems translucent, fading. I think perhaps it might vanish during the night, only returning at dawn. Farther down, I turn south at the levee's lock system, installed to vent the overflow of water should the Atchafalaya threaten to tear down the stinging violation of the levee. On south, under the bridge, I turn west again and find my way home. It's nearly dark. Back on Grande Avoille Cove, if it's still even there, I imagine the canal is completely cloaked now. Perhaps the entire cove is covered by darkness. Are ancestors dancing there, wraiths on the surface of the water, lifting themselves through the trees and into the stars just twinkling on high?

We once occupied these waters and lands from east to west, from the gulf to the junction of the two great rivers, but now we are spread thin across time and space, hidden from the sun in the back ends of dark canals.

MIKE TIDWELL

Bayou Farewell: The Rich Life and
Tragic Death of Louisiana's Cajun Coast (2003)

Mike Tidwell (b. 1956) has spent most of his adult life advocating for the environment and making people aware of pressing global warming issues. His prescient book *Bayou Farewell: The Rich Life and Tragic Death of Louisiana's Cajun Coast*, excerpted here, was published in 2003 and was one of the earliest books to call attention to the loss of the wetlands in Louisiana. In *Bayou Farewell*, Tidwell is in conversation with a number of Louisiana Cajuns who have lived and worked on the Louisiana bayous for generations and know the bayou's moods and changes intimately. They point to the physical progress of the ocean's rising through the loss of a favorite tree or shrimping area. These conversations are revelatory and, in many cases, foretell what is occurring today in southeastern Louisiana's imperiled landscape to an even greater degree.

A year before the publication of *Bayou Farewell*, Tidwell founded the Chesapeake Climate Action Network, and he serves as its director. Tidwell is the author of *Amazon Stranger* (1996), *In the Mountains of Heaven* (2000), and *Ravaging Tide: Strange Weather, Future Katrinas, and the Coming Death of America's Coastal Cities* (2007). In 2003 the Audubon Naturalist Society awarded Tidwell its coveted Conservation Award.

We're almost done picking the shrimp when another somber subject comes up: the vanishing land. News of this phenomenon has deeply colored my trip so far and part of me is still hoping it isn't true, that everything I've heard along Bayou Lafourche is a bad dream and over here along Petit Caillou I'll somehow wake up to find people have no idea what I'm talking about. Everything will be okay. The terrible thing won't be happening.

But of course it is.

"See dis big lake all around us, Cap?" Charlie says, pointing 180 degrees to the left and then to the right using only his nose while his hands continue to throw tiny crabs overboard. "Dis lake, in de 1960s, didn't have no shrimp. De water was too fresh. So when I was a kid you didn't come here. You went furdder sout' for shrimp. Now look."

Again, with his nose, he points, this time to the dozen or so trawlers scattered in all directions, hauling in shrimp just like us.

Charlie picks up a small shovel from against a gunwale. "Nope," he says, scooping several thousand shrimp off his deck and into an ice hold, "not a single shrimp here when I was a kid."

The problem, he says, is more than just the sinking land and the massive erosion spawned by all the oil-company canals.

Those canals also provide highwaylike avenues for the saltier water of the Gulf to travel north through the marsh. This saltwater "intrusion," as it's called, wreaks havoc on fresh and brackish-water ecosystems, pickling whole forests of swamp cypresses and pushing such species as alligators and oysters farther and farther north. Canals, in fact, are a big part of the reason Lake Boudreaux is now salty enough for shrimp while being inhospitable to the same species when John F. Kennedy was elected president. The entire marine zone is shifting north toward an inevitable collision with higher, more stable, nonalluvial land, where roads and towns and subdivisions and hurricane levees will block any further advance, spelling the death of the entire estuarine ecosystem. If the fantastic land loss continues, the famous ragged edge of the Louisiana coast will simply flatten out, eventually coming to look more like coastal Mississippi, Alabama, and Florida, i.e., made up mostly of narrow beaches with only small pockets of wetlands that produce only a fraction of the fisheries wealth of the current, vast Louisiana system.

Charlie drops his nets back into the water, having just finished icing down all the shrimp below deck. But the haulback twenty minutes later brings almost nothing. "De shrimp have gone into de marsh," he says. "We'll have to wait for low tide, after sunset, to flush dem out." It's only midafternoon right now. "We got some time to kill," he says.

He decides to make an escape into a series of obscure bayous north of the lake. These lead to his favorite resting place: a grassy bend in the middle of nowhere where three idle shrimp boats are already tied together, including Big Wayne Belanger's Lady Desiree skiff. Wayne is an exceedingly handsome man with a trim silver beard and silver hair. Over his shoulder, atop the wheelhouse, sits a great blue heron so close it looks like Wayne's pet.

Wayne, forty-six, has the largest hands I've ever seen, nearly rivaling catcher's mitts and inches thick at the palms. The size makes his missing ring finger even more conspicuous. He was picking shrimp one day, he says, when a catfish fin sunk deeply into the fleshy digit. "I did just what de old-timers tell you: make it bleed to get de poison out," Wayne says. "So I bled it and a lot of blood sure came out and I t'ought dat should do it, but damned if my finger didn't turn black anyway and dey finally had to take it off."

Wayne's sun-bronzed face is a study in fatigue from last night's hard shrimping and today's equally long morning repairing his boat winch. He's taking an afternoon break right now, quaffing a few cold Buds. These Cajun shrimpers, away for days at a time in distant waters, rest by tying up together in groups of three or four boats in the shelter of remote back-country bayous, cooking big communal Cajun meals and drinking beer and talking about shrimp and helping repair each other's boats and talking about women—and that's basically what we do for the rest of the day, hour after unhurried hour. An overflying plane would have seen a knot of dirty boat decks and shirtless men surrounded by a watery world of Everglades vastness with interconnecting bayous and lakes and marshland set ablaze in the gleaming reflection of late afternoon sun. It's something that's almost completely gone in America: the fellowship of working men in a wild place.

At one point a four-foot alligator swims past the boat, and Wayne tells me there are lots more up here north of the lake, some reaching twelve and fourteen feet. Last year he got a five footer caught in his shrimp net. These cold-blooded reptiles hatch their eggs by cleverly piling big mounds of grass and leaves over them, then letting the heat of decomposition incubate the eggs. People around here still hunt the adults each September, Wayne explains, by tossing out raw chicken parts on huge hooks. They then sell the skins and eat the meat.

"You eat it?" I ask.

"Sure," Wayne says. "A good sauce piquante wit' gator meat over rice? You got Cajuns swear by it. Dere's not much, you know, a coon ass won't eat."

Coon ass. It's a name I've heard Cajuns apply to themselves repeatedly on this trip, a moniker employed not unlike the way some African-Americans use the word "n——"; for years it was employed as a slur against Cajuns until these French descendants claimed it for themselves. Linguists pretty much agree that the word has nothing to do with raccoons, but derives instead from the no-longer-used conasse, a French cussword for a prostitute who has not had her regular health inspection. Today, the use of "coon ass" reflects a certain Cajun pride in their traditionally rural and rough-hewn way of life, and it pokes a little fun, expressing Cajuns' own perception of themselves as just a little bit backward. Thus, a beat-up pair of rubber deck boots are called coon-ass Reeboks. A ruler for measuring fish is a coon-ass computer. An elaborately jury-rigged boat repair job is coon-ass engineering. But again, when a Cajun tells you he's an RCA (registered coon ass), he's positively taking pride in who he is. He's not apologizing for anything.

"If you like coon-ass food," Charlie says, turning matters back to cooking, "you gotta come down for de Blessin' of de Fleet. That's when people really eat down here. You got your gumbo, your jambalaya, your shrimp boulettes, your crawfish etouffee, your boiled crabs. It's all dere."

The Blessing of the Fleet, Charlie and Wayne explain, is an old and venerable bayou tradition where a town's Catholic priest, riding at the head of a parade of boats, blesses the community's fishing vessels with holy water just prior to opening day of shrimp season. Before the parade, a mass is held where shrimpers are given blessed medallions to protect them from the season's inevitable storms. Afterward there's usually a feast on church grounds with lots of French music and a traditional Cajun dance, a *fais-do-do*.

The images of holy water and boiled crabs and washboard rhythms resonate in my mind as I sit on Wayne's Lafitte skiff surrounded by prowling gators and Wayne's onboard blue heron. The ceremony these men have just described seems as foreign as anything I've heard so far on this trip. What could be more out of place in a nation where meaningful community rituals have all but vanished thanks to television, the decline of rural America, the weakening of the church in community life, and the generally obliterating sameness of mass culture?

But somehow nothing has derailed the Blessing of the Fleet ceremony in small towns all across Louisiana's bayou country. For many Cajuns "the Blessin'" is second only to Mardi Gras as a chance to throw a party, be with family and friends, and show off valued cultural traits. I keep asking Wayne and Charlie more and more questions about the ceremony until I can almost taste the okra-laced gumbo, hear the pearl-buttoned accordions, and see the parade of shrimp boats decorated in colorful bunting and triangular flags that snap with pride in the salty breeze.

"But you know," Wayne says, "it's all dying down here. De fishing industry and all de towns. Everyt'ing is passing away."

His words draw me back to the blunt facts of coastal Louisiana.

"We've already been talking about it," Charlie tells Wayne.

"So did Charlie show you my favorite tree?" Wayne asks.

I shake my head. "What tree?"

Everyone down the bayou has a favorite land-loss anecdote, it seems, and Wayne's involves a large oak tree near the northeast corner of Lake Boudreaux. The dead and leafless tree, which Wayne shows me later that afternoon, is submerged at its base in lake water, the body a forlorn sculpture of silvery-white branches reaching like fingers toward the sky in a gesture that seems to ask "Why?" Twenty years ago this tree was on a solid bank of land near where Wayne and his brother flipped over in a small motorboat one winter day.

"My brudder, he was being a couillon [clown] and turned too fast and we hit de water," says Wayne. "So we went onto de shore, totally wet, and gathered up some firewood, and built us a fire under de shelter of dat tree, which was totally alive, and we had us some sit-down until we warmed up and dried off. Now it's gone, dat land. Twenty years, and de tree is in water where we built a fire. Dere's no more land. I never t'ought I'd live to see anyt'ing like dat," Wayne says.

For more than two days I've listened to dark stories like this, all presented with an air of fatalism, a firm sense of fait accompli, the causes of decline seemingly too monumental and rooted in too many decades of destructive momentum to allow any hope for change.

"Is there nothing that can be done to stop all this?" I finally ask Wayne and Charlie. "Is there no way to make the land stop sinking and eroding? To make it stop disappearing?"

"Sure dere is," Wayne says, rubbing his silver beard with his enormous hands as his voice dips into sharp sarcasm. "All you have to do is fill in all de oil company canals, build up all de barrier islands to de size dey were a hundred years ago, and den let de Mississippi River flood again. Dat's all."

The remedies are fantastically ambitious, of course, each carrying such huge price tags and posing technical challenges as to render them nearly impossible. For his part, Wayne is especially doubtful about letting the Mississippi flow from its banks again. Too many potential flood victims keep the politicians scared.

But I later learn that some isolated efforts were under way to fill in certain oil-field canals or otherwise mitigate the erosion they cause. And a few barrier islands had been shored up temporarily with new sand and the planting of protective grasses. And, most important, there was a plausible plan already developed to let the Mississippi breach its banks in a controlled way, a move that would resume the process of sedimentation and land creation and so save large parts of the coast without flooding homes.

But this "controlled diversion" of the river, the Holy Grail of coastal restoration hopes, was expensive and politically complicated in the extreme and time was rapidly running out for it to have any chance of success.

Time was also running out for about two million Louisianans who depend on the state's coastal wetlands as a buffer against hurricane damage. As conservationists, scientists, and public officials make excruciatingly slow progress toward possible solutions, the marsh continues to disappear at a rate of 25 square miles per year. This, Wayne points out to me, means that hundreds of Louisiana towns and cities, all just a few feet above sea level, lie increasingly prone to that deadly wrecking ball of hurricane force known as the storm surge. Coastal wetlands, it turns out, provide more than just a critical nursery for shrimp, crabs, and fish. Every 2.7 miles of marsh grass absorbs a foot of a hurricane's storm surge, that huge tide of water pushed inland by the storm's winds. For New Orleans alone, hemmed in by levees and already on average eight feet below sea level, the apron of wetlands between it and the closest Gulf shore was, cumulatively, about 50 miles a century ago. Today that distance is perhaps 20 miles and shrinking fast. With very slow evacuation speed virtually guaranteed (there are only three major exit bridges that jump over the encircling levees for central New Orleans' 600,000 people), it's not implausible that a major hurricane approaching from the right direction could cause tens of thousands of deaths.

This is to say nothing of the literal disappearance of entire towns like Leeville and Chauvin and Golden Meadow which have even less—dramatically less—marsh protection. After the Really Big One hits and drifts up the Mississippi Valley, spending itself over land, there might be nothing left behind under the clearing skies except a sunny expanse of open water and bright waves where bayou people and houses once stood, the land finally battered and scoured of every last handful of ancient and fragile Mississippi soil.

Then the tortured process, at long last, would be complete. Or, as one shrimper tells me, "Dere won't be no more nothin' left anymore, forever."

STEVE LERNER

Diamond: A Struggle for Environmental Justice
in Louisiana's Chemical Corridor (2005)

What is it like to have your community surrounded by large petrochemical facilities whose pipes and towers recall an urban landscape more than a small farming community? Diamond, Louisiana, is a fenceline community, a town that butts up to the edge of industrial chemical processing plants. In 2002, Steve Lerner, research director of Commonweal, a health and environmental research institute, collected oral histories from community members in Diamond on their experiences living between two giant industrial facilities. These oral histories form the basis of *Diamond: A Struggle for Environmental Justice in Louisiana's Chemical Corridor*, a book that amplifies the voices of the residents while also giving a wide context of the petrochemical industries' history, practices, and (sometimes violent) strategies for dealing with fenceline communities.

Diamond is one of many towns across the United States that has sued large multinational companies to keep their towns healthy, pollution-free environments. In Robert Bullard's excerpt in this anthology, low-income Houston communities populated largely by people of color have been disproportionately affected by toxic pollution from solid waste disposal facilities. Lerner shares a similar story here. Margie Richards, a teacher and community leader from Diamond, was able to organize her Louisiana community and implement air quality monitors that revealed high levels of chemical toxins that Shell had failed to report to the state's environmental agency. In 1999, Richards was invited to speak at the United Nations about the problem of chemical pollution in Diamond. While there, she met with a Shell official, and soon afterward, Shell changed its position and offered to purchase the homes of community members. It is important to note that though Richards accomplished her goal, Shell consented only because of public attention in the press, not because it was ethically obligated to provide a safe environment. Margie Richards and her community worked for many difficult and determined years to successfully advocate for their health, though many communities throughout the Gulf South continue to be exposed to toxic pollution in their own backyards.

Work Sourced

Adamson, Joni. "What Winning Looks Like: Critical Environmental Justice Studies and the Future of a Movement." *American Quarterly*, vol. 59, no. 4, 2007, pp. 1257–1267.

Diamond is not a place where most people would choose to live. Located in the heart of the "chemical corridor" between the mouth of the Mississippi River and Baton Rouge, the four streets of this subdivision are hard up against fencelines with a Shell Chemical plant and the huge Shell/Motiva oil refinery. Residents here have long breathed the fumes from these two plants, suffered illnesses they attributed to toxic exposures, and mourned neighbors and friends killed by explosions at these facilities.

The view from the homes in Diamond is of heavy industry at work. There are catalytic cracking towers, stacks topped by flares burning off excess gas, huge oil and gasoline storage tanks, giant processing units where oil and its derivatives are turned into a wide variety of useful chemicals, and a Rube Goldberg maze of oversized pipes. The clanking and crashing of railroad cars coupling and uncoupling can be deafening, and the eerie sight of the superstructures of gargantuan oil tankers soundlessly moving up the Mississippi to dock and unload their crude oil completes the industrial landscape.

The streams of chemicals pouring out of the plants in the vast, sprawling Shell/Motiva Norco Complex are used in factories around the United States. Truly, these two mammoth plants are part of the front end of the system that has forged the American lifestyle by making products cheap and convenient. One cannot help but be in awe of the ingenuity, tenacity, and hard work that built these technological behemoths.

What seemed an incongruous sight, however, was a small residential community sandwiched between these two giant plants. The terrible cost of introducing heavy industry into a residential neighborhood soon became apparent. In the homes of Diamond residents there were many signs that this was not a healthy place to live. On many days the plant stank. Shell officials said that the smell was not dangerous and was caused by an organic digester unit that became backed up and gave off a rotten odor as millions of micro-organisms died. They were working on a solution to the problem, they said. But on some days the smell emanating from the plants had a toxic bouquet. Not infrequently, there was an acrid, metallic odor than caused headaches, sinus problems, and stinging eyes. There were even days, residents and visitors reported, when they could actually see a chemical fog swirling around their legs and seeping through the cracks into the houses.

And while it was notoriously difficult to prove that there existed a causal link between the toxic chemical released from the plant and the health of neighboring residents, inside the homes of Diamond residents were a disturbing number of children with asthma; young adults with severe respiratory, allergic, and unusual skin problems; and older people whose breathing had to be aided with oxygen tanks.

Then there was the history of periodic explosions. A 1973 explosion took the lives of two Diamond residents. A 1988 explosion that killed seven Shell workers blew out windows and doors and brought down sheet-rock ceilings in many homes. Diamond was evacuated in the middle of the night. Many homes required extensive reconstruction.

If it was so poisonous and dangerous to live there, why didn't the residents of Diamond just move? The answer was that few of those who lived in Diamond stayed because they wanted to. Given an opportunity to sell their homes and move they would do so, but without getting decent prices for their homes they could not afford to leave. Living next to the Shell plants had not only been bad for their health, they said; it also had been lethal·to property values. As the chemical and oil plants expanded to an area just across the street, residents who wanted to sell their homes and relocate could not find buyers who were foolish enough to want to purchase their homes. In other words, they were stuck: they could not bear living where they were because of the bad air, but they could not afford to move elsewhere. Faced with this dilemma, a small group of Diamond residents decided to organize and demand that Shell give them enough money for their homes so that they could relocate elsewhere in St. Charles Parish, away from the fumes and the danger of explosion. They began picketing the Shell facilities, seeking face-to-face meetings with Shell officials, and talking to the press. One 80-year-old woman who joined the picket lines told me that she just wanted to be relocated so she could live the rest of her life in peace: "I would go. I'm not particular [about the replacement house] as long as it is not raining in there and the plumbing and floors is good. I am not a picky person. I am just looking to get away. I just want to be gone."

If this were a script for a Hollywood movie, I could stick with a simplistic story line: a group of neighbors living near two petrochemical plants become sick of breathing toxic fumes and decide to organize a relocation campaign. But reality is rarely as neat as a simple plot. The fact was that not everyone in the vicinity of these two Shell plants agreed that a relocation program was warranted. Tellingly, opinion on the subject was divided along racial lines. Those who lobbied long and hard for relocation lived in Diamond, where all the residents were black. Their community was separated from the adjacent white community of Norco by a wooded strip of land and railroad tracks. And many of those on the white side of Norco dismissed these complaints, arguing that the town was a great place to live where they and their neighbors were healthy and lived to a ripe old age. Diamond residents who claimed that the plants were making them sick were either lying or at the very least exaggerating the problem in order to make a buck, some of them said.

There was also the perspective of Shell officials in Norco, at Shell's Louisiana headquarters in New Orleans, at Shell's national headquarters in Houston, and at Shell's international headquarters in London and The Hague. They vehemently denied that their facilities were hazardous to the health of their neighbors. They contended that their plants were meeting regulatory standards, that they were permitted to operate by federal and state regulatory agencies, and that their emissions were harming no one. But Diamond residents who had to breathe the fumes from these facilities daily held a very different view of the facts. They laughed at Shell's assertion that the emissions were harmless.

Some Diamond residents traced their history on the land back to plantation days. Their story started during the days of slavery, when many of their ancestors worked the sugarcane fields of the Trepagnier Plantation that subsequently became the Diamond Plantation, Belltown, and finally the Diamond subdivision of Norco. After the Civil War, when the plantation was abandoned by its owners, many of the freed slaves continued to occupy their old slave cottages; others moved into the plantation house. In 1916, when Shell Oil began to build its refinery near this African-American enclave, some of the residents hoped they would find employment at the new facility. Few of them were hired, however, and most of those who did find employment at Shell were relegated to menial jobs.

When Royal Dutch/Shell purchased the land that the freed slaves lived on in the early 1950s and began to build the Shell Chemical plant, residents were forced to move off the land they had worked for decades. They tore down their homes and rebuilt them a quarter of a mile away on what became the fenceline with the giant Shell refinery and the adjacent chemical plant. Again there was renewed hope that they would find employment in the vast new facility that was being built on their doorstep; again, however, they found themselves on the receiving end of the fumes from the plant but with few of the jobs.

Over the years the plant expanded ever closer to their homes. In the mid 1970s, unable to sell their homes for a reasonable price and move elsewhere, a small group of Diamond women began to organize protests and to demand that Shell buy them out. In the late 1980s, as the grassroots movement (led by a tenacious local schoolteacher named Margie Richard) gathered steam, people outside of the parish began to hear of this David and Goliath struggle between the world's third-largest petrochemical company and a tiny black community on its fenceline. Over time, Norco became a "poster child" for environmental racism and environmental justice activists, and toxics activists began to provide support for the struggle.

Shell officials denied that their plants were causing illness and pointed out that there were more white people in Norco than there were blacks in Diamond and that the former had few complaints about living next to their plants. But the plight of Diamond residents on their fenceline continued to receive sympathetic treatment from the press, and the pressure built on Shell to relocate them.

DIANE WILSON

An Unreasonable Woman: A True Story of Shrimpers,
Politicos, Polluters, and the Fight for Seadrift, Texas (2005)

Diane Wilson (b. 1948) is an activist who writes with an authority that comes from someone whose livelihood was directly connected to the environment; she knows the waters intimately. Before the 2005 publication of her book *An Unreasonable Woman: A True Story of Shrimpers, Politicos, Polluters, and the Fight for Seadrift, Texas*, Wilson was a fourth-generation shrimp boat captain in the town of Seadrift, Texas, about eighty miles from Corpus Christi. In 1989, she read a newspaper article that said that Calhoun County, Texas, had the most toxic waste disposal of anywhere in the country. The article made her wonder if there was a connection between that and the dying fish and sea animals she had seen. From that moment on, Wilson threw herself into the role of investigator, advocate, organizer, and eventually, writer.

As with so many of the stories of individuals trying to call to account corporate polluters, her writing is laced with the frustration and antagonism she encountered in her struggles. Yet, Wilson struggled on and in 1994 won a "zero discharge" agreement from Formosa, an industrial facility that was polluting those waters and air. However, Formosa has continued to be a serial offender. A Texas judge ruled in 2019 that Formosa was in "enormous" violation of state and federal clean air and water laws and that the Texas Commission on Environmental Quality was unwilling or unable to make the company comply. Though this ruling was a win, Formosa is still trying to expand into other Gulf states such as Louisiana, where the company might find a more lenient political environment.

In this excerpt, Wilson, her friend Donna Sue, her son Crockett, and a few shrimpers discover that their catch is either acting funny or dying. Wilson begins to organize her community, and a county commissioner arrives for a visit to convince her that she should be happy Formosa is coming to their town.

Work Sourced

Collier, Kiah. "Federal Judge Rules against Formosa Plastics in Pollution Case, Calling Company a 'Serial Offender,'" *The Texas Tribune*, June 28, 2019.

It was the second week after the meeting and the second week into the fall shrimp season, and no surprise to anyone, it had disintegrated into another calamity. It was what shrimping was: a series of calamities. Then Jumpin' Junior (named for his peculiar habit of saying he was in one bay one minute, then ten minutes later showing up in another bay) hauled up in his pickup to the front door of the fish house and, with his head hanging out the window, yelled at the top of his lungs, "Why don't you gals find out what's goin' on down in that channel!"

I was sewing a net from a bent nail at the door and Donna Sue was on the back dock, and we both heard him. She came around the front with her hands on her hips and said, "Now, what in the hell do you want?"

"*Whadda I want? Whadda I want?* I want you gals to see what's goin' on out there in that bay! Go on, looky back there in that basket at what I got. Dead, rotten shrimp! Now, where did I get dead, rotten shrimp? Whyyy, I got 'em in the channel, is where I got 'em, and what's dead, rotten shrimp doin' out there? Tell me that, would ya!"

So I got Jumpin' Junior's dead, rotten shrimp and I stuck them in a plastic bag and labeled them with a black magic marker, and then I put them in Donna Sue's freezer. Later I would say that day was the day that something as familiar as a child's voice coming over the backseat of a car became nothing but a frozen Ziploc bag in Donna Sue's freezer.

Then on another day not much different (except that it was raining and cold), I stood on a makeshift wharf. A norther had blown in, and the rain splashed slow on the yellow pine boards. The wharf was just big enough for one shrimper to get on and off his boat in the early morning hours, so I didn't move any farther down the wharf than I had to. I certainly didn't try to go inside the cabin with the men in their wet slickers. I just turned and watched a flatbed truck haul off two dead dolphins.

The shrimpers stood on their boat, looking at me like they were deciding what they wanted told and what they thought was better left unsaid.

"How many more dead dolphins were out there?" I asked. The men said nothing. One shrimper looked down at a knotted rope like it mattered, and the rain came down off his ears and fell onto his already soaked shirt.

"This ain't no family secret here," I said, and put my boot against a rotten piling that the new boards were nailed to. It was black all the way into the water. When I looked up the shrimpers were out on the back deck and folding up the oyster sacks they had laid over the dolphins.

"Ain't it?" the skinny one said. "Who you think they're gonna blame for them being dead? First off, who's it gonna be? I told *him*" and he jerked a thumb to the other shrimper—"we just oughta leave 'em dolphins out there to rot to pieces. Who they gonna blame but us?"

"Those dolphins didn't have bullet holes! And who catches dolphins in their nets? Nobody! Ain't a single shrimper I've ever seen. And they damn sure weren't knocked cold by a shrimp door. So nobody's thinkin' it."

"No?" he said.

"No," I said.

"Shit. Then I guess we should've got them first ones we seen last week."

The shrimpers weren't fooling. The dolphin count *had* started the week before. A newspaper account detailed the progress, saying a helicopter pilot returning from offshore spotted four dead dolphins on a single flyby. The dolphins were washed up in the shallow marshes of the bay, all male and all over three hundred pounds. Then the pilot called the Coast Guard and the Coast Guard called the game warden, and by then the pilot had counted eleven on a second check.

I didn't know how many the shrimpers found but didn't report. One gill netter left me a penciled message hammered to the fish-house door, and on the back dock a dead redfish wrapped in old newspaper. The note said, *This fish acted funny. He swum at the surface in a slow circle, and all I did was reach out and grab him. There was an alligator acting funny, but I didn't bring him.*

I took the redfish wrapped in the newspaper and froze it. Donna Sue didn't want nothing to do with the redfish because a redfish—dead, alive, or blackened in a skillet—was *big* trouble for a commercial fishing person. "You know what a game warden's gonna do if he catches us with that damn fish?"

"It's evidence," I said.

"Evidence, hell! It's illegal! They'll string us to that high line pole out there."

I wasn't worried and didn't believe Donna Sue was either. She just wouldn't admit it, and hung on to her game warden tangent like she'd hang on to an old sweater she liked. But sure enough, like an old wound that festers and heals, then festers again, the game wardens seemed to arrive overnight. I couldn't remember when I had last seen that much single-mindedness from Parks and Wildlife, and I suppose it could have been over the dolphin sightings, but the local shrimpers weren't so sure. They figured the arrival of the game wardens was to hammer another nail in their coffins, and they hung around the tailgates of their trucks and talked long and hard about it.

Sanchez figured it was him. He said if there was one thing a game warden couldn't stand worse than a commercial fisherman, it was a commercial fisherman that wouldn't stand still while they were handing out the tickets. And it didn't matter that his trial was over and done with; game wardens had mighty long memories. So I wasn't surprised when Sanchez wanted the three tires up on the piling again and he wouldn't come to the docks until way past everybody else, and I had to bring Crockett down to the bay because he was up and running the house anyhow, so it might as well be the fish-house floor he was running. Sanchez's paranoia wasn't totally out of line. Earlier in the day four game wardens in two army-green Range Rovers stationed themselves outside the fish house under our wild mulberry tree, and there they waited out the fishermen while me and Donna Sue waited out the whole mess—game wardens and shrimpers alike. Finally the game wardens grew tired of messing with shrimpers, and they cleared out with only one handwrote ticket costing one shrimper five hundred dollars. Only Sanchez remained in the bay.

Donna Sue had been closemouthed since the game wardens left, and still silent, she swept up the dead shrimp that had fallen off the weighing bucket and ramp where shrimp are hauled from the boats. When she finished she dumped the trash shrimp outside and fed the thundering cloud of hardheads in the harbor. Then she turned on the water hose and poured bleach all over the fish-house floor. In her jeans spotted with bleach and under the raw yellow lights yawning from the fish-house rafters, Donna Sue slung water like she hardly knew what she did.

I told her to go home. I could finish up. Sanchez was tied to a piling, probably eating M&M's and drinking coffee. "He ain't sufferin' none," I said. So Donna Sue gathered her belongings; took her magazines and her half-eaten candy bar and her purse and stomped out of the fish house.

Then the fish house got quiet, and I stood and breathed in the silence. Scattered shrimp still hid in a cement wash gutter, and their bay smell and the lingering bleach smell were two things under the yellow lights of the fish-house rafters that I couldn't put my hands on. The night air did that sometimes; what seemed solid enough an hour ago—the shrimpers, the boats, diesel motors, ropes being thrown—now fled like ghosts leaving nonbelievers. I was alone with my Davy Crockett—my antelope baby. No ghost, for sure. The bayou and the high-hung nets smelt to the high heavens, and me and Crockett waited out Sanchez. Once I heard a motor and went through the fish house and looked out on the docks and down the harbor. Nothing. Ten o'clock. Eleven. I took Crockett's hand and we walked to the end of the shell road and stopped at the water's edge. The other fish houses were dark. Across the harbor, two lights hung from a two-by-four nailed to a pier. If Sanchez had seen either he would have knocked 'em both out.

Crockett was restless and grabbed my shirt to pull me down the street. He jumped on the truck-pulverized oyster shell, first one foot, then the next, then again. His hair was wet and his shirt was limp as a crumpled rose. I looked past Crockett, then beyond the docks to the boats. Above the boats mast poles and A-frames and jerked-up try nets moved slowly this way and that. Eventually it was a movement too little or not quite right that stopped me. Then I saw the game warden truck. It was pulled into the shadow of a closed fish house, and inside were two men, and one moved and the other did nothing.

"What is that, Crockett? Is that the game wardens? Think we oughta warn Sanchez? Should we, should we?"

I talked to Crockett, and his eyes were wide open and hot looking, but as I went to grab his hand, he was gone. He ran down the middle of the road, upright and high in the night air. Then for no reason, he stopped and his feet came together like a dance step remembered. His feet started drumming again. It wasn't a loud drum, just a low, monotonous one where the oyster dust took a beating. I grabbed his hand while he still danced and walked him off the road so the sound of our feet wouldn't carry across to the game wardens.

Crockett and I were the cavalry all war-telling is full of! Not holstered or sabered, just hoping for one VHF radio to warn Sanchez. *Beware los federales!* We went from shrimp boat to shrimp boat, tromping over winches and deck buckets and oil buckets and wet ropes and wetter nets. I rattled one cabin door after another, one lock after another. Most cabins were open, but with radios missing. Finally I found an open door and a working radio, and I shoved Crockett inside and held him tight with my knees. I reached for wires and the feel of a cold metal radio.

Twice I called Sanchez, but no answer. Then he did, and I said next to nothing. Calling was enough. Sanchez wanted to know how long it would take me to meet him. Not long, I said. You know where? He said, and I said, Shore, shore. Another secret kept from enemy game wardens. So I left the fish house lit and the Sears van in plain sight of the game wardens and walked down the road with Crockett until I found Sanchez's truck.

I was lucky I found it. Sanchez never left his truck in the same place twice and the key was always hidden. I unlocked the truck and reached inside and shoved Sanchez's bayonet underneath the seat, then picked up Crockett and set him inside. I drove the truck in first gear past the fish houses and past the game wardens. Crockett hardly budged. His tight body faced the windshield, and only two hands twisting said he was alive and with me.

We rode silently through main street, past Seadrift's city limits sign, past open fields of ranch land and rice farms, then finally across an open field and onto a dirt road that smelt of salt grass and wet cow pens. The sand was tight and puckered from rain the day before and when we drove over, little clumps of succulent plants burst like Christmas bulbs. Ahead was the intercoastal canal, and beyond that was the open bay, with its cool water and silver and black fish. When I came to the edge of the canal, I stopped the truck. The air was dead, and Crockett was quiet too. Maybe asleep. I leaned my head against the window and watched Crockett and the west end of the channel, and thought nothing at all until Sanchez's diesel motor killed the silence by degrees.

His bow came fast, high, and hard, and it rammed the canal bank, but from the stern a soft foam came like an old woman's wash water.

Sanchez walked out of the cabin in his bare feet and stood quietly near the bow. "Where's the game wardens?" he said.

"Sittin' in the dark. Waitin' on you." I could see Sanchez's tanned face and his hair clustered soft as a woman's. His lips came away from his teeth like he was laughing at something.

"Can you keep my shrimp in my truck overnight? I can give you extra ice."

"Sure, but what's the matter with yore shrimp that you can't bring 'em in?"

"Ain't nothin' the matter with them. I just don't trust those friggin' game wardens. You lose thirty thousand dollars to Austin and see how much you trust them after that. I'm not giving those bastards one single excuse to screw me again!"

Sanchez turned and drug baskets of shrimp from inside the cabin. His was a common enough maneuver for a captain nervous about his shrimp. Whether his shrimp were undersized or over the pound limit, or whether the captain was just plain nervous or neurotic and imagined game wardens around every bend, a shrimper always felt better if he kept shrimp in the cabin, where a near and ready boot could dump a load in the unfortunate event that a game warden's boat surprised him on the bay. A shrimper would lose everything before he'd let a game warden confiscate his shrimp, then fine him for them, then sell the shrimp and use the money to buy more game wardens to chase shrimpers.

So I got out and helped Sanchez load the baskets onto the truck tailgate and sling them up next to the rear window. Sanchez filled two empty shrimp baskets with ice and I dumped them on the shrimp, then covered them with oyster sacks. After Sanchez pulled out, I watched his boat disappear down the canal. It was after midnight, but I wasn't tired. I was only stopped like a clock's second hand was stopped, and I glanced towards the truck, and Crockett's head hadn't moved either.

The next morning I caught Sanchez on his boat and told him for that little midnight arrangement, he owed me a big one. I needed a director on my environmental group, and he was my male quota. After the conversation with Formosa's plant manager at the fish house, I had decided the time had arrived for directors and everything legal an environmental group needed. Right off the bat Donna Sue said she wasn't being president, so just look elsewhere for that donkey. She did have a daughter old enough to do something, though. With all our connections (I had a cousin and she had a daughter and a friend), and after a phone call to Blackburn, we made Sanchez and the daughter directors, and the cousin and the friend became the secretary and treasurer. So much for voting rights.

When Sanchez reached the fish house the next afternoon for our first organizational meeting, the cousin and the daughter and the friend had been there for over half an hour. Sanchez came in and sat down on the edge of the desk I was sitting behind, and put a thermos of coffee in the middle of the table and proceeded to pour me a cup of coffee without asking. Then he looked around at the women. "Is this the directors?" he said.

"Just you and me and Donna Sue and Sabrina. Blackburn said all we needed was three or four. The rest here are officers."

"Nobody can sue us, can they?"

I looked up from my coffee cup and said, "Now, who in the hell would want to sue us?"

Donna Sue's friend, who was our new secretary and a large-boned woman with a quiet enough hairdo, sat up straight in her chair. Her eyes got big and she said, "Nobody told me nothing about getting sued."

I looked hard at Sanchez and squinted my eyes, then I looked back at the woman. "Sanchez is just talkin' to be a talkin'. Ain't that right, Sanchez? Nobody's got nothing to worry about. We got us a lawyer, don't we?"

Sanchez moved off the desk and walked halfway across the room. Then he remembered his thermos and came back. "Hey, don't take my coffee, there. Listen, tell me what y'all decide, all right? Just give me a call tonight and tell me what all y'all decided. I trust you ladies. I always trust the women."

Then without a backwards glance, he went and left the door wide open in the going. I could see the sun hammering on the street from where I sat, then ten minutes more, I could see it again when all the other women left. We had barely made it halfway through the meeting, and half of the directors and all of the officers had taken Sanchez's direction and left. I crossed my legs and moved Froggie's old coffee cup in a slow circle. Then Donna Sue turned and all I saw was her white neck, so I listened to her white neck like it was her mouth that was talking. She said, "Well, why don't we just put out an open invitation in the newspaper? Just invite everybody in!"

Donna Sue was looking through the door at a man standing in the middle of the fish house. It was the county commissioner, another elected official that didn't make my meeting. He didn't move out of his spot in the fish house. It was like he was superglued. Then after he still said nothing and didn't move any closer, just giving Donna Sue a sideways glance now and then, Donna Sue frowned and said she was leaving. Then she went into the ice vault and slammed the door.

"Looks like y'all gonna need a traffic cop down here just to let the traffic past," the commissioner said. He looked around the fish house, then at me, and for a second we were face-to-face. There was something about the lines around his mouth and I thought he might be fixing to smile, but he didn't.

"What can I do for you, Mister Hahn?"

"Well, nothing really. I've just been meaning to come down here, is all. Tell you why I didn't make that meeting of yours. It went all right, didn't it?"

"Sure, Mister Hahn. It went just fine."

"I figured it would. That's what I was thinking." He stared at the floor awhile, then he looked up and his words seemed to hit out of nowhere.

"You know I went to Taiwan, don'tcha?"

I said I sure didn't. So he proceeded to tell me how he and a few of the county's best had went to Taiwan on a business deal, intending to get a little offer of a few million dollars for a chemical expansion and instead got billions. Billions. Myyy, but wasn't that chairman a wonderful man. Even sent him a birthday cake down to the office without nobody having to say so. Just up and sent the cake.

"Who's this Chairman fella? I've never heard of him."

"*The Chairman*! You've never heard of Formosa's Chairman? Whyyy, he's one of the richest—eleventh, I believe—richest men in the world! Comes from Taiwan. Great humanitarian. Great. Just great. Builds hospitals, chemical plants. Into all kinds of stuff. Real name isn't the Chairman, though. That's just what they call him 'cause . . . I guess he's such a great fella and rich and all."

The commissioner was talking pretty fast, obviously thinking my question was a plenty good avenue to say what he really came for, so I got the spill on Wang Yung-Ching—*the Chairman, the owner, builder, man extraordinaire*. In a world where large, faceless multinational corporations were the norm, Formosa was one of the biggest family-owned dynasties around. Probably in the world! And it was his family that owned the Formosa chemical plant that my environmental group was requesting a hearing on.

The commissioner stopped talking and looked at me, like if I wanted to jump in and say something, then I could, but I didn't, so he blurted out, "You know why he left Taiwan and came all this way down here to Texas, don'tcha?"

"Are you talkin' about the Chairman and Formosa? Why Formosa has all those permits out there?"

"That's it! That's it!" the commissioner said, and his face got red like a woman had slapped him good. Then that same hand that had got the commissioner was now up to my face, and I saw either I ducked or I got slapped, so I backed up.

"Look, all we went to Taiwan for was a little county business. A little something extra going on at that tiny plant of his down here. But what we got . . . what he *offered was three billion dollars! Three billion!* We nearly fell out of our chairs. He offered us more than the whole county's worth! *And he did it because he hates communists.*"

"Three billion dollars' worth because the Chairman hates communists? I didn't know there were communists in Taiwan," I said.

"Whyyy, shore there is. Wang just figured, why not get out of Taiwan altogether? Come to the United States. He got his start in the first place from us. Got a little economic starter loan after we—well, it wasn't we, not me and you, it was U.S. *bombers* flying during World War II that blew his rice mill to kingdom come that did it. So after that blowing-up deal he got his half-million-dollar loan, and here we sit in Calhoun County, three billion dollars richer."

The commissioner stepped closer and said he had to get real personal with me. Formosa only had one window of opportunity. Things had to be put into motion fast. The Chairman had asked them—well, them that went—to *personally* see to a few things. See if those state and federal agencies couldn't speed up the permitting. "'Cause, you know," he said, "you gotta go when the train leaves the station, or else you get left behind."

"So where did y'all go to do all this asking?" I said.

"Oh, Austin. Dallas . . . that's where the EPA's regional office is, you know. Dallas. We were *quite* a little delegation. Told those agency heads, 'We may be little, but we've come a *long* way, and you can't just go around holding up economic development like this. Let's put a little grease on this thing!' 'Cause it's not like we're getting this three billion-dollar offer for nothing! We have to give a little too. That's what the Chairman said. A few incentives on our part. Besides, Formosa could just as easy take this deal to Louisiana. We don't have it sewn up entirely, and I don't think Louisiana would kick him out either. Probably offer him a better deal, is all. So you see what I mean? What I'm talking about. It doesn't hurt to have a little friendly persuasion coming down the tube on our part. Make things friendly. What does it hurt?"

Donna Sue opened the ice vault and came out with a bottle of bleach and poured it on the fish-house floor. I watched the bleach trail get closer and closer to the commissioner's shoes, until finally he said, "Well, I won't pester you no more." His breath came slow—not easy, but slow like it was borrowed air to begin with and it didn't know the way out. Then he turned and went through the fish house in a cautious way, as though he thought at any moment Donna Sue might hit him with the water hose she was washing everything down with. But Donna Sue payed him no mind and looked content over the fact that a man interrupted was a man stopped. Then, as I watched from the door, the commissioner got in his official county car with the words COUNTY COMMISSIONER stenciled in black so nobody in the county would ever be confused over whose car it was, and the smell of bleach came over my shoulder like near-rain right before it hits.

MICHAEL GRUNWALD

The Swamp: The Everglades, Florida,
and the Politics of Paradise (2006)

> Michael Grunwald (b. 1970) has worked as a *Time* senior correspondent and
> a reporter for *Politico* and *The Washington Post*, and he is the author of two
> books. In *The Swamp: The Everglades, Florida, and the Politics of Paradise* (2006),
> Grunwald explores the history of the Everglades, chronicling its natural sys-
> tems and their twentieth-century destruction as Florida's population and
> industries boomed; he also covers the movement led by Marjory Stoneman
> Douglas to reclaim the Everglades as a national park and now its deterioration
> to the point that 90 percent of its bird population is gone and its ecosystems
> show signs of severe stress. *The Swamp* chronicles the massive environmental
> changes in the Everglades over such a short time.
>
> In the excerpt here, Grunwald writes about the ancient history of south-
> ern Florida. Only in recent decades have archaeologists found evidence that
> humans have lived for centuries in what is now called the Everglades, and
> little is yet known of its precolonial peoples.

Yes, man was native to the Everglades, too. In fact, the southwest edge
of the Everglades may have been man's first permanent home in North
America.

Until 1989, archaeologists believed that all Archaic peoples on the continent were nomadic, that year-round settlements only appeared after
the introduction of agriculture. Then a graduate student named Michael
Russo excavated Horr's Island, a squiggle-shaped clump of mangrove keys
at the head of the Ten Thousand Islands. Russo found evidence of centuries of permanent occupation by a complex society, including traces of
wooden posts used in dwellings and huge shell mounds used for rituals
and burials.

Russo then carbon-dated the site to the late Archaic period—right
when the Everglades and its estuaries were taking form.

Russo's findings were archaeological heresy. It seemed inconceivable
that primitive hunter-gatherers with the run of the continent would have

settled down on a swampy outpost off the tip of Florida, separated from the mainland by ten miles of tangled mangroves and tidal flats, in a humid archipelago where a twentieth-century entomologist would catch a record-breaking 365,696 mosquitoes in one trap in one night. But that's what happened. Russo revealed why when he dug up the island's food remains, which included seventy-four varieties of fish and shellfish: Horr's Island was an all-you-can-eat seafood buffet. The fishing at the edge of the Everglades was so good that its residents did not need to leave in the off-season to find more food, so good that it forced the archaeology establishment to revise its assumptions about Archaic man.

The people of Horr's Island sometimes ventured offshore to harpoon whales, sharks, marlins, and manatees, paddling canoes they fashioned from hollowed-out cypress logs, but they found most of their food in south Florida's sheltered near-shore estuaries. They hauled in tiny pinfish, catfish, and herring with nets woven from palm fibers, and gathered mollusks that provided raw material for their shell mounds as well as protein for their diets. They harvested different species in different seasons, like reliable underwater row crops: oysters in winter, scallops in summer, fish all year long. Most of the world's ancient societies had agricultural origins, but the bountiful fringes of the Everglades, where mangrove roots and seagrass meadows provided shelter and nutrition for hundreds of estuarine species, proved that cultivation was not a prerequisite for civilization.

By the time Europeans arrived in the sixteenth century, the people of Horr's Island were gone. The Calusa Indians controlled southwest Florida, and exacted tribute from weaker tribes scattered around the peninsula. None of these native people were farmers, either. Most were coastal fishermen. Many also maintained hunting camps in Big Cypress uplands or Everglades tree islands, and some may have even lived year-round in drier pockets of the interior—eating more turtles, mammals, and freshwater fish, but thriving just the same. The Europeans marveled at the imposing height, powerful physiques, and rich diets of the Calusa, the ultimate tribute to the bounty of the Everglades. Hernando d'Escalante Fontaneda, a Spanish shipwreck survivor who spent seventeen years as a Calusa prisoner, called his captors "men of strength" in his memoirs. "The people are great anglers, and at no time lack fresh fish," he wrote.

Fontaneda catalogued the marine cuisine of the Glades Indians, including lobsters, oysters, manatees, "enormous trout, nearly the size of men," and eels as thick as thighs. He also noted that the Tequesta Indians, who occupied the high ground of the Atlantic ridge, collected nuts and fruits and made bread out of "coontie," a starchy root abundant in the pinelands. They hunted deer, birds, snakes, alligators, "a certain animal that looks like a fox, yet is not," presumably raccoons, "an animal like a rat," probably opossum, "and many more wild animals, which, if we were to continue enumerating, we should never be through."

The Indians of the Everglades had enough food that they didn't need to spend every waking moment hunting and gathering; they had plenty of time for construction, religion, and art. The Calusa built enormous mounds from their discarded clam, conch, and oyster shells, including the 150-acre island of Chokoloskee, and topped them with palmetto-thatched homes. They crafted hammers, bowls, toys, and pendants out of wood, shell, and bone. They attended rituals in elaborate costumes, and sculpted ceremonial masks and statuettes depicting turtles, pelicans, panthers, and gators. One archaeologist was amazed by the "startling fidelity" of the inner ears, hair tufts, and other details he found on a Calusa deer carving: "The muzzle, nostrils and especially the exquisitely modeled and painted lower jaw were so delicately idealized that it was evident the primitive artist who fashioned this masterpiece loved, with both ardor and reverence, the animal he was portraying."

The Glades Indians have often been romanticized as wild savages with hip-length hair and skimpy clothes, worshipping natural creatures and living in harmony with the land. The Calusa certainly were fierce warriors. "Calusa" meant "fierce"—and it is true that they did not overdress in the heat. "The men onely use deere skins, wherewith some onely cover their privy members," gasped a British observer named John Sparke. But the Glades Indians were sophisticated people, and they did not follow the Leave No Trace ethic of the outdoors. They built impressive engineering projects that molded nature to their needs—not just the shell mounds that still dot the Gulf coast, but seawalls, jetties, weirs, fish traps, and reservoirs. They dug canals to create canoe routes to their hunting grounds, including a three-mile cut from the Caloosahatchee River to Lake Okeechobee that would be reopened centuries later for one of the first Everglades drainage ditches. The Calusa burned prairies to attract deer, chopped down cypress trees for their canoes, butchered the animals they idealized in their art, and preyed on baby fish that would be untouchable under modern catch-and-release rules. Native people had an impact on the Everglades environment, just as gators did when they dug their holes, or birds did when they ate seeds in the tropics and deposited them in south Florida.

But the natives had an extremely modest impact. For one thing, there weren't many of them—perhaps 20,000 in south Florida at the time of European contact. They did not slaughter for sport, and their way of life was sustainable without the hunting limits, pollution controls, water restrictions, and wetlands protections associated with modern eco-sensitivity. It wasn't necessarily an admirable lifestyle—Calusa chiefs performed human sacrifices, married their sisters, kidnapped additional wives from conquered villages, and murdered subjects who tried to snoop around their secret meetings with gods—but there is no evidence that it significantly depleted the region's natural resources. "In view of the fact that they lived there for about 2,000 years, the Calusa left surprisingly little impress upon the development of the area," one historian wrote.

The Everglades was still the Everglades before white men arrived.

CYNTHIA BARNETT

Mirage: Florida and the Vanishing Water of the Eastern U.S.
(2008)

The Gulf South has long been the wetlands of the United States, a place where at times there is more water than land. In *Mirage: Florida and the Vanishing Water of the Eastern U.S.*, Cynthia Barnett explores the water systems of Florida and sounds an alarming call for attention to new sources of water scarcity. Visiting with politicians, farmers, artists, homeowners, and a host of characters, Barnett combines the personal experiences of everyday people with large-scale policy research. In this excerpt, we meet Clyde Butcher, a photographer of the Everglades who, after the death of his son, creates epic photos of the disappearing landscapes. Barnett provides an example of the ways people can find hope and solace through their connection to the environment. This piece provides a moment of optimism; despite Butcher's grief, there is an undaunted optimism to his work. It is a reminder to keep working toward a better way of photographing, of living, of being a part of the world.

Barnett is an award-winning environmental journalist and author. She followed *Mirage* (2007) with *Blue Revolution* (2011) and *Rain: A Natural and Cultural History* (2015), which was long-listed for the National Book Award. Her new book, *The Sound of the Sea* (2021), is a global story of seashells and the mollusks that make them.

Twenty-five years ago, a bankrupt commercial photographer from California did what so many other down-on-their-luck Americans have done when they needed to make a fresh start. He packed all his stuff into a truck, loaded up his family, and drove down to Florida.

Clyde Butcher had earned his living mass-producing color lithographs of natural scenes for American living rooms. Sold through J.C. Penney, Sears, and other department store chains whose sales records told him what photos would sell—seagulls yes, mountains no—some of Butcher's images would sell 250,000 times over. But the man so good at making beautiful pictures was not so at finances. Things as mundane as accounts receivable brought him down, even as his photographs sold in the thousands.[1]

A cross-country road trip with their nine-year-old daughter and seven-year-old son was not a bad thing for Clyde and Niki Butcher. They were hippyish nature lovers who had lived in a tent trailer in California's state parks when the kids were babies, aboard a twenty-six-foot sailboat when the children were a little older and Butcher was making money. The couple wanted to find a place where they could sail with their son and daughter, and where Butcher could take the sorts of sunset and seagull shots that make Americans reach for their wallets. South Florida had the seagulls and the sunsets. And it was a sailor's paradise, with quiet bays and gentle waters compared to California's violent waves.[2]

The Butcher family's early years in Florida were not smooth sailing. As everyone who runs to Florida figures out eventually, you cannot leave your troubles at the state line. When they first arrived, in 1980, creditors from California tracked them to Fort Lauderdale. Repo men hauled off their car, van, and motor home.

But over time, with the help of a friend, they started selling Butcher's photographs once again. Back then, his photos were known for little clocks mounted in the corners. He and Niki cranked them out in a rented garage in Lauderdale. Eventually, the Butchers turned to the artshow circuit, selling the clock pictures at weekend festivals up and down the eastern United States. The family began to thrive again. They settled in Fort Myers, on Florida's southwest coast.

Butcher did not get much satisfaction from his work. He knew his pictures were sappy and commercial. He also was not enamored with Florida—except, that is, for the sailing. "Whatever there once was of value," he used to say, "had been turned by the plow or paved over."[3]

But Butcher was not a big complainer. He and Niki had everything they moved to the Sunshine State for: the sunset-that-sells scenery, the sailing, the closeness (sometimes too much) with children Jackie and Ted, now teenagers.

They would have all that until Father's Day in 1986, also Clyde and Niki's twenty-third wedding anniversary. The knock on their door came at midnight. Their son, the sweet and introspective Ted, was dead at seventeen. He had been killed in a car crash, by a drunk driver.

The story of Florida's vanishing water is not just one of senseless waste. It is also a story of redemption. Redemption can take many forms. For some, it is as easy as a baptism in the Suwannee River, an instant washing away of sins. For others, it is a lifelong struggle. Some find redemption in a child, others in a church. Still others find it in nature.

Clyde Butcher found it in the Florida Everglades.

In the weeks following Ted's death, Butcher began to wander Big Cypress National Preserve, taking solace in its beauty and solitude. He found a Florida he never knew existed: waves of marsh grass as far as he could see; cypress stands as stately as California's Avenue of the Giants; the huge, primeval tree islands and the tiny, delicate orchids; all under a sky as wide as an African savannah.

After enduring funerals for first his son and then his father just weeks later, Butcher gathered up his life's work—color negatives and prints worth more than $100,000—and tossed them. He bought an eight-by-ten-inch box camera that he could not afford. And he started shooting the Big Cypress in black and white. It was the way he used to shoot California's mountains when he was young, before J.C. Penney told him that mountains do not sell.

Butcher's new, oversized photos of Florida were haunting and primal, not a seagull or a sunset in sight. The first time he showed them in public, at an art festival near Orlando, people swarmed his booth. "Is this Africa?" they would ask. "Is this the Amazon?" And he would answer, "No, it's just out in the Everglades."

"People had never seen pictures that allowed them to feel the Everglades," Butcher says. And the pictures sold. Better than his sappy, clock-affixed pictures ever had.

Today, Butcher is one of the best-known photographers in the United States. His work hangs in the homes of movie stars and U.S. senators. When *Popular Photography* recently asked, "Who is the next Ansel Adams?" the magazine named Butcher one of the nation's four "keepers of the large-format flame."[4] His business, now run by his daughter Jackie, has grown as large as his photos, as big as his three-hundred pound frame.

But for Butcher, photography is no longer business. As he trudged deeper and deeper into the Everglades, he came to see that the swamp was dying—a victim, like his son, of human carelessness. In this case, Butcher might be able to do something about it.

In the 1870s, landscape artist Thomas Moran's paintings of Yellowstone cinched the campaign to make it a national park. In 1938, Ansel Adams's book of wilderness photographs, *Sierra Nevada: The John Muir Trail*, helped convince Franklin Roosevelt's administration that national parks should support wilderness, not resorts.[5]

Butcher's Everglades photos became popular just as the notion of "Save Our Everglades," Governor Bob Graham's restoration project, was taking hold in Tallahassee and Washington, D.C. Butcher became a champion of Everglades restoration, a particularly effective one because he could show someone who would never step foot in the Glades why they were worth saving.

As he sold thousands of prints, Butcher also gave his photos away to any environmental organization or government agency that needed them for education or promotion. His ancient-looking forests, rivers, and prairies helped change the way Americans saw the Everglades. The photos were too beautiful to reveal the destruction of the ecosystem—even his photos of cattails, which signal pollution. But they made people fall in love with a swamp that previous generations had disdained and destroyed.

It was, for Butcher, redemption. "Before the death of our son, the images were products," he says. "After Ted's death, they became art that could educate people about the loss of the world around them. When something like that happens, you can either become positive or negative.

"If you become negative, you've wasted a soul."

NOTES

1. Tom Shroder and John Barry, *Seeing the Light: Wilderness and Salvation; A Photographer's Tale*. Random House, 1995, 37–41.

2. Author interview with Clyde and Niki Butcher.

3. Shroder and Barry, *Seeing the Light*, 54.

4. "Who Is the Next Ansel Adams?" *Popular Photography*, July 2004.

5. Roderick Frazier Nash, *Wilderness and the American Mind*, Yale University Press, 2001, 326–327.

OLIVER HOUCK

Down on the Batture (2010)

Oliver Houck (b. 1939) is a professor of law at Tulane University, the author or editor of eight books, and an environmental advocate who has been closely involved in the environmental movement since the 1970s when he served as general counsel to the National Wildlife Federation. Houck also figures prominently in John McPhee's "Atchafalaya," excerpted in this volume. Houck is quoted as saying, "The third-greatest arrogance is trying to hold the Mississippi in place," just behind stealing the sun and running rivers backward. Houck's book *Down on the Batture* explores the batture, the small strip of land between the large levees and the Mississippi River. Houck tells stories that reveal the history of this small sliver of land and how it shapes the future of the river.

In this excerpt, he leaves the batture for the woods. Houck writes about his search for the gorgeous ivory-billed woodpecker, now assumed to be extinct. Responding to a possible sighting on Louisiana's Pearl River, Houck sets out to see for himself. At one point, he hears what he believes is the bird's characteristic double thump of its famous white bill striking a tree. He does not see the bird, however, and leaves disheartened. Of its apparent extinction he implores, "Just give us another chance." One wonders how often this lament will be written in one form or another for other creatures in the future.

"The owls, they'll eat your dog!" Ricky says, poking the fire with a stick.

I say I didn't know that.

"Hell, yes," he explains, "come right down and take 'em away."

I say a man I know over by the Atchafalaya shoots owls because he says they take his chickens, but taking dogs is news to me.

"Oh, yeah," he says, as if it happens several times a week.

We are both listening for another call. One had sounded upriver, not too far, and that's what triggered the conversation. It was a barred owl, the one that looks like a sack of laundry in a tree, and they tend to start calling right at sunset as their night vision kicks in and they are getting ready to hunt. Sometimes they chatter back and forth to each other in hoo-hoos and haw-haws like an argument of crows. Come pure dark, though, like coyotes and other wild things that need to get serious about catching something to eat, they quiet down.

I say I wonder how they eat a dog, and he says, "Skin 'em, like a catfish," and I say that sounds pretty complicated. Poking the fire again, he says, "Owls are smart," adding as a clincher, "Ever see their beak?"

I was, however, sidetracked onto skinning catfish, and how many people knew that you skinned them at all. I mean, if you were starving and someone gave you a big catfish from the river, what would you do? The skin is the consistency of a Goodyear tire and it clings to the flesh like superglue. What they do is nail the catfish to a tree, head up, cut a ring around the neck, and then pull the skin down over the body with a pair of pliers like a pair of tight jeans. The nail had better be secure because it is more of a battle than shaving the family cat. I see nails in the trees along the river bank sometimes. My thought is that, given a catfish, I'd probably still starve.

The owl sounds off again, this time farther away. The call is unmistakable, a burst of hoots that rise like a question mark and then fall into sadness. It is the call you hear in the lost-in-the-woods movies where scared teenagers huddle in their tents until the monster creeps a hairy foot inside. But what I hear more is loneliness. As long as people believe that this bird kills their dogs, then barred owls have a problem.

On the other hand, at least they are around. The pelicans are back, too, bred from recruits from Florida. They tend to favor water with a little more salt in it, but from time to time a line of them led by a silver-headed adult will come gliding up the Mississippi, rising and falling like a game of follow-the-leader, and you simply have to stop and look. Sometimes a bald eagle gets this far downriver, and where you are most likely to spot one is in the open, over the power lines, above the gulls, bigger than the vultures and circling absolutely motionless, unperturbed, the lion king of the sky. The bird you will not see here anymore is the one we have eliminated from all of these river bottoms and perhaps the world: It was the signature bird of the southern forests, the ivory-billed woodpecker, also called Elvis because your chances of seeing it now are about the same. And yet, I did. Or maybe I did, I'll never know. It was just east of here along the Mississippi River's little sister, the Pearl.

I blame my dog. The Pearl runs down from northern Mississippi to form the border with Louisiana, where it braids out and floods a wide forested swamp. The lower Mississippi used to look like this, too, and the early towns like New Orleans hugged the banks of natural levees and hung on. Back behind them in the flooded woods was a woodpecker so spectacular in its size and coloring that locals named it the Lord God! bird, because that is what people would exclaim when they saw it. It is intensely wild by nature, and James Audubon tells of one chained to a desk in a hotel room where it proceeded to destroy the desk leg, its own leg, and die.

The ivory bill lived in tall cypress trees past their prime, infected by grubs, and that was where she fed, hammered out her nesting holes, and raised her young.

We wiped them out. We shot them, of course; they were big and pretty so it was not hard to kill them, but, in the end, we cut down their trees. All of them. The last ivory-bill families were up in Avoyelles Parish, and their woods were logged to liquidate some debts of the Singer Sewing Machine company. One of the last people alive to see the Lord God bird was George Lowery, a young ornithologist at the time, who joined an expedition to record it in the 1930s. They got some grainy photographs and an even more grainy phonograph disk. The call on the disk went "Yank yank!" followed by a distinctive drumming. It was not machine-gun rapid like the pileated woodpecker, which is common in these parts, but a slow, loud couplet, like two sledge hammers on a log. The bird was not seen again. But it is the call that matters here.

By the 1950s Lowery was a leading ornithologist at LSU. Visiting the state wildlife agency one day, he heard a conversation about the ivory bill, whose mystique had lingered on, and he remarked that they were extinct. "That's not so," said another visitor who happened by. "I've got 'em on my place by Alexandria." Lowery said that it wasn't possible, which would have ended things except that the following week the same man showed up at his office and dropped a dead ivory bill on his desk. He'd shot it that morning. Proof the old, incontrovertible way that they were still on this earth. No others were ever found.

More than a decade later, Lowery received another visit, this time from a man who had two photographs of an ivory bill on a tree. Lowery was unable to confirm the sightings, but he presented the photos as evidence of the bird's possible existence at the next meeting of the American Ornithologists' Union, the supreme court for all matters pertaining. This is a conservative body, as it should be, skepticism is how science proves its theories, and it treated Lowery's photographs roughly. Some said that they showed dummies on a tree. The question of the photographs was never resolved. Lowery died not long afterwards, and the ivory-bill woodpecker retreated again to the obit section of the news.

It simply would not stay there. In the 1990s a hunter reported seeing one by the Pearl River. It was not an ordinary siting. The hunter was a graduate student at LSU, an NRA member, and the kind of fellow who went hunting in order to be in the woods. He described characteristics of the bird he saw that were not open source material, but were in the notes of those who had last seen it up on the Singer tract a half century before. As a matter of genetics alone, the survival of the ivory bill seemed impossible; a population that limited could not escape the death spiral of inbreeding and mutations over so many generations. But here was the report.

Nikon funded a search throughout the lower Pearl. National Public Radio visited the search team, and that broadcast came to me one morning when I was standing in the bathroom shaving.

I remember the moment as clearly as if it happened today, twelve years later. When I turned on the radio, I'd heard none of the run up to the story. They were playing a recording taken in the Pearl just a few weeks earlier. It did not have the yank yank! call, which would have been dispositive, but it had caught, several times, the slow, loud couplet of a hammer on trees. I had heard the Singer tract recording which included this couplet; it was on a record I'd listened to once when I was very ill, and it was grooved into my brain like the multiplication tables. When that same sound came over the radio, I dropped my razor into the washbasin and said, holy shit! so loudly that Lisa called out to see if I was hurt. I was not hurt. I was in wonderland.

So we went into the Pearl River swamp to look for it, my friend Jay in his canoe, and my dog and I in ours. Ms. Bear is not too good at seeing birds; for one, they are usually up too high in the trees, but she can sense an animal before I do and that, too, is important to what happened. It was late spring but the Pearl runs more on local rainfall than the Mississippi does, and it had rained a lot. You could paddle about anywhere on the high brown water, moving swiftly more like a river through trees. We crossed the forest entirely from west to east, often out of sight of each other, lost in the scene, thick yellow-top at water level topped by red maple seeds, green cypress trees in the background, under a blue sky. The primary colors of our lives.

By mid-afternoon we had drifted into a lake that we could not locate on our maps. Jay saw a fisherman in the distance and drifted over to him to get our bearings. That is when I heard it, two distinct chops, loud as two sledgehammers and very close by. Not daring to breathe, I kept my paddle in the water and feathered the canoe slowly to point towards the sound. There was a total silence, and then an answering rap, two strikes, at a considerable distance, deep in the trees. I pushed the canoe towards a tiny cove in the trees, Ms. Bear alert on the bow like a black hood ornament, she had heard something, too, maybe scented it, who knows what she knew. Then it happened again, very close ahead, a loud double blow, no machine gun, a pause, and then two answers way out in the distance. At this point I was in the cove, and the sound seemed to be coming from low near the water, straight ahead, around the spread of a wide buttonbush. The water was quiet here and littered with floating branches. I began poking the nose of the canoe past the bush; Ms. Bear could already see beyond, I had about four feet to go, and just then a turtle to the side slid off its log with a loud plop! It startled Bear, who gave a small woof! which in turn startled whatever was ahead of us because it rose with a huge rush of wings straight up through the trees and I saw no color, only a shape, fast, and it was gone.

I sat still and listened for several minutes. Jay came back. I asked whether he had seen anything, and he said no but he had heard the two raps. We examined the far side of the buttonbush and found a crooked stump up out of the water, torn up by something. A large bill.

The next day I called up an ivory-bill expert at LSU and asked him about the double raps. He said it was probably an accident. There were Navy SEALs practicing out there, he told me, and it could be that they had heard about the Nikon recordings and were playing tricks on people, pounding on trees. I think I said something like, "anything's possible," not knowing whether I meant the SEALs or the bird. To be sure, some things are not possible. It is just hard to say which things they are.

I will tell you this, though. The pull of this one bird is so strong that there are thousands of us, maybe millions, who would go down on our knees and promise never to do this to such a creature again if we knew the ivory-bill woodpecker were still alive. Just give us another chance. We would not even have to see it. Seeing it is not the point.

BOB MARSHALL

"A Paradise Lost"

PART 3

The Times-Picayune (2010)

> Born and raised in Louisiana, Bob Marshall is a New Orleans journalist whose
> reporting on Louisiana coastal issues at *The Times-Picayune* and *The Lens* has
> been recognized by two Pulitzer Prizes. Marshall is also the recipient of the
> John H. Oakes Prize for Distinguished Environmental Reporting from Colum-
> bia University and the Keck Award for best science reporting from the Na-
> tional Academies of Sciences. Marshall has been deeply devoted to the Louisi-
> ana coastline and community and has led canoe tours into the bayous to help
> educate the public about coastal land loss.
>   Excerpts from two of his in-depth pieces are included in this anthology.
> "A Paradise Lost," about the travails of the residents of Delacroix Island in
> southeastern Louisiana, is excerpted here. In it, Marshall recounts the stories
> of fishermen and their families, many of whose ancestors arrived from the
> Canary Islands in the 1700s, facing the aftereffects of the BP oil spill in 2010
> and the uncertain future of their way of life.

Lloyd Serigne was 10 when his mother took the family on a trip to New
Orleans to shop for items the natural bounty of their bayou home couldn't
provide.

The city was just 30 miles away, but among the forested ridges and thick
marshes of eastern St. Bernard Parish, their life was so complete, if isolated, that they only needed the city every year or two.

At the Woolworth's on Canal Street in the late 1950s, young Lloyd
turned the faucet to wash his hands, and yanked them back, baffled.

Hot!

He turned the faucet on and off several times to see if it would happen
again. It did, and he left the bathroom thoroughly confused. Only a few
houses on Delacroix Island had indoor plumbing at the time, and even
they had to heat water over a fire.

He asked his mother: How does the hot water get in there?

She stared at him for a few seconds before dismissing him, in Spanish—"Oh, don't bother me with things like that!"

She didn't know how the water got hot, either. The water heater, invented some 60 years earlier by Edwin Ruud, had yet to infiltrate life on the Island.

"It was a different world on the Island back then," Serigne said, recalling the story. "We did things the old ways."

OLD TIMERS, NEW TIMES

Now 70, Serigne and his lifelong buddy Henry Martinez, 67, page through memories from a Delacroix childhood in the 1940s and '50s with smiles of amazement. Such "in-my-day" stories are the stuff of cliché in most places, but they are hardly hyperbole in the case of the bayou communities surrounding New Orleans. Their worlds didn't merely change in a generation: They disappeared.

The Delacroix of today resembles those childhood memories in name only. The dense, rich wetlands that provided sustenance and livelihoods have become a crumbling salt marsh with yawning open bays leading right to the Gulf. The thriving village is gone, replaced by a thin line of mostly sport fishing camps and the temporary chaos of the BP oil cleanup army.

But the original name of this barren landscape provides a clue to the natural bounty that once thrived here: Terre aux Boeufs, or "land of the buffalo."

"The name was given by Bienville," said William de Marigny Hyland, president of Los Isleños Heritage and Cultural Society and St. Bernard Parish historian. "The wild cattle were buffalo—bison—that he saw in some numbers all over this area."

It was high land, some of the most fertile on earth, with thick bottomland hardwood forests extending from the bayou ridges, followed by cypress swamps, then freshwater marshes. The salty Gulf was still many miles away.

Serigne's ancestors pioneered the landscape after the Civil War. Their forebears were Spanish immigrants from the Canary Islands who arrived in New Orleans between 1778 and 1779 and worked on plantations along the northern end of Bayou Terre aux Boeufs, which flowed from the Mississippi River. When the war destroyed the plantation culture, they migrated down the bayou, where they found unsettled property owned by the absentee French landlord Francois du Suau de la Croix. The untamed land had plenty to offer.

The Islanders, as the new residents were called, had settled in one of North America's greatest natural shopping malls. The vast delta of the Mississippi was still growing into the Gulf of Mexico, a vibrant ecosystem building plenty of high ground for farms and settlements, and also producing enormous volumes of seafood, ducks and geese, upland game such as deer and elk, cypress and oak for boats and houses, and fur bearers such as otter, mink and muskrat. What Los Isleños didn't need for home consumption, they exported to the city for manufactured goods and cash.

By the 1950s that lifestyle, like the wetlands, had changed little. Life—commercial as well as social—followed nature's calendar, moving from shrimp to trapping to fishing and back to shrimping again—with crabbing throughout.

The wetlands had been healthy not just for survival, but for growth. The Delacroix of Serigne's childhood featured houses three and four deep, shaded and sheltered by oak, hackberry, maple and sycamore trees. As many homes and businesses were constructed on the west side of Bayou Terre aux Boeufs as the east side, which is the only settled bank today. The community bustled, and grew.

"We had three dance halls, churches, small groceries—everything we needed," Martinez said. "It was a great place for kids. We had woods to play in, the bayou to swim in. We could go fishin', and huntin', and trappin'.

"And it was a very, very tight-knit place. Everyone knew everybody else. For kids, it was like you had 700 parents," so closely knit was the community of the 1950s. "If you misbehaved on one end of the bayou, your parents knew about it before you got home."

A WORLD APART

Children and teens in nearby New Orleans, like other American kids, may have been worrying about the latest TV show, which fashions to wear to the Saturday hop or how to convince their parents to let them drive, but Delacroix kids were still connected to the land. School came only between seasons. Classes started in September, but when trapping season started in December most of the kids moved with their parents to distant cabins in the marsh, where they helped harvest muskrat, mink, otter and nutria.

They seldom left before April. Serigne, his eight siblings and parents lived in a one-room cabin about 12 feet wide and 24 feet long—about the size of a FEMA trailer.

"The boys old enough would help my daddy run the traps and fish crabs, and the younger boys, the girls and my mother, we would skin the rats, and put the skins on (frames) for drying," Serigne said.

They'd pack the meat in barrels to use for crabbing, which started when they got back to Delacroix in March.

"Our camp was on a bayou with several other families," Serigne said. "And the marsh back then was solid enough to walk on, so you didn't have to spend all your time in a pirogue."

And they had other visitors. Fur buyers made the rounds to purchase pelts, and grocers steered their floating markets to the outposts so families could restock their staples.

Formal education suffered, of course, but with marsh life so successful, a lack of book knowledge wasn't considered a handicap.

"Most of us didn't speak English until we went to the first grade, and that was something we needed to learn if we traveled to the outside," said Martinez, who still crabs commercially. "But most kids became fishermen and trappers like their daddies, got married to local girls and raised their own families there—just like it was always done."

Trapping season was followed by a spring shrimp season that was profitable, but dangerous.

Fisherman stayed out weeks at a time back then, because shrimp dealers would meet them out in the bays, buying their catch straight from the boat.

"Well, to stay out, you needed to carry plenty of extra gas," Serigne recalled. "We'd have it in barrels tied to the boat, and it was always leaking, and of course guys were smoking or engines were sparking." One or two boats would explode every year, he said.

"You'd hear this big boom and see a red glow, and you knew someone was in trouble," Serigne said.

'CHIVOS' COMING DOWN

Summer was crabbing time, but also the season for the "chivo" migration.

"We called the sports fishermen from the city 'chivos,' which is Spanish for goat," Serigne recalled with a laugh. "They would come down on the weekends and hire our fathers to take them out fishing.

"Visitors from the city always seemed to like to stand on top of the boat cabin or on boxes, probably to see across the marsh. So they were always wobbling like goats and often fell over.

"Look at that silly chivo," one of the locals would say, or "I got some chivos coming down."

Serigne and Martinez remember the security they felt on the bayou, the confidence that life would always be that way.

But change was coming, and at a pace that would stun them. They can pinpoint now what set the demise in motion: the arrival of hard surface roads and canal dredging.

JOSH NEUFELD

A.D.: New Orleans After the Deluge (2010)

Josh Neufeld's *A.D.: New Orleans After the Deluge*, the only graphic novel in this anthology, combines the visual and textual to tell the stories of Hurricane Katrina's arrival, devastation, and then lingering impacts on New Orleans. The introduction, which we have included here, is nearly mute—only a few words place the location and the date as we see the hurricane approach Louisiana and Mississippi. We need few words to understand the oncoming destruction that will play out throughout the book.

As the book unfolds, Neufeld braids the stories of seven characters together, each of whom experiences the human failures exposed by Hurricane Katrina. We follow Leo and Denise, a young couple who flee to Texas during the storm; Abbas, the Iranian-born father of two and owner of a convenience store uptown, and Abbas's friend Darnell; Denise, a social worker whose apartment collapses in Central City; Kwame, a high school student from New Orleans East; and the Doctor, a French Quarter–dwelling bon vivant who refuses to leave in the face of the storm.

Neufeld worked for many years gathering interviews and photos to tell a complex story that weaves characters' experiences together as if to say that disaster is experienced in many different ways, often revealing the deep race, gender, age, and class differences that so often define their experiences.

Work Sourced

Hoefer, Anthony Dyer. "A Re-Vision of the Record: The Demands of Reading Josh Neufeld's A.D.: New Orleans After the Deluge." *Comics and the U.S. South*, edited by Brannon Costello and Qiana J. Whitted, U P of Mississippi, 2012, pp. 293–323.

THE STORM

Monday, August 22, 2005.

New Orleans, Louisiana.

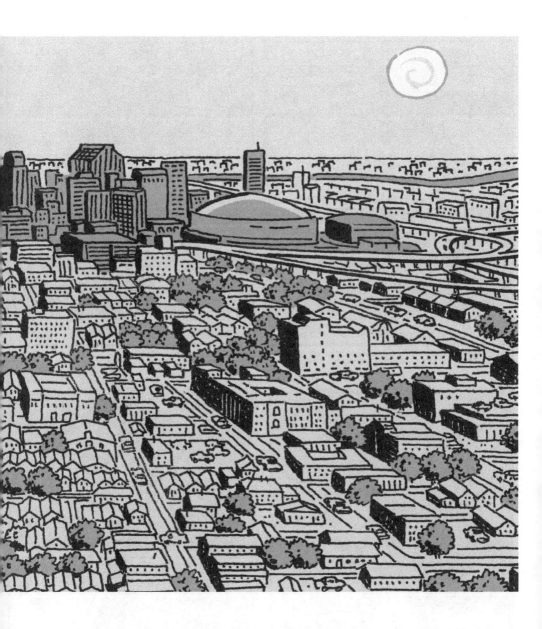

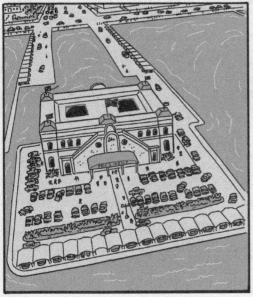

New Orleans.

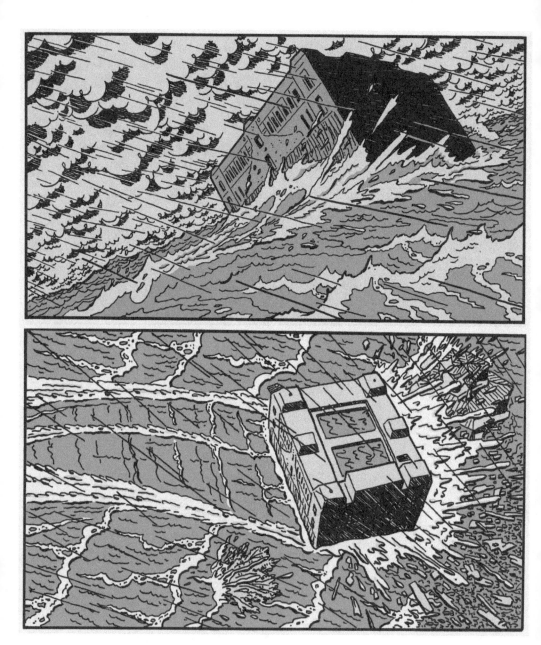

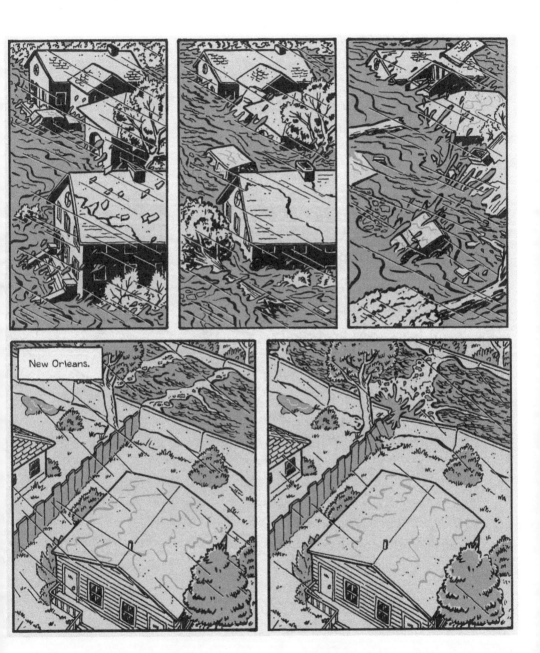

Tuesday, August 30.

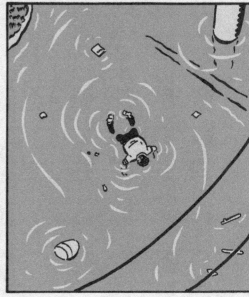

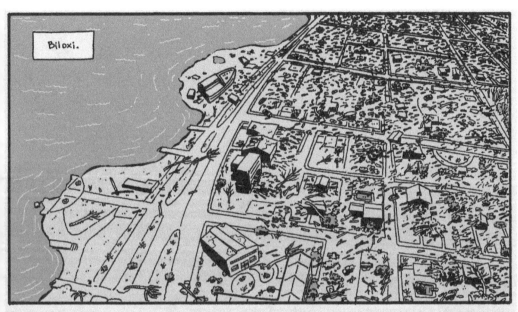

NATASHA TRETHEWEY

Beyond Katrina: A Meditation on the Mississippi Gulf Coast
(2010)

Memoir has a quicksilver element to it, something almost unattainable in the space between how a place and a time were versus how the writer wants to remember them. This is one of the great strengths in Natasha Trethewey's *Beyond Katrina*—it does not overlook the conflicts and questions that arise from remembering. In truth, this book is only part memoir; it is also a book of poetry and a liturgy for a lost home, a hybrid text, to put a name to it. In this space between genres, between memories, Trethewey discovers new narratives to share about her home after Hurricane Katrina. She writes about her grandmother after the storm: "She has layered upon the old story of Camille the new story of Katrina. Between the two, there is a suggestion of both a narrative and a meta-narrative—the way she both remembers and forgets, the erasures, and how intricately intertwined memory and forgetting always are." Memory is not a fixed vantage point here; instead it invites in the emergence of new perspectives of history, creating common ground between poetry and nonfiction and between a place that was and a place that will be after the storm.

Trethewey, born in 1966 in Gulfport, Mississippi, has been recognized for her blending of autobiography and history, examining the complexity of her own biracial identity through the lens of twentieth-century American history. Trethewey was the Poet Laureate of the United States from 2012 to 2014. She won the Pulitzer Prize for *Native Guard* (2007) and the Cave Canem prize for *Domestic Work* (2000).

Work Sourced

Goad, Jill. "Throwaway Bodies in the Poetry of Natasha Trethewey." *South: A Scholarly Journal*, vol. 48, no. 2, Spring 2016, pp. 265–282.

The morning after the storm, hundreds of live oaks still stood among the rubble along the coast. They held in their branches a car, a boat, pages torn from books, furniture. Some people who managed to climb out of windows had clung to the oaks for survival as the waters rose. These ancient trees, some as many as five hundred years old, remain as monuments not only to the storm but to something beyond Katrina as well—sentries, standing guard, they witness the history of the coast. Stripped of leaves, haggard, twisted, and leaning, the trees suggest a narrative of survival and resilience. In the years after the storm, as the leaves have begun to return, the trees seem a monument to the very idea of recovery.

Such natural monuments remind us of the presence of the past, our connection to it. Their ongoing presence suggests continuity, a vision into a future still anchored by a would-be neutral object of the past. Man-made monuments tell a different story. Never neutral, they tend to represent the narratives and memories of those citizens with the political power and money to construct them. Everywhere such monuments inscribe a partic- ular narrative on the landscape while—often—at the same time subjugat- ing or erasing others, telling only part of the story. In Auburn, Alabama, a plaque in the center of town, meant to describe how the city was founded, reads simply "After the Indians left . . ." As I write this, determined citi- zens in Gulfport are working to erect, on Ship Island, some kind of mon- ument to the Louisiana Native Guards—the first officially sanctioned regiment of African American Union soldiers in the Civil War—who were stationed there and to whom no monument exists alongside the monu- ment for Confederate soldiers. According to historian Eric Foner, "Of the hundreds of Civil War monuments North and South, only a handful depict the 200,000 African Americans who fought for the Union." That's only one example of our nation's collective forgetting. With such erasures common- place on the landscape, it is no wonder that citizens of the Gulf Coast are concerned with historical memory. And no wonder the struggle for the national memory of New Orleans—and the government's response in the days after the levees broke—is a contentious one.

Political contests over the public memory of historical events undergird the dedication of particular sites, the objects constructed, funds allocated, and the story that is to be told. These contests, rooted in power and money, undergird the direction of rebuilding efforts as well—how the past will be remembered, what narrative will be inscribed by the rebuilding. Many of the people I spoke with on the coast were concerned not only about how the storm and aftermath would be remembered but whether it would be remembered at all. A woman waiting in line at a store worried that people were forgetting the victims on the Mississippi Gulf Coast, what they had endured and endure still. "There's a difference between a natural disaster and the man-made disaster of New Orleans," she said. "Don't forget about us." Though she acknowledged that more attention has been given to New Orleans because of the travesty of the aftermath, her own need to inscribe a narrative into our national memory prevailed. "We have suffered too," she said.

The first monument erected on the coast to remember Katrina and the victims of the storm stands on the town green in Biloxi. Part of the memorial is a clear Plexiglas with found and donated objects—shoes, dolls, a flag, pieces of clothing, a cross, a clock. They suggest the ordinary lives of the people and the kinds of things that can be recovered or regained. Taken another way, they symbolize things lost: childhood, innocence, faith—national or religious—and time. A wall of granite in the shape of a wave replicates the height of the storm surge. Even more telling is the dedication: not for whom but by whom the monument was commissioned. A gift donated to the city of Biloxi by ABC's Extreme Makeover: Home Edition, the memorial not only remembers the storm and the people but also inscribes on the landscape a narrative of the commercialization of memory. The show, broadcast to millions of viewers, must have garnered millions of dollars in advertising. Even as it commemorates the experiences of the hurricane victims, as well as the seeming generosity of the TV show's producers, the benefits to the network cannot be ignored; people will recall the storm, but they will also recall the network and its programming. Still, the monument is small compared to the giant replica of an electric guitar that looms nearby; across the street from the town green, the new Hard Rock Casino and Resort has opened. When sunlight hits the chrome and bounces off the building, it's the only thing you can see.

Inside, the Hard Rock Casino offers a strange counterpoint to the collection of homely objects in the Plexiglas memorial; the walls are covered with memorabilia—all of it supposedly authentic: shoes of famous rock stars, their clothing, instruments, jewelry. The casino had been set to open just before Katrina hit, and some memorabilia washed away in the storm. A small collection of what has been recovered—muddy and misshapen still, showing the effects of the disaster—reminds us that the casinos have suffered too, that they are like us in their appreciation of loss.

Farther down the beach a different kind of monument anchors the memory of the destruction of Katrina: live oaks that did not survive the storm. Rather than seeing them removed, a local chainsaw artist is transforming the dead trees into sculptures that depict the native species of animals on the coast—pelicans, turtles, dolphins, herons—all shaped to suggest movement and perhaps hope for the coast's environmental future.

The future of the Mississippi Gulf Coast's environment is tied to the stability of the wetlands, the possibility of rising tide levels—due, in part, to global warming rates—and the potential impact of humans and development along the coast. Since Mississippi governor Haley Barbour signed a new law allowing onshore gaming, returning casinos such as the Biloxi Grand, the Island View in Gulfport, and Treasure Bay have reopened on land. In March, Harrah's announced plans to construct Margaritaville Casino and Resort on the shores of Biloxi. Taking the place of a historic neighborhood, the project is expected to cost more than $700 million and is the single largest investment in Mississippi since the hurricane. The huge casino, hotel, and retail complex will claim prime, historic property near the Point Cadet area of Biloxi.

When I ask about the future of development in the area, Aesha tells me about the new FEMA requirements for housing elevation levels. "It makes rebuilding too expensive for many poor people," she says. The new regulations stipulate that homes can only be rebuilt twenty yards back from the road, but many homeowners' lots don't extend that far. "Now," she says, "it's likely that they'll be pushed out." It's not hard to imagine a future for the coast in which their absence in the face of the casinos transforms forever the historic character of the area into a glitzy corporate landscape. With the damage wrought by the storm to the seafood industry, the casinos are now the creators of the dominant economic narrative on the coast. They are visually dominant too.

This is perhaps one of the most apparent changes to the Gulf Coast. My brother imagines a future for the coast that resembles that of a resort and vacation town like Panama City. He says Biloxi will be "a nice city—but it just won't look like the old Biloxi." One of the hardest things Joe thinks the future holds for residents of the Gulf Coast is the cost of living. He has little confidence in the development of affordable housing. Only one person he knows lives in an apartment where the landlord didn't raise the rent by the roughly 70 percent that was commonplace in the months following the storm.

Even as he imagines a "nice city," Joe laments the commercial development of the coast by what he calls "out-of-towners"—corporations with big-business interests in the ports and the gaming industry. "So many landmarks are gone," he says, "replaced by something commercial. Everything seems artificial now, and there are only two local restaurants left on the beach—the rest are casino restaurants." Sitting with him in the bar of the Beau Rivage, I see the evidence of this, sometimes in small ways: a glass of wine I order—and pay more for—comes as a completely different, lesser one when we order a second round. When I say this to the bartender, he shrugs, then opens the bottle to pour me what I asked for. It seems a kind of fake, bait-and-switch culture of the new coast: maybe the bartender thought I wouldn't recognize the difference. Perhaps the notion that drives this idea will undergird the inscription of a new coast narrative. As visitors arrive—not knowing the former culture, the architecture, or the landscape—corporate narratives can prevail, cross-written over the small-town story.

Still, as much as Joe worries about the impact of the decisions of "out-of-towners," he points to the coast's growing diversity—its influx of newcomers—as one of the best outcomes of the rebuilding effort. I can see his point; in a region where the vestiges of racism hang on, played out in debates about "heritage" and the Confederate flag, and where only business leaders vote to do away with a symbol that divides rather than unites coast citizens under one banner, the arrival of newcomers must also signal a new coast, a new Mississippi. In their attempts to gain the patronage of all residents and visitors to the coast, businesses are helping to inscribe a more liberal narrative—at least one in which the only color is money green. Immigrants from Jamaica and Mexico are helping to inscribe a more multiethnic narrative, as did the Vietnamese immigrants of the 1970s and the Slovenian and Yugoslavian immigrants—and others of European and African descent—more than a century before that.

Conversely, the biggest loss to the coast Joe measures is in the displacement of the people. "I've lost a lot of friends," he says, describing a social network—a group of people with whom he gathered after work—that has all but disappeared.

People carry with them the blueprints of memory for a place. It is not uncommon to hear directions given in terms of landmarks that are no longer there: "turn right at the corner where the fruit stand used to be," or "across the street from the lot where Miss Mary used to live." Aesha tells me there are no recognizable landmarks along the coast anymore, and I see this too as I drive down the beach. No way to get your bearings. No way to feel at home, familiar with the land and cityscape. In time, the landmarks of destruction and rebuilding will overlap and intersect the memory of what was there—narrative and meta narrative—the pentimento of the former landscape shown only through the memories of the people who carry it with them. With fewer people in the area who remember the pre-Katrina landscape and culture, there's a much greater chance that it will be forgotten. Too, the memory of such events requires the collective efforts of a people—each citizen contributing to the narrative—so that a fuller version of the story can be told. In that way, one hope we can have for the future, beyond the necessities with which we must concern ourselves—environmentally sound rebuilding, fair and equal recovery—is the continuity of culture and heritage fostered by ongoing change and honest, inclusive remembrance of the past.

Rituals of commemoration serve to unite communities around collective memory, and at the second anniversary of the storm people gathered to remember—some at church or community centers, others at locations that held more private significance. Personal recollections are equally integral to the larger story. Johnny, a card dealer at one of the casinos—a friend of my brother's who did not leave—says that he stayed home to watch the national news. He wanted to see how the anniversary and the recovery were being understood outside the region. Then he took a kind of memorial drive—"just riding down the beach," he said, "trying to find places I used to go." Aesha marked the anniversary by donating blood. When I ask them both about what they do year round to keep the memory of the storm and its aftermath and about whether there is a danger in forgetting, Johnny takes the diplomatic approach:

"You have to learn from history," he says. Shaking her head, Aesha is more adamant about the memory of the storm. "There is no forgetting," she says. "You can't forget—you won't." In her words, an imperative, a command.

Some time ago—before the storm—my grandmother and I were shopping in Gulfport, and we met a friend of hers shopping with her granddaughter too. The woman introduced the girl to us by her nickname, then quickly added the child's given name. My grandmother, a proud woman—not to be outdone—replied, "Well, Tasha's name is really Nostalgia," drawing the syllables out to make the name seem more exotic. I was embarrassed and immediately corrected her—not anticipating that the guilt I'd feel later could be worse than my initial chagrin. Perhaps she was trying to say Natalya, the formal version, in Russian, to which Natasha is the diminutive.

At both names' Latin root: the idea of nativity, of the birthday of Christ. They share a prefix with words like natal, national, and native. "I write what is given me to write," Phil Levine has said. I've been given to thinking that it's my national duty, my native duty, to keep the memory of my Gulf Coast as talisman against the uncertain future. But my grandmother's misnomer is compelling too; she was onto something when she called me out with it.

I think of Hegel again: "When we turn to survey the past, the first thing we see is nothing but ruins." The first thing we see. The fears for the future, expressed by the people I spoke with on the coast, are driven by the very real landscape of ruin and by environmental and economic realities associated with development, but they are driven by nostalgia too. When we begin to imagine a future in which the places of our past no longer exist, we see ruin. Perhaps this is nowhere more evident than in my own relationship to the memory of my home.

Everywhere I go during my journey, I feel the urge to weep not only for the residents of the coast but also for my former self: the destroyed public library is me as a girl, sitting on the floor, reading between the stacks; empty, debris-strewn downtown Gulfport is me at the Woolworth's lunch counter—early 1970s—with my grandmother; is me listening to the sounds of shoes striking the polished tile floor of Hancock Bank, holding my grandmother's hand, waiting for candy from the teller behind her wicket; me riding the elevator of the J. M. Salloum Building—the same elevator my grandmother operated in the thirties; me waiting in line at the Rialto movie theater—gone for more years now than I can remember—where my mother also stood in line, at the back door, for the peanut gallery, the black section where my grandmother, still a girl, went on days designated colored only, clutching the coins she earned selling crabs; is me staring at my reflection in the glass at J. C. Penney's as my mother calls, again and again, my name. I hear it distantly, as through water or buffeted by wind: Nostalgia.

Names are talismans of memory too—Katrina, Camille. Perhaps this is why we name our storms.

When Camille hit in 1969, I was three years old. Across the street from my grandmother's house, the storm tore the roof off the Mount Olive Baptist Church. A religious woman, my grandmother believed the Lord had spared her home—a former shotgun to which more rooms had been added—and damaged, instead, the large red-brick church and many of the things inside, thus compelling her to more devotion. During renovation the church got a new interior: deep red carpet and red velvet draperies for the baptismal font—made by my grandmother, her liturgy to God's House. In went a new organ and a marble alter bearing the words Do This In Remembrance Of Me. As a child I was frightened by these words, the object—a long rectangle, like a casket—upon which they were inscribed; I believed quite literally that the marble box held a body. Such is the power of monumental objects to hold within them the weight of remembrance.

And yet I spent so little time in the church when I was growing up that I'm surprised now that so much of my thinking comes to me in the language of ceremony. But then, when I look up the word liturgy, I find that in the original Greek it meant, simply, one's public duty, service to the state undertaken by a citizen.

I am not a religious woman. This is my liturgy to the Mississippi Gulf Coast:

LITURGY

To the security guard staring at the Gulf
thinking of bodies washed away from the coast,
    plugging her ears
against the bells and sirens—sound of alarm—
    the gaming floor
on the coast;

To Billy Scarpetta, waiting tables on the coast,
    staring at the Gulf
thinking of water rising, thinking of New Orleans,
    thinking of cleansing
the coast;

To the woman dreaming of returning to the coast,
    thinking of water rising,
her daughter's grave, my mother's grave—underwater—
    on the coast;

To Miss Mary, somewhere;

To the displaced, living in trailers along the coast,
    beside the highway,

in vacant lots and open fields; to everyone who stayed
   on the coast,
who came back—or cannot—to the coast;

To those who died on the coast.
This is a memory of the coast: to each his own
recollections, her reclamations, their
restorations, the return of the coast.

This is a time capsule for the coast: words of the people
—*don't forget us*—
the sound of wind, waves, the silence of graves,
the muffled voice of history, bulldozed and buried
under sand poured on the eroding coast,
the concrete slabs of rebuilding the coast.

This is a love letter to the Gulf Coast, a praise song, a dirge,
invocation and benediction, a requiem for the Gulf Coast.

This cannot rebuild the coast; it is an indictment,
   a complaint,
my *logos*—argument and discourse—with the coast.

This is my *nostos*—my pilgrimage to the coast, my memory,
   my reckoning—

native daughter: I am the Gulf Coast.

Nine months after Katrina, I went home for the first time. Driving down Highway 49, after passing my grandmother's house, I went straight to the cemetery where my mother is buried. It was more ragged than usual—the sandy plots overgrown with weeds. The fence around it was still up, so I counted the entrances until I reached the fourth one, which opened onto the gravel road where I knew I'd find her. I searched first for the large, misshapen shrub that had always showed me to her grave, and found it gone. My own negligence had revisited me, and I stood there foolishly, a woman who'd never erected a monument on her mother's grave. I walked in circles, stooping to push back grass and weeds until I found the concrete border that marked the plots of my ancestors. It was nearly overtaken, nearly sunken beneath the dirt and grass. How foolish of me to think of monuments and memory, of inscribing the landscape with narratives of remembrance, as I stood looking at my mother's near-vanished grave in the post-Katrina landscape to which I'd brought my heavy bag of nostalgia. I see now that remembrance is an individual duty as well—a duty native to us as citizens, as daughters and sons. Private liturgy: I vow to put a stone here, emblazoned with her name.

Not far from the cemetery, I wandered the vacant lot where a church had been. Debris still littered the grass. Everywhere, there were pages torn from hymnals, Bibles, psalms pressed into the grass as if they were cemented there. I bent close, trying to read one; to someone driving by along the beach, I must have looked like a woman praying.

JESMYN WARD

Salvage the Bones (2011)

When Jesmyn Ward (b. 1977) writes of Bois Sauvage, a semifictional town on the Mississippi Gulf Coast, she writes of red dirt, seeping streams, and the undulating exchange between water and earth. In Ward's novel *Salvage the Bones*, Esch and the Batiste family live on the Mississippi coast at the edge of the Gulf during a precarious moment in time when Hurricane Katrina is approaching. Just as Faulkner's prose is deeply influenced and inspired by his part of Mississippi, so Ward's is by hers. In this selection, we encounter the family preparing for and then experiencing Hurricane Katrina. What is captivating about this writing is that it shows, in patient, poetic detail, the effects of this catastrophic event on a single family. It is almost an hour-by-hour description of how the family tries to contend with an unstoppable force and how tenuous the systems of support are for so many people along the coast. Ward's fiction is a testament to how the effects of climate change, even when not directly spoken about, inform the very creation of her literature. The growing intensity of storms and the lived experience of them direct the plot, affect the characters, and color the prose of this book.

Jesmyn Ward was raised in DeLisle, Mississippi, on the Gulf Coast. She is the author of three books of fiction and a memoir, and she edited the collection *The Fire This Time*. She has won two National Book awards, one in 2011 for *Salvage the Bones* and again in 2017 for her novel *Sing, Unburied, Sing.* Ward was awarded a MacArthur Fellowship in 2017. She is a professor of creative writing at Tulane University.

Works Cited

opher. "Creaturely, Throwaway Life after Katrina: *Salvage the Bones* and *Beasts of the Southern Wild.*" *South: A Scholarly Journal*, vol. 48, no. 2, 2016, p. 246-264.

first explained to me what a hurricane was, I thought that all the animals ran away, that they fled the storms before they came, that they put their noses to the wind days before and knew. That maybe they stuck their tongues out, pink and warm, to taste, to make sure. That the deer looked at their companions and leapt. That the foxes chattered to themselves, rolled their shoulders, and started off. And maybe the bigger animals do. But now I think that other animals, like the squirrels and the rabbits, don't do that at all. Maybe the small don't run. Maybe the small pause on their branches, the pine-lined earth, nose up, catch that coming storm air that would smell like salt to them, like salt and clean burning fire, and they prepare like us. The squirrels pack feathers, pack pine straw, pack shed fur and acorns from the oaks in the bowels of their trees, line them so that they are buried deep in the trunks, so safe they can hardly hear the storm cracking around them. The rabbits stand in profile, shank to shank, smell that storm smell that hits them all at once like a loud sound, and they tunnel down through the red clay and the sand, down until the earth turns black and cold, down past all the roots, until they have dug great halls so deep that they sit right above the underground reservoirs we tap into with our wells, and during the hurricane, they hear water lapping above and below while they sit safe in the hand of the earth.

Last night, we laid sleeping pallets in the living room, whose windows we'd lined with mismatched wood. Randall and I, side by side, on the floor, and Junior on the couch. We brought our own limp pillows, our flat and fitted sheets, and our old electric blankets short-circuited cold long ago. We piled them to create mattresses so flimsy we could feel the nubby carpet on the floor underneath us when we sat. We washed all the dishes. We filled the bathtub, the kitchen and the bathroom sinks to the brims with water that we could use for washing and flushing the toilet. We ate a few of the boiled eggs, and Randall cooked noodles for all of us. We balanced the hot bowls in our laps and watched TV. We took turns picking shows. Randall watched a home improvement show where a newlywed couple converted a room in their house from an office into a mint-green nursery. I chose a documentary on cheetahs. Junior picked last, and once there were cartoons on the screen, even after Junior fell asleep, we let them turn us bright colors in the dark. Daddy stayed in his room, but he left the door open. Skeetah stayed in his room with China and the puppies, but that door was closed.

Before I fell asleep, in the flickering light from the television and one dusty lamp, I read. In ancient Greece, for all her heroes, for Medea and her mutilated brother and her devastated father, water meant death. In the bathroom on the toilet, I heard the clanking of metal against metal outside, some broken machine tilting like a sinking headstone against another, and I knew it was the wind pushing a heavy rain.

On the day before a hurricane hits, the phone rings. When Mama was living, she picked it up; it is a phone call from the state government that goes out to everyone in the area who will be hit by a storm. Randall has answered it since we lost Mama; he lets it play at least once each summer. Skeetah answered once and hung up before the recording could get beyond the hello. Junior never has picked it up, and neither has Daddy. I picked it up for the first time yesterday. A man's voice speaks; he sounds like a computer, like he has an iron throat. I cannot remember exactly what he says, but I remember it in general. Mandatory evacuation. Hurricane making land fall tomorrow. If you choose to stay in your home and have not evacuated by this time, we are not responsible. You have been warned. And these could be the consequences of your actions. There is a list. And I do not know if he says this, but this is what it feels like: You can die.

This is when the hurricane becomes real.

The first hurricane that I remember happened when I was eight, and of the two or three we get every year, it was the worst I've ever been in. Mama let me kneel next to the chair she'd dragged next to the window. Even then, our boards were mismatched, and there were gaps we could peer out of, track the progress of the storm in the dark. The battery-operated radio told us nothing practical, but the yard did: the trees bending until almost breaking, arcing like fishing line, empty oil drums rattling across the yard, the water running in clear streams, carving canyons. Her stomach was big with Junior, and I laid a hand on it and watched. Junior was a surprise, a happy accident; she'd had me and Skeetah and Randall a year apart each, and then nothing else for nine years. I kneeled next to her and put my ear to her stomach and heard the watery swish of Junior inside her, as outside the wind pulled, branch by root, until it uprooted a tree ten feet from the house. Mama watched with her eye to the slit formed by the board over the window. She rocked from side to side like the baby in her would not let her sit still. She stroked my hair.

That storm, Elaine, had been a category 3. Katrina, as the newscaster said late last night after we settled in the living room, echoing Daddy, has reached a category 5.

During Elaine, Randall and Daddy had slept. Skeetah had sat on the other side of Mama, opposite me, and she'd told us about the big storm when she was little, the legend: Camille. She said Mother Lizbeth and Papa Joseph's roof was ripped off the house. She said the smell afterward was what she remembered most clearly, a smell like garbage set to rot, seething with maggots in the hot sun. She said the newly dead and the old dead littered the beaches, the streets, the woods. She said Papa Joseph found a skeleton in the yard, gleaming, washed clean of flesh and clothing, but she said it still stank like a bad tooth in the mouth. She said that Papa Joseph never took the remains down to the church, but carried it in an oyster sack out into the woods; she thought he buried the bones there. She said she and Mother Lizbeth walked miles for water from an artesian well.

She said she got sick, and most everybody did, because even then the water wasn't clean, and she had dreamed that she could never get away from water because she couldn't stop shitting it or pissing it or throwing it up. She said there would never be another like Camille, and if there was, she didn't want to see it.

I fell asleep after everyone else did last night, and now I wake before everyone. Daddy snores so loudly I can hear him from his room. Randall sleeps with his face turned to the sofa Junior is asleep on, his back to me, curved like he hides something. Junior has one arm off the sofa, one leg, and his cover hangs from him. The TV is dead. The house is quiet in a way it never is, its electric hum silent; in our sleep, the arriving storm has put a strangling hand over the house. We've lost power. Through the crack in the living room window, the morning is dark gray and opaque as dirty dishwater. The rain clatters on the rusted tin roof. And the wind, which yesterday only made itself known by sight, sighs and says, Hello. I lay here in the dark, pull my thin sheet up to my neck, stare at the ceiling, and do not answer.

Mama had talked back to Elaine. Talked over the storm. Pulled us in in the midst of it, kept us safe. This secret that is no longer a secret in my body: Will I keep it safe? If I could speak to this storm, spell it harmless like Medea, would this baby, the size of my fingernail, my pinkie fingernail, maybe, hear? Would speaking make it remember me once it is born, make it know me? Would it look at me with Manny's face, with his golden skin, with my hair? Would it reach out with its fingers, pink, and grasp?

The sun will not show. It must be out there, over the furious hurricane beating itself against the coastline like China at the tin door of the shed when she wants to get out and Skeet will not let her. But here on the Pit, we are caught in the hour where the sun is hidden beyond the trees but hasn't escaped over the horizon, when it is coming and going, when light comes from everywhere and nowhere, when everything is gray.

I lie awake and cannot see anything but that baby, the baby I have formed whole in my head, a black Athena, who reaches for me. Who gives me that name as if it is mine: Mama. I swallow salt. That voice, ringing in my head, is drowned out by a train letting out one long, high blast. And then it disappears, and there is only the sound of the wind like a snake big enough to swallow the world sliding against mountains. And then the wind like a train, again, and the house creaks. I curl into a ball.

"Did you hear that?"

It is Skeetah; I can barely see him. He is only a wash of greater darkness that moves in the dark opening of the hallway.

"Yeah," I say. My voice sounds like I have a cold, all the mucus from my crying lodged in my nose. *A train*, Mama said. *Camille came, and the wind sounded like trains.* Then Mama told me this, I put my nose in her knee. I'd heard trains before when we went swimming on the oyster shell beach, and the train that ran through the middle of St. Catherine would sound loudly in the distance. I could not imagine wind sounding like that. But now I hear, and I can.

"Where's the lamp?"

"On the table," I squeaked. Skeetah walked toward the table, bumping into things in the half-light, and fumbled the kerosene lantern to light.

"Come on," Skeetah says, and I follow him to the back of the house, to his and Randall's room, which seems smaller than it is, and close and hot and red in the light of a smaller kerosene lamp that Skeet must have found in the shed. He shuts the door behind us after eyeing Daddy's open door. The wind shrieks. Trees reach out their arms and beat their limbs against the house. Skeet sits on his bed next to China, who sprawls and lifts her head to look at me lazily, and who licks her nose and mouth in one swipe. I climb onto Randall's bed, hug my knees. The puppies' bucket is quiet.

"You scared?"

"No," Skeetah says. He rubs a hand from the nape of China's neck over her shoulder, her torso, her thigh. She lets her head roll back and licks again.

"I am," I say. "I never heard the wind sound like that."

"We ain't even on the bay. We back far enough up in the trees to be all right. All these Batistes been living up here all these years through all these hurricanes and they been all right. I'm telling you."

"Remember when Mama told us that the wind sounded like that when Camille hit?" I squeeze tighter. "Elaine wasn't nothing like this."

"Yeah, I remember." Skeetah rubs his fingers under China's chin, and it is like he is coaxing something from her because she leans toward him and grins, tries to kiss him. "I can remember her saying it." He stops rubbing

China, leans forward to put his elbows on his knees, rubs his hands together, looks away. "But I can't remember her voice," he says. "I know the exact words she said, can see us sitting there by her lap, but all I can hear is my voice saying it, not hers."

I want to say that I know her voice. I want to open my mouth and have her voice slide out of me like an impression, to speak Mama alive for him as I hear her. But I can't.

"At least we got the memory," I say. "Junior don't have nothing."

"You remember the last thing she said to you?"

When Mama was birthing Junior, she put her chin down into her chest. She panted and moaned. The ends of her moans squeaked, sounded like bad brakes grinding when a car stops. She never screamed, though. Skeetah and Randall and I were sneaking, standing on an old air-conditioning unit outside her and Daddy's window, and after she pushed Junior out, once he started crying, she let her head fall to the side, her eyes like mirrors, and she was looking at us, and I thought she would yell at us to get down out of the window, to stop being nosy. But she didn't. She saw us. She blinked slow. The skin above her nose cracked and she bit her lip. She shook her head then, raised her chin to the ceiling like an animal on the slaughter stump, like I've seen Daddy and Papa Joseph hold pigs before the knife, and closed her eyes. She started crying then, her hands holding her belly below her deflated stomach, soft as a punctured kickball. I had never seen her cry. But she hadn't said anything, even after Daddy called some of their friends, Tilda and Mr. Joe, to the house to watch us, even after he carried her and Junior out to the truck and she slumped against the window, watching us as Daddy drove away. Shaking her head. Maybe that meant no. Or *Don't worry—I'm coming back.* Or *I'm sorry.* Or *Don't do it. Don't become the woman in this bed, Esch,* she could have been saying. But I have.

"No," I say. "I don't remember."

"I do," Skeetah says, and he props his chin on his fists. "She told us she loved us when she got into the truck. And then she told us to be good. To look after each other."

"I don't remember that." I think Skeetah is imagining it.

"She did." Skeetah sits up, leans back in the bed again, and lays a still hand on China's neck. She sighs. "You look like her. You know that?"

"No."

"You do. You not as big as her, but in the face. Something about your lips and eyes. The older you get the more you do."

I don't know what to say, so I half grimace, and I shake my head. But Mama, Mama always here. See? I miss her so badly I have to swallow salt, imagine it running like lemon juice into the fresh cut that is my chest, feel it sting.

"Did you hear that?"

"What?" I sound stuffed again. Leaves slap the roof in great bunches. The rain is heavy, endless, hits the roof in quick crashing waves. At least the wind doesn't sound like a train again.

"That," Skeetah says, his head to one side, his ear cocked toward the window. His eyes gleam in the light of the lamp. He stands up, and China stands up with him, ears straight, tail pointed, tongue gone. Somewhere out in the storm, a dog is barking.

"Yeah," I say, and then all three of us are at the window, peering out of the light edge left by the boards. We hear the dog but can't see it; what we do see is the pines, the thin trees bending with the storm, bending almost to breaking. Even the oaks are losing leaves and branches in the gray light, the beating rain. The dog barks loudly, fast as a drum, and something about the way the bark rises at the end reminds me of Mama's moans, of those bowing pines, of a body that can no longer hold itself together, of something on the verge of breaking. The high notes are little rips. It circles the house, its bark near and far. Is it one of Junior's mutts, his mangy family member, seeking shelter, the cool bottom of a house and a knobby-kneed boy and no rain?

"We can't." Skeetah leans toward the window as if he could push his way through the glass and board and save that invisible dog, who for him, I know, must be China. She drops from where she has been standing on her hind legs with her paws pressed against the wall and leans into Skeetah's side, head-butts his thigh, her smooth white head and floppy ears as soft as the swaddling blankets that Daddy brought Junior home in after he returned from the hospital and Mama didn't. *This your little brother. Claude Adam Batiste the second. Call him Junior.* And then, *Your mama didn't make it.* The searching dog barks one last time before the rain and wind tighten like a choke collar and silence him. China growls in answer, but swallows it when Skeetah kneels before her, takes her face in his hands, and smoothes her ears back so that her eyes are slits and she grins and her skin pulls tight and her head could be a naked skull.

China squeals and jumps up into a bark, skitters back and forth across Skeetah's bed, over his knees; this is what makes me look up from my crouch on Randall's bed, from my stomach, from me trying to burrow into myself, to safety. China looks to the ceiling, her teeth gleaming in the dark, ripping barks.

"China, what's . . . ?" Skeetah reaches out to grab her, to stop her from curling and running, and there is a loud, deafening boom. When it comes, China leaps from Skeetah's bed and rushes to the door as if she would rip the wood to splinters with her teeth. Skeetah yanks the door open, and Randall is running into Daddy's room with a lantern, Junior clinging to his waist while the wind yells outside and the house shudders. There was no need for the lamp; there is a hole in the ceiling in Daddy's room, the trunk and branches of a tree tossing in the opening. It is a large bush growing wrong. China barks, her nose to the wind.

"Daddy!" Randall runs forward into the wind and rain streaming through the gaping hole, the gray day fisting through it. Daddy is on his knees in front of the dresser, pushing an envelope down his pants. He stands and sees us.

"Go on!" Daddy says. He waves at us, the bandage on his wounded hand flashing light. He is slack and then tight like a clothesline catching in the wind, and he shoves us out of the ruined room and into the hallway, pulling the door shut behind him. Junior will not let go of Randall.

"We'll stay in the living room." Daddy says this as he slumps over on the sofa, pushing his head back into the cushion like Mama pushed hers back into the pillow, baring his neck. He's blinking too much.

"Your hand," Randall says.

"It's fine," says Daddy. "We going to stay here until the storm's over."

"When you think?" Skeetah asks.

"A few hours."

China squeals and barks again.

"She knew," I say.

"Knew what?" Daddy's face is wet, and I don't know whether it is water or sweat.

"Nothing," Skeetah says.

"About the tree," I say at the same time. Skeetah rubs China's neck, and she gives a swallowed growl and sits, lays her head along Skeetah's thigh and up his hip, her nose to him.

"She didn't know nothing," Skeetah says, and then he and China step as one, a new animal, toward the light opening of the hallway where the wind whistles in a thin sheet under Daddy's door. They are going back to Skeetah and Randall's room.

"Come in the living room, Skeet," Daddy says. He rolls his eyes, closes them. Bares his teeth. "Please."

I pick my blankets up, wrap them around me, and sit where I had lain. Skeetah walks back in with China, sets the bucket and China's food and leashes and toys in the corner of the living room farthest away from Daddy, next to the TV. Skeetah lays his blanket against the corner, makes a chair, and China drapes herself across his lap, long and white, and lays her head along her paw and begins licking the pink pads of her feet. Skeetah rubs her, sets his small kerosene lamp down, and in the half-dark, China gleams butter yellow with the flame.

"Junior," Randall says, "I know you ain't pee yourself."

Junior leans over, touches the ground beneath his butt, his face in his thighs.

"I didn't do that."

"Then why it's all wet over here?"

We have been sitting in the living room, terrified and bored. I'm trying to read by the oil lamp, but the sound of the words are not coming together over the sound of the wind and the rain relentlessly bearing down on the house; they are fragments. Jason has remarried, and Medea is wailing. *An exile, oh God, oh God, alone.* And then: *By death, oh, by death, shall the conflict be decided. Life's little day ended.* I shut the book, don't even mark my place, and sit on it. I am cold. Skeetah and China look like they've fallen asleep, his hand on her flank and her breastbone on his knee, but when Randall says this, their eyes open to slits at the same time. The half deck of UNO cards that Randall had been attempting to teach Junior how to play stick to the floor around Junior's legs. I shrug out of my covers; the thin stream of air that whispers from under Daddy's door brushes past me like a boy in a school hallway, insistent and brusque, and *Why are my shorts wet? Is it gone? Am I bleeding? Shouldn't I be cramping?* I stand. The floor underneath me is dark.

China rolls to her feet, her teeth out, and Skeetah grabs her by her scruff as she lunges. He holds her still. He stands, looking calmly about the room.

"It's water. It's coming in the house," Skeetah says.

"Ain't no water coming in the house. Wood just getting a little damp from the rain," Daddy says.

"It's coming up through the floor," says Skeetah.

"Ain't nowhere for it to come from." Daddy waves at the room, waves like he's stopping one of us from giving him something he doesn't want: his antibiotics, a letter from a teacher, a school fundraising brochure.

"Look," Randall says, and he walks over to the window facing the street and bends like an old man, peering out. "Lot of trees on the road."

"But you don't see no water," Daddy says.

"No."

Skeetah and China walk past Junior, who stands where Randall left him in front of the sofa. Junior is picking up each foot, setting it down; he looks at the bottoms as if he cannot believe that he has feet and that they are wet. He pulls his shorts away from him, but they stick anyway. Skeetah peers out of the window, with China next to him.

"There," Skeetah says. Randall and I run to the window at Skeetah's side, but Junior is there first, and we are all over each other, our feet wet, the carpet a soaked sponge where we stand, Daddy looking at the window like it isn't boarded up, like he can see through it.

There is a lake growing in the yard. It moves under the broken trees like a creeping animal, a wide-nosed snake. Its head disappears under the house where we stand, its tail wider and wider, like it has eaten something greater than itself, and that great tail stretches out behind it into the woods, toward the Pit. China barks. The wind ripples the water and it is coming for us.

There is water over my toes.

"The Pit," Randall sighs.

Daddy gets up then, walks slowly over to the window, each bone bent the wrong way in each joint. Randall moves so Daddy can see out of the crack.

"No," Daddy says.

I shift, and the water licks my ankles. It is cold, cold as a first summer swim. China barks, and when she jumps down from the window and bounces, there is a splash.

"Daddy?" Randall says. He puts his arm over Junior, who, cringing with his eyes wide, hugs Randall's leg. But for once, Randall's arm doesn't look like metal, like ribbon, like stone; it bends at the elbow, soft, without muscle, and looks nothing but human.

"Daddy!" Junior squeals, but he buries his face in Randall's hip, and Randall's hip eats the end of the word. Junior rises an inch or so; he must be on his toes. The water is up to the middle of my calf.

"Look," I say.

There is something long and dark blue between the trees. It is a boat. Someone has come to save us. But then I squint and the wind lags clear for one second, and it is not a boat, and no one has come to save us. It is Daddy's truck. The water has picked it up, pushed it from the Pit. The snake has come to eat and play.

"Your truck," Skeetah says.

Daddy begins to laugh.

The snake has swallowed the whole yard and is opening its jaw under the house.

"Open the attic," Daddy says.

The water is lapping the backs of my knees.

"It's stuck," Randall says. He is pulling at the string that hangs from the door of the attic, which is in the ceiling of the hallway.

"Move," says Skeetah.

The water is tonguing its way up my thighs. Skeetah hands me the puppies' bucket.

"Hurry," Randall says.

The three puppies squeal little yips that sound like whispered barks. These are their first words.

"Pull down," Daddy says. He frowns, holds his hand up like he is pulling the cord.

The water slides past my crotch, and I jump.

"All right!" Skeet yells. He pulls himself up on the cord, like he is swinging from a swing rope in a tree, and the attic door groans downward.

"Up!" Randall says, and he is shoving Junior up the ladder into the attic. China is swimming next to Skeetah, her head bobbing like a buoy.

"Go!" Skeetah says, and he pushes me toward the ladder. I float on the water, my toes dragging on the hallway carpet. He grabs my back and steadies me as I slog into the attic with the bucket. "Esch," Junior says.

"I'm here." Junior's eyes are white in the dark. The wind beats the roof, and it creaks. Randall is next, then Daddy, and last, Skeetah and China. I cup the bucket with my knees, sit on a pile of boxes, fish out a broken ornament that is digging into my thigh. Christmas decorations. Randall is sitting on an old chain saw, Junior cowering next to him. Daddy takes out the package he put in his pants after the tree fell into his room. It is a clear plastic bag. He opens the packet, pulls out pictures. Just before Skeetah pulls shut the attic door, seals us in darkness, Daddy makes as if he would touch one of the pictures, hesitant, as lightly as if he is dislodging an eyelash, but his glistening finger stops short, and he wraps the pictures again and puts them in his pants. *Mama*.

The attic door moans shut.

The roof is thin; we can hear every fumbling rush of the wind, every torrent of rain. And it is so dark that we cannot see each other, but we hear China barking, and her bark sounds like a fat dog's, so deep, like dense cloth ripping.

"Quiet, China!" Skeetah says, and China shuts her jaw so quickly and so hard, I can hear the click of her teeth shuttering together. I put my face down in the bucket; the puppies do not hear. They mewl still. I feel them with my hand, still downy, their coats just now turning to silk, and they squirm at my touch. The white, the brindle, the black and white. They lick for milk.

"The house," Randall says, and his voice is steady, calm, but I can hardly contain the panic I feel when the house tilts, slowly as an unmoored boat.

"It's the water," Skeetah says. "It's the water."

"Shit!" Daddy yells, and then we are all bracing in the dark as the house tilts again.

"Water," I say.

"It never came back here." Daddy breathes. "The damn creek."

"Daddy," I say, and I'm surprised at how clear my voice is, how solid, how sure, like a hand that can be held in the dark. "Water's in the attic."

The water is faster this time; it wraps liquid fingers around my toes, my ankles, begins creeping up my calves. This is a fast seduction. The wind howls.

"There was a family . . . ," Randall says.

"We know," Daddy says. Fourteen of them drowned in Camille. In their attic. The house lifts up off of its bricks again, and rocks.

"We're not drowning in this fucking attic," Skeet says, and I hear a banging, again and again. I look up and debris falls in my eyes. He is beating at the inside of the roof. He is making a way.

"Move," Randall says. "Junior, go by Esch." And I feel Junior's little pin fingers on my wrists, and he bangs into something, and he is a monkey on top of the bucket, locked to my lap. "I got it."

Randall is swinging something in the dark, and when it crashes into the roof, it makes a dent, a chink of light. He bashes the wood, grunts.

Whatever he swings is making a hole. He swings it again, and the wood opens to a small hole no bigger than my finger, and I see that he is swinging the chain saw, hitting the roof with the blunt end.

"Any gas"—Randall bashes—"in here?"

"Can't remember," Daddy yells. The storm speaks through the hole, funnels wind and rain through. We squint toward it. The water is over my crotch. The house lists.

Randall cranks once, twice. He pulls the cord back a third time and it catches, and the saw buzzes to life. He shoves it through the finger-wide opening, cuts a jagged line, draws it back out, cuts another jagged line, a parenthesis, before it chugs to a stop. He tries to crank it again, but it will not start. He swings it instead, an awkward hammer, and the wood cracks, bends outward. He swings again, and the closed eyelid he drew with the cutting saw, with the blows, flutters, and the roof opens. The storm screams, I have been waiting far you. Light floods the flooded attic, close as a coffin. Randall grabs Junior, who swings around and clings to his back, his small hands tight as clothespins, and Randall climbs out and into the hungry maw of the storm.

It is terrible. It is the flailing wind that lashes like an extension cord used as a beating belt. It is the rain, which stings like stones, which drives into our eyes and bids them shut. It is the water, swirling and gathering and spreading on all sides, brown with an undercurrent of red to it, the clay of the Pit like a cut that won't stop leaking. It is the remains of the yard, the refrigerators and lawn mowers and the RV and mattresses, floating like a fleet. It is trees and branches breaking, popping like Black Cat firecrackers in an endless crackle of explosions, over and over and again and again. It is us huddling together on the roof, me with the wire of the bucket handle looped over my shoulder, shaking against the plastic. It is everywhere. Daddy kneels behind us, tries to gather all of us to him. Skeetah hugs China, and she howls. Daddy's truck careens slowly in the yard.

Skeetah is hunched over, picking at his jeans. He takes off his pants, tries to hold them still in front of him; the legs whip in the wind. He shoves China's back legs into the crotch, and then he flings one pant leg over his shoulder, and the other he tucks under his underarm.

"Tie it!" Skeetah yells.

I tie it in a knot. My fingers are stiff and numb. I pull the wet fabric as hard as I can, test it. China's head and legs are smashed to his chest, pinned under the fabric. She is his baby in a sling, and she is shaking.

"Look!" Skeet says and points. I follow his finger to the hollow carcass of Mother Lizbeth and Papa Joseph's house. The top half and the eaves of the house are above water. "It's on a hill!" Skeetah screams.

"How are we going to get there?" Randall yells.

"The tree!" Skeetah is inching down the roof to a spreading oak tree that touches our house and stretches to MaMa's house.

It rises like a jungle gym over the seething water. "We're going to climb the tree!"

"No!" Daddy yells. "We're going to stay here!"

"What if the water keeps coming?" Randall asks. "Better for us to take that chance than stay here and drown!"

Junior's teeth are sealed together, his lips peeled back. His eyes are blasted open. As Randall picks his way down the roof toward the branch, Junior looks back. Randall braces an arm across his chest, holds Junior's arm.

"Just like the first time we swam in the pit, Junior! Hold on!" Randall crouches at the edge of the roof with Skeetah, both of them hunched like birds, feathers ruffled against the bad wind, both of them holding their bundles closely. Skeetah leaps.

He catches the closest ricocheting branch, lands half in and half out of the water. China yelps and begins to struggle, but Skeetah grips her harder with one arm and pulls himself down the branch until it bows to the water. And then he leaps again, for the next whipping branch. He jumps and grabs. I reshoulder my bucket, pick my way toward the edge. The wind flattens me down to the roof. Randall leaps, lands on the same close branch with his stomach, his arms iron again, binding Junior to him. Both Skeetah and Randall scramble along the half-naked branches of the oak with one arm and both legs, using the limbs to pull themselves and their burdens until they reach water, when they kick their feet, scoot back up the branch, and leap for the next whipping limb. Randall stops, braces himself on the branch, looks back.

"Come on!" he yells.

I grip the tin with my toes, my fingers, crouched on my haunches at the edge of the roof. Readjust the bucket. My heart is a wounded bird, beating its wings against the cage of my ribs. I don't think I can breathe.

"Jump," Daddy says.

I lean out and leap.

The hurricane enfolds me in its hand. I glide. I land on the thickest branch, the wood gouging me, the bucket clanging, unable to breathe, my eyes tearing up. I scramble at the wood, pull myself along the branch, my feet in and out of the water, the steel handle to the bucket digging into my shoulder, my living burden already so heavy. The bare bones of Mother Lizbeth's house are so far away; I do not know if I can carry it that far. I inch to the end of the branch where it plunges beneath the water to join the trunk of the tree, and I dig in with my hands and feet. Clutch. Jump. Catch the next branch, where Randall is waiting. The branches we are grasping and grabbing shudder, twist in the water and air. The little branches whip like clotheslines come unpinned. It is an animal, alive, struggling against the water, trying to shove us off its back.

I look back to see Daddy hurtling through the air. He hits the branch so hard with his torso that his body jack knifes and his face is almost in the water. He is shocked still; he's knocked the wind out of himself. He looks up at us, blinks. Whispers it, but we cannot hear it, only see it. Go.

Skeetah has worked his way to the middle of the tree, which buds out of the water, and he is swimming and thrusting from branch to branch. We follow him through the whipping branches, the undulating water. Through plastic bags that skim the surface of the flood like birds. Through the clothesline that knots the branches like fishing net. Through our clothes, swept from the flooded house. Through the plywood, ripped from the windows, pried away by the teeth of the storm. Through the rain that comes down in curtains, sluicing against Daddy's lazily spinning truck, the detritus, until we cluster at the end of the farthest-reaching branch, the one closest to the grandparents' house. We clutch each other and the swaying branches. China is pawing at Skeetah's breast, snapping her head back and forth. She is jerking away from him, and he clutches her with one white-tipped hand. The bucket feels like it's tearing the skin on my shoulder, feels like I'm carrying three grown dogs instead of three puppies. Where barely the top of the tree had been visible at our house, the branches here are clearly above the flood. The water here comes up to the middle of the closest window: the house must have been built on a small hill, and we never noticed it.

"I'ma swim, break the window. Y'all come in," Skeetah says.

"Hurry," Randall says.

"Esch, you come with me!" Skeetah says.

"This ain't the time!" Daddy yells.

"This ain't about the puppies!" Skeetah squints at me.

"She too small!" Daddy hollers. He grabs my free elbow with his good hand. Grips.

"She's pregnant." Skeetah points.

Daddy's face shuts, and he pushes.

Daddy saw it, that second before he pushed me. My big T-shirt and my shorts fitting me like a second skin, sodden with water. Where I used to be all sharp elbows and thighs straight as pines and a stomach like a paved road, my wet clothes show the difference. Daddy saw the curve of a waist, the telltale push of a stomach outward. Daddy saw fruit. I'm flailing backward with the bucket, the squeaking puppies. And in that second after he pushes me, Daddy is reaching out with his good hand, his bad hand hooked to the branch he crouches on, his eyes open and hurt and sorry as I haven't seen him since he handed Junior over to me and Randall, said, Your mama—and I kick, grasping at the air, but the hurricane slaps me, and I land in the water on my back, the puppies flying out of the bucket, their eyes open for the first time to slits and, I swear, judging me as they hit.

"Esch!" Randall yells, and Junior tightens his legs like a looping shoe-string across Randall's waist. Randall grips Junior's shins, those legs thin as rulers. Randall can't jump in. "Swim!" he screams.

I kick my legs and palm water, but I can barely keep my head above it. It is a fanged pink open mouth, and it is swallowing me.

"Fuck!" Skeetah yells. He looks down at China, who is thrusting up and against his sling.

"Esch!" Junior screams, and the water is dragging me sideways, away from the window, out into the yard, toward the gullet of the Pit. I snatch at the puppy closest to me, the brindle, which is limp in my hand, and shove it down my shirt. The white and the black-and-white have disappeared.

"Fuck!" Skeetah screams. He grabs China's head, whispers something to her as she scrabbles against him. Her teeth show and she jerks backward away from him. She writhes. Her torso is out of the sling he has made. Skeetah grabs China by the head and pulls and her body comes out and she is scrambling. She flies clear of him, twists in the air to splash belly first in the water. She is already swimming, fighting. Skeetah jumps.

The water swallows, and I scream. My head goes under and I am tasting it, fresh and cold and salt somehow, the way tears taste in the rain. The babies, I think. I kick extra hard, like I am running a race, and my head bobs above the water but the hand of the hurricane pushes it down, down again. Who will deliver me? And the hurricane says sssssssshhhhhhhh. It shushes me through the water, with a voice muffled and deep, but then I feel a real hand, a human hand, cold and hard as barbed wire on my leg, pulling me back, and then I am being pushed up and out of the water, held by Skeet, who is barely treading, barely keeping me and him afloat. China is a white head, spinning away in the relentless water, barking, and Skeetah is looking from her to me, screaming, Hurry up! Hurry up! at Randall, who is breaking what was left of the glass and wood of the window with his hands, his shoulders, his elbows, and diving through, while Junior clings to him close as a shell, and Skeetah is pushing me through the window, his hand a leash loop wrapped too tightly around my arm, his other hand treading, and he is calling, China, come China, but she is nowhere, and Daddy is swimming and sinking and jerking toward us, his bad hand flashing, and he is through the window and we are all struggling, grabbing at walls, at broken cabinets, at wood, until Randall stretches his way up to the open ceiling and hauls himself and Junior into the half-eaten attic, where the hurricane fingers the gaping roof, and Skeet pushes me up and through while Randall almost breaks my wrist with his grip as he hauls me up, and then Skeetah kicks off of something buried under the flood and is up and through the opening, and Daddy is on his back in the water below, treading with one hand and two feet, and Randall is hollering, Help him! and Skeet is laying next to the hole in the attic floor, looking at us, his face sick, twisted, and he is reaching a hand down to Daddy, hoisting him up, and the puppy must be dead in my shirt because it is not moving and I pull it out as I cough and cough up the water and the hurricane and the pit and I can't stop and Skeetah is braced, looking out the ravaged roof calling China, watching her cut through the swirling water straight as a water moccasin into the whipping, fallen woods in the distance, and Junior is rocking back and forth, squatting on the balls of his feet, his hands over his eyes because he does not want to see anymore; he is wailing NoNoNoNoNoNoNoNoNoNoNO.

DAVID GESSNER

*The Tarball Chronicles: A Journey Beyond the Oiled Pelican
and Into the Heart of the Gulf Oil Spill* (2011)

In 2010, David Gessner (b. 1961) drove his pickup from Florida to Louisiana, following the Gulf Coast to talk with fishermen, restaurant workers, journalists, and scientists about the effects of the explosion of the Deepwater Horizon oil rig and the BP oil spill and its persistent impact on the Gulf. *The Tarball Chronicles: A Journey Beyond the Oiled Pelican and Into the Heart of the Gulf Oil Spill*, published in 2011, grew out of this trip. In the book, Gessner investigates why BP sprayed powerful chemical dispersants to sink oil to the Gulf floor and for what reasons the international company directed the effort instead of local or federal government, among other questions. His narration questions the way American energy systems control the economy, while recognizing that he himself is fueling up his vehicle despite his deep concern for the environment. In the excerpt included here, Gessner accompanies a scientist on a walk through a marsh near Mobile, Alabama, in an effort to determine the effects of the oil spill. The walk is enlightening if only to demonstrate the complexity of nature's reaction to such devastation and ultimately, the difficulty of knowing what that will be in the long run. *The Tarball Chronicles* won the 2012 Reed Award for Best Book on the Southern Environment and the 2013 Association for the Study of Literature and Environment's Best Book Award.

David Gessner has proven to be a compelling and versatile environmental writer. Among his ten books, *Return of the Osprey: A Season of Flight and Wonder* in 2001 cast him on the national scene as an important new voice. Gessner is founder of *Ecotone Magazine* and teaches at University of North Carolina, Wilmington.

Fall is coming and the world jitters with movement. Right now up in Minnesota loons are stirring. Soon they will leave the Northern lakes for which their calls serve as a signature and fly down to the Gulf for the winter. These sleek, dark diving birds will arrive by the millions and will plunge deep into the oily Gulf. Meanwhile Ryan's ducks are already on the move, blue-winged teal and scaups among them, and by late August they, too, will pour into the Gulf.

The early waves of birds are sweeping through, an advance wave of a massive exodus that will funnel down the great corridor of the Mississippi before making the bold move across the Gulf, linking the northern hemisphere to the southern. "Bird migration is the world's only true unifying natural phenomenon," writes Scott Weidensaul, "stitching the continents together in a way that even the great weather systems fail to do." The birds might as well trail thread behind them and hold needles in their bills, so obvious is this stitching.

Before I left for this trip I talked to as many bird people as I could about the coming migration.

"Imagine running a marathon in bad air," said Laura Erickson, of the Cornell Lab of Ornithology. "Well, for many species this is their marathon and conditions need to be just right."

For some birds the marathon includes a six-hundred-mile water crossing over the Gulf. Which means a marathon following the supermarathon that is the overland central corridor migration itself. Over a billion birds flying down the middle of the country, a migration containing not just a stunning number of birds but also a stunning variety.

Migration is always a gambit where everything has to be perfect, birds building up body fat from high-quality sources of food at certain stopover points. Imagine if the fish a migrating bird eats is compromised, or if a certain sandpiper can't find a certain crustacean, or an abundance of certain crustaceans, where it has reliably found them before.

Of course none of the scientists I've talked to claim to know exactly what the results of the spill will be, either short-term or long. They are cautious, and everyone I speak to is understandably quick to use caveats and qualifiers, which leads to other questions. Not only do we not know the results, but we may not know them for years. How will we gauge the ultimate effects of the spill?

Back in Alabama, at the Dauphin Island Sea Lab, I spoke with Senior Marine Scientist John Dindo. His was a brand new building but the air-conditioning had died on July 1 so fans blasted us as we talked.

"There is a whole lot of unaccounted oil out there and what happens to that oil is the big question."

He adjusted one of the fans on his desk so that it pointed straight at me. I was grateful.

"I'm not too worried about animals. Animals are highly resilient. For the most part they can repopulate an area in a short time. But habitats are not resilient. Habitats that get affected by the oil cause a cascade effect. All the way up and down the food chain."

But Dindo stopped short of pronouncing that the oily apocalypse was upon us. He was reluctant to make any grand conclusions and was skeptical of those who were doing so.

"Scientists should not be making bold, definitive statements at this time. It is tempting, but what we should really be concerned with is not today or tomorrow, but a potential decadal situation. Anyone who makes a bold statement at this point doesn't know what they're saying."

I liked this. BP's great flaw was certainty, and scientists and environmentalists should be wary of mirroring this flaw. It seems to me that the only real conclusion at this point, the only truly scientific conclusion, can be summed up in five words: we just don't fucking know.

This morning I begin a migration of my own. I am not driving home, however, not yet. What I am doing makes no sense really. Yesterday my wife and I were supposed to close on our new house, our first after years of migrating from north to south. We've decided to settle on, and in, a home off a salt marsh in North Carolina.

The seller is upset that I'm not back and is threatening to pull out. I swear to him and the Realtor and to my wife that I'll be back, even if I have to hitchhike or crawl. I will be back Monday, I tell them, though to be honest I still hate the thought of leaving this place. Maybe it's just that end-of-a-trip feeling, but I decide that before I leave I need to make one more stop. And so, rather than immediately heading north and east as I should, I point the car west toward Texas. My goal is to get to Galveston. The trouble is that it just happens to be eight hundred miles in the wrong direction. I drive fast and turn up the music.

One reason I'm heading to Galveston is that it almost perfectly embodies the theories of the straight-line thinkers like Orrin Pilkey's bete noire, the Army Corps of Engineers. The story of the city, its early drowning and recent redrowning during Hurricane Ike, is as simple and powerful as a fairy tale, though a grim old-fashioned fairy tale of the sort New Orleanians might read to scare their children. Or you could imagine Orrin Pilkey taking the owner of some coastal condo on his knee and telling the story in a frightening whisper. Either way it's the story of a people who believed in straight lines, a story of a people who built high walls, thinking they could stop the sea, and a story of how those walls ultimately doomed the city. In the summer of 1900, Galveston, which was then a thriving port town, was struck by a storm that remains the deadliest hurricane in United States history, killing 20 percent of the city's people and destroying all of its buildings. The town responded by vowing "never again" and constructing a massive seawall. But the wall has ultimately acted, as geologists like Orrin and others have warned it would, by destroying Galveston's beaches, its natural buffer and protection, leaving it beachless and therefore defenseless. Which led to this decade's disaster when Ike struck and wiped out the city again.

By heading this way I'm also following the refugee route of those who left New Orleans to spend their years in the diaspora of the Lone Star State. Cajuns among cowboys. Like Glennis of the Ninth Ward, they passed the years in trailers while back home their houses lay underwater or in soggy tatters.

Homes and homelessness are much on my mind. Back when I lived on Cape Cod, John Hay talked to me a lot about the idea of home. He had lived in the same place for almost sixty years and he spoke of our need to "marry" the places where we live, to spend a lifetime learning the land and people. He also believed that many of our national troubles spring from a "great epidemic of homelessness."

"People are on the run everywhere these days," he told me. "As if they don't know where they live. Everyone seems intent on dispossessing themselves."

As I travel, I can't help but feel this is true. Most of us don't know where we live and those who do know are uprooted by circumstances beyond their control. We move and float, rootless and out of place. We have become a homeless nation, drifting, uprooted, unsure of where we are.

I want to be wary, however, of mere theoretical homelessness. At a time when more people are losing their actual homes, I need to watch my metaphors. I think of my brother, who was homeless for a while on the streets of Austin. His time on the streets affected him in many ways, but one of the smaller consequences was literary. He could no longer stand to read Jack Kerouac.

"I read *On the Road* when I was in a homeless shelter in Texas," he said. "I hated it. Kerouac was *playing* at being a bum. He doesn't know anything about it." Rootlessness was no longer a playful thing to him.

In the book *Turtle Island*, Gary Snyder exhorts his readers to "find your place on the planet. Dig in, and take responsibility from there." Two people who have taken his advice—to dig in and fight, in Mobile, Alabama—are Bill Finch and Bethany Kraft. They both impressed me deeply on the day we saw the great sand mounds of Dauphin. Earlier on that same day, Bill had taught me some things about migration by reminding me that the invisible is also part of the so-called real world. We drove into Bayou La Batre and turned up University Road, which within seconds happily de-volved from a paved street into a bright orange-red clay road. We stopped to examine a small body of water on the roadside, more puddle than pond. Bill brought up the subject of carnivorous plants, and I boasted, with new-found regional pride, that my current home in southeastern North Caro-lina was a kind of unofficial capital for bug-eating plants.

"Yes," Bill admitted, "you have almost a dozen species of carnivorous plants."

And then he dropped his naturalist's hammer. "Here we have over a hundred. This is the world's capital."

He went on to prove his point as we hiked into the longleaf pine sa-vanna, pointing and giving Latin names until I was ready to cry "No mas!" The plants were beautiful, especially the tiny sundrop, bringing dewy death to bugs who thought they had struck water, as well as a larger red-veined beauty that looked like it took pleasure in its work. Bill kneeled down by a pitcher plant and broke it open to show me its innards where an insect was being digested. "Darwin said he cared more for his work with carnivorous plants than all the rest of his work combined." You could see why: this was a miraculous and miniature world that almost no one was aware of. Before we left the savanna, Bill offered each of us a piece of toothpick grass, a spirally, brownish-beige grass that numbed our gums.

But the real treat was just ahead: A couple miles down the road we climbed out of the car and cut through a slash of pine forest and into the marsh itself. We walked through grasses that were up to our waists, with no way of seeing where we were planting our feet. The only thing keep-ing us from stomping on a cottonmouth was luck, that and the fact that maybe we were loud enough for them to slither off and avoid us. Of course I didn't utter a peep about my fears. Birders and other nature types are regarded as somewhat geeky by the general populace, if they are regarded at all, but we have our own sort of unspoken machismo rules.

I can say with confidence that I've spent more time tramping around marshes than most people, but I usually stick to the mucky earth. Not Bill. When he reached the marsh's edge he waded right in without hesita-tion. He, like Bethany and me, was wearing long pants and sneakers, but soon he was up to his knees, and then thighs, sloshing through the water of the salt pan that bordered the taller grasses of the marsh. We followed suit, each of us splashing along, fanning out into different parts of the landscape. Bethany stopped to take pictures and I followed Bill for a while before drifting off and staring out at the endless prairie of tall grasses.

We were walking into one of the most miraculous inventions in the history of the planet: the salt marsh. The salt marsh, a great nursery where almost every fish in the nearby sea is born. The salt marsh, whose moods change every six hours or so, transforming it from a rushing river to a landscape of stranding muck. A true edge between land and sea, fresh and saltwater, forest and ocean.

"Alabama the Beautiful," the license plates say, but I wasn't buying it when I first drove into the state. Alabama was toothless folks listening to Skynrd and getting frisky with their cousins out by the still, and their landscape was as scraggly and dirt poor as they were. But here was the real Alabama: the grasses soughed in the winds, and the Gulf beyond roiled and crashed against the marsh, and the birds—egrets, herons, sandpipers, ospreys—shot overhead, and other than our small group there wasn't a human being for miles and I was starting to feel that old familiar exhilarated feeling.

Just then Bill called out. He'd struck oil. We all sloshed over to him. And there it was. Not the goopy black variety of our nightmares, the kind I'd imagined before coming down here, but a light blue sheen, beautiful really if it weren't for what it was. The oil weaved and curled through the marsh grasses. Bill touched it and rubbed it in his fingers and it left a rusty red film. I did the same.

Bill was cautious. Marsh plants create their own natural oil, a kind of vegetable oil that has a sheen much like what we were seeing. After all, Bill stressed, oil also comes from plants and the marsh is adept at breaking down oil.

"Oil isn't alien," he said.

But the volume and residue argued that the oil we were seeing was from the spill. And it had worked its way into the deepest recesses of the marsh. When Bill and I talked by phone, back when I was still in North Carolina, his voice sounded pained when he considered the prospect of a great volume of oil smothering the marshes, the home for so much fish and bird life, and the stopping point for migrating birds. We worried that the very complexity of the landscape might doom it; that while the oil might roll off a beach, or be cleaned by humans, this would be impossible in a marsh, where the variety of grass—cordgrass and needlerush and eelgrass and other spartinas—and the terrain of mud and muck are built for trapping nutrients, and would therefore trap oil as well.

Though the oil we had found was troubling enough, we were both relieved that it wasn't thicker. Psychologically, it was an interesting moment for us. That earlier phone call had been full of emotion. It was a different world then, right after the oil started spilling, and we imagined gooping Valdez quantities of oil smothering the marsh. Though we, as environmentalists, have something invested in resisting the notion that "it's better than we hoped," the fact is that it was now better than we hoped. And yet how much of this was due to the dispersants? We didn't know. What was the price we would pay in the future? Again, we didn't know.

Bill cut through the taller grasses to the shore of the Gulf itself. I followed, thinking a machete would have come in handy. When we finally pushed through to the Gulf waters we were relieved to see no obvious signs of oil coming in with the tide.

We splashed back to the salt pan and Bill pointed to tiny fish below the surface—sailfin mollies—with backs that flashed a blue that mirrored the color of the slick above them.

While Bill was glad we were looking at a sheen, not a thick black slick, he was still worried.

"People want to see dead animals," he said.

I didn't understand him at first.

"They want an obvious symbol of the devastation to rally around," he continued. "And that means dead, oiled birds. But what we are likely to get is going to be a lot more subtle than that."

What we are likely to get, he went on, are invisible changes that will make it harder to match cause and effect. He pointed to the brown and white periwinkles that clung to the tops of marsh grasses.

"How many periwinkles do you see?" he asked me.

I looked around.

"Millions," I said.

"That's right, millions. And while they look nice they are really trying their best to swallow the whole marsh. They actually have a weird way of eating plants. They slice them open and introduce a fungus and then they eat what the fungus digests. And the marsh supports these periwinkles in huge numbers. But to support them the marsh has to be growing at full speed and if it slows down the periwinkles devour it. What happens when the oil gets in here, and begins to take the oxygen out of the soil, and suddenly the marsh periwinkles, which the marsh had supported just fine, start swallowing the marsh. Then consider what happens if this year's crab population—the young are somewhere out in the middle of the Gulf right now, just starting to migrate back—gets whacked by the oil. So we see fewer crabs over the next year or two. Guess what is the only significant predator of periwinkles?"

"Crabs?"

"Crabs. It's not as obvious as a fish floating belly-up, but it's one way for the marsh to die. And then two years from now when the marsh is dead everyone says periwinkles are to blame. But, oh no, they're not. Things have been thrown out of balance."

Why did it really matter if the marsh died? After all, there wasn't another human being in sight for twenty miles or so, and most of those humans were clustered over in Bayou La Batre, puttering out to sea in Vessels of Opportunity. Well, one reason it might matter was that the marsh was both birthplace and preschool for almost all the fish that, in better times, those same boats harvested. In other words, whether they knew it or not, the townspeople depended on periwinkles.

Complications multiply. A damaged marsh would no longer support sailfin mollies. Which could mean that a green heron, exhausted in its migratory journey and eager to reach what it knew would be a bountiful stopover point, would go hungry. I drive through a sunken land, at times crossing more bridges than regular road. I don't know if I am getting across how attractive this Gulf landscape is, how visceral its appeal is to a man who loves birds and water. By even the most conservative of scientific estimates, this place won't exist or rather will exist underwater—in two hundred years. From the looks of it, it could happen in two. It's so low, so marshlike, so permeable, so inconstant. In other words, perfect. It seems to me an accurate map of what the world is really like, even if you live in South Dakota. These days you don't need water around to know that things will be changing soon, likely tomorrow.

The world is on the move and so we build things with straight lines—highways, toasters, oil derricks—anything to stop it from moving. But wait, here's an idea: what if instead we just accepted that things are constantly in movement?

Easier said than done. Perhaps I am a better preacher than a doer. All morning, as I drive toward Texas, I've experienced a kind of free-floating anxiety. In my cupholder is the blue EPA stress ball that I got at the meeting in Buras, and I take it out and squeeze it a few times in my right hand.

Then my vague anxiety becomes less so, specifying itself when the dashboard lights up again. The little illustrated engine catches fire and blinks red. I curse Ali, though not Allah. What the fuck? Now my house and hearth and home, and wife and daughter, feel farther away than ever. My anxiety spikes and won't go away no matter how I squeeze my ball.

And so finally good sense, a rare visitor to my mind over the last few weeks, gets the better of me. It is time to turn around and head home. Galveston was my goal but now the town of Grosse Tete, Louisiana, becomes my end and westernmost point. In Grosse Tete I find a ramshackle little building called the "Doc-Your-Dose Pharmacy" and I chat with an older white woman by the river who assures me that the destruction of the mostly African American lower Ninth Ward was "God's will." Then I find a mechanic whom I somehow trust despite the fact I can barely understand his accent. He assures me that what is causing the light is the catalytic converter, and he thinks I can make it home to North Carolina.

"Yull make it," he drawls.

So the day, which began with grand intentions, becomes what amounts to a 160-mile U-turn.

On the return trip, I almost manage to show great discipline and drive right past New Orleans. Until something makes me tug the wheel to the right and, before I know it, I'm taking the last exit and bumping back down through the narrow streets of the French Quarter in search of French 75 and one final Daisy. To counteract or complement (depending on your take) the drink, I also request a road cigar, and a bartender named Cindy (who seems every bit as professional and a whole lot nicer than the famous, haughty Chris) promises me that the cigar she clips and hands me will be a "long burn," which it indeed proves to be since I smoke it, on and off, for most of the way home. Before we left the marsh on Grand Bay, I took a break from gloom and doom to just watch the birds. Willets—large, elegant sandpipers with sharply patterned underwings flew by and let go with crazy seesawing cries. A tricolored heron fished patiently. Its colors startled: white throat and caramel neck stretched up high against the backdrop of the vibrant green marsh grass. Suddenly it stepped forward and its blade of a bill flashed and the life of a small fish ended.

Bill pointed down at a green, wormlike plant called glasswort, which has a celery taste. He described a miniature tomato that actually tasted more like tomato sauce than a tomato itself, as if it had already been salted and cooked.

"We would come here and mix that up with the glasswort and some wolfberry and then get a couple of oysters and have a great lunch. It was delicious. Savory."

No one needed to point out that we wouldn't be lunching on marsh plants today. We looked out toward the sea, where ospreys and gulls hovered, and where the young fish of the marsh would eventually migrate. Then we hiked back up to dry land, walking out through a forest of charred bark like turtle shells and through long grasses and plants called rose pink that made the place look like the poppy field in Oz.

We gradually made our way back to the cars and headed out the red clay road. The road, Bill explained, served as a dividing line between freshwater and salt.

"I wish they'd take it out," he said. "It acts as a causeway and doesn't allow for interaction between fresh and saltwater habitats. Without it you'd have a lot rougher edges between the two."

"You have to listen to what the marsh wants," Bill continued, pointing at the way the road blocked the proper flow of water. "This marsh has deep connectivity issues."

It occurred to me that those words applied to me and to all of us. That I—and Bill, and Bethany, and the tricolored heron and BP and our country and the sailfin mollies and the periwinkles and the crabs—have deep connectivity issues, too.

I am not the only writer to be leaving these parts. The mass migration has begun, reporters taking their pens and cameras with them, off to the next place. You can feel the great national spotlight swinging away, the news cycle ending. We are all tired of oil. Time for the next disaster.

As the writers leave, the birds arrive. I picture the millions of migrating birds streaming through the dark overhead, toward the degraded marshes and waters.

Before I left the Buras headquarters, I decided to call Scott Weidensaul to talk about the fall's migration.

"It's hard to think of a species of migrating bird east of the Rockies that doesn't fly through the Gulf," he said. "And these birds, already stressed, are going to be flying into uncertainty."

He pointed to the ways that migrations were already strained. Even in a non-oiled year, new development could ruin a bird's chances. Imagine returning to a copse of woods where your kind had landed for generations only to find a mall or housing development.

"We have been hearing that the worst of the oil is over," Weidensaul continued. "But that oil went somewhere and those toxins went some-where and that somewhere is the food chain."

He pointed to an example that was quite similar to the one that Bill Finch described back on the Grand Bay marsh. While Bill talked about crabs and periwinkles, Scott talked about whooping cranes. Whooping cranes feed almost exclusively on blue crabs. Blue crabs, as it turns out, have been one of the few species that have been tested extensively at this early date. What scientists have discovered is that almost 100 percent of the crab larvae have traces of oil and dispersant.

"It will be very hard to tease out," Weidensaul continued. "To connect cause and effect. To say this is clearly because of the oil spill."

I have come to better understand what Bill Finch meant by saying that people "want to see dead animals." The reporters and cameramen have fo-cused their cameras on single birds, covered in oil, unable to fly. It is a powerful image, beamed all over the world, and pointedly tells a story of the tragedy of many embodied in one. But it is also a mistelling. Cameras can't tell the larger, deeper story. That's because nature is not merely a se-ries of connections, but also a series of perfectly timed connections. Like a symphony. A symphony whose invisible conductor is time, time on a level humans can't imagine. When that conductor points its baton, the trum-pets blare or the flutes sing.

Phenology is a word coined by naturalists for nature's impeccable sense of timing, for the way that, as the year progresses, a fish will spawn in April just after the smaller fish it dines on have spawned, or the swallows will return north just as the insects appear. One of the climaxes of this great symphony is migration. As bad as it is right now on the shores of the Gulf, the coming migration promises a different level of impact. Birds from the north may land at a certain time to find what is not there. We can't and won't know the results of these journeys, since they are largely invisible to us. But we worry that the music may stop.

There are already tears in a web that took millions of years to create. If the whooping crane can't eat crabs, they either can't fly or do so severely weakened. If the crabs don't prey on the periwinkles, the periwinkles eat the marsh. And while this may not be the sort of disaster we first envi-sioned, that does not mean the results aren't disastrous.

At around eight o'clock, still puffing on my cigar, I drive into Hatties-burg, Mississippi, for dinner. I push on and sleep in a hotel in Meridian, Mississippi. I drive all the way through the next day, my thoughts dulled by the road. Migration barely enters my mind, except once when I pull up behind a truck with oversized tires and Georgia plates and a bumper sticker that reads "Hey Audubon, identify this bird." Blearily, I obey, trying to make out the creature with the swanlike neck, only gradually realizing that it's a middle finger.

I arrive home on Saturday night. A glorious reunion with my wife and little girl. On Monday it turns out the seller of the house has calmed down and we sign the papers. We now own our first home. The next three weeks are a marathon of moving all of our belongings to start our new life by the salt marsh. For once we will be settling for longer than a single year, though we are also well aware that hurricane season is now in full swing and so have few illusions of permanence. Still, when I am out in my new backyard I feel like I've found a good camping spot, only this is a camping spot where we can stay for years. Fairly quickly we add a second home when I build a Hadley, a fort at the base of a magnolia tree.

One day a friend helps me move my two kayaks from my old place to my new. We do this by water, paddling along the Intracoastal Waterway and camping on a dredge spoil island for the night. I watch the blazing orange ball rise near the same spot where the moon—red also, but darker and not as fiery—came up the night before. The next day I paddle home, and see a bittern, usually solitary, in the reeds behind the house. Kingfishers ratchet along above the water, occasionally stopping in midair before diving. I eye the spot out on the marsh where I will soon build an osprey platform so that the birds can nest here in the spring. By the time we have settled into the house the signs of migration flow through the marsh: the early swirls of tree swallows and Canada geese honking overhead.

Sure enough the first hurricane isn't long in coming. I have been keeping my eye on the weather, wondering if a storm will stir up the oil in the Gulf. But this storm veers northward instead of west and for a while we are in the bull's-eye of Hurricane Earl, briefly a category five. Earl slows and stays out to sea and though I dutifully bring in the lawn furniture, barely a pinecone stirs in our yard. So far we have been lucky, as has the Gulf. There is talk of dodging a bullet followed by much knocking of wood.

It feels bizarre to settle after the unsettledness of the summer. But in the face of coming storms, in the face of a country caught in a crisis of homelessness, and in the face of my own uncertain self, I begin to root down.

"The first flush of rootedness can't be repeated," a friend on Cape Cod once said to me.

All fall long I am deep in that flush. While I've never owned a house before, I have spent my whole adult life dreaming of having a place to call home. It is strange that that house turns out to be in North Carolina, but less strange that it turns out to be on a salt marsh. Not only is the marsh a miraculous ecosystem where I now daily hear the applause of clapper rails, but it connects me by water to the many other coastal places I have come to love over the years. I don't mean this mystically, but practically. If one day I am feeling particularly ambitious, I can hop in my kayak, hang a right, and paddle south to Florida before hooking around to Ryan's lodge or Anthony's fish camp.

As we begin to settle here, I think often of John Hay and his neighbor, Conrad Aiken, the Pulitzer Prize–winning poet. I dip into Aiken's Collected Letters and learn that Aiken and his wife, Mary, moved to Cape Cod in 1940. On May 21, 1940, the day the Aikens bought their house in the town of Brewster, Conrad wrote to Malcolm Lowry:

> Ourselves, we pick off the woodticks, and pour another gin and French, and count out the last dollars as they pass, but are as determined as ever to shape things well while we can, and with love. Nevertheless, I still believe, axe in hand, I still believe. And we will build our house foursquare.

The rest of the letters from Brewster are the sort of combination of pastoral and grumble common to those tackling renovating an old house in the country. Conrad spent his time "weeding the vegetable garden, mowing lawns, cutting down trees, shooting at woodchucks and squirrels, attacking poison ivy with a squirt gun," as well as "scything the tall grass," and, as usual, drinking copious amounts of alcohol. The poet, then fifty-one, had a good deal of pride in what he and Mary were accomplishing— "We both thrive on hard physical work, and feel extremely well" and exalted in his new surroundings, surroundings that would soon make their way into his best poetry.

To shape things well while we can. I write Aiken's line down on a note card and tape it above my desk. It seems to me as good a credo as any in these uncertain times as we try to make this place our own.

MOIRA CRONE

The Not Yet (2012)

Science fiction writers have long imagined how human actions can have profound consequences on the environment. Before anyone used the expression "climate change," science fiction novels were imagining drastic changes to seasons and weather in the world as well as in invented worlds. Ursula Le Guin's *The Earthsea Cycle* and N. K. Jemisin's *Broken Earth Trilogy* offer examples of how science fiction, by asking where the world might end up, preceded many other literary genres in imagining how to live in an environment no longer hospitable to humans and other species.

Following in this tradition, Moira Crone (b. 1952), author of six novels and countless short stories, invites the reader to imagine the Gulf South of the future in *The Not Yet*. The Gulf South, and specifically Louisiana, is a mostly underwater place inhabited by those willing to live on the edge. In this excerpt, the main character, Malcolm, travels with his new acquaintance Serpenthead to the Sunken Quarter, modeled after the French Quarter in New Orleans, to find Malcolm's old boss Lazarus and track down the inheritance Lazarus left. Crone points clearly to the contradictions of living in the Anthropocene—the lost inheritance will be the very places that defined so much of modern American history.

5:30 PM October 12, 2121
New Orleans Islands, Northeast Gulf De-Accessioned Territory,
UA. Protectorate

PONTCHARTRAIN SEA-RIM SKY RAIL
CLOSED UNTIL FURTHER NOTICE
BOATS: DETOUR BAYOU ST. JOHN LINK TO
NAPOLEON TRENCH /PROCEED AT YOUR OWN RISK
ENTERING NORTHEAST GULF DE-ACCESSIONED
TERRITORY. U.A. PROTECTORATE. SUBJECT TO
SECURITAS PATROLS.
HAVE VISAS, ID'S, ENCLAVE CARDS READY FOR
INSPECTION

It had been two and a half years since I'd seen the city and at that time, the Sky Rail system had still been working reasonably well. Now it was half-submerged. The Y-shaped supports for the cables were poking up from the waters like deformed, yellow trees. Seagulls and brown pelicans were perched on every artificial branch. We passed what was left of the station platform and saw two bulb-shaped gondolas lying on their sides on it—humongous, rusted onions, the gray blue sea slapping at their hulls.

Serpenthead maneuvered our tub with some skill, into the Trench. He knew his way, even with so many landmarks under water. In a little while, we passed a few hipped roofs peeking out, what was left of the old shore homes. Not long ago, they'd been handsome, on their high stilts, and the Sea of Pontchartrain could wash underneath in tidal surges. Water birds—egrets I guessed—flew in a low V formation over our heads. It was clear they thought of this place as their exclusive territory now. Once, it had been for people, only.

A mile or so inside, we came upon our first occupied house, and then our second, then a row of five. These were really just the tops of old two- and three-story houses—Outliar compounds. No enclaves here. I made out the rotting, fan-shaped attic windows of the tall Victorians, the humps of the camelbacks. It looked as if the occupants had moved to the upper rooms, and turned eaves into living space, former upper balconies into front porches, abandoned the flooded lower floors, and managed to seal them off. Ringed by rails and gates, which served as the lounging spaces, docks, and security perimeters, these rickety homesteads could be taken for stationary houseboats. On the gatepost of one, the sign: "Leave a Wake, You Won't Wake." And the skull and bones.

When I had been through here last, those houses stood on muddy patties of land, still fending off the sea most of the time. Now they had succumbed. Yet the occupants had not fled. Their very existence was illegal, in a sense—here, no one persecuted them exactly, but no one helped them either.

Lazarus had always complained the problem was the territory had been let go by the United Authority years back, but they never allowed it the freedom they'd promised. "Always some limbo," he'd say. True independence was not the fact.

I was totally depressed about the question about my Trust. Why had Lazarus not answered? This landscape didn't help. When we came to a wide expanse of water, the Broad Marsh, Serpenthead stopped, pushed in the throttle, and said, "We are almost on empty, and we'll use the current here."

The motor stopped chugging so we drifted. Suddenly everything was quiet. A little past the open water there were houses again—rougher, more fortified. Outliar camps surrounded by high fences, guarded by bigger dogs. No water birds here. On a few of the houses, the balcony columns were wrapped in barbed wire mesh forming the cages for fuel tanks.

I could hear things from inside now—human shouts, guitars, the rough harmony of semi-wild dogs, the rattle-roar of generators—a cacophony, almost pleasing over water. I was sorry when we had to accelerate to veer into the Tchoupitoulas Canal. From there we cut into the Old River at the Napoleon Segue.

"Bandits this way," he shrugged. "Different neighborhood."

We glided past the great floodwall of the Museum City. It was guarded by sentries, Securitas. I'd never gotten inside, but I had heard of the wonders there. In my heyday as an actor, many of my fans lived in those mansions, but they never actually invited me in.

The light was getting low. I was tired. Of course, I had not eaten.

The pain in my jaw, my ear, and my neck was a little worse. I went to the cot below decks for a few minutes, put up with the stench.

I must have dozed, for I startled when Serpenthead said, "The Quay, Malcolm. Coming up."

I climbed the stairs. The setting sun bit at my eyes.

It took me a while to realize what I was seeing, for the water reflected the lowering sun, flashing orange and blue and gold. But then something sorted itself out. It was wet and shining as the water, but smooth. It might have been the flat back of a sea monster for it had something like scales. Then I saw the "scales" were paving slates—it was a curving road at the edge of the Old River. Big thick poles the size of children poked up from it. When we were close enough, Serpent threw a rope over the head of one the pylons, and called it "a bollard."

This was a busy place. Around us were other craft-boats with bigger wheelhouses, several with multiple swivel seats for fishing. Along the slate road were stalls and stands selling provisions.

"But where is the Quarter?" I asked. Surely it had to be nearby.

"Sunken Quarter," Serpenthead called out. "Over there."

But I looked and saw nothing, save for a pointed narrow tower, which stuck up out of nowhere. For a second I thought this "Quarter" might be made up. There were so many stories about it, it might as well be. "I don't see anything," I said.

"Over there, and down," Serpenthead said, excited.

I looked.

The paved road I discerned wasn't a road at all, or a proper bank. It was the wide top of a huge, encircling barrier. We had pulled up to the top of an amphitheater, a bowl, the irregular perimeter that held back the Old River.

Below, the wonder.

What I saw first were bronze roofs with steep dormers. Next, the crowns of palms, which I'd never seen from above before—lush, green blooms. Underneath, buildings with bright shutters. The old cathedral, an ancient edifice, in the middle. Its spire pierced the horizon, the one structure taller than the level of the Quay. It alone caught natural light. Everything below in that valley set into the water had already descended into an almost garish, electrified night. All of it gleamed, for it was coated in glazes. The city itself seemed to be made of porcelain, like something kept in a cabinet for a giant's delight. I felt I was breaking a law, coming to visit this place everyone in my boyhood talked about in whispers.

KATE GALBRAITH
AND ASHER PRICE

The Great Texas Wind Rush: How George Bush,
Ann Richards, and a Bunch of Tinkerers Helped the Oil
and Gas State Win the Race to Wind Power (2013)

Kate Galbraith and Asher Price, both environmental journalists, explore the potential of Texas as a major producer of energy through the wind in their book, *The Great Texas Wind Rush*. Since the beginning of the twentieth century, Texas has been known for first wildcatters, then oil magnates, and now massive petrochemical corporations. *The Great Texas Wind Rush* tells a surprising story of how a state known for fossil fuels is perfectly situated to develop a booming wind energy system. Because the offshore oil industry has significant infrastructure and knowledge about how to operate industry offshore, the local resources of associated shipyards, fabrication shops, supply vessels, and skilled workers all make Texas perfectly situated to take advantage of the wind boom. Throughout this book, Galbraith and Price explore the complicated machinations of energy policy, but they also know how to find compelling and strange characters from environmentalists with car dealerships to oil magnates turned sustainable-energy tycoons. In this excerpt, we meet Herman Schellstede, a sort of contemporary wildcatter of the wind industry. While a turn toward sustainable energy would be a significant improvement in the region, this text also raises the question of how to overcome climate change if the environment is still seen as a commodity to be bought and sold.

Galbraith and Price are deft observers of the culture and landscape of Texas. They write of the Texas plains all the way to the flat horizons of the Gulf Coast, all with a chilling stillness and beauty, as in this passage about West Texas: "Awful and exhilarating, the land is a smoothed-out, washed-out territory that seems as if it has been ground down by a giant mortar. Apart from mesas here and there or the Big Bend peaks and the Guadalupe Mountains, born of an ocean reef, there is nothing. It is a hard, unromantic land of caliche and scrub, of tumbleweed and bluestem, of flatness and endless sky." The prose of the authors combines not just deep investigation into the policy of energy on the Gulf Coast but also the poetry of the environment

that surrounds oil rigs and wind turbines. In the excerpt included here, Galbraith and Asher reveal some of the possibilities for adapting to climate
change, recognizing some of the potential successes of the environmental
movement as well as the challenges still ahead.

Along the Gulf Coast, an aging entrepreneur named Herman Schellstede,
whose father in 1947 had helped construct the first offshore oil rig in the
Gulf of Mexico, had begun thinking about wind after decades of designing
offshore oil and gas platforms. A Sierra Club friend who owned a Cadil-
lac dealership, as Louisiana environmentalists are wont to do, had told
him that wind was the next big thing, and Schellstede, who knew how
wind could batter isolated rigs in the water, took him seriously. And so in
2004 the man whom the Financial Times would later describe as "an oil
man's oil man" got into the business of offshore wind power and searched
around at banks and oil companies for over $300 million to build a sixty-
two-turbine farm nine miles off Galveston, in fifty-foot water. It was a lot
of money—offshore projects cost considerably more than onshore ones—
but the winds, he knew, were far stronger and steadier than the ones in
West Texas. Near to shore, the Gulf is relatively shallow, which "gives us
a big advantage over the New England boys," says Schellstede. In a convenient quirk, Texas waters extend up to ten miles offshore, considerably
farther than most states, due to historical reasons relating to how Texas
joined the union. This means that developers like Schellstede had plenty
of room to plant turbines without hitting federal waters and triggering a
cascade of new rules. Also, an enormous offshore service industry already
existed in Houston, Galveston, and Corpus Christi.

In 2007 Schellstede's company, Wind Energy Systems Technology, put
up a meteorological tower to measure the wind. A year later Hurricane
Ike struck. "As the hurricane approached us, the winds went up to 110
miles per hour," says Schellstede. "Then they went down to zero as the eye
passed over." Then the other wall came, with sustained winds of 140 miles
per hour and gusts that may have reached 200 miles per hour. "The gusts
are the really ferocious items that really tear things apart," he says. Somehow the tower survived, and Schellstede emerged with plenty of new details for his "wind profile" of the site. Later, one local asked if Schellstede
would put a restaurant on top of his tower so diners could see the turbines
when they were up and spinning. Otherwise, "You could barely see them if
you were standing having a margarita in Galveston," Schellstede said.

Schellstede had hoped to get the wind farm up and running by 2010, and he secured five leases from the Texas General Land Office, which controls the state's offshore lands. "Oil and gas is a diminishing resource," was a favorite saying of Jerry Patterson, the land commissioner who took great pride in arguing that Texas could build wind farms in the Gulf faster than Massachusetts's Cape Wind project or other wind farms planned off the East Coast. Patterson put it this way to the magazine Fast Company in 2008: "We don't have Ted Kennedy in Texas, so we don't have anybody with the hypocrisy of 'I'm in favor of green power. Oh, but you're going to put it here off my house? No, no, no we don't want that.' We have people who are realists. I don't even get into the debate about global warming. It's an argument that has no justification because we need to be doing the same things whether global warming is man-made or not. We're running out of hydrocarbons." Asked about birds—a big concern for environmentalists, because the Texas Gulf Coast lies in the pathway of major migrations—Patterson told the reporter, "I talked to the Audubon Society and told them, 'Don't worry about this, after several generations we'll have smarter birds.' They did not think that was funny. The other thing I told them was wind farms in the Gulf of Mexico would be the first line of defense against avian flu. These people have no sense of humor. You can't break the ice with them."

So far Schellstede's plans, like Pickens's, have fallen short. In 2008 the credit crisis struck, wiping out potential investors like Lehman Brothers and Wachovia. That event "put us on our knees," said Schellstede. The plunge in natural gas prices also made it harder for an offshore project to compete against more mainstream technologies, as have the uncertainties related to federal policies on renewable energy. Schellstede remains a perpetual optimist, predicting in early 2011 that he would have a turbine in the waters off Galveston by the end of the year. Also that year, an Austin-based company, Baryonyx, proposed erecting 200 offshore wind turbines between Corpus Christi and Brownsville. Neither plan has yet been realized. In early 2012, unfazed, Schellstede was still determined to put up that solitary turbine, and he spoke eagerly about the day that five offshore wind farms built by his company would line the Texas coast.

PEGGY FRANKLAND

Women Pioneers of the Louisiana Environmental Movement
(2013)

Peggy Frankland, like a few other authors included in this collection such as Diane Wilson, was thrust into her role out of necessity. Frankland, who moved to Sulphur, Louisiana, when she was eighteen years old, saw on the national news that forty-one train cars carrying toxic waste had crashed and caught fire, releasing burning chemical fumes into the air. The next month, when she found out the remaining toxic waste was being shipped to a landfill very near to her home, Frankland helped organize and lobby for the right to a clean environment. She and the MacArthur Fellow scientist Wilma Subra founded the Calcasieu League for Environmental Action Now (CLEAN) in Lake Charles, Louisiana.

Frankland's book, *Women Pioneers of the Louisiana Environmental Movement*, published in 2013, turns upside down the idea that the Gulf South had not been active in the environmental movement throughout the twentieth century. Frankland interviews women from Louisiana who organized around environmental sustainability between 1976 and 1996 and got laws, policies, and major land use projects changed; each woman operated without institutional support. Each of these stories is told as oral history in the activist's own words. The stories reveal the years of struggle, personal sacrifice including health at times, and immense amount of work these women took on to make their communities a bit healthier.

Narrative from Rose Jackson (b. Ironton, Louisiana, 1942)

I was born and raised in Ironton. My mom and my dad were also born and raised there, and so were my grandfather and grandmother. As far as I know, my great-great-grandfather came here from France. And we have a home in Ironton, built on that strip of property where my great-great-grandfather settled, about a block from the Mississippi River. I was told that my great-grandfather was a slave master on my father's side of the family. I knew my great-grandfather on my mother's side. He was in his eighties and he had been a slave. All of that area was plantation property.

When I was a little girl he used to tell us about how hard they had to work. They talked about how hard it was to get an education and work and try to take care of their families. And the families were pretty large. Both sides of my family were religious.

My great-grandfather was also a minister. Back then they had to baptize in the Mississippi River. So I got baptized in the Mississippi River in Ironton. People are no longer baptized there because it is too polluted. For many years that is where we got our water supply. We filled barrels and rolled them down the levee. We used to pick wild berries near the river and sell them. We would go out on the riverbank on the day the banana boats would be going up and down the Mississippi River. They [crew] would throw bananas and we would stay out until the waves would wash them in. We used to catch catfish from the river. We used to go crabbing. We would catch (river) shrimp. But you can't get that out of the river anymore because it is so polluted. Back then you didn't see the oil slicks all over the place.

My grandfather had fruit trees and raised chickens. We had to pick up eggs every day. He had ducks, geese, and turkeys. He had two pigs. He raised bell peppers, peas, squash, cucumbers, tomatoes, cabbage, mustard greens and turnip greens, and corn. So we had all of the basic foods we needed. My grandfather never used pesticides. The only thing I remember him using on his plants, to kill bugs was baking soda. And for fertilizer he would take shrimp [peels] and mix them up with soil. My grandmother used to make her own preserves. She canned okra, green beans, and even corn. She taught me how to cook when I was seven years old. I can vaguely remember her going to the grocery store. It wasn't that much she had to purchase. My dad used to fish, trap, and hunt. My dad used to trap for muskrats. I remember him fussing about these big nutria rats, but then he found out that he could sell the hides.

As far as trash, there was not that much that had to be thrown away. My grandmother always found some way that paper could be reused. We would get the newspaper and we cut it up in little strips and put it in the hen houses. All of the cold drinks came in bottles. We would wash them and carry them back to the grocery store and get the deposit. Then we would buy cookies and candies. My grandmother would cut the top clean out of cans. And she would wash them out and take the labels off. She would then go and buy these big pieces of wax and we would take those cans and make candles. And we would use those candles until we couldn't use them anymore. I had a work ethic instilled in me at an early age.

In 1953, Plaquemines Parish built three schools for the African American children. That eliminated the kids from going to school in churches, but church is where we started our education. My mom also went to school in a church. My grandmother went to school in a church. My dad went to school in a church, and so did his parents. They opened the public schools to us in 1955 [when I was thirteen].

One of the teachers that made a difference was Mrs. Nelson. She was the type of teacher that could put an impact on any child's life. If that child couldn't read, trust me, she took that kid in her classroom for a month and when that kid came out, he could read. That was the type of teacher that she was. She was dedicated. However, the one that really had an impact and influence with me was Miss Washington. She was my music teacher. I started singing at an early age as a small child in church, and it was something that I didn't want to continue to do. Miss Washington found out because she would take each child in the class and she would make them sing so many notes of a song, and she picked it up right away that I had a soprano voice. And she wrote my mom a letter. And she told my mom that she was going to train my voice. And she did.

I met my husband in church. When he heard me sing he told my aunt, "I want to meet that young lady." We dated for almost two and a half years and then we got married. We've lived in Oakville, which is eleven miles from Ironton, since we got married. We have four girls, and if my son were living now, he'd be almost forty-two. [Rose lost her son to an accidental drowning.]

Now, three weeks before my son died I almost lost my daughter too. She had a ruptured cyst and then about three months after that she got another one. A month after that she was back again. She had two that were side by side on her thigh. It was about two and a half months after that and she had two others removed. The doctor told me, "Your daughter has some type of bacteria that is in the environment where you live and whatever it is, she is allergic to it." He said, "The best thing that I can tell you to do is to keep her inside." I said, "You mean to tell me that I have to keep my baby locked up in the house?"

That's when I went after Industrial Pipe, I mean, much harder than what I was doing before because now it was causing my child too much misery. I found out about the five hundred transformers [containing PCBs] that were buried at the site and all of that toxic waste. And the Industrial Pipe dump was burning. During this time, 1986 or 1987, a lady named Mrs. Lois Lowery came to me and told me, "Something is going wrong over at that place." She said we had to do something because whatever was burning back there was poison. I went out that evening when it was getting dark, and you couldn't stand the odor burning your throat.

So I called the Plaquemines Parish Sheriff's Department and the firehouse. They had fire truck after fire truck trying to put that fire out. They told me they couldn't put it out because it was underground combustion. The sheriff's office told me to tell all the people to get their kids inside because whatever was burning over there was toxic and it was going to make a bunch of the kids sick. I told them it was their job and that they were supposed to notify the people in the community that what was burning was toxic. I also told them to tell the fire department to make a report. But three months passed and I saw where there wasn't anything being done about it. So, when someone told me about Miss Ann Williams, I contacted her. She gave me Willie Fontenot's number. He in turn gave me a number to call, which was the Tulane Environmental Law Clinic, and I spoke to Audrey Evans and they came out immediately. Mr. Fontenot also told me to contact the media, and I did.

Then I sat down with several other parents and we drew up a petition. We took those petitions out and we got them signed. I contacted the local government, which at that time was Mr. Luke Petrovich, who was president of the Plaquemines Parish Commission Council. He set up a meeting for the residents of Oakville. I went to the council meeting along with the Tulane Environmental Law Clinic, Willie Fontenot, Marylee Orr, and Ramona Stevens. I didn't know that the Department of Environmental Quality had so many charges on the owner of the landfill. The Tulane lawyers pulled out all of this documentation of the extensions and fines that he had within a year's time. He had violation after violation. I couldn't believe that my local government knew this was going on, because it had been brought before them, and they wouldn't stop it. And that landfill burned for seven and a half years. It might still be burning.

During that time my youngest daughter had a baby girl and she was living here with me. And that baby broke out all the way up her back and under her arms; it was like somebody had scalded her. She would scratch, scratch, and scratch. It was to the point where I had to wrap her in Ace bandages and give her Benadryl. She was miserable. I sat down and talked to my daughter one day and I told her, "Look, you are going to have to move from here with this baby." The baby was having one asthma attack after another. And my other daughter Leslie has asthma also and my granddaughter. They all have respiratory diseases.

In my opinion, the landfill was causing harm to so many families. I have a neighbor that buried her only son. He had lung cancer. And this kid never smoked. My neighbor up the street had breast cancer. We had young women twenty-one years old that had to have their uteruses removed. There were miscarriages on top of miscarriages. I had one little girl that was working with me, only twenty-three years old and she had to have a complete hysterectomy—cancer. My youngest daughter ended up having surgery because they found cancer cells in the uterus and cervix. She was twenty-eight years old. As a young mother, when I was thirty-two years old, I also had to have a hysterectomy.

Linda King and I went through the community and did [an unscientific] medical survey. Linda sent the documentation to Dr. Legator, who found this community was overwhelmed with children with respiratory problems and cancer. I went to my local government officials and I told them that I found a 49 percent rate of respiratory problems in the community. They told me that I didn't know what I was talking about. So Audrey Evans suggested they do a survey. When the Health Department did their own study, they found a 69.5 percent rate of respiratory problems in Plaquemines Parish.

Anyone who figures that what comes out of smoke incinerator stacks is not going to come back down, then, there is something wrong with them. It is contaminated. This whole community is. I can remember planting flowers in my front yard and they would stand up so pretty for about two or three days and then I would go back out there and they were dead. And the ones that were not dead and had leaves on the plants were not green but white. It was like a white film or paint.

Narrative from Liz Avants (b. Brulie, Louisiana, 1950)

When I was an infant, we moved to [the city of] Plaquemine where my relatives lived. That is where I spent all of my growing-up years. I can remember going to my grandparents' on Sundays on a two-lane highway. There were big, beautiful oak trees on either side of the road and sugarcane fields beyond that.

Dow located here in 1956, when I was a child. When they came in, it prompted other industries to locate in our area. Industry was already in

Baton Rouge with the Essa Standard Oil Refinery, and Dow got cranked up in 1958. The reason they came here was because they had access to the river with barge transportation and rail transportation and the other lagniappe that came with the state of Louisiana in the way of tax exemptions.

I graduated in 1968 from Saint John High School. In the years that I was going to school there, especially in middle school and upper elementary, there was a third floor to the school building, and from there we could see plumes and plumes of smoke coming from Dow Chemical every day. It was like burning waste, and not just plumes from the stacks. It was kind of like I never really thought about it [being harmful].

After I graduated, I went to Baton Rouge Vocational Technical School for a year. I took a secretarial course and then worked in the office for seven years. While I was at the trade school I married Rusty Avants. We had five children.

In the 1980s, the Community Alert Network, the CAN system, came on line, and they used to tell us to "cocoon," which was the thing then. If you heard the sirens, you needed to go into your home and shut off the heat and cooling system and close your windows. Sometimes it meant putting rags under the doors and in the windows because we have many people that have cracks in their floors and windowpanes missing. I mean that was a really scary thing. I guess if you really thought about it, nobody would live here, because at any second of any day we could have an accident like Bhopal, India. So I tell people that God has been really good to us. I mean, if you want to look at the reality of it—that is the reality.

I kind of got involved in the environmental movement but not by a conscious decision because I was really busy raising my family. My husband left when my youngest child was not quite two weeks old. It was all I could do to continue maintaining a full-time job and keeping up with my kids and just the regular routine of living every day.

In January 1986, it was in the newspaper that the EPA was conducting a public hearing and taking comments on a feasibility study as to how to clean up the CLA site (Clean Land, Air, and Water). The site was located in Bayou Sorrel, which is about thirty miles from where I live. It was shut down and became a Superfund site because in 1978 an eighteen-year-old young man dropped dead at a waste [hazardous] pit. He was hauling waste and when he opened the valve on the truck to let the waste loose in this open pit, with the combination of the toxins, he just dropped dead right there.

I heard about this and I said, "Let me go see what is going on." I went to the meeting and I took two or three of my kids with me. I was amazed at the people from Bayou Sorrel who came and who had gone to so much effort to see about getting this site cleaned up.

At the hearing the engineering firm and the EPA were proposing a solution that the people really didn't like. They proposed to dig the waste up and install geothermal liners, which were plastic. They would then put the chemicals back in, cover it [pit] with an eighteen-inch clay cap, and monitor the site for thirty years. And that would be the end of it. But that was not a viable solution; at least that is what the people thought.

I met Willie Fontenot from the Attorney General's Office in Baton Rouge at the meeting, and Les Ann Kirkland, a distant cousin of mine, was also there. The EPA meeting was in January 1986, and then in March of 1986 Dow proposed to do a commercial incineration at their site. So Les Ann drags me off to Willie's office one afternoon [to discuss the proposal] and he was saying, "You all really need to start a group and Louisiana Environmental Action Network (LEAN) is forming and you need to come to the conference." We went to the conference and started our own [environmental] group Alliance against Waste and Action to Restore the Environment (AWARE).

So anyway, we come back home and we were fighting DOW, who wanted a commercial incinerator. Dow had done what Dow wanted all along. From 1956 to 1986, thirty years, they had no opposition or negative publicity. If they had a little spill, a little fire, a little problem, it made a little news, but it was not a big deal. Some folks worked out there, so it was like everything was hunky dory. We knew a little bit about the Rollins incinerator, in North Baton Rouge, and that was not the way we wanted to go. We had had enough of the production of toxic chemicals. Then all of a sudden we said, "No! Commercial incineration is not the way to go. You already have two incinerators out there and that is not what we want for our community." And when we said that—they backed off.

In 1987 or 1988, they came out with the Toxic Release Inventory [TRI] program that forced industries to quantify all 313 chemicals. Well, actually it was 100 of the worst of the worst. Then it kind of expanded—since there is something like 80,000 chemicals out there. So this is what is required by the TRI. You have to say what your inventory is and how much you are releasing of these specific chemicals. However, there is no means to gather that data in accumulation—and how it mixes together like a toxic soup. It is measured chemical for chemical. And when you read those numbers from 1987, you'll see major, major reductions. But if you think back before the TRI, what Dow was spewing out all those years hadn't been monitored, and we were not even talking about Esso or Exxon, or Standard Oil in North Baton Rouge, in operation since the 1930s and 1940s. And so Dow was not monitored or required to report what they were releasing for a lot of years. This is where their minds were: "The people do not want to look at this, so we are going to build a levee around the site and they really will not see what is going on." God! How was that going to contain the poisons that might come out of these things? What is that going to do in a worst-case scenario?

I would go almost every Saturday and do a little bit of homework. Those records of emissions and other data related to Dow and others were in our local library. If there were a particular permit for a public comment period that I needed to be doing research on, I would do that. At other times I would be looking at what was there to see if I had missed anything and how I could pull future data. The information on the library shelves went back to the early 1980s.

Well, it was the end of July and I went to the library to look things up and they had moved the files. The assistant librarian told me the EPA took the data. But I said, "Most of the data was not EPA, it was DEQ data. And so he replied, "That's probably who it was then." I was so ticked because all they left was a tiny bit of data, which was up for public comments right then I had used the public records for hearings related to a number of issues. Now we don't have any of those documents.

I tried calling Dale Givens at the DEQ, but there was no listing for him. I tried to call three other people because I was so infuriated, but I couldn't reach anyone. And the library's reasoning for them taking the material was to make space in the library. Finally, I was able to contact the DEQ, and a spokesperson said, "It just got disposed of." They did send me an inventory—four single-spaced pages identifying volumes of information that were gone.

RICHARD M. MIZELLE JR.

Backwater Blues: The Mississippi Flood of 1927
in the African American Imagination (2014)

> Richard M. Mizelle Jr.'s book *Backwater Blues: The Mississippi Flood of 1927 in the African American Imagination* reads the blues music of the South as a document of the 1927 Mississippi River flood and how the inundation affected African Americans. Mizelle notes that blues music provides first-person accounts of the event that often cannot be found in historical records. He studies songs such as Bessie Smith's "Back-Water Blues" as a record of the black experience and a powerful medium for reading the environmental transformations wrought. Further, Mizelle contributes new information on the ways African Americans were forced into the military and Red Cross relief efforts to save white lives, businesses, and properties. In this excerpt, Mizelle documents the deliberate explosion of the Caernarvon levee downriver from New Orleans. This explosion was done to prevent flooding in the city of New Orleans, a richer and more populous area, at the cost of thousands of people's homes. This reading would be well paired with the excerpt "Old Man" by William Faulkner.
>
> Richard McKinley Mizelle Jr. is associate professor of history at the University of Houston. He is a coeditor of the book *Resilience and Opportunity: Lessons from the U.S. Gulf Coast after Katrina and Rita* and has works published in numerous academic journals.

LIVING UNDER THE SHADOW OF LEVEES

The 1927 flood is fundamentally a story of worthiness and unworthiness in a powerfully racialized society. Charity, displacement, and race-based peonage were powerful markers of social worth in 1927. But we can also see markers of social worth embedded within a part of the flood that is not as easily accessible. The artificial construction of massive levees, including the one involved in the Mounds Landing crevasse that set the federal government in motion, was blamed for creating the suffering that black and white Mississippians experienced. Levees were not simply structures of concrete, wood, and dirt, disconnected from social history, and their construction and presence were far from a disentangled social theory of decisions by engineers and politicians regarding flood control. The control of the Mississippi River and construction of levees was about more than the United States Army Corps of Engineers. Levees were designed to protect people and the Yazoo Delta cotton-growing economy. But the process was not unilateral; people physically and psychologically fell through the gaps of levee coverage, a point that emerges in the blues archive. Still, how might we take note of 1927 technology and the ways in which it shaped life? In his classic work *The Whale and the Reactor: A Search for Limits in an Age of High Technology*, social theorist Langdon Winner asks whether "artifacts have politics" and how we might imagine culture, politics, class dynamics, and race within the theoretical and practical development of technological systems. "At issue is the claim that the machines, structures, and systems of modern material culture can be accurately judged not only for their contributions to efficiency and productivity and their positive and negative environmental side effects, but also for the ways in which they can embody specific forms of power and authority," Winner writes.[1] Ultimately, people made choices about levees, deciding when and how to build them, the appropriate height and width, and whether certain communities would be protected. The failure of levees was not simply happenstance, an occurrence devoid of human culpability, but rather demonstrated the power certain groups held over other groups in the shaping and creation of suffering.

New Orleans during the 1927 flood represents a powerful marker of social worth, pitting country against city, and urban metropolis against rural hinterland. From its founding by Jean-Baptiste Le Moyne Sieur de Bienville, in 1718 as the French capital of Louisiana, it was a vulnerable environmental landscape. Surrounded by the Mississippi River and another body of water later named Lake Pontchartrain, the French capital was called L'Isle de la Nouvelle Orleans.[2] Bienville and the settlement's boosters hoped that New Orleans would become the most important city in the South and the commercial gateway to Europe and the Atlantic world. What the physical landscape of New Orleans provided in spatial location as a commercial gateway it also took away as a uniquely vulnerable environment, becoming a city in the middle of a fishbowl surrounded by fifteen-to twenty-foot-high levees.[3] As the height and breadth of levees continued to grow, the vulnerability of living under its shadow was not lost on residents and visitors to the region. In New Orleans, elevated levees and the Mississippi River that flowed behind them provided a heightened sense of insecurity. T. L. Nichols visited New Orleans in the late nineteenth century and described the unsettling environmental landscape, juxtaposing the low-lying landscape of New Orleans surrounded by water with the massive levees that protected the city. Making a conscious connection between the river and the artificiality of technology, he wrote that "hundreds of ships and steamers were floating far above the level of the streets—as high, indeed as the roofs of the houses in the back streets of town." For some, the sight of commercial ships floating high above their heads was unnatural and surreal, even ghastly, while others questioned the ability of artificial levees to keep floodwaters out of the city. John Hammond was jarred by the size of levees when he visited the city in 1916, noting in his writings how seemingly inconsequential the levees were in relation to the Mississippi River, "a mound of earth that somehow made me think of the Pyramids." After climbing the levee and seeing the Mississippi River's power, he describes his impression: "The city lay back of me, far beneath the level of the mighty river upon whose brink I stood. It seemed so easy for the river to dash away the barrier of earth, imposing as that had seemed a few minutes ago."[4]

Greenville residents had similar experiences. The sight of large steamers hovering above the city's physical landscape was not uncommon. In his book *Where I Was Born and Raised*, Mississippi writer and cultural critic David Cohn talks about the shadowing presence of levees surrounding the low-lying Queen City of Greenville in the early twentieth century: "In the springtime when the waters of the river are high against the levees, [residents of Greenville gaze] at the yellow flood and ponder the possibilities of disaster." Cohn's description of elevated artificial levees surrounding Greenville is equally powerful when situated within a theory of vulnerable landscapes and levee construction. Cohn paints Greenville, like New Orleans, as a defenseless city where "steamboats on the swollen stream pass high above the level of the earth like monstrous birds in slow flight."[5] Artificial levees had grown into massive technological structures that could have a pervasive, even intrusive, presence in the lives of Yazoo Delta residents. Levees designed to protect the economy and protect human life were, at times, transformed into mechanisms for the creation of suffering that became part of living under the shadow of levees.

For New Orleanians during the 1927 flood, the vulnerability of living under the shadow of levees was a reflection of the built environment and manipulation of technology. New Orleans politicians and businessmen, including the recently elected Democratic mayor Arthur O'Keefe, considered the Crescent City the most important economic city of the South. As floodwaters barreled down the Mississippi River and its tributaries toward New Orleans in late March, correspondence between city, state, and local officials reflected an adamancy that a flooded New Orleans would be disastrous for the region, if not the entire nation.[6] The business-friendly *Times-Picayune* hoped to quell fear within the city and the rest of the world about the city's impending crisis. One headline read, "Safety Assured in New Orleans: Merchants and Residents Concerned over False Reports about City." The article opened by noting that "New Orleans is and has been doing business as usual. Residents and merchants are pursuing their vocations and avocations without interruption. The levees surrounding the city are intact and not one drop of flood water from the river has touched the city and no such intrusion is expected."[7] This proved to be false bravado; city leaders did not have complete faith in the levees surrounding the city. Instead, behind closed doors city officials gathered support for a plan to ensure that vulnerable New Orleans would be safe from the flood.

On Good Friday city officials initiated a new civic organization called the Citizens Flood Relief Committee (CFRC), composed largely of the city's business elite. Its primary goal was to protect the valuable waterfront and commercial interests of the city. Their biggest fear was that a tarnished image would keep visitors and investors from the city even if floodwaters stayed clear.[8] O'Keefe and Marcel Garsaud, New Orleans's dock board manager, presented a resolution to the Mississippi River Commission (MRC) to destroy the levee at Poydras, twelve miles downstream, flooding the New Orleans hinterland parishes of Plaquemines and St. Bernard. This would have been unthinkable before, but now the future of New Orleans was at stake. Historian Ari Kelman describes the MRC's initial reaction to this idea as "chilly," primarily because such an action would effectively "jettison decades of policy and admit culpability in raising the river."[9] At the same time, CFRC delegate James Thomson met with President Calvin Coolidge, Edgar Jadwin of the Corps of Engineers, and Secretary of War Dwight Davis in Washington. Somewhat reluctantly, all parties agreed to the proposal, with the contingency of a 100 percent reimbursement of adjusted claims filed by displaced residents of the proposed blast. The vast majority of the ten thousand residents were the Acadian descendants of ancestors who had migrated from Nova Scotia over a century before and worked in the Louisiana fur-trapping industry.[10]

On Tuesday, April 26, Democratic Louisiana governor Oramel Simpson signed the order to cut the Poydras levee, setting the stage for one of the more baffling moments in the history of environmental disasters. Residents of the two doomed parishes had three days to collect their belongings and leave for what was supposed to be a temporary displacement. For most, the displacement was anything but temporary.[11] They refused to go quietly into the night; armed citizens in St. Bernard and Plaquemines Parishes began patrolling the Poydras levee, showing they were willing to use violence to protect their property and livelihood. On a few occasions shots were fired by patrollers as a warning to unknown individuals coming too close to the levee, and in a well-publicized incident shots were even fired near Secretary of Commerce Herbert Hoover. When rumors circulated that the angry residents from St. Bernard and Plaquemines were planning to sabotage New Orleans levees in a preemptive strike, New Orleanians took no chances and formed their own round-the-clock armed levee patrols, calling in the National Guard to provide additional protection.[12] Moving day was April 26: residents drove and walked out of the parishes in what one observer wryly described as an "endless caravan which streamed out of the doomed area."[13] Those displaced would be temporarily housed at an army base inside New Orleans city limits, one floor for blacks and another for whites. People were forced together by the actions of others, but racial customs and norms were nonetheless maintained during this human-made disaster.

Three days later, during the early morning hours of April 29, officials blocked entrance into the two parishes while military planes flew above looking for last-minute evacuations. Reporters, journalists, and interested bystanders gathered at the Caernarvon levee twelve miles away from a portion of Canal Street at high noon; some traveled across the country to witness an event likened to a strategic military maneuver that would spill floodwaters over an estimated seventy thousand acres of economically viable Louisiana landscape in a visually fantastic show of human's control over nature. The end result was successful, but the show itself was rather pedestrian. It took three separate blasts until a fifteen-foot-wide stream of water finally began to emerge from the levee, hours after the first blast. It was perhaps disappointing to those whose lives and livelihoods had not been destroyed in an instant. As one witness observed, "There was to be a mighty wall of water suddenly unleashed, Niagara-like, ripping, tearing all before it; whirling down toward the Gulf of Mexico like the onrush of Attilla's horde of Huns. Was there? There was not."[14] One thing did fantastically explode with the Caernarvon crevasse—the much-maligned "levees only" policy. The dirty secret had once and for all been brought into the open with this act, and no longer could the Corps of Engineers and the Mississippi River Commission deflect the criticism that a narrowly conceived policy of flood control had brought such pain to thousands of people. One of the few lasting images of the event shows the act of human-created suffering with a trickle of floodwater coming through the levee.

The numbers were staggering. Close to ten thousand people were displaced, and 70 percent of the region's muskrat population was destroyed. It took several years for the muskrat population to come back and even longer for the trapping and fur pelt industry economy to recover. Muskrats are nocturnal creatures, and the blast forced them out of their natural habitat and routine. Those not among the hundreds of thousands that drowned eventually perished from overexposure to sunlight.[15] The return of a viable trapping industry was significantly hampered by a depleted muskrat population and bureaucratic obstacles put in place to deny paying 100 percent reimbursement.

Settlements proved more costly than the city anticipated, and lawyers for the CFRC found loopholes in settlement agreements to enable the CFRC to withhold payment. The CFRC agreed to bear the cost of housing and feeding victims displaced from the blast while temporarily residing in New Orleans, but it also deducted food allotments from final settlements. Over $35 million in claims was quickly reduced to $2.9 million by CFRC lawyers, and most of this amount went to the Acme Land and Fur Company.[16] Most of those displaced received somewhere in the range of $300, while others received nothing. Rather than face uphill and costly court battles they could little afford, St. Bernard and Plaquemines Parish residents accepted meager payments for their suffering and began the slow process of rebuilding their lives from scratch. Most would never recover.[17]

NOTES

1. Langdon Winner, *The Whale and the Reactor: A Search for Limits in an Age of High Technology* (Chicago: University of Chicago Press, 1986), 19.

2. Ari Kelman, *A River and Its City: The Nature of Landscape in New Orleans* (Berkeley: University of California Press, 2006), 4.

3. John Martin Hammond, *Winter Journeys in the South* (Philadelphia: JB Lippinscott, 1916) 115–17; TL Nichols, *Forty Years of American Life* (London: Longmans & Green 1874), 132; Kelman, *River and Its City*, 158, 161–72.

4. Hammond, *Winter Journeys in the South*, 115–17.

5. David Cohn, *Where I was Born and Raised* (Notre Dame: University of Notre Dame Press, 1935), 43.

6. Arthur O'Keefe Papers, New Orleans Public Library, Louisiana Room; Kelman, *River and Its City*, 171–71.

7. "Safety Assured in New Orleans: Merchants and Residents Concerned over False Reports about City," *New Orleans Times-Picayune*, May 4, 1927.

8. Kelman, *River and Its City*, 161.

9. Ibid., 174.

10. Arthur O'Keefe Papers; Kelman, *River and Its City*, 171–96.

11. "Red Cross Appeal," *New York Times*, April 30, 1927; *Memphis Commercial Appeal*, April 20, 1927; "Cut Levee is Order of Governor," *Plaquemines Protector*, April 30, 1927; Kelman, *River and Its City*, 161.

12. Arthur O'Keefe Papers; Kelman, *River and Its City*, 178–80.

13. Kelman, *River and Its City*, 179.

14. Ibid., 182.

15. Ibid., 171–96; *New Orleans Evening*, April 29, 1927; *St. Bernard Voice*, April 30, 1927.

16. Kelman, *River and Its City*.

17. Ibid., 171–96; "Cut Levee," *Plaquemines Protector*; "Government Financial Aid Assured Flood Zone Farmers," *Christian Science Monitor*, May 4, 1927; "Reparations Body Decides Methods to Handle Claims," *Plaquemines Protector*, May 14, 1927; "Prompt Action Needed," *Plaquemines Protector*, June 25, 1927.

BOB MARSHALL, BRIAN JACOBS, AND AL SHAW

"Losing Ground"

The Lens, ProPublica (2014)

Bob Marshall is one of Louisiana's most respected environmental writers. (For his full bio, see the earlier excerpt from "A Paradise Lost.") This is a selection from "Losing Ground," a groundbreaking, multimedia collaboration with Brian Jacobs and Al Shaw about land loss in Louisiana. It was originally published in partnership with *ProPublica* and *The Lens*.

In this excerpt, Marshall lays out, starkly and simply, and with historical context, the inexorable, bleak future of southeastern Louisiana. He reports on the 2013 lawsuit issued by the Southeast Louisiana Flood Protection Authority (of which John Barry, an author included in this anthology, was a board member) against ninety-seven oil and gas companies in Louisiana. He writes that since 2013, approximately 2,000 square miles of land have disappeared in Louisiana; various studies say the oil and gas industry is responsible for anywhere from 16 to 50 percent of that. This lawsuit, dubbed by *The New York Times* the most ambitious environmental lawsuit ever, was thrown out in 2015. But that was not the end. In 2019, twelve parishes in Louisiana sued gas and oil companies for their part in land loss; Freeport-McMoRan, one of the companies, settled out of court, agreeing to pay $100 million dollars toward coastal restoration. The legal battles will continue for many years to come.

Work Sourced

Wendland, Tegan. "Freeport McMoRan Settles Coastal Lawsuits." WWNO, October 3, 2019.

Louisiana is drowning, quickly.

In just 80 years, some 2,000 square miles of its coastal landscape have turned to open water, wiping places off maps, bringing the Gulf of Mexico to the back door of New Orleans and posing a lethal threat to an energy and shipping corridor vital to the nation's economy.

And it's going to get worse, even quicker.

Scientists now say one of the greatest environmental and economic disasters in the nation's history is rushing toward a catastrophic conclusion over the next 50 years, so far unabated and largely unnoticed.

At the current rates that the sea is rising and land is sinking, National Oceanic and Atmospheric Administration scientists say by 2100 the Gulf of Mexico could rise as much as 4.3 feet across this landscape, which has an average elevation of about 3 feet. If that happens, everything outside the protective levees—most of Southeast Louisiana—would be underwater.

The effects would be felt far beyond bayou country. The region best known for its self-proclaimed motto *"laissez les bons temps rouler"*—let the good times roll—is one of the nation's economic linchpins.

This land being swallowed by the Gulf is home to half of the country's oil refineries, a matrix of pipelines that serve 90 percent of the nation's offshore energy production and 30 percent of its total oil and gas supply, a port vital to 31 states, and 2 million people who would need to find other places to live.

The landscape on which all that is built is washing away at a rate of a football field every hour, 16 square miles per year.

For years, most residents didn't notice because they live inside the levees and seldom travel into the wetlands. But even those who work or play in the marshes were misled for decades by the gradual changes in the landscape. A point of land eroding here, a bayou widening there, a spoil levee sinking a foot over 10 years. In an ecosystem covering thousands of square miles, those losses seemed insignificant. There always seemed to be so much left.

Now locals are trying to deal with the shock of losing places they had known all their lives—fishing camps, cypress swamps, beachfronts, even cattle pastures and backyards—with more disappearing every day.

Fishing guide Ryan Lambert is one of them. When he started fishing the wetlands out of Buras 34 years ago, he had to travel through six miles of healthy marshes, swamps and small bays to reach the Gulf of Mexico.

"Now it's all open water," Lambert said. "You can stand on the dock and see the Gulf."

Two years ago, NOAA removed 31 bays and other features from the Buras charts. Some had been named by French explorers in the 1700s.

The people who knew this land when it was rich with wildlife and dotted with Spanish- and French-speaking villages are getting old. They say their grandchildren don't understand what has been lost.

"I see what was," said Lloyd "Wimpy" Serigne, who grew up in the fishing and trapping village of Delacroix, 20 miles southeast of New Orleans. It was once home to 700 people; now there are fewer than 15 permanent residents. "People today—like my nephew, he's pretty young—he sees what is."

If this trend is not reversed, a wetlands ecosystem that took nature 7,000 years to build will be destroyed in a human lifetime.

The story of how that happened is a tale of levees, oil wells and canals leading to destruction on a scale almost too big to comprehend—and perhaps too late to rebuild. It includes chapters on ignorance, unintended consequences and disregard for scientific warnings. It's a story that is still unfolding.

SPECK BY SPECK, LAND BUILT OVER CENTURIES

The coastal landscape Europeans found when they arrived at the mouth of the Mississippi River 500 years ago was the Amazon of North America, a wetlands ecosystem of more than 6,000 square miles built by one of the largest rivers in the world.

For thousands of years, runoff from the vast stretch of the continent between the Rockies and the Appalachians had flowed into the Mississippi valley. Meltwater from retreating glaciers, seasonal snowfall and rain carried topsoil and sand from as far away as the Canadian prairies. The river swelled as it rushed southward on the continent's downward slope, toward the depression in the planet that would become known as the Gulf of Mexico.

Down on the flat coastal plain, the giant river slowed. It lost the power to carry those countless tons of sediment, which drifted to the bottom. Over thousands of years, this rain of fine particles gradually built land that would rise above the Gulf.

It wasn't just the main stem of the Mississippi doing this work. When the river reached the coastal plain, side channels—smaller rivers and bayous—peeled off. They were called "distributaries," for the job they did spreading that land-building sediment ever farther afield.

The delta had two other means of staying above the Gulf. The plants and trees growing in its marshes and swamps shed tons of dead parts each year, adding to the soil base. Meanwhile, storms and high tides carried sediment that had been deposited offshore back into the wetlands.

As long as all this could continue unobstructed, the delta continued to expand. But with any interruption, such as a prolonged drought, the new land began to sink.

That's because the sheer weight of hundreds of feet of moist soil is always pushing downward against the bedrock below. Like a sponge pressed against a countertop, the soil compresses as the moisture is squeezed out. Without new layers of sediment, the delta eventually sinks below sea level.

The best evidence of this dependable rhythm of land building and sinking over seven millennia is underground. Geologists estimate that the deposits were at least 400 feet deep at the mouth of the Mississippi when those first Europeans arrived.

By the time New Orleans was founded in 1718, the main channel of the river was the beating heart of a system pumping sediment and nutrients through a vast circulatory network that stretched from present-day Baton Rouge south to Grand Isle, west to Texas and east to Mississippi. As late as 1900, new land was pushing out into the Gulf of Mexico.

A scant 70 years later, that huge, vibrant wetlands ecosystem would be at death's door. The exquisite natural plumbing that made it all possible had been dismantled, piece by piece, to protect coastal communities and extract oil and gas.

ENGINEERING THE RIVER

For communities along its banks, the Mississippi River has always been an indispensable asset and their gravest threat. The river connected their economies to the rest of the world, but its spring floods periodically breached locally built levees, quickly washing away years of profits and scores of lives. Some towns were so dependent on the river, they simply got used to rebuilding.

That all changed with the Great Flood of 1927.

Swollen by months of record rainfall across the watershed, the Mississippi broke through levees in 145 places, flooding the midsection of the country from Illinois to New Orleans. Some 27,000 square miles went under as much as 30 feet of water, destroying 130,000 homes, leaving 600,000 people homeless and killing 500.

Stunned by what was then the worst natural disaster in U.S. history, Congress passed the Flood Control Act of 1928, which ordered the U.S. Army Corps of Engineers to prevent such a flood from ever happening again. By the mid-1930s, the corps had done its job, putting the river in a straitjacket of levees.

But the project that made the river safe for the communities along the river would eventually squeeze the life out of the delta. The mud walls along the river sealed it off from the landscape sustained by its sediment. Without it, the sinking of land that only occurred during dry cycles would start, and never stop.

If that were all we had done to the delta, scientists have said, the wetlands that existed in the 1930s could largely be intact today. The natural pace of sinking—scientists call it subsidence—would have been mere millimeters per year.

But we didn't stop there. Just as those levees were built, a nascent oil and gas industry discovered plentiful reserves below the delta's marshes, swamps and ridges.

At the time, wetlands were widely considered worthless—places that produced only mosquitoes, snakes and alligators. The marsh was a wilderness where few people could live, or even wanted to.

There were no laws protecting wetlands. Besides, more than 80 percent of this land was in the hands of private landowners who were happy to earn a fortune from worthless property.

Free to choose the cheapest, most direct way to reach drilling sites, oil companies dredged canals off natural waterways to transport rigs and work crews. The canals averaged 13 to 16 feet deep and 140 to 150 feet wide—far larger than natural, twisting waterways.

EFFECTS OF CANALS RIPPLE ACROSS THE WETLANDS

Eventually, some 50,000 wells were permitted in the coastal zone. The state estimates that roughly 10,000 miles of canals were dredged to service them, although that only accounts for those covered by permitting systems. The state began to require some permits in the 1950s, but rigorous accounting didn't begin until the Clean Water Act brought federal agencies into play in 1972.

Researchers say the total number of miles dredged will never be known because many of those areas are now underwater. Gene Turner, a Louisiana State University professor who has spent years researching the impacts of the canals, said 10,000 miles "would be a conservative estimate."

Companies drilled and dredged all over the coast, perhaps nowhere more quickly than the area near Lafitte, which became known as the Texaco Canals.

This fishing village 15 miles south of New Orleans had been named for the pirate who used these bayous to ferry contraband to the city. For years, the seafood, waterfowl and furbearers in the surrounding wetlands sustained the community. As New Orleans grew, Lafitte also became a favorite destination for weekend hunters and anglers.

Today those scenes are only a memory.

"Once the oil companies come in and started dredging all the canals, everything just started falling apart," said Joseph Bourgeois, 84, who grew up and still lives in the area.

From 1930 to 1990, as much as 16 percent of the wetlands was turned to open water as those canals were dredged. But as the U.S. Department of the Interior and many others have reported, the indirect damages far exceeded that:

Saltwater creeped in: Canal systems leading to the Gulf allowed saltwater into the heart of freshwater marshes and swamps, killing plants and trees whose roots held the soils together. As a side effect, the annual supply of plant detritus—one way a delta disconnected from its river can maintain its elevation—was seriously reduced.

Shorelines crumbled: Without fresh sediment and dead plants, shorelines began to collapse, increasing the size of existing water bodies. Wind gained strength over ever-larger sections of open water, adding to land loss. Fishers and other boaters used canals as shortcuts across the wetlands; their wakes also sped shoreline erosion. In some areas, canals grew twice as wide within five years.

Spoil levees buried and trapped wetlands: When companies dredged canals, they dumped the soil they removed alongside, creating "spoil levees" that could rise higher than 10 feet and twice as wide. The weight of the spoil on the soft, moist delta caused the adjacent marshes to sink. In locations of intense dredging, spoil levees impounded acres of wetlands. The levees also impeded the flow of water—and sediments—over wetlands during storm tides.

If there were 10,000 miles of canals, there were 20,000 miles of levees. Researchers estimate that canals and levees eliminated or covered 8 million acres of wetlands.

All this disrupted the delta's natural hydrology—its circulatory system—and led to the drowning of vast areas. Researchers have shown that land has sunk and wetlands have disappeared the most in areas where canals were concentrated.

In the 1970s, up to 50 square miles of wetlands were disappearing each year in the areas with heaviest oil and gas drilling and dredging, bringing the Gulf within sight of many communities.

As the water expanded, people lived and worked on narrower and narrower slivers of land.

"There's places where I had cattle pens, and built those pens . . . with a tractor that weighed 5,000 or 6,000 pounds," said Earl Armstrong, a cattle rancher who grew [up] on the river nine miles south of the nearest road. "Right now we run through there with airboats."

There are other forces at work, including a series of geologic faults in the delta and the rock layers beneath, but a U.S. Department of Interior report says oil and gas canals are ultimately responsible for 30 to 59 percent of coastal land loss. In some areas of Barataria Bay, said Turner at LSU, it's close to 90 percent.

Even more damage was to come as the oil and gas industry shifted offshore in the late 1930s, eventually planting about 7,000 wells in the Gulf. To carry that harvest to onshore refineries, companies needed more underwater pipelines. So they dug wider, deeper waterways to accommodate the large ships that served offshore platforms.

Congress authorized the Corps of Engineers to dredge about 550 miles of navigation channels through the wetlands. The Department of Interior has estimated that those canals, averaging 12 to 15 feet deep and 150 to 500 feet wide, resulted in the loss of an additional 369,000 acres of coastal land.

Researchers eventually would show that the damage wasn't due to surface activities alone. When all that oil and gas was removed from below some areas, the layers of earth far below compacted and sank. Studies have shown that coastal subsidence has been highest in some areas with the highest rates of extraction.

PUSH TO HOLD INDUSTRY ACCOUNTABLE

The oil and gas industry, one of the state's most powerful political forces, has acknowledged some role in the damages, but so far has defeated efforts to force companies to pay for it.

The most aggressive effort to hold the industry accountable is now underway. In July 2013, the Southeast Louisiana Flood Protection Authority–East, which maintains levees around New Orleans, filed suit against more than 90 oil, gas and pipeline companies.

The lawsuit claims that the industry, by transforming so much of the wetlands to open water, has increased the size of storm surges. It argues this is making it harder to protect the New Orleans area against flooding and will force the levee authority to build bigger levees and floodwalls.

The lawsuit also claims that the companies did not return the work areas to their original condition, as required by state permits.

"The oil and gas industry has complied with each permit required by the State of Louisiana and the Corps of Engineers since the permits became law," said Ragan Dickens, spokesman for the Louisiana Oil and Gas Association.

State leaders immediately rose to the industry's defense. Much of the public debate has not been about the merits of the suit; instead, opponents contested the authority's legal right to file the suit and its contingency fee arrangement with a private law firm.

"We're not going to allow a single levee board that has been hijacked by a group of trial lawyers to determine flood protection, coastal restoration and economic repercussions for the entire State of Louisiana," said Gov. Bobby Jindal in a news release demanding that the levee authority withdraw its suit.

"A better approach," he said in the statement, "to helping restore Louisiana's coast includes holding the Army Corps of Engineers accountable, pushing for more offshore revenue sharing and holding BP accountable for the damage their spill is doing to our coast."

The industry's political clout reflects its outsized role in the economy of one of the nation's poorest states. The industry directly employs 63,000 people in the state, according to the federal Department of Labor.

Many of those employees live in the coastal parishes that have suffered most from oil and gas activities and face the most severe consequences from the resulting land loss.

Legislators in those areas helped Jindal pass a law that retroactively sought to remove the levee authority's standing to file the suit. The constitutionality of that law is now before a federal judge.

CONSEQUENCES NOW CLEAR

Even as politicians fought the lawsuit, it was hard to deny what was happening on the ground.

By 2000, coastal roads that had flooded only during major hurricanes were going underwater when high tides coincided with strong southerly winds. Islands and beaches that had been landmarks for lifetimes were gone, lakes had turned into bays, and bays had eaten through their borders to join the Gulf.

"It happened so fast, I could actually see the difference day to day, month to month," said Lambert, the fishing guide in Buras.

Today, in some basins around New Orleans, land is sinking an inch every 30 months. At this pace, by the end of the century this land will sink almost 3 feet in an area that's barely above sea level today.

Meanwhile, global warming is causing seas to rise worldwide. Coastal landscapes everywhere are now facing a serious threat, but none more so than Southeast Louisiana.

The federal government projects that seas along the U.S. coastline will rise 1.5 to 4.5 feet by 2100. Southeast Louisiana would see "at least" 4 to 5 feet, said NOAA scientist Tim Osborn.

The difference: This sediment-starved delta is sinking at one of the fastest rates of any large coastal landscape on the planet at the same time the oceans are rising.

Maps used by researchers to illustrate what the state will look like in 2100 under current projections show the bottom of Louisiana's "boot" outline largely gone, replaced by a coast running practically straight east to west, starting just south of Baton Rouge. The southeast corner of the state is represented only by two fingers of land—the areas along the Mississippi River and Bayou Lafourche that currently are protected by levees.

FINALLY, A PLAN TO REBUILD—BUT NOT ENOUGH MONEY

Similar predictions had been made for years. But Hurricane Katrina finally galvanized the state Legislature, which pushed through a far-reaching coastal restoration plan in 2007.

The 50-year, $50 billion Master Plan for the Coast (in 2012 dollars) includes projects to build levees, pump sediment into sinking areas, and build massive diversions on the river to reconnect it with the dying delta.

The state's computer projections show that by 2060—if projects are completed on schedule—more land could be built annually than is lost to the Gulf.

But there are three large caveats.

The state is still searching for the full $50 billion. Congress so far has been unwilling to help.

If the plan is to work, sea-level rise can't be as bad as the worst-case scenario.

Building controlled sediment diversions on the river, a key part of the land-building strategy, has never been done before. The predictions, then, are largely hypothetical, although advocates say the concept is being proven by an uncontrolled diversion at West Bay, near the mouth of the river.

Some of the money will come from an increased share of offshore oil and gas royalties, but many coastal advocates say the industry should pay a larger share.

In fact, leaders of the regional levee authority have said the purpose of the lawsuit was to make the industry pay for the rebuilding plan, suggesting that state could trade immunity from future suits for bankrolling it.

That idea is gaining momentum in official circles, despite the industry's latest win in the state Legislature.

Kyle Graham, executive director of the Louisiana Coastal Protection and Restoration Authority, said recently that the industry understands its liability for the crumbling coast and is discussing some kind of settlement. "It's very difficult to see a future in which that [such an agreement] isn't there," he said.

Graham has said current funding sources could keep the restoration plan on schedule only through 2019. He was blunt when talking about what would happen if more money doesn't come through: There will be a smaller coast.

"There are various sizes of a sustainable coastal Louisiana," he said. "And that could depend on how much our people are willing to put up for that."

A VANISHING CULTURE

Trying to keep pace with the vanishing pieces of southeast Louisiana today is like chasing the sunset; it's a race that never ends.

Lambert said when he's leading fishing trips, he finds himself explaining to visitors what he means when he says, "This used to be Bay Pomme d'Or" and the growing list of other spots now only on maps.

Signs of the impending death of this delta are there to see for any visitor.

Falling tides carry patches of marsh grass that have fallen from the ever-crumbling shorelines.

Pelicans circle in confusion over nesting islands that have washed away since last spring.

Pilings that held weekend camps surrounded by thick marshes a decade ago stand in open water, hundreds of yards from the nearest land—mute testimony to a vanishing culture.

Shrimpers push their wing nets in lagoons that were land five years ago.

The bare trunks of long-dead oaks rise from the marsh, tombstones marking the drowning of high ridges that were built back when the river pumped life-giving sediment through its delta.

"If you're a young person you think this is what it's supposed to look like," Lambert said. "Then when you're old enough to know, it's too late."

ANTONIA JUHASZ

"Thirty Million Gallons Under the Sea

FOLLOWING THE TRAIL OF BP'S OIL
IN THE GULF OF MEXICO"

Harper's Magazine (2015)

Antonia Juhasz literally goes under water in this riveting investigation of the 2010 BP oil spill and its massive impact on the ecosystem of the Gulf of Mexico. "Thirty Million Gallons Under the Sea" was published in *Harper's Magazine* in 2015, four years after the BP Macondo well explosion and following debacle that allowed 170 million gallons of oil to seep into the Gulf for eighty-seven days, the largest offshore-drilling oil spill in history. Juhasz, a policy analyst and investigative journalist, goes into a deep-sea submersible, the *Alvin*, with a group of scientists who are trying to determine the extent of the damage of the remaining 30 million gallons of oil left on the seabed. What they discover is a moonscape, devoid of the natural plant and animal life that should be on the rich seabed of the Gulf.

Though there were many great stories—and now some not so great movies—written about the BP oil spill, Juhasz's willingness to go where few people, let alone storytellers, have gone and bring back the images and characters surrounding the ongoing research of this massive corporate debacle illuminates parts of this story never before seen. With this information, one would hope that new policies would keep such a massive disaster from happening again, but Juhasz does not sugarcoat the prospects. She reports that a Louisiana-based oil company purchased the area from BP and is now drilling into the Macondo reservoir. The extraction of oil in the Gulf continues unabated.

One morning in March of last year, I set out from Gulfport, Mississippi, on a three-week mission aboard the U.S. Navy research vessel *Atlantis*. The 274-foot ship, painted a crisp white and blue, stood tall in the bright sunlight. On its decks were winches, cranes, seafloor-mapping sonar, a machine shop, and five laboratories. Stowed in an alcove astern was *Alvin*, the federal government's only manned research submarine. "Research vessel *Atlantis* outbound," A. D. Colburn, the ship's captain, reported into the ship radio.

The water was calm and the bridge crew quiet as they steered us into open water. For the next fourteen hours, we would sail toward the site of BP's Macondo well, where, in April 2010, a blowout caused the largest off-shore-drilling oil spill in history. Once there, *Atlantis*'s crew would launch *Alvin* and guide it to the bottom of the ocean, reaching depths as great as 7,200 feet below the surface. Over the next twenty-two days they would send the submersible down seventeen times, to gather animal, plant, water, and sediment samples. Their goal was to determine how BP's spill had affected the ocean's ecosystem from the seabed up. I would get the chance to join them in the submarine as they went closer to the Macondo well-head than anyone had gone since the blowout.

Data gathered by the *Atlantis* would likely be used in the federal legal proceedings against BP, which began in December 2010. A few months after our mission, U.S. district judge Carl Barbier found the company guilty of gross negligence and willful misconduct. In January 2015, he ruled that the amount of oil the company was responsible for releasing into the Gulf totaled some 134 million gallons, a decision both sides have appealed. By the time this article went to press, Barbier had yet to make his third and final ruling, which will determine how much BP owes in penalties under the Clean Water Act. (If his judgment about the size of the spill is not overturned, the company will face a $13.7 billion fine.) Meanwhile, the Environmental Protection Agency, the National Oceanic and Atmospheric Administration, the Department of Agriculture, and the Department of the Interior are concluding an ecological-damages assessment to determine how much BP must pay to restore the Gulf Coast. The trial and the assessment are likely to result in the largest penalty ever leveled against an oil company.[1]

Dr. Samantha Joye, a biogeochemist at the University of Georgia and the lead scientist on the mission, estimated that 30 million gallons of oil from the BP spill remain in the Gulf—the equivalent of nearly three *Exxon Valdez* spills—and that about half of this amount has settled on the ocean floor, where its ecological effects could be devastating. A BP spokesman told me that most of the spilled oil had been removed, consumed, or degraded, and that there had been "very limited impact from the oil spill on the seafloor." But Joye's research indicates that any damage the oil has done to creatures inhabiting the deep-sea waters—from tube worms to sperm whales—threatens the ecosystem, harming organisms that rely on those species. Among those at risk are phytoplankton, the sea vegetation that produces about half of the planet's oxygen. "If you short-circuit the bottom, you threaten the entire cycle," Joye told me. "Without a healthy ocean, we'll all be dead."

The Gulf of Mexico is one of the world's most ecologically diverse bodies of water, home to more than 15,000 marine species. Its coastal areas contain half of the wetlands in the United States—some 5 million acres—which provide habitat for a variety of birds and fish. Mangrove forests line the Gulf shore, and its shallow waters are filled with sea grass. Before the oil spill, more than 60 percent of all oysters harvested in U.S. waters were caught in the Gulf. Today that share has dropped to about 40 percent. Many threatened and endangered species also live in the Gulf: sea turtles, Florida manatees, whooping cranes, and bald eagles. Dolphins are a frequent sight. Giant squid, jellyfish, and octopuses swimming through the Gulf's waters pass some of America's lushest and most imperiled coral reefs.

As *Atlantis* carried us farther from shore, the fishing boats dropped away and we gradually entered clear, open ocean. Mississippi and Florida are the only Gulf states that do not allow offshore drilling in their coastal waters, which extend several miles out from shore. But as soon as we entered federal waters, oil rigs and drilling platforms began to appear. We sailed through the rigs for twelve hours and, near eleven o'clock at night, arrived at our destination, Mississippi Canyon Block 252 (MC252). This was the roughly 5,760-acre lease area that contained the Macondo oil well.

Much of the western and central Gulf of Mexico has been parceled into a patchwork of oil and natural-gas lease blocks. A web of underwater pipelines carries the fuel to shore. MC252 sits in an industrial corridor that is occupied by the world's largest oil companies—including ExxonMobil, Chevron, Shell, Eni, Noble Energy, Hess, and BP. Some 17 percent of U.S. oil comes from the Gulf, nearly 80 percent of that from depths of 1,000 feet or more below the ocean's surface. In 2008, BP leased MC252 from the Department of the Interior, paying $34 million for ten years. The company then leased the Deepwater Horizon, a semisubmersible oil rig, from Transocean, which also ran the rig's daily operations. On February 15, 2010, the crew of the Deepwater Horizon started drilling at the Macondo site, some 5,000 feet below the ocean's surface. Eventually they dug through more than two miles of rock and sediment, to a depth of 18,360 feet.

The Gulf of Mexico's high concentrations of methane, along with other natural features, make it an especially dangerous place to drill. Natural gas, which is lighter than oil, can get into oil pipes and overwhelm a well's pressure-control systems, leading to a blowout. At 9:45 on the night of April 20, 2010, as the crew worked to prepare the well, methane escaped from the Macondo and shot up the steel pipe that connected it to the Deepwater Horizon. Inside the rig, sparks from machinery ignited the gas, setting off a series of explosions. The two men who were working near the pipe, in the rig's mudroom, were quickly incinerated. They were the first of eleven crew members to die. At 10:21 a.m. on April 22, the Deepwater Horizon collapsed into the ocean. Its wreckage remains strewn around the well to this day.

When the Macondo well blew, none of the oil companies operating in the deep waters of the Gulf were prepared, even though the largest among them—ExxonMobil, Chevron, Shell, and BP—had claimed to the Department of the Interior that they could handle a far worse deepwater blowout. So BP applied methods designed for smaller, shallow-water spills. In May, employing what were known as the "top kill" and "junk shot" approaches, BP dumped drilling mud, golf balls, and tire rubber onto the well. Nothing worked. In the eighty-seven days it took to secure the well with a temporary cap, more than a hundred million gallons of oil and half a million tons of natural gas—most of which was methane—escaped into the Gulf. Eventually, BP performed the one operation that, however risky and time-consuming, it knew how to do: it drilled another well. One hundred and fifty-two days after the blowout, BP's relief well intersected the Macondo borehole, allowing the company to pump in mud and cement. This remains the only proven method for permanently sealing a blown-out well in deep water.

By May 2011, BP's oil had sickened or killed more than 100,000 Gulf animals: 28,500 sea turtles, 82,000 birds, and more than 26,000 marine mammals, including several sperm whales. Too small or too numerous to count were the vast numbers of dead fish, crustaceans, insects, and plants that washed up onshore. Most of the other organisms initially killed by the spill died at sea and were never seen.

The creatures that inhabited the coldest and darkest realms of the Gulf were not spared, either. Until the nineteenth century, when a pioneering British naval expedition was able to collect living samples from the seafloor, there was no evidence that animals could survive in the ocean's deepest waters. In 1977, more than a century later, researchers used *Alvin* to explore the Galápagos Rift, in the Pacific Ocean, at depths never before visited. To their surprise, they observed a broad diversity of life, including many previously unknown species. A 1984 *Alvin* dive revealed abundant populations thriving in the deepest parts of the Gulf, as well. In December 2010, Joye and her crew surveyed the sea life near the Macondo wellhead. The view from the submarine revealed a barren landscape. The spill had chased out or killed anything that had been living down there. "It's so strange to see nothing along the seafloor, particularly at this depth and in this area," Joye wrote in her 2010 *Alvin* dive report. "I saw nothing on the bottom that was living," she told me.

When we arrived at MC252, *Atlantis*'s twenty-four-person science party, most of them women in their twenties, immediately got to work. One group began deploying equipment from the decks, including sampling tools so large they had to be lowered into the water by crane. A device called a MOCNESS—the Multiple Opening and Closing Net with Environmental Sampling System—floated alongside the ship like a green sea monster, gathering tiny creatures to analyze how oil and gas were being taken up into the food web. Joye and her team disappeared belowdecks to prepare for the next day's dive.

Life aboard *Atlantis* revolved around *Alvin*. A twelve-person team of pilots, engineers, and technicians was constantly at work on the sub. *Alvin* was commissioned by the Woods Hole Oceanographic Institution (which continues to operate it, on behalf of the Navy) and built by General Mills in 1964, six years after the establishment of the U.S. space program. In 1966 *Alvin* located a lost hydrogen bomb in the Mediterranean Sea; in 1986 the sub surveyed the wreckage of the *Titanic*. For many of the scientists, a key payoff for their long hours and grueling working conditions (they rarely slept during their three weeks at sea) was the chance that they would get to take part in a dive.

Since Joye's 2010 mission, *Alvin* had undergone a three-year overhaul that replaced 75 percent of its components and cost $41 million. Despite the work, the sub proved finicky. On a test dive a few weeks before we set sail, the oxygen scrubber, which removes carbon dioxide from the air, had failed, requiring *Alvin*'s three passengers to put on oxygen masks during their rapid return to the surface. Technicians later fashioned a simple umbrellalike device to temporarily fix the problem—just one of many contrivances that kept the sub running. (In a workroom one day I found a box

filled with condoms. An *Alvin* technician explained that they were especially useful for protecting electrical wiring from exposure to seawater.)

Alvin is twenty-three feet long, round and squat with a bright white
shell, a red hatch, and long metal arms reaching from its sides. The sub
was named for Allyn Vine, a pioneering submersibles engineer, but members of its crew, following nautical tradition, refer to *Alvin* as "she," or
sometimes "the Ball." They never call *Alvin* "it." The language they use is
that of a very demanding and complicated personal relationship. At a media event the day before we left port, *Alvin* had appeared on deck, slowly
rolling out on yellow tracks. I caught myself and several other reporters
turning our recorders and microphones toward her, as if we expected her
to speak.

By five o'clock on the morning of April 1, the day I was scheduled to dive,
the *Alvin* crew was already up and preparing the sub. My dive would be the
second of the trip, and the first to approach the Macondo wellhead.

After it rolled out to the stern's edge at seven o'clock, *Alvin* was tethered
to a mechanical winch with a thick white rope that would lower it into the
water. During my time on the *Atlantis* I had learned how to maneuver my
way into an oversize red rubber survival suit (the "Gumby suit") in case we
had to abandon ship. I'd learned, too, how to use the emergency-breathing
device, which looked like a cross between a 1940s gas mask and a canister
vacuum cleaner, in the event that the sub's scrubber failed again. I knew
not to bring shoes on the dive, and to wear thick socks and warm clothing,
because we'd be sitting still for eight hours. It gets very cold at the bottom
of the ocean.

Bruce Strickrott, the *Atlantis* expedition leader, became an *Alvin* pilot in
1997, after retiring from the navy. He compared diving in the sub to space
travel, and *Alvin*'s silver and black interior does indeed resemble a space-
craft. The top half is packed with computers, monitors, electrical cables,
and dashboards covered with red and black buttons and silver switches.
Most of the sub's volume is given over to thrusters, banks of lead-acid bat-
teries, and bundles of electrical wiring. Its three passengers share a sphere
seven feet in diameter. Inside the sphere are five viewing portholes—three
at the sub's nose, in front of the pilot, and one on each side—and the walls
are draped in black insulated fabric to keep out the cold. As Joye, Bob Waters—the pilot for my dive—and I entered the sub in socks, sweats, and
wool hats, I felt as though we were settling in to a cozy camping tent. A

more sinister feeling crept in, however, when *Alvin*'s ladder was drawn up and the hatch closed securely behind us.

After Strickrott gave us permission to depart, we gently descended underwater. Through my tiny circular window I saw the sunlight and clouds give way to bubbling blue liquid.

"Damn it!" Waters grumbled, after we'd dropped just a few feet below the surface. Out the front window, we watched as a pair of milk crates, which had been secured to the front of the sub to carry the tubes used to collect samples, sank into the deep. A pair of crew members in swim trunks, riding atop the sub in case of just this sort of situation, dove after the crates. They saved one, but the other got away.

Once the salvaged crate was reattached, Strickrott's soothing voice came back over the radio. "Let's do this again," he said, and we descended once more.

Joye and I are both small, and we sat with our legs stretched out on the cushioned floor. Waters crouched on a low stool that faced the computers he used to pilot *Alvin*. Once we reached the bottom, we were to identify any visual changes from the December 2010 dive and to collect water and sediment samples for further study. The scientists from Joye's research consortium wanted to know how much oil was on the ocean floor, whether microbes were consuming the oil that remained, and how the sea life was faring in the depths.

Our descent took two hours, at a pace that felt motionless. We could see no farther than a few feet from our windows, and there was little change in the scenery. Waters reported regularly to the *Atlantis* via an underwater telephone, and the digital display on the Fathometer marked off our continuing dive, but the only visible sign of our depth was the color of the water—powder blue became turquoise and then navy, before fading into total darkness.

At 1,223 feet, the gloom was suddenly illuminated by zooplankton, which appeared as sinuous black lines with glowing tops. Joye explained that these tiny animals hosted luminescent bacteria that lit up when the zooplankton were surprised or alarmed. When we reached 3,609 feet, two thirds of the way down, I asked Waters if he was excited.

"About what?" he responded. This was his 120th dive, give or take. He'd started working with *Alvin* in 1995, after building a laser-tag system for a Defense Department training program. Much of the rest of the *Alvin* crew was also composed of engineers, because, as Waters told me, "you've got to be able to fix it, not just fly it."

At 5,272 feet, we hit bottom. *Alvin's* LEDs came on. If there was oil down here, we couldn't see it. Outside was an endless gray underwater desert: barren, flat, and stark. Through our tinted windows it looked like a vast moonscape.

Our dive brought us within two nautical miles of the wellhead. Any nearer and we would have risked getting caught in the wreckage of the Deepwater Horizon. We traveled about a mile and a half in five hours, tracing half a circle around the site, and stopped periodically to collect samples. By manipulating *Alvin's* robotic arms and fingers, Waters was able to remove each sample tube from the crate, push it into the sediment, and delicately return it to its place.

On the previous day's dive, Joye and Joseph Montoya, a biological oceanographer at Georgia Tech, had been disturbed by their observation of dead and damaged coral—healthy coral provides habitat for thousands of species; dead coral is home to nothing. Today, however, there was a bit of good news: we saw a handful of sea cucumbers, small white fish, red crabs, blue eels, and pink shrimp. Etched along the seafloor we noted little pencil-shaped lines, evidence of organisms called infauna, which burrow, wormlike, into the sediment. As we passed, sea creatures struck attack poses: eels hung vertically in the water; crabs extended their claws and hind legs in our direction. Joye exclaimed at the sight of a vampire squid, a rare cephalopod, which showed us its bright red body and small webbed tentacles as it sped past. Later we saw a giant isopod, which Joye described as a "swimming cockroach." These gave her hope. But she told me that before the oil spill, we would have expected to see many more of these and other creatures: fish, urchins, sea fans, and perhaps even whales and sharks.

After a few hours we stopped to eat lunch. Outside the sub, it was 39 degrees Fahrenheit. The cold seeped in, causing condensation along the walls that soaked anything pressed against them.

Shortly after we resumed our journey, the flat seabed topography was broken by a set of mounds running in straight, parallel lines. They were too symmetrical not to be human-made. "Someone's been messing around down here," said Joye. We followed the lines for a while, then returned to our sampling.

At three in the afternoon, Waters announced the completion of our mission to the *Atlantis*, which gave us clearance to ascend. The sub had no toilet, so Joye, who was in need of one, was forced to use the dreaded pee bottle. I held up a blanket, Waters turned up the music—Adele—and Joye regaled us with the story of "the first guy to poop in the sub." When we reached the surface, we spent twenty minutes bouncing in the waves until the *Atlantis*'s swimmers were able to hook us onto the winch. Once we were back on deck, Montoya and another researcher dumped two giant buckets of seawater over my head, initiating me into the exclusive club of *Alvin* divers.

Over the next ten days I spent dozens of hours in the ship's labs, watching the researchers sort and analyze specimens. The sediment samples we'd gathered were, it turned out, virtually identical to the ones collected in 2010. The layer of oil residue deposited four years earlier was still there. "It looks the same no matter where you are," Joye said. "And it hasn't changed."

Today a coating of degraded oil, as much as two inches thick, extends across nearly 3,000 square miles of ocean floor. It is expected to remain there forever. In the *Atlantis*'s computer lab, Andreas Teske, a microbial ecologist at the University of North Carolina at Chapel Hill, told me, "When another expedition comes here in a hundred or a thousand years, they will say, 'Ah, okay. Here is the 2010 oil spill.'"

There are many reasons that oil remains on the seafloor. The cold, dark bottom of the ocean is a naturally preservative environment. In addition, Joye found that microbes that consumed some of the oil and methane in the first few months after the spill have largely stopped eating. What they've left behind—the parts they have not yet broken down—are among the most toxic components of the oil, including polycyclic aromatic hydrocarbons, which are known human carcinogens. The microbes have also been inhibited by Corexit, a toxic chemical dispersant that was supposed to keep the oil from drifting ashore. Nearly two million gallons of the dispersant were used in the aftermath of the spill. Joye's research now suggests, however, that Corexit was not only environmentally harmful; it was also counterproductive.

What does it mean that a blanket of oil remnants will cover thousands of miles of ocean floor for the foreseeable future? "We don't know exactly," Joye told me. Nothing close to the size and duration of this disaster has ever been studied, and it will take years to fully understand the spill's effects. But the data collected so far is alarming. Last June I talked to Dr. Paul Montagna, a marine ecologist at Texas A&M University who studies benthic organisms. He had found significant declines in a range of species that live on the Gulf seafloor. Within a nine-square-mile area around the Macondo wellhead, he measured a 50 percent loss in the biodiversity of tiny invertebrates called meiofauna and slightly larger species called macrofauna. These species are a critical food source for larger organisms. Meiofauna and macrofauna have suffered losses as far as ten miles from the well. A die-off at any link in the food web threatens the species that depend on it, but it can also affect those farther down. Phytoplankton, for instance, rely on seafloor macrofauna such as tube worms to help decompose organic matter and release nutrients back into the water.

The increase in sea life that we had observed on *Alvin* could signal the start of an ecological recovery, Montagna said. But those returning species were now also being exposed to the oil on the seafloor, which they would pass along to the creatures that ate them. Joe Montoya's research on phytoplankton has uncovered clear evidence that oil and gas carbon are moving through the food web. Ultimately, these contaminants, in potentially harmful concentrations, could reach "things like big fish that people are commercially interested in," Montoya told me.

One study has already demonstrated that the spill was followed by immediate declines in the larval production of tuna, blue marlin, mahi-mahi, and sailfish. Macondo oil has also been linked to life-threatening heart defects in embryonic and juvenile bluefin and yellowfin tuna, as well as in amberjack. Perhaps even more troubling has been the effect on dolphins, which are predators at the top of the food chain and therefore indicators of the ecosystem's degradation. In 2011, dolphins were stillborn or died in infancy at rates six times the historical average. Last year, the number of dolphins found dead on the Louisiana coast was four times higher than the annual average before the spill.

The effects of BP's disaster have now spread far from the Gulf. Traces of oil and Corexit, for instance, have been found in Minnesota, Iowa, and Illinois, in the eggs of white pelicans that were in the Gulf at the time of the spill. Nor are humans immune to the damage. In January 2013, BP agreed to a medical-benefits settlement that provides twenty-one years of health monitoring and potential monetary compensation—up to $60,000 per person—to Gulf Coast residents and cleanup workers who can demonstrate spill-related respiratory, gastrointestinal, eye, skin, and neurophysiological conditions. (Researchers have also found that crude-oil contamination can lead to cancer, birth defects, and developmental and neurological disorders such as dementia, though none of these are covered by the settlement.) Of the more than 200,000 people who were potentially eligible for remuneration, however, only 12,144 had filed claims by the end of 2014, a spokesperson for the court-appointed medical-benefits-claims administrator told me. Of those, a mere 1,304 have been approved for payment.[2]

In June of last year, a tar mat composed of degraded BP oil that weighed more than a thousand pounds was found on a beach near Fort Pickens, Florida. BP's oil also remains lodged in shoreline marshes, where it is killing plants and intensifying coastal erosion. In March, another tar mat, this one weighing 29,000 pounds, was found buried in the marshes of East Grand Terre Island, Louisiana. The beaches of Bay Jimmy and Bay Batiste, also in Louisiana, are still so heavily oiled that they remain closed to shrimping, crabbing, fin fishing, and oystering. "Our catch is down by a hundred percent," Byron Encalade, a Louisiana oysterman, told me in March. And although the Food and Drug Administration declared in fall 2010 that many Gulf fish products were safe for human consumption, one 2011 study found that people who ate a diet heavy in Gulf seafood (or who were medically vulnerable) could be at risk of developmental disorders and cancer. "When people say, 'Oh, the oil spill is over,'" Joye told me, "they're not realizing that the full impacts are on a very long timescale, of decades or more."

NOTES

1. Some of the funding for the *Atlantis*'s mission came from a $500 million initiative to study the effects of the spill. The program was endowed by BP in 2010, under pressure from the White House and Congress.

2. Sixty-five percent of the filed applications were returned with requests for additional information; the rest were denied.

ARLIE HOCHSCHILD

Strangers in Their Own Land: Anger and Mourning
on the American Right (2016)

> Berkeley professor of sociology Arlie Hochschild wrote *Strangers in Their Own*
> *Land: Anger and Mourning on the American Right* in the years prior to the 2016
> Trump and Clinton presidential campaigns. Hochschild wondered why those
> on the political right often voted for candidates who did not serve their in-
> terests. She began to focus on what she called a "keyhole issue"—the envi-
> ronment. She visited Lake Charles, Louisiana, over a number of years to meet
> with Tea Party Republicans who loved the land; they went hunting and fish-
> ing, raised animals, swam in lakes and bayous, and more, yet they adamantly
> were against environmental regulation, even when they had been exposed
> to high levels of toxic pollution. She chronicles the plight of people whose
> homes have been destroyed by pollution and families whose health has suf-
> fered. Hochschild brings together a wealth of information and thought on
> why some politically right-leaning Louisianians do not take a stand against
> the loss and degradation of their land. *Strangers in Their Own Land* is a tes-
> tament to why environmentalism has become a politicized issue rather than
> one that unites communities. Hochschild's "Great Paradox" asks why red states
> continue to vote red despite their people being poorer, in worse health, and
> dying on average almost five years earlier than those in blue states. In this ex-
> cerpt, Hochschild listens to Lee Sherman, previously a worker at a petrochemi-
> cal company, describe his experience while employed there.

There he is, seated on his wooden front porch overlooking a trim yard
in suburban DeRidder, Louisiana, watching for my car. He rises from his
chair, waving with one arm and steadying himself on his walker with the
other. A large-chested, six-foot-three man with a gray crew cut and jet-
blue eyes, Lee Sherman, age eighty-two, beams me a welcoming smile. A
player for the Dallas Texans football team (later renamed the Kansas City
Chiefs) for two years, an honoree in *Who's Who of American Motorsports*, a
NASCAR racer who drove 200 miles an hour in a neck brace and fire suit,
and the proud purchaser of a waterski boat once owned by TV's Wonder

Woman, Lee shakes my hand, apologizing, "I'm sorry to be on this thing," he points to his walker, "and not take you through the house properly." He doesn't feel like his old self, he says, but accepts his feeble legs good-naturedly. Given his dangerous work at Pittsburgh Plate Glass, he is happy to be alive. "All my co-workers from back then are dead; most died young," he tells me as he slowly leads me through a tidy home toward the dining room table on which he has set coffee cups, coffee, cookies, and a large photograph album.

Driving north from Lake Charles through southwest Louisiana to De-Ridder, I had passed a miscellany of gas stations, Family Dollar stores, pay-day loan offices, diners, and lush, green rice fields—crayfish were some-times cultivated in the wet canals between rows of rice—flat on all sides to the horizon. Some 200 miles west of DeRidder, on land bordering Texas, lay a vast pine wilderness, once a no-man's-land where the legendary out-laws Bonnie and Clyde robbed and roamed. To the north lay soy, sugar-cane, and bean fields, oil derricks nodding in the far distance. Southeast of DeRidder by 130 miles sat Baton Rouge, the capital of Louisiana. Along the great Mississippi, between it and New Orleans, stand majestic plan-tation manor houses surrounded by gracious skirts of green lawn where once lived the richest families in America. Now tourist sites, they are over-shadowed by giant neighboring petrochemical plants, such as Shintech, Exxonmobil, and Monsanto.

Lee has also become an ardent environmentalist due to things he had suffered, seen, and been ordered to do as a pipefitter in a petrochemical plant. Calcasieu Parish, in which he had worked for fifteen years at the Lake Charles–based Pittsburgh Plate Glass company, is among the 2 per-cent of American counties with the highest toxic emissions per capita. Ac-cording to the American Cancer Society, Louisiana has the second highest incidence of cancer for men and the fifth highest male death rate from cancer in the nation.

But Lee has recently volunteered to post lawn signs for Tea Party congressman John Fleming, who earned a score of 91 on the right-wing FreedomWorks scorecard and favors cutting the Environmental Protec-tion Agency, weakening the Clean Air Act, and drilling on the outer con-tinental shelf, as well as opposing the regulation of greenhouse gases and favoring less regulation of Wall Street. Lee is a regular at meetings of the DeRidder Tea Party, wearing his red, white, and blue party T-shirt featur-ing an eagle sharpening its talons. So why was Lee the environmentalist eager to plant lawn signs for a politician calling for cuts in the EPA? If I could answer this question, maybe I could unlock the door to the Great Paradox.

Maybe I could also find the keys to Lee's own journey from left to right. For years, back when he worked in a naval shipyard outside Seattle, Washington, he had campaigned for Senator Scoop Jackson, a Cold War–era liberal Democrat who championed civil rights and human rights. Brought up by a single mother who fought in the shipyards for equal pay for equal work, Lee describes himself as "an ERA baby." When he came south for work in the 1960s, however, he turned Republican, and after 2009 he joined the Tea Party.

We seat ourselves, pour our coffee, and I ask him to tell me about his childhood. Lee speaks slowly, deliberately, as if for posterity.

"I was a dare-devil kid, one of seven boys. At around age seven, I roped down a bunch of poplar tree branches, tied myself to them, and released them so I could *fly*," Lee recalls with a laugh. "I flew pretty high"—he describes a broad arc with his arm—"and landed in a prickly blackberry thicket. It hurt. But my mom didn't come get me because she wanted me to learn a lesson. I didn't though," he added. Lee drove cars long before he had a license, and at age twelve stole, flew, and safely landed a neighbor's biplane.

Even at a younger age, Lee was an active child. "When I was about five, I got pneumonia and had to stay in bed for three months. My great grandma (a Native American who lived on a Crow reservation in Montana) sat *on* me, not *with* me, so I wouldn't get up. That's how she kept me still so I could learn to crochet."

As a young man, Lee trained as a coppersmith in the U.S. naval shipyards outside Seattle, where his dad worked as an electrician. When traveling south for work in 1965, Lee was hired by Pittsburgh Plate Glass as a maintenance pipefitter and soon earned a workroom reputation as a mechanical genius. "He can make nuts and bolts and rods and pipes and estimate lengths to the millimeter without having to measure or re-measure them," Mike Tritico, the environmental activist, told me, when he put the two of us in touch. And on weekends Lee raced cars, one of his plant supervisors always asking on Monday how Saturday's race had gone.

Lee was fearless and careful, a good fit for his dangerous job at PPG—fitting and repairing pipes carrying lethal chemicals such as ethylene dichloride (EDC), mercury, lead, chromium, polycyclic aromatic hydrocarbons (PAHs), and dioxins. Mysteriously, these same chemicals found their way into a nearby waterway called Bayou d'Inde—a bayou on which a Cajun family, the Arenos, had lived for many generations, and greatly suffered, and whose extraordinary connection to Lee we will learn.

At one point, Lee narrowly escaped death, he tells me, taking a careful, long sip of coffee. One day while he was working, cold chlorine was accidentally exposed to 1,000 degree heat, which instantly transformed the liquid to gas. Sixteen workers were in the plant at the time. Noting that the company was short of protective gear, Lee's boss instructed him to leave. "Thirty minutes after I left," Lee says, "the plant blew up. Five of the fifteen men I left behind were killed." The next afternoon, Lee's boss asked him to help search for the bodies of the five dead workers. Two were found, three were not. Acid had so decomposed the body of one of the three victims that his remains came out in pieces in the sewer that drained into Bayou d'Inde. "If someone hadn't found him," Lee says, turning his head to look out his dining room window, "that body would have ended up floating into Bayou d'Inde."

In the 1960s, safety was at a minimum at PPG. "During safety meetings," Lee tells me, "the supervisor just gave us paperwork to fill out. Working with the chemicals, we wore no protective facial masks. You learned how to hold your nose and breathe through your mouth."

"The company didn't much warn us about dangers," Lee says, adding in a softer voice, "My coworkers did. They'd say, 'You can't stand in that stuff. Get out of it.' I wouldn't be alive today, if it weren't for my co-workers."

The pipes Lee worked on carried oxygen, hydrogen, and chlorine, and when a pipe sprung a leak, he explains, "I was the guy to fix it."

"Did you use your bare hands?" I ask.

"Oh, yeah, yeah."

Eventually the general foreman issued badges to the workers to record any overexposure to dangerous chemicals, Lee says, "but the foreman made fun of them. It's supposed to take two or three months before the gauge registers you've reached the limit. My badge did in three days. The foreman thought I'd stuck it inside a pipe!" Such was the scene in the late 1960s at the PPG plant in Lake Charles, Louisiana.

Accidents happened. One day, Lee was standing in a room, leaning over a large pipe to check a filter, when an operator in a distant control room mistakenly turned a knob, sending hot, almond-smelling, liquid chlorinated hydrocarbons coursing through the pipe, accidentally drenching him. "It was hot and I got completely soaked," Lee tells me. "I jumped into the safety shower and had the respirator in my mouth, so I wasn't overcome. But the chemical was burning pretty bad. It really gets you worst underneath your arms, in between your legs, up your bottom." Despite the shower, he said, the chemical ate off my shoes. It ate off my pants. It ate my shirt. My undershorts were gone. Only some elastic from my socks and my undershorts remained. It burned my clothes clean off me."

Lee's supervisor told him to go home and buy another pair of shoes, socks, undershorts, Levis, and work shirt—and to bring in the receipts, to be reimbursed. A few days later, he brought his receipts into his supervisor's office. The bill was about $40.00. But his supervisor noted about the incinerated clothes that he had already put some wear into them. "You got about 80 percent use of the shoes and about 50 percent use of the pants," he told Lee. "In the end, taking into account discounts for previous wear," Lee notes wryly, "my supervisor gave me a check for eight dollars. I never cashed it."

Lee's work at PPG was a source of personal pride, but he clearly did not feel particularly loyal to the company. Still, he did as he was told. And one day after his acid bath, he was told to take on another ominous job. It was to be done twice a day, usually after dusk, and always in secret. In order to do this job, Lee had to wield an eight-foot-long "tar buggy," propelled forward on four wheels. Loaded on this buggy was an enormous steel tank that held "heavy bottoms"—highly viscous tar residue of chlorinated hydrocarbon that had sunk to the bottom of kitchen-sized steel vessels. A layer of asbestos surrounded the tank, to retain heat generated by a heater beneath the buggy. Copper coils were wound around its base. The hotter the tar, the less likely it was to solidify before it was dumped. Inside was toxic waste.

Working overtime evenings, under cover of dark, his respirator on, Lee would tow the tar buggy down a path that led toward the Calcasieu Ship Channel in one direction and toward Bayou d'Inde in another.

Lee would look around "to make sure no one saw me" and check if the wind was blowing away from him, so as to avoid fumes blowing into his face. He backed the tar buggy up to the marsh. Then, he said, "I'd bend down and open the faucet." Under the pressure of compressed air, the toxins would spurt out "twenty or thirty feet" into the gooey marsh. Lee waited until the buggy was drained of the illegal toxic waste.

"No one ever saw me," Lee says.

THE BIRD

Lee helps himself to a cookie, eats it slowly, and lingers over an event that occurred one day while he was alone on the bank with his secret. "While I was dumping the heavy bottoms in the canal, I saw a bird fly into the fumes and fall instantly into the water. It was like he'd been shot. I put two shovels out into the mud, so I could walk on them into the marsh without sinking too far down. I walked out and picked up the bird. Its wings and body didn't move. It looked dead, but its heart was still beating. I grew up on a farm, and I know about birds. I walked back on the shovels to the bank with the bird. I held its head in my right hand and its wings and body in my left hand. I blew into its beak and worked it up and down. Then it started breathing again. Its eyes opened. But the rest of its body still didn't move. I put it on the hood of my truck, which was warm. Then I left the bird to go check my tar buggy. But when I got back, the bird was gone. It had flown away. So that was one thing good."

During the afternoon, Lee circles back to the story of the bird, alternating between it and the story of the tar buggy. "I knew what I did was wrong," he repeats. "Toxins are a killer. And I'm very sorry I did it. My mama would not have wanted me to do it. I never told anybody this before, but I knew how not to get caught." It was as if Lee had performed the company's crime and assumed the company's guilt as his own.

But, like the bird, Lee himself became a victim. He grew ill from his exposure to the chemicals. After Lee's hydrocarbon burn, "My feet felt like clubs, and I couldn't bend my legs and rise up, so the company doctor ordered me put on medical leave. I kept visiting the company doctor to see if I was ready to come back, but he kept saying I shouldn't come back until I could do a deep knee bend." Lee took a medical leave of eight months and then returned to work. But not for long.

After fifteen years of working at PPG, Lee was summoned to an office and found himself facing a seven-member termination committee. "They didn't want to pay my medical disability," Lee explains. "So they fired me for absenteeism! They said I hadn't worked enough hours! They didn't count my overtime. They didn't discount time I took off for my Army Reserve duty. So that's what I got fired for—absenteeism. They handed me my pink slip. Two security guards escorted me to the parking lot." Lee slaps the table as if, decades later, he has just gotten fired again.

The Fish Kill and the Showdown

Seven years later, Lee would meet an astonished member of that termination committee once again. There had been an enormous fish kill in Bayou d'Inde, the bayou downstream from the spot where Lee had dumped the toxic waste and rescued the overcome bird, a bayou on which the Areno family lived. A Calcasieu Advisory Task Force met to discuss the surrounding waterways, to describe them as "impaired," and to consider issuing a seafood advisory warning people to limit their consumption of local fish.

Local waterways had long been contaminated from many sources. But in 1987, the state at last issued a seafood advisory for Bayou d'Inde, the Calcasieu Ship Channel, and the estuary to the Gulf of Mexico. The warning was shocking, the first in memory, and it called for limits "due to low levels of chemical contamination." No more than two meals with fish a month, it said. No swimming, water sports, or contact with bottom sediments. It was a very belated attempt by the state of Louisiana to warn the public of toxins in local waters.

Instantly fishermen became alarmed. Would they be able to sell their fish? Would residents limit what they ate? Were they now being asked to look at fish not with relish for a scrumptious gumbo, jambalaya, or all-you-can-eat fish fry, but as dubious carriers of toxic chemicals? The carefully cultivated notion of harmony between oil and fishing—all this was thrown into question, and not just in Louisiana; one-third of all seafood consumed across the nation came from the Gulf of Mexico, and two-thirds of that from Louisiana itself.

Many livelihoods were at stake. From net to plate—fishermen, grocery stores, trucking companies, and restaurant workers—all were furious at the government officials who had declared the seafood advisory. The government was a job killer, and many jobs were at stake:

Shrimp provided 15,000 jobs,
oysters 4,000 jobs,
crab 3,000 jobs, and
crawfish provided 1,800 jobs, including
1,000 crawfish farmers and the 800 commercial fishermen who catch wild crawfish.

By 1987 several things had transpired that would affect the fishermen's response to the edict. For one thing, PPG was not alone. Other industries had been polluting so much that Louisiana had become the number-one hazardous waste producer in the nation. For another thing, the U.S. Congress had established the Environmental Protection Agency (1970), the Clean Air Act (1970), and the Clean Water Act (1972). In addition, many small grassroots environmental groups had sprung up throughout the state, led by homemakers, teachers, farmers, and others appalled to discover backyard toxic waste, illness, and disease. Around the time of the advisory, local activists were rising up against toxic dumping around Lake Charles and nearby Willow Springs, Sulphur, Mossville, and elsewhere, part of the "front-porch"—or "kitchen-sink"—politics of the 1970s and 1980s.

Peggy Frankland, a lively woman now in her early seventies, the daughter of farmers, and a former homecoming queen in eastern Texas who now lives on a pecan farm in Sulphur not far from PPG, describes the scene at the time of the seafood advisory: "We tore up my station wagon and my friend's husband's copy machine. We talked in churches, schools, met with Boy Scout leaders and officials in Lake Charles, Baton Rouge, and Washington D.C. People said we weren't Christian but animists who worshiped the Earth instead of God. We were called 'zealots' and 'country goats.' We tried to meet state legislators, who ignored us as silly housewives." As Frankland tells the story in her book *Women Pioneers of the Louisiana Environmental Movement*, "companies were treating our land and rivers like toilets, and we were standing up to it."

As Frankland, a Democrat, noted, "We could say, 'Hey, there's a federal law about clean water. You've contaminated our water. How're you going to clean it up?" But most of Frankland's activists are now Tea Party Republicans and, like Lee Sherman himself, are averse to an overbearing federal government, and even to much of the EPA. There it was: the Great Paradox through a keyhole.

In the meantime, the Louisiana Department of Health and Human Services posted warning signs about fishing and swimming, signs promptly riddled with bullets or stolen. This, then, was the context when a member of the PPG termination committee had a surprise encounter with Lee Sherman.

As Lee continues his story, we each take another cookie. Burton Coliseum, the largest public meeting place in Lake Charles at the time, was filled "with about a thousand angry fishermen and others in the fish industry." Lee continues, "When the meeting was called to order, it was standing room only. I could hear murmuring in the crowd. Oh, they were ready to kill the government."

A row of company officials, including two from Pittsburgh Plate Glass, company lawyers, and state officials, all sat behind a table on a stage in front of the crowd. A state official stood to explain the reason for the seafood advisory: the fish had been contaminated. Citizens had to be informed. What had caused it? The officials from PPG seated on stage feigned ignorance. The meeting went on for twenty or thirty minutes, cat-calls to the government officials rising from the crowd.

Then, to everyone's astonishment, uninvited, Lee Sherman—long since fired by Pittsburgh Plate Glass—climbed on stage. With his back to the officials, he faced the angry fishermen, lifted a large cardboard sign, and slowly walked from one side of the stage to the other, so all could read it: "I'M THE ONE WHO DUMPED IT IN THE BAYOU."

The entire coliseum went silent.

Officials tried to get Lee to leave the stage. But a fisherman called out, "We want to hear him."

"I talked for thirty-six minutes," Lee recalls. "Someone said, 'Sherman, you gotta sit down, it's so-and-so's turn to talk!' But another guy said, 'No, I want to hear him!' I told them I had followed my boss's orders. I told them the chemicals had made me sick. I told them I'd been fired for absenteeism. The only thing I didn't tell them was that sitting behind the front table on stage was a member of the PPG Termination Committee that had fired me. He had even once placed bets on my weekend NASCAR races. That was the best part—the PPG guys had both hands over the backs of their heads."

Now the fishermen knew the fish were truly contaminated. Soon after the meeting, the fishermen filed a civil lawsuit against PPG and won an out-of-court settlement that gave a mere $12,000 to each.

NEENA SATIJA, KIAH COLLIER, AL SHAW, JEFF LARSON, AND RYAN MURPHY

"Hell and High Water"

The Texas Tribune, Reveal, ProPublica (2016)

Houston, Texas, is the fourth-most populous city in the United States and home to a massive petrochemical industry situated along the Gulf Coast. Houston narrowly missed a monster hurricane named Ike in 2008. The near miss raised questions: How were politicians, scientists, and residents preparing for an unavoidable perfect storm in a major city with few levees and no zoning codes to control development? What actions were being taken to safeguard the Houston Ship Channel, one of the world's busiest shipping lanes? How were dozens of chemical manufacturing plants protecting their facilities from storm surge? These are some of the questions posed in the two-part article "Hell and High Water," a multimedia collaboration between *ProPublica*, *Reveal*, and *The Texas Tribune* that won a Peabody Award in 2016. The journalists who worked on the project had the foresight to question safety precautions in advance of a major hurricane.

Just a year after this article was published, Hurricane Harvey made landfall in Texas, on August 25, 2017. An estimated thirteen million people were affected, nearly 135,000 homes were damaged or destroyed in the historic flooding, and eighty-eight people were killed. Harvey ranked as the second-most costly hurricane to hit the US mainland since 1900 and proved "Hell and High Water" a tragically prescient article. This reporting deftly synthesizes complex storm models and predicts many of the civic infrastructure issues of Harvey. It also forewarns many Houston residents to leave their homes, an instance in which environmental writing may have actually saved lives.

IT IS NOT IF, BUT WHEN HOUSTON'S PERFECT STORM WILL HIT . . .

They called Ike "the monster hurricane."

Hundreds of miles wide. Winds at more than 100 mph. And—deadliest of all—the power to push a massive wall of water into the upper Texas coast, killing thousands and shutting down a major international port and industrial hub.

That was what scientists, public officials, economists and weather forecasters thought they were dealing with on Sept. 11, 2008, as Hurricane Ike barreled toward Houston, the fourth-largest city in the United States and home to its largest refining and petrochemical complex. And so at 8:19 p.m., the National Weather Service issued an unusually dire warning.

"ALL NEIGHBORHOODS, AND POSSIBLY ENTIRE COASTAL COMMUNITIES, WILL BE INUNDATED," the alert read. "PERSONS NOT HEEDING EVACUATION ORDERS IN SINGLE FAMILY ONE OR TWO STORY HOMES WILL FACE CERTAIN DEATH."

But in the wee hours of Sept. 13, just 50 miles offshore, Ike shifted course. The wall of water the storm was projected to push into the Houston area was far smaller than predicted—though still large enough to cause $30 billion in damage and kill at least 74 people in Texas. Ike remains the nation's third-costliest hurricane after Katrina and Superstorm Sandy.

Still, scientists say, Houston's perfect storm is coming—and it's not a matter of if but when. The city has dodged it for decades, but the likelihood it will happen in any given year is nothing to scoff at; it's much higher than your chance of dying in a car crash or in a firearm assault, and 2,400 times as high as your chance of being struck by lightning.

If a storm hits the region in the right spot, "it's going to kill America's economy," said Pete Olson, a Republican congressman from Sugar Land, a Houston suburb.

Such a storm would devastate the Houston Ship Channel, shuttering one of the world's busiest shipping lanes. Flanked by 10 major refineries—including the nation's largest—and dozens of chemical manufacturing plants, the Ship Channel is a crucial transportation route for crude oil and other key products, such as plastics and pesticides. A shutdown could lead to a spike in gasoline prices and many consumer goods—everything from car tires to cell phone parts to prescription pills.

"It would affect supply chains across the U.S., it would probably affect factories and plants in every major metropolitan area in the U.S.," said

Patrick Jankowski, vice president for research at the Greater Houston Partnership, Houston's chamber of commerce.

Houston's perfect storm would virtually wipe out the Clear Lake area, home to some of the fastest-growing communities in the United States and to the Johnson Space Center, the headquarters for NASA's human spaceflight operation. Hundreds of thousands of homes and businesses there would be severely flooded.

Many hoped Ike's near miss would spur action to protect the region. Scientists created elaborate computer models depicting what Ike could have been, as well as the damage that could be wrought by a variety of other potent hurricanes, showing—down to the specific neighborhood and industrial plant—how bad things could get.

They wanted the public to become better educated about the enormous danger they were facing; a discussion could be had about smarter, more sustainable growth in a region with a skyrocketing population. After decades of inaction, they hoped that a plan to build a storm surge protection system could finally move forward.

Several proposals have been discussed. One, dubbed the "Ike Dike," calls for massive floodgates at the entrance to Galveston Bay to block storm surge from entering the region. That has since evolved into a more expansive concept called the "coastal spine." Another proposal, called the "mid-bay" gate, would place a floodgate closer to Houston's industrial complex.

But none have gotten much past the talking stage.

Hopes for swift, decisive action have foundered as scientists, local officials and politicians have argued and pointed fingers at one another. Only in the past two years have studies launched to determine how best to proceed.

A devastating storm could hit the region long before any action is taken.

"That keeps me up at night," said George P. Bush, the grandson and nephew of two U.S. presidents and Texas' land commissioner. As head of an agency charged with protecting the state's coast, he kickstarted one of the studies that will determine the risk the area faces and how to protect it.

But the process will take years. Bush said, "You and me may not even see the completion of this project in our lifetime."

It's already been eight years since Ike and Houston gets hit by a major storm every 15 years on average.

"We're sitting ducks. We've done nothing," said Phil Bedient, an engineering professor at Rice University and co-director of the Storm Surge Prediction, Education, and Evacuation from Disasters (SSPEED) Center. "We've done nothing to shore up the coastline, to add resiliency . . . to do anything."

To this day, some public officials seem content to play the odds and hope for the best.

Houston's new mayor, former longtime state lawmaker Sylvester Turner, declined an interview request for this story. Turner's office released a statement from Dennis Storemski, the city's public safety and homeland security director.

"Only a small portion of the city of Houston is at risk for major storm surge," it said. In a second statement, Storemski placed the onus primarily on the federal government to safeguard the Houston region from a monster hurricane. He said the city "looks forward to working with the responsible federal agencies when a solution is identified and funded."

"Until then, we continue to inform our residents of their risk and the steps they should take when a significant tropical cyclone causes storm surge in the [Ship] Channel, and evacuations become necessary," the statement said.

The pressure to act has only grown since Ike, as the risks in and around Houston have increased.

The petrochemical complex has expanded by tens of billions of dollars. About a million more people have moved into the region, meaning there are more residents to protect and evacuate.

"People are rushing to the coast, and the seas are rising to meet them," said Bill Merrell, a marine scientist at Texas A&M University at Galveston.

"We're all at risk"

The Houston Ship Channel and the energy-related businesses that line it are widely described as irreplaceable. The 52-mile waterway connects Houston's massive refining and petrochemical complex to the Gulf of Mexico.

For all its economic importance, though, the Ship Channel also is the perfect conduit to transport massive storm surge into an industrial area that also is densely populated.

"We're all at risk, and we're seriously at risk," said Craig Beskid, executive director of the East Harris County Manufacturers Association, which represents ExxonMobil, Chevron, Shell and other major companies that operate 130 facilities in the area. "Not only are the people here in this region at risk, but significant statewide economic assets and national assets are also at risk."

Half of the Ship Channel, which is 45 feet at its deepest, cuts through Galveston Bay, while the other half is landlocked, snaking inland at about 400 feet wide. Its slim and shallow nature would intensify the height and impact of potential storm surge.

The effect would be similar with Clear Lake, another narrow channel jutting off the bay that is surrounded by affluent suburban communities.

The storm models that scientists have created show that Houston's perfect storm would push water up the Ship Channel, topping out at a height of more than 30 feet above sea level. The surge would be only slightly lower in Clear Lake.

That's higher than the highest storm surge ever recorded on the U.S. coast—27.8 feet during Hurricane Katrina. And it would be almost entirely unabated. Unlike New Orleans, whose levee system failed during that 2005 storm and was rebuilt after, Houston has no major levee system to begin with. (A 15-foot earthen levee and flood wall surrounds one low-lying town on the Ship Channel, but that would be inadequate to protect against a worst-case storm.)

"You're talking about major, major damage," said state Sen. Sylvia Garcia, a Houston Democrat. "And it seems like every year they tell us that we're overdue for one."

Each monster hurricane model that scientists provided to *The Texas Tribune* and *ProPublica* is slightly different. One model, nicknamed "Mighty Ike" and developed by the SSPEED Center and the University of Texas at Austin, is based on Ike but increases its wind speeds to 125 mph. Researchers also refer to that as "p7+15."

Another storm, modeled by the Federal Emergency Management Agency and the U.S. Army Corps of Engineers, is physically smaller but has much higher wind speeds—145 mph. Still, neither the FEMA model nor Mighty Ike is classified as a Category 5 storm, which would have wind speeds of at least 157 mph.

Both would make landfall at a point near the western end of Galveston Island, where Ike was originally projected to come ashore.

For Houston, that's the worst place a hurricane could hit, positioning the counterclockwise-spinning storm to fling the most water into the Ship Channel and Clear Lake.

The scenarios are rare, scientists say, but by no means impossible.

Mighty Ike is considered a 350-year event, according to the SSPEED Center, and the FEMA model is what is referred to as a 500-year storm.

Such events have a small, but measurable, chance of occurring in any given year. For example, there is a 1-in-500, or 0.2 percent, chance that a storm portrayed by the FEMA model will occur in the next hurricane season. Over the next 50 years, that translates to a likelihood of about 10 percent.

Scientists widely believe the method of calculating the probability of such storms may no longer be valid, in part because of climate change. "100-year" events might occur as often as every few years, while "500-year" events could every few decades, climate scientists say.

As scary as the models are, they are based on current sea levels. That means such storms will be even more damaging in the future as sea levels continue to rise in the wake of climate change.

Each model projects nothing short of catastrophe. Total damage could easily top $100 billion, scientists say. That is about how much damage Katrina inflicted on Louisiana, Florida and Mississippi a decade ago.

Galveston Island and low-lying communities in the Houston metro area would be completely underwater hours before the hurricane even hit.

Once the storm makes landfall, hurricane-force winds would meet rising waters to blow 25- to 35-foot storm surges up Clear Lake and the Houston Ship Channel.

The rushing water would be strong enough to knock homes and even sturdier commercial buildings off their foundations. The models incorporate base land elevation and even some small levees or barrier systems, though not whether structures are elevated on slabs or stilts. They show that many industrial areas along the Ship Channel would be inundated with enough water to cover a two- or even three-story building.

For more on how the models work, read our complete methodology. The communities and industrial plants around the Ship Channel and Clear Lake are typically elevated to only 10 to 20 feet above sea level, said Bedient of Rice University.

That means for many who haven't evacuated, "you're seeing people scrambling for their lives off of that first floor into the second floor," Bedient said. "And then when it's 20 feet high, you're going to see water in the second floor as well."

Sam Brody, a marine scientist at Texas A&M at Galveston who has studied the vulnerability of Clear Lake, says many people living there have no idea of the risk.

"It's a great place to be," he said of the region. "The last thing you think about is 20 feet of water coming up here."

An economic and national security issue

Beyond the pain a scenario like Mighty Ike would inflict locally, a storm that cripples the region could also deeply damage the U.S. economy and even national security.

The 10 refineries that line the Ship Channel produce about 27 percent of the nation's gasoline and about 60 percent of its aviation fuel, according to local elected and economic development officials. The production percentage is by most accounts even higher for U.S. Department of Defense jet fuel. (Official production figures are proprietary.)

In 2008, Ike caused widespread power outages that shuttered refineries for several weeks and forced operators to close a vast network of pipelines that delivers gasoline made in Houston to almost every major market east of the Rocky Mountains. Days after the storm hit, Houston Congressman Gene Green said concern over jet fuel was significant enough that a Continental Airlines executive and an Air Force general showed up to a local emergency response meeting to assess the situation.

"We can't stand it when they shut down," Green, a Democrat, recalls the general telling him. "We need to see what we can do to help."

The airline executive, meanwhile, told him that commercial planes that usually gassed up in Houston were flying out with partially empty tanks.

If Houston's refineries closed, some experts envision something like $7pergallon gasoline across the country for an indefinite period of time—particularly in the southeast, which is "highly dependent" on two pipelines fed by Gulf refineries, according to the U.S. Department of Energy.

"We would definitely see the price of gasoline, aviation and diesel fuel skyrocket," not only domestically but probably globally, said Jankowski, of the Greater Houston Partnership.

Other analysts are less concerned, saying that refineries elsewhere would meet demand.

"Price spikes influenced by major storms/hurricanes tend to be shorter lived than most think," said Denton Cinquegrana, chief oil analyst for the Oil Price Information Service, in an email.

Still, the Houston region's 150 or so chemical plants are even more central to U.S. and global manufacturing than its refineries are to fuel production. They make up about 40 percent of the nation's capacity to produce basic chemicals and are major makers of plastics, specialty chemicals and agrochemicals, including fertilizers and pesticides.

They export tens of billions of dollars' worth of materials every year to countries such as China, which turn them into consumer goods—toys, tires, Tupperware, pharmaceuticals, iPhone parts, carpet, plumbing pipe, polyester fabric and all manners of car parts.

A lot of those products are shipped back to U.S. ports, including the Port of Houston, the busiest container port on the Gulf and the sixth-busiest in the United States.

"The phone I'm holding in my hand is made of plastic, which probably came out of one of the plants on the Ship Channel, and it was shipped to someplace overseas and then came back in the form of a molded phone and was installed in my office," Jankowski said.

In 2014, during a climate change workshop held in Houston, staff from the White House and the Federal Emergency Management Agency outlined the potential implications of a monster hurricane shuttering Houston's refining and petrochemical complex.

"Any disruption lasting longer than several days will negatively affect U.S. energy supplies. Any disruption lasting longer than several weeks will negatively affect the food security of the United States and our trading partners," according to a workshop handbook, which envisioned a massive hurricane producing a 34-foot storm surge in the Ship Channel in 2044, when sea levels will be higher.

FEMA declined to make someone available to further discuss the risks.

An analysis of the FEMA 500-year storm model by the Institute for Regional Forecasting at the University of Houston shows that 52 facilities on the Houston Ship Channel, including two refineries, would flood by as much as 16 feet of water.

Flooding is the most disruptive type of damage an industrial plant can experience from a hurricane. Salty ocean water swiftly corrodes critical metal and electrical components and contaminates nearby freshwater sources used for operations. Even plants that aren't flooded would likely have to shut down because they depend on storm-vulnerable infrastructure—electric grids, pipelines, roads and rail lines.

After a storm like Mighty Ike, the Ship Channel itself—a crucial lifeline for crude imports and chemical exports—would probably be littered with debris and toxins, officials say. It would have to be cleaned up before ships and tankers could move safely again.

The U.S. Coast Guard briefly shutters all or parts of the Ship Channel dozens of times a year, often because of fog, but the costs of doing so are enormous: More than $300 million per day, as of 2014. (Experts say that number likely has fallen somewhat, along with the price of oil.)

Most plants keep about a month's worth of inventory on hand, said Douglas Hales, a professor of operations and supply chain management at the University of Rhode Island. "As goods and supplies run out after about 30 days, you're going to start feeling it."

Ascend Performance Materials would burn through its inventory in two weeks, said Carole Wendt, its chief procurement officer. It is one of only two companies in the world capable of fully producing Nylon 66, a strong, heat-resistant plastic that goes into products such as tennis balls, airbags and cable ties.

That's even after the company pads its inventory, which it does every hurricane season.

A worst-case scenario storm is "a really hard thing to plan for," Wendt said. "It's in our minds, it's important, but there's really no way to plan for it."

Houston's refineries and chemical plants have taken measures to protect themselves from hurricanes since Ike and Katrina, constructing floodwalls and relocating and elevating certain buildings and sensitive infrastructure.

These steps will likely protect them from a weaker hurricane, but not the worst-case storms depicted in the SSPEED Center or FEMA models.

Protecting against anything beyond a 100-year storm is uncommon in the United States but not in other parts of the world. Systems in the Netherlands that inspired the "Ike Dike" concept are built to protect against a 10,000-year storm.

Industry officials say building a system to guard against these types of events would be cost prohibitive, especially given their comparatively low likelihood. They say it's up to government to fund and execute such plans.

"That's really a political question and a question for the federal government and the state government to decide upon," said Beskid of the East Harris County Manufacturers Association.

Last year, his group endorsed the "coastal spine" concept. The Texas Chemical Council, which represents most of the chemical manufacturing plants in the Houston area, has not endorsed a particular project but says it supports studying the issue.

"Nothing's changed"

With so much at stake, many public officials readily agree not nearly enough has been done to protect the Houston region from hurricane damage.

And if anything is ever approved for construction, it's at least a decade away from breaking ground.

"Here we are—what is this, eight years after Ike?—and nothing's changed," said Annise Parker, who stepped down as Houston's mayor in January. "I don't think we've done enough, and I don't think we made enough progress."

For years, scientists bickered over the cost and feasibility of the "Ike Dike," a Dutch-inspired concept Merrell proposed in the months after Ike that has evolved into the "coastal spine."

With a pricetag of at least $8 billion, the coastal spine would extend Galveston's century-old, 17-foot seawall down the entire length of the island and along the peninsula to its north, Bolivar. It also would install floodgates at the entrance to Galveston Bay to block storm surge from entering.

The SSPEED Center has warmed to the coastal spine concept, but it's also proposed a few alternatives, most recently, a $2.8 billion barrier dubbed the "mid-bay" gate that would stretch across Galveston Bay. As tall as 25 feet, the gate would be constructed closer to Houston than Merrell's proposal. The proposal also includes another levee to protect Galveston.

Local officials have blamed scientists for not working together on a single plan. Congressional representatives for the area say they have been waiting on the state to give them a proposal to champion.

"These things come from our local government," said Green, the Houston congressman who represents part of the Port of Houston. "I don't have the capability to say, 'This is what we need to do.'"

At a 2014 hearing in Galveston, members of the state's Joint Interim Committee to Study a Coastal Barrier System blasted the SSPEED Center and Texas A&M for failing to agree on what to build.

"Hurricane Ike is now six years ago, and we're still talking about trying to come up with consensus," said state Sen. Larry Taylor, a Republican who represents Galveston and suburban Houston, at the meeting. "We've spun our wheels since 2008, and it's time to get moving."

It was the only time the committee, created by the Texas Legislature in

2013, has ever convened, although Taylor said he thinks that meeting was key to getting Merrell and the SSPEED Center to work together.

Today, many coastal communities and industry groups have embraced the "coastal spine" concept.

Still, scientists and the business community fault state and federal elected officials for a lack of leadership in executing it or any other plan.

"I have begged some of our local officials to take this more seriously and take the lead," said Bob Mitchell, president of the Bay Area Houston Economic Partnership, whose mission is to recruit businesses to the area and help them expand.

Six county executives formed a coalition in 2010 to study the issue, but for years it had no funding to do so.

Parker, the former Houston mayor, said the number of jurisdictions involved has complicated things but that "It's absolutely going to take state leaders stepping up. No question in my mind."

Taylor acknowledged that state lawmakers have dragged their feet on the issue, and said the congressional delegation isn't at fault because "we've given them nothing to work with." But he also said there have been legitimate organizational obstacles.

"Of course I'm frustrated it's taken this long," he said. "I think we all kind of picked it up a little late. It wasn't like we had a plan sitting on the books when Hurricane Ike hit. It's been a learning curve."

State leaders had known the specifics of a worst-case hurricane years before Ike.

In the mid-2000s, then-Gov. Rick Perry's office asked researchers at the University of Texas at Austin's Center for Space Research to imagine monster storms pummeling the Texas Coast. They predicted that such a storm hitting the Houston area could cause $73 billion in damage and harm hundreds of industrial and commercial structures.

"Very likely, hundreds, perhaps even thousands would die," the Houston Chronicle wrote in 2005, describing the scenario. The storm would also flood the homes of about 600,000 residents of Harris County, home to Houston, the newspaper said.

Around the same time, Harris County hired a local firm to do similar work and engineers there reached much the same conclusions, the article noted.

Officials presented the research all across the state's coast in 2005. Soon after, hurricanes Katrina and Rita hit the Gulf Coast, prompting national discussions on storm preparedness and response. But all that work did not result in any concerted effort to build a storm surge barrier.

Inaction persisted even after Ike, some say.

"There was not a whole lot of support from the state as far as seeking—or even expressing the importance of seeking—funds" to study a solution, said Sharon Tirpak, project manager for the Army Corps' Galveston District.

A Perry spokesman insisted the state made strides to prepare for hurricanes under his leadership.

"Over Governor Perry's 14-year tenure, Texas enhanced and expanded its ability to respond to disasters across the state, with an emphasis on planning ahead and moving swiftly to save lives and protect as much property as possible," said spokesman Stan Gerdes.

The office of Texas' current governor, Greg Abbott, did not make him available for an interview.

The slow path forward

After years of delay, officials say they're optimistic that a consensus plan to protect the region will emerge soon.

Since 2014, two studies have launched to determine how best to proceed, one led by the six-county coalition formed in 2010.

The local engineering firm the coalition hired with a $4 million state grant is examining the coastal spine, mid-bay gate and any other alternatives. The coalition is expected to make a final recommendation in June on how best to proceed.

It will then be up to someone else to do something with it.

"We were never chartered to build anything or to lobby for anything—only to study and to make recommendations," said Galveston County Judge Mark Henry, the district's chairman.

He said the final proposal likely will incorporate some aspects of the coastal spine.

But the multibillion-dollar idea will need approval from the Army Corps, which will borrow from the six-county district's work for its own study.

For years, the Army Corps didn't have the money to study protecting the Houston-Galveston region. But last year it finally found a willing state partner in the Texas General Land Office, which agreed to split the cost with the Army Corps for a $20 million study that will span the entire Texas coast.

"The Texas coast powers the nation," Bush, the Texas land commissioner, said in a statement announcing the partnership. "Its vulnerability should be considered a national security issue."

But the Army Corps has yet to secure its half of the funding for the study, which will take five and a half years. Every year, it will have to ask Congress for a portion of that $10 million, and if Congress says no, the study could take longer.

"It's a lot of money. It'll be competitive," said Olson, the Houston-area congressman. "It starts with the Corps doing their job."

The five-and-a-half year timeline is "disappointing," members of Texas' congressional delegation wrote in a November 2015 letter to the Army Corps and the White House.

"Progress on this study is long overdue," they wrote. "This effort is important, not just to our state but to the entire nation."

Even if the Army Corps study gets done, the agency will need a local partner to construct a project and pick up at least 35 percent of the tab under its normal rules.

Assuming everything goes perfectly, the Army Corps will identify a "tentatively selected plan" in the next two years. It then would embark on the arduous process of getting Congress to fund the plan. If that pans out, construction wouldn't begin until about 2025. There's a 1 in 50 chance that a 500-year storm will happen before then.

Those are a lot of ifs. Most projects carried out under the process that the Army Corps just started for Texas take years—even decades—to complete, if they get done at all, said Col. Leonard Waterworth, the former head of the Galveston District of the Army Corps.

"It's a system that doesn't work," said Waterworth, who now is coordinating storm surge protection research at Texas A&M.

Bush, the land commissioner who kickstarted the Army Corps study, said he's trying to "manage expectations," noting that "we've got a long way to go."

When a project is approved, Texas will need a political heavyweight to fight for billions of dollars from Congress to build it—probably a high-ranking federal lawmaker.

But no one seems willing to step up just yet.

Asked if he had anyone in mind, Bush responded, "Not at this time."

Congressman Randy Weber, a Republican whose coastal district spans Galveston and some Houston suburbs near the coast, said he's fully committed to securing funding for a project.

"I've been pushing as much as I can," Weber said. "Obviously, if we could get one of the senators to step up and champion it, it would go a great way." He specifically mentioned U.S. Sen. John Cornyn, the second-highest-ranking Republican in the Senate.

Cornyn's office declined to make him available for an interview. A staffer in the office of U.S. senator and presidential hopeful Ted Cruz said only that he supports the Army Corps' study.

The Texas Tribune contacted every member of Texas' 36-member U.S. House delegation. Only four made time for interviews: Two Republicans, Olson and Weber, and two Democrats, Green and Eddie Bernice Johnson of Dallas.

Asked if she thinks a storm surge barrier will be built, Johnson replied, "That's an interesting question, and much of it will depend on Mr. Weber's party."

Some local officials remain skeptical.

Harris County Judge Ed Emmett, a former state lawmaker who was widely praised for his leadership during Ike, says he is not convinced that anything should be built at all and is waiting to hear what the six-county district recommends.

"What level of protection do we want? What level of risk is acceptable? That's going to be part of the decision," said Emmett, a Republican.

Most think the best hope of getting something done may be a devastating storm, bringing national attention to the issue and galvanizing politicians at every level of government.

"We will have a project six years after the next disaster," Waterworth predicted.

That is how long it took to rebuild the levees near New Orleans after Katrina. The devastation prompted Congress to abandon the normal rules and fast-track the project, with the federal government picking up the entire $14 billion tab.

Merrell, too, predicted something will be built four years after the next hurricane.

"People who lose their relatives, [their] property, and they're going to say, 'why did that have to happen?'"

"Right Up There with the BP Oil Spill"

Vulnerable storage tanks could devastate the area.

DEER PARK—Thousands of cylindrical storage tanks line the sides of the narrow Houston Ship Channel. Some are as small as residential propane tanks, others as big as the average 2-story house.

Inside them sits one of the world's largest concentrations of oil, gases and chemicals—all key to fueling the American economy, but also, scientists fear, a disaster waiting to happen.

Hundreds of thousands of people live in industrial towns clustered around the Ship Channel, in the path of Houston's perfect storm. And if flooding causes enough of what's inside the storage containers to leak at even one industrial facility nearby, scientists say, the damage could be far-reaching.

A chemical release could fuel an explosion or fire, potentially imperiling industrial facilities and nearby homes and businesses. Nearly 300,000 people live in residential areas identified by one scientist as particularly at risk to a chemical or oil spill.

And if hazardous material spills into the Ship Channel and ends up in Galveston Bay, it could harm one of the region's most productive estuaries and a national ecological treasure.

"It will be an environmental disaster right up there with the BP oil spill," said Phil Bedient, who co-directs the Severe Storm Prediction, Education, and Evacuation from Disasters (SSPEED) Center at Rice University.

What companies keep in many of the storage facilities on the Ship Channel and what measures they take to protect them is difficult to pin down, both for national security reasons and to maintain trade secrets. That leaves scientists and advocates unsure of the true risk. But virtually all would agree the government standards and regulations in place would not protect against major oil and chemical spills if a monster storm were to hit.

Industry groups said they take hurricanes seriously and don't deny they are at risk. They said that's why the region needs a coastal barrier system.

"Hurricanes are devastating meteorological events, and when they hit . . . they will cause massive impact all over the Gulf Coast," said Craig Beskid, executive director of the East Harris County Manufacturers Association, which represents ExxonMobil, Chevron, Shell and other major companies that operate 130 facilities in the area.

"Our facilities will be impacted. There will be severe impact to all of us because of that storm. We should be planning now to prevent those kinds of things," Beskid said.

But no plans are in place to build a coastal barrier. And the risk is only increasing as companies have invested tens of billions of dollars in building new plants or expanding existing ones in the area, capitalizing on the cheap and plentiful natural gas that's come with the shale boom.

James Stokes is the city manager for Deer Park, a town near the Houston Ship Channel where more than 30,000 people live. He said he thought most people in town understood the risk posed by the more than 1,500 storage tanks there.

"They see the tanks. They know that we're in a petrochemical complex environment here," Stokes said. "I think everyone's aware that the tanks are there. That's not a surprise."

Jana Pellusch, a Deer Park resident who works at the Shell Oil Refinery, isn't so sure. The tanks are so ubiquitous in Deer Park that they've become "part of the landscape," she said. Most people hardly notice them.

"As a community, it would be good if we could come together and have a discussion about this," she said.

With tanks, no guarantee

No single government agency keeps track of all the industrial storage tanks on the Houston Ship Channel, but tanks do show up on Google Earth as tiny dots. Scientists at the University of Houston examined aerial imagery and satellite data from 2008 to find more than 3,400—a number that is likely higher today.

Usually made of steel plates welded together, the structures may not appear vulnerable to severe weather. But many elsewhere on the Gulf Coast have been damaged during hurricanes in the past decade, causing major spills.

High winds or rushing water can cause storage tanks to partially or completely collapse, rupture, or lift up off their foundations and float—turning into battering rams that can cause more damage.

"It's not uncommon for tanks to fail like this in hurricanes," said Jamie Padgett, a scientist at Rice University who has studied the hardiness of storage tanks on the Ship Channel. "It's been sort of a repeated issue."

One of the most famous examples of a tank damaged in a hurricane happened in 2005 at the Murphy Oil Refinery in Meraux, La., when Hurricane Katrina hit.

Floodwaters rushed into the refinery, overwhelming the earthen levees around a large oil tank and ripping it from its foundation. The tank, which was wider than a football field, floated to the west and ruptured, eventually pouring out more than 1 million gallons of oil.

That oil traveled a mile through receding floodwaters to the densely populated town of Chalmette, about 10 miles from New Orleans. It contaminated more than 1,700 homes that were already devastated by flooding. Murphy Oil reached a $330 million settlement with home and business owners, but many say the area will never be the same.

Experts say that Houston's perfect storm could cause a much bigger disaster on the Ship Channel.

Using a version of "Mighty Ike," the hurricane model developed at the SSPEED Center and the University of Texas at Austin, University of Houston researchers found that thousands of storage tanks along the Ship Channel could be impacted by storm surge. A few hundred may be especially in danger because they are so close to the water and are at a low elevation.

"It only takes one of those" to leak and create a major problem, turning the Houston Ship Channel into "a dead water body" and impacting wildlife in Galveston Bay, said Hanadi Rifai, a scientist at the University of Houston who has led the research.

The situation would be similar in a hurricane scenario developed by the Federal Emergency Management Agency and the U.S. Army Corps of Engineers. Both the FEMA model and Mighty Ike imagine a hurricane with wind speeds of at least 125 mph (a Category 3 storm). Each scenario would cause a storm surge of more than 25 to 30 feet above sea level on the Ship Channel.

Such storms are rare, scientists say, but not impossible; there is a 9.5 percent to 13.3 percent chance that one of the two particular storms modeled will occur in the next 50 years.

The findings disturbed Pellusch, who has worked at Shell since 2004 maintaining the refinery's instrumentation. It's a job she loves.

"It makes me look at everything differently, having to do with the petrochemical industry in this area," Pellusch said. "This is something people need to see."

Experts want better protections

Murphy Oil's tank wasn't the only one to fail in 2005, and it didn't even cause the largest spill; tanks damaged during Hurricanes Katrina and Rita caused more than 8 million gallons of oil to spill in Louisiana, Mississippi and Texas, according to government estimates.

Some tanks on the Houston Ship Channel were even damaged during Hurricane Ike in 2008, though the storm surge was far smaller than originally anticipated. About 15 feet of water covered the eastern part of Magellan Terminals Holdings' oil storage terminal in Galena Park, right on the Ship Channel, the company reported to the Texas Commission on Environmental Quality.

The storm surge and high winds caused damage to several tanks and a spill of nearly 1 million gallons of oil. Some was recovered, but about 300,000 gallons were released into the Ship Channel and "lost at sea," Magellan reported. (The spill didn't appear to impact any homes or businesses in Galena Park.)

Asked about its hurricane preparedness, Magellan spokesman Bruce Heine said that the company has a robust hurricane plan in place and follows all regulations. That also appears to have been true for Murphy Oil in Meraux (which has since been bought by Valero).

When companies store oil in hurricane-prone areas, they have to write spill prevention plans and follow certain regulations. But none of those regulations address protecting specifically against storm surge, which scientists say is one of the gravest threats. And no government standards exist in Texas for how to design the tanks to withstand storm surge from hurricanes.

The spill prevention rules simply ask companies to follow the standards developed by the American Petroleum Institute—standards that focus on withstanding high wind speeds, not surge, Padgett and other experts say.

The federal government requires oil tanks to have "secondary containment," which usually means walls built around a tank. Those are usually not high enough to withstand surge in a storm like Mighty Ike, however. The 8-foot-high earthen walls around the Murphy Oil tank were easily overtopped during Katrina, according to the settlement agreement the company later reached with the community.

In general, the rules "more or less just leave it to the owner's discretion as to how to consider any kind of surge or flood loads," Padgett said. "It pushes all of the onus onto the owner."

While Padgett and other experts think the design standards for industrial storage tanks should include better protection from storm surge, some don't think it makes sense to require them to protect against every storm scenario.

"If you get a direct hit, there's nothing you can do," said Marshall Mott-Smith, who once ran Florida's storage tank safety program and is now an industry consultant. "You wait till it's all over, you go pick up the pieces, and you go pick up your tank . . . it would be cost-prohibitive to build tanks that withstand those forces."

After the large tank spills during Katrina in 2005, a group of state and federal emergency officials looked for potential policy improvements. They released a fact sheet that advises companies to anchor tanks to the ground, replace oil or chemicals with water before a storm and keep tanks full enough so that they are too heavy to be moved by the force of rushing water. Those were just recommendations, however.

"You can only plan so large," said Bryant Smalley, an emergency management official with the Environmental Protection Agency. "From an engineering standpoint, my question would be, what would it take to withstand a 25-foot storm surge down there?"

Smalley said the EPA could revisit one gap in the current rules on spill prevention: They apply to the storage of oil but not to other materials. The agency is now being sued over that and may reconsider, Smalley said.

Some storage tanks on the Ship Channel that carry toxic and potentially deadly chemicals are regulated under Texas' air pollution programs, but no rules exist requiring them to protect against storm surge, experts say.

Some states require companies to add protections to oil and chemical tanks to guard against spills in natural disasters. In California, storage tanks must be anchored to the ground to prevent damage during earthquakes. But experts say Texas has no such laws for chemical storage tanks on the Ship Channel.

Communities in harm's way, with little information

Based on Rifai's analysis, residential areas on the Ship Channel at risk of damage from a chemical or oil spill include Deer Park, Galena Park, Pasadena, Baytown, and parts of southeast Houston—where nearly 300,000 people live.

The exact risks they face in a hurricane scenario are unclear, Rifai said, because it's so hard to get specific information about what industrial facilities keep in their storage tanks and how well they're protected. Residents may not understand the importance of evacuating or realize the added risk of living near refineries and chemical plants.

"My district is working-class, Latino, and [has] many people in poverty," said state Sen. Sylvia Garcia, D-Houston, who represents many of the industrial towns along the Ship Channel, including parts of Galena Park and Pasadena. "Even if we told them to move to safe harbor, they don't have the car or the way to get there."

Companies that store certain dangerous chemicals have to file "risk management plans" with the federal government that explain the most catastrophic accidents that could occur, but the plans do not require details about vulnerability to flooding or high winds.

Facilities that store significant amounts of oil near waterways also have to file special documents with the EPA that demonstrate how they would respond to a spill and how they're working to prevent one.

The Tribune and *ProPublica* requested those documents for more than 15 facilities on the Houston Ship Channel under the Freedom of Information Act. But as of publication time, the EPA had not fulfilled the request.

The EPA said that while those documents are generally public, some individual companies said their plans had information relevant to national security, prompting the delayed response.

The Texas Tribune and *ProPublica* also contacted nearly two dozen facilities that store large amounts of oil and chemicals on the Ship Channel which could be inundated by at least several feet of storm surge if a major hurricane directly hit the area. One company, Chevron, offered specifics, saying its 40- to 50-foot-tall storage tanks in Galena Park were surrounded by containment berms roughly 8 feet high.

Vopak's bulk oil terminal in Deer Park has 243 storage tanks on the Ship Channel that can carry nearly 300 million gallons of oil, according to the company's website. The worst-case-scenario models project that the area around the terminal could be inundated by more than 12 feet of water.

Vopak's spokeswoman Liesbeth Lans said the bulk liquid storage company has calculated the amount of liquid necessary to prevent the tanks from floating. She added that the company has plans to fill empty tanks with water in a storm event. She did not specify what level of storm surge Vopak is prepared for.

"A great amount of this information is commercially sensitive," Lans wrote in an email. "As such, our preference is not to provide more specifics for the Vopak Terminal Deer Park."

Several companies referred any questions about storm preparedness to the Texas Chemical Council, which represents most of the 150 chemical manufacturing plants in the Houston area.

"Chemical manufacturing plants along the Texas Gulf Coast are inherently designed and engineered to withstand hurricanes and other events, utilizing hardened equipment, as well as dikes and levees to provide added protection from storm water and containment in the event of a spill," the council wrote in a statement.

Hector Rivero, the council's president and CEO, argued that when it comes to the most serious risks posed by a hurricane, the focus should be on schools and neighborhoods. Industrial facilities have more means to protect themselves than most of the community, he said.

"Think about the thousands and thousands of cars that are now leaking gasoline and oil out because they're underwater," Rivero said.

For Pellusch, though, the unique risks to the petrochemical industry on the Houston Ship Channel should be better understood.

A common saying among workers is that the smell of petrochemicals and hydrocarbons that is ubiquitous along the Ship Channel is "the smell of money," she said.

"You just brush it off like that," she said. "I know people that work at these plants, and they make their living that way. So it's something that we accept. It's a big part of the economy."

But, she added: "It comes with hazards."

EDWARD O. WILSON

Half-Earth: Our Planet's Fight for Life (2016)

Few scientists have left such a large legacy in both the science and literature fields of the Gulf South. Edward O. Wilson, born in Birmingham, Alabama, in 1929, is one of the world's experts in the study of ants and has been called the father of sociobiology, the study of the genetic basis for the social behavior of animals, including humans. The author of more than twenty books, Wilson is a two-time Pulitzer Prize winner for his books *On Human Nature* (1979) and *The Ants* (1991).

In the excerpt included here, Wilson proposes that by giving half of the planet's land and ocean surface to nature, millions of species as well as humanity will survive the developing biological mass extinction. While this vision requires a radical global change, Wilson offers a wealth of evidence and data that contradict Anthropocene optimism that humans can survive without nature and that technology and human ingenuity might save us. Instead, Wilson offers anecdotes of successful ways humans have worked to preserve natural ecosystems for the future. Here, we meet MC Davis, a businessman from Alabama whose love of the longleaf pine led him to purchase land and plant a million trees to restore the balance of the ecosystem. Again, this excerpt reveals an optimism that with significant changes to human perspectives and approaches to living within the Earth's ecosystem, humans can shrink ecological destruction.

There are true wildernesses around the world that, if simply left alone, will endure as wildernesses. In addition there are mostly wild places whose living environments can be returned close to their original condition, either by the removal of a few invasive species or the reintroduction of one to several extirpated keystone species—or both. At the opposite extreme are landscapes so degraded that their original life must be restored from the ground up, by inserting soil, microorganisms, and eukaryotic species (algae, fungi, plants, animals) in certain combinations and in particular sequences.

For a large minority of conservation projects, some amount of restoration, meaning human intervention, is necessary. Each project is special unto itself. Each requires knowledge and love of the local environment shared by partnerships of scientists, activists, and political and economic leaders. To succeed, it needs every bit of their entrepreneurship, courage, and persistence.

Large conservation programs, like new scientific disciplines, start with a heroic age. A few individuals push forward, risking failure and harm to their own security and reputations. They have a dream that does not fit the norm. They accept long hours, personal expense, nagging uncertainty, and rejection. When they succeed, their idiosyncratic views become the new normal. Their individual stories are then rightfully seen as epics. They become part of environmental history.

During my work in nature parks and reserves, I have had the privilege of working with two such pioneers in biodiversity conservation. Their heroic endeavors unfolded on different continents. The landscapes they restored had problems that at first seemed polar opposites, but these conservationists were motivated by the same prime movers: the love of the habitats they befriended and the perceived need to bring back keystone species earlier destroyed by human action.

MC Davis of Miramar Beach, Florida, was (until his death from cancer in 2015) a very successful business entrepreneur whose wealth was built in good part from property management and the rehabilitation of small businesses. At first his way of life, focused on capital investment and development, seemed typical for an American businessman. But he was also an outdoorsman who explored the wild environments of his native Florida Panhandle with a special passion for science and education. Learning ecology and natural history on his own, MC discovered that the biodiversity of most of the Panhandle woodlands was in a seriously disturbed condition. The principal cause, he learned, was the disappearance of the longleaf pine (*Pinus palustris*), the signature tree of the southern U.S. wildlands.

The longleaf pine is a tall, stately tree that yields lumber of high quality, ranked with white pine and redwood among the best in the United States. Before the coming of Europeans, it was the dominant species on 60 percent of the Southern wild lands. Longleaf was not tightly arrayed into a forest, nor was it the most abundant tree within small hardwood forest groves scattered across the landscape. Rather, it ruled over an open savanna. Other tree species in its midst were kept sparse by frequent lightning-sparked fires. Longleafs survived because they evolved special resistance at the seedling stage, including rapid aboveground growth and deep roots. It is relatively easy to walk through an old-growth stand of longleaf pine, because the understory consists primarily of low herbs and shrubs, representing a great variety of flowering species also adapted to survive the frequent fires.

Following the U.S. Civil War, Northern entrepreneurs and newly impoverished Southerners began harvesting longleaf pine as a principal source of income. By the end of the twentieth century, less than 1 percent of the pristine original cover remained.

The clear-cutting resulted in more than the severe reduction of the dominant species. It changed the entire structure of the remaining savanna. Previous "weedy" tree species, including fast-growing slash pine and loblolly pine, took over from the commercially more valuable longleaf. Higher understory shrubs replaced much of the original species-rich understory. They and the newly dominant pines allowed the accumulation of thick, dried-out leaf litter and masses of flammable dead branches caught and held well above ground level. The result was that natural fires no longer crept along close to the ground and burned themselves out among vegetation adapted to resist them. Aided by even a slight wind, they instead swept upward through the understory and raged outward through the canopy as full-blown wildfires. I know this degraded environment very well. I spent the bulk of my boyhood wandering through it in southern Alabama and the western Florida Panhandle. Only as an adult did I understand the full picture of its decline.

MC Davis recognized that restoring the longleaf pine was the key to the health and sustainability of the Florida Panhandle and a substantial region of the southern United States beyond. Other environmentalists, including forestry professionals in the Longleaf Alliance and similar environmental organizations, had also grasped the problem well and begun to address it. But it was Davis who as a private citizen chose single-handedly to do something dramatic about this problem. And he did. He noticed that undeveloped property away from the beach zone of the Gulf of Mexico coast, having been shorn of its longleaf and left with soil relatively poor for farming, could be purchased cheaply. In partnership with a fellow business entrepreneur, Sam Shine, he bought up large sections of land and put them into a permanent conservation trust.

Then came the even harder part, restoration of the longleaf savanna. Davis acquired big-timber equipment and set out to cut down the intrusive slash and loblolly pines. He arranged to sell the timber to help pay for the operation. His crews used other, specialized machines to claw out the dense fire-prone parts of the understory. When the cleared land was ready, they planted more than a million longleaf seedlings. Where the South's premier timber species began to return, the rich ground flora resumed its original unimpeded growth.

In the course of restoring to life a part of northern Florida's original habitat, MC Davis conceived another idea. While we're at it (he said in a good-old-boy Deep Southern drawl), we might create a wildlife corridor, consisting of a narrow but continuous strip of natural environment along the Gulf of Mexico coast from Tallahassee west to Mississippi. The corridor would allow larger animals, including bears and cougars, to reoccupy regions from which they had disappeared decades ago. It would also make possible a moderation of damage due to climate change, which was expected to include an eastbound wave of drying along the Gulf Coast. Such a linkage is now viewed as a possibility. Even better, its creation is under way. The parts, achieved and planned, include state and federal woodland, coastal river floodplain forests, military buffer property, and privately-owned wild land tracts.

JUSTIN NOBEL

"The Louisiana Environmental Apocalypse Road Trip"

Longreads (2017)

There is a long history of travel literature about driving across the Gulf Coast: Walker Percy's *The Moviegoer* features a drive along the Gulf; David Gessner's *The Tarball Chronicles*, excerpted in this book, centers on his driving along the coast to explore the BP oil spill; here, Justin Nobel continues that tradition in a macabre sense. "The Louisiana Environmental Apocalypse Road Trip" is a ride through the environmental destruction of Louisiana. New Orleans, Bossier City, Lake Charles, and other cities across the state are stops along Nobel's trip as he catalogues health defects, crippled communities, and loss of critical wetlands. The prose of this piece is filled with anger at the state of the state. Much can be summed up in Nobel's interview with a retired military man and environmental activist: "We have some of the most profound natural resources in America, and we are the second largest energy producer, but we are the second poorest state," says the General. "Now what the fuck is wrong with that picture?"

Justin Nobel's work has been published in *Rolling Stone, Orion, Tin House,* and *Virginia Quarterly Review* as well as *Best American Science and Nature Writing* 2014 and *Best American Travel Writing* 2011 and 2016. Nobel cowrote *The Story of Dan Bright* with Dan Bright, a death-row exoneree. Nobel's forthcoming book on oilfield radioactivity will be published with Simon & Schuster.

If you're visiting New Orleans and want to see something truly amazing, take your beer or daiquiri to-go and walk a few blocks past the Superdome—you'll find a school being constructed on an old waste dump.

"All the toxic chemicals from the landfill are still there," says toxicologist Wilma Subra. This includes lead, mercury, and arsenic, exposure to which can lead to reproductive damage, and skin and lung cancer. Even more astonishing, Subra says hundreds of schools across Louisiana have been built on waste dumps. Why? Dumps represent cheap land often already owned by a cash-strapped town or city, plus serve as rare high ground in a flood-prone state. And this is just the beginning of Louisiana's nightmare.

The risk of cancer in Reserve, a community founded by freed slaves, is 800 times the national average, making the community, by one EPA metric, the most carcinogenic census tract in America—the cause is a DuPont/Denka chemical plant adjacent to the town that annually spews 250,000 pounds of the *likely carcinogen* chloroprene into the air. If you think the situation in Flint is bad, there are approximately 400 public water systems in Louisiana with lead or other hazardous substances leaching into the drinking water. Meanwhile, hundreds of petrochemical plants peppered across the state's lush swampy interior freely emit carcinogens, endocrine disruptors, and neurotoxins into the air and water, as well as inject them deep into the earth.

Perhaps it's no surprise that Louisiana is ranked, according to different surveys, 47th in environmental quality, third in poverty, and 49th in education. Are you still gushing about your latest trip to New Orleans for *Jazz Fest Presented by Shell*, or *French Quarter Festival presented by Chevron*? "New Orleans is the best," one visitor recently wrote to me, "you are so smart to live there!" But how smart is it to allow children to attend school built on toxin-laced waste? How smart is it to allow a community's cancer rates to shoot off the charts? Louisiana is rich in culture, spirit, and faith, yet what type of state knowingly poisons its own people? What type of country stands by and allows it to happen?

While it is fashionable to critique President Trump for his scientific ignorance, science was misdirected long before Trump laid hands on it. It is time to open our eyes and see what is really going on in this world, to critique our society's dinosaur methods, then step back and imagine what a new path forward might look like. It is with this aim that I begin a science column for Longreads. In my first story I'll tour us through a land America should have never allowed to materialize—it's what I'm calling the *Louisiana Environmental Apocalypse Road Trip*. As the Trump administration chucks environmental science out the window, evaporates industry regulations, and cripples agencies charged with protecting the environment, this tale is relevant for all Americans, because the poisoning happening in Louisiana could happen in your state too—in fact, it is probably already happening.

But for now sit back, enjoy a signature New Orleans cocktail from the comfort of your couch or chair, and get ready to keep reminding yourself: Yes, this is occurring in 2017 in the United States of America.

We begin beneath a shade tree on Croydon Street, in the state capitol of Baton Rouge, where Lieutenant General Russel Honore shares with us a one-line lesson in Louisiana economics. "We have some of the most profound natural resources in America, and we are the second largest energy producer, but we are the second poorest state," says the General. "Now what the fuck is wrong with that picture?"

The General is an epic Louisiana hero. In the dark violent days after Hurricane Katrina, he was tapped to lead Joint Taskforce Katrina and roared into the beleaguered city to control the chaos. A *Times-Picayune* reporter called him a "salty-mouthed, cigar-chompin' guardian angel in camouflage." Now, at age 69, rather than winding his career down with rum and cokes on some tropical beach, the General has transformed himself into a venom-spitting environmental warrior. He leads a (guerrilla) posse of activists called the GreenARMY, whose aim is to rescue Louisiana's poisoned communities and environment. Soldiers tirelessly crisscross the state, chastising toxic corporations and lame duck regulatory agencies at public meetings and standing up for the people. We lay out a map of Louisiana and the General, dressed in Army cap, navy blue blazer, and leather boots hurls out a laundry list of catastrophes.

"This is about as stupid as stupid gets!" he spits, diving into a story that conveys how Louisiana's lax oversight can actually lead to things exploding. A military facility in northern Louisiana called Camp Minden contained 18 million pounds of old explosives, much of which had been stored improperly by a military contractor, including gigantic 880-pound sacks of propellant left outdoors and exposed to the baking Louisiana sun. On October 15, 2012, a tremendous explosion rocked the site, shattering windows in homes four miles away, generating a toxic mushroom cloud that rose 7,000 feet into the atmosphere. The local sheriff told people the cause may have been "a meteor."

One hundred miles south in Colfax, a company called Clean Harbors has been burning old military and industrial explosives out in the open on metal sheets, releasing arsenic, lead and radioactive strontium into the environment. "Here we are in the 21st century and they're using Roman army methods," fumes the General. The burns are illegal under the Clean Air Act but *Clean Harbors* was granted an exemption by Louisiana's

Department of Environmental Quality. "This is one of the few places in America an open air burn of military explosives would even be permitted," he says. Activities too toxic for other parts of America are regularly shuttled to Louisiana, often at the eager request of the state's politicians. "Louisiana," says the General, "is a dumping ground."

Near Alexandria, in central Louisiana, two plants that use coal-tar creosote and pentachlorophenol to pressure-treat and preserve wooden objects like rail ties and telephone poles operate directly adjacent to communities. Historically, wood was cooked with these chemicals then laid outside, where chemicals escaped into the air and leaked into the soil and groundwater, often flowing from these facilities in open ditches. One plant drained into a schoolyard. Pentachlorophenol can cause severe irritation to the skin and may be carcinogenic. As for creosote, exposure, according to the Agency for Toxic Substances and Disease Registry, can lead the outer layers of skin to flake off and peel away. Regulators have continued to reject the plants as a health hazard. "Please," the General begged city officials at one 2015 meeting, citing a man with strange blotches across his face, "please, please, please on behalf of these poor people, do something."

Residents in Bossier City, Louisiana, near the Arkansas border, have also suffered from living adjacent to a wood preservation plant. A Louisiana State University toxicologist found leukemia rates here to be 40 times the national average. In 2001, a reporter visited the community and spoke to Harold Quigley, who grew up beside a ditch the plant used to funnel away creosote waste. "He spent summer nights sleeping on the side porch, breathing the fumes from the plant," the reporter noted. Harold's family health history: two cousins lost to leukemia; sister had breast cancer and also suffered an aneurism; mother developed four different types of cancer; two brothers both got skin cancer and both bore sons with birth defects; a nephew's wife has birthed two stillborn babies.

The wind whistles through our shade tree. Even this pleasant late spring morning breeze feels suspicious. "Here we are," the General sighs, paraphrasing Ansel Adams, "fighting our own government for clean air."

The General grew up on a farm in tiny Lakeland, Louisiana, one of 12 children. "We never worried about having enough money because we never had enough money," he said during a May 2016 Ted Talk. About 7 miles from his home, in New Roads, the Big Cajun II coal-burning power plant continues to spray the fine country air with neurotoxins, mutagens—compounds that can alter an organism's DNA—and teratogens—compounds capable of disturbing the development of a fetus. In a nearby parish is Belle River, a fishing community of 107 households on the edge of the Atchafalaya Basin, the largest bottomland hardwood swamp in America. Since the mid-1980s an *environmental service* company has been shipping industrial waste from across the nation and injecting it deep beneath the swamp. "What a great fucking concept," smacks the General.

Travelling west to Mossville, a 30-minute drive from the Texas border, a once vibrant 230-year-old African American community is now surrounded by 14 industrial facilities, including petroleum refineries, vinyl chloride manufacturers and a coal-fired power plant—"There are no fucking birds in Mossville," says the General. In 1998 the federal government tested the blood of Mossville residents and discovered dioxin levels to be among the highest ever seen in the country. The South African fuels company Sasol, looking to expand their petrochemical facility, is now buying residents out, one by one. "The poor people never get a break in this state," says the General. "With no help from the state of Louisiana, none!"

Marylee Orr, director of the Louisiana Environmental Action Network and one of the General's main allies, brings us mugs of water. Instead of being seen as environmental advocates, people like the General and Orr are often regarded by legislators as a threat to the state's tourism and commerce. "A lot of people are concerned that if we over-speak it'll make our seafood suspicious," quips the General. "What we're talking about here is atypical information warfare—psychological operations. Our democracy has been hijacked."

The General must run to the capitol building, where he'll be presenting to the House's Health & Welfare Committee on a bill intended to make Louisiana Tumor Registry information, now kept confidential and only accessible at the parish level, available at the community-level. The bill was passed by the House last May and signed into law by the governor in June. Effective August 1, 2017, House Bill 483 could prove monumental, potentially pulling back the curtain on cancer clusters across the state.

Zooming south out of the capital we enter a squiggly 85-mile stretch of the Mississippi River between Baton Rouge and New Orleans that contains more than 150 petrochemical plants. This is infamous Cancer Alley, and to help explain how it came to be we turn onto a country road in New Iberia and park in the gravel drive of Wilma Subra, toxicologist, environmental consultant, and winner of the prestigious MacArthur "Genius

Grant." Behind bulletproof glass she hums about a bunker-like room filled with tables completely occupied by neatly stacked piles of documents; each stack is a different community that is being poisoned. At any given time she has between 100 and 150 cases, though not all are from Louisiana. But this state is home. Subra grew up in the nearby oil town of Morgan City, and got her masters at the University of Southwestern Louisiana in 1966. She has been fighting for the health of Louisianans ever since.

Subra explains to us that 200 years ago Cancer Alley was a fertile belt of river-front land occupied by sugarcane and cotton plantations, and worked by enslaved African American men and women. The plantations extended inland from the Mississippi River in long rectangular plots. With Emancipation, in 1863, former slaves settled in shacks along the lanes bordering the plantations. These rows of shacks became communities, like Diamond, St. James, Morrisonville, Reveilletown, and Reserve. But this scenic sleepy stretch of the Mississippi was of magnificent industrial value, as a ready-made port with quick access to the grain and corn fields of the Midwest, the oil and gas reserves of the Gulf Coast, and the deposits of salt that layer southern Louisiana and contain chlorine, a necessary component in the production of many fertilizers and plastics.

In the 1970s, notoriously corrupt Louisiana Governor Edwin Edwards (he spent eight years in federal prison on racketeering charges) invited, "all these industries to relocate to Louisiana," Subra says. "He granted them benefits and permits that weren't restrictive, the corporations came and these facilities just operated however they wanted." When neighboring communities began complaining about bad air and water, the petrochemical companies—as is presently happening in Mossville—began buying them out. Reveilletown was swallowed by the Georgia Gulf Corporation in the late 1980s; Morrisonville devoured by Dow Chemical around 1990; And the community of Diamond, squeezed between a Shell refinery and a Shell chemical plant, and forced to suck down decades of noxious emissions, was at last digested by the company in the early 2000s—Shell, to remind you, is the official sponsor of Jazz Fest; Diamond and environs where famous jazz musicians Tubby and Minor Hall hailed from, as well as James Brown Humphrey, referred to by some as "the grandfather of jazz."

With natural gas presently booming in the U.S., Cancer Alley is buzzing with activity. Earlier this year Houston-based Yuhuang Chemical, a subsidiary of China-based Shandong Yuhuang Chemical broke ground on a massive methanol plant in St. James Parish, in the middle of Cancer Alley and right beside the community of St. James. Following the American way, Yuhuang simply bought the town. The plant, to be completed next year, will cook natural gas into methanol, used as the feedstock in many plastics. "The process creates so much pollution," says Subra, "that they can't even do this in China."

So plantations become petrochemical plants to produce fuels and products we all use daily, yet rarely do we stop to consider that they are made in a place, and that place is a Louisiana community founded by freed slaves, and these communities are being poisoned, and now corporations that own the plants are buying up these communities and turning them into "buffer zones." Can we all put down our cocktails for just a moment, and think about that?

But there is a resistance. It is bold and beautiful and we curve through Cancer Alley on Highway 44 to find it, passing facilities operated by Cargill, Marathon, and Kinder Morgan, one of the (self-described) largest energy infrastructure companies in North America. In Reserve, one of the most cancer-ridden towns in America, 76-year-old Robert Taylor Jr. welcomes us into his home, where we politely step past his sick wife and daughter, who are watching the Will Smith movie *Collateral Beauty* in the living room, and take a seat at the kitchen table. Taylor was born in Reserve and remembers when DuPont began neoprene production in 1969, and the unexplainable wave of sickness and death that followed. Production of neoprene—dive wetsuits, insulated lunch boxes, beer koozies—emits toxic chloroprene, and this is the only plant in America that produces it.

Taylor, in jeans and black T-shirt, is well-spoken and furious. One of his main concerns is the Fifth Ward Elementary School, which borders the plant, and where just this past January chloroprene concentrations in the air were recorded at 332 times the federal guidelines. "If we can commit an act of war against another country for chemically poisoning their children," says Taylor, "how can we stand by and do nothing when chemicals are poisoning our own children?"

Taylor was born in 1940. As a teenager in the 1950s he played electric bass on Bourbon Street in New Orleans, where bars and restaurants were still legally segregated by skin color. In 1963, he got married, and in 1966 he began building the home we're presently seated in. Taylor worked as an electrician, a general contractor, had four children and numerous grandchildren. "This has been our community," says Taylor, "all my life."

He tells us that the DuPont/Denka plant appears to emit large spurts of chloroprene in the wee hours of the night, "when they figure everyone's asleep and they can get away with it."

We have also noticed, Taylor adds, "that if it rains you better get inside, because they are going to dump that stuff out in quantities that are unbelievable."

"What does chloroprene smell like?" we ask him.

"I can't describe it," says Taylor. "It has a real and immediate effect on you, the kids know to look out for it. They'll be outside playing basketball and run in with their eyes and throat burning. Your chest starts hurting, you start breathing differently."

"When we call 911," he continues, "we get hostilities. The last time I called 911 they came and were totally unconcerned. They said, 'What do you want us to do?'"

Taylor pressed St. John the Baptist Parish emergency preparedness officials on whether or not they had plans for an evacuation should some type of disaster occur at the plant—they have no plans. And the school board, he says, has no plans on how to evacuate the children. "It goes beyond complacency," says Taylor. "It's complicity. They are gassing people, and then do a language trick and call it emissions. There has to be some consequences to this."

The looming fear in Cancer Alley is not so much the slow leak of emissions and the cancer it causes, but a swift burning chemical death, like what happened in Bhopal, India in 1984, when a Union Carbide pesticide plant leaked highly toxic methyl isocyanate gas into the night, killing nearly 4,000 people. "I'll be awake at two or three in the morning and hear a loud noise coming from that plant and I'm panicking," says Taylor, "should I be waking my family and run?"

But the most tragic story involves the schools. Not only are Reserve children being poisoned with a known carcinogen but, "they're not teaching our black boys anything except sports," says Taylor. "They've taken out shop, they've taken out home economics, they've taken out music!" Remember, Wilma Subra had said, "the industries in these community become partners in education and have total control over the topics that are taught. If you have a student who wants to do a project about plant emissions, they get told, 'No.' And the school board members need money to run for election, and where do you think their money comes from . . . ?"

Louisiana is intentionally raising a generation devoid of the knowledge necessary to comprehend their own toxic situation. Not only is the state poisoning its people, but it is taking away their means of being able to understand that they are being poisoned. And it doesn't stop there. Louisiana State University and many reputable institutions across America receive large sums of money from the petrochemical industry, so who, Subra asks, is going to do the research that actually critiques these corporations?

"Do you have some time?" Taylor asks me, "I want to take you to our meeting."

At a church in Reserve, every two weeks, a group of local citizens—diverse in race, age and gender—gather to strategize. They are the Concerned Citizens of St. John the Baptist Parish, a group co-founded by Taylor in October to fight back against DuPont/Denka. Every two weeks Wilma Subra meets with the group for a public toxicology class of sorts, aimed at arming the community with an education on the chemicals that are killing them. On alternate weeks—like when we are there—the group meets on its own.

There is Shondrell Perrilloux, a vivacious young mother who says her 10-year-old son, "has been getting sick, fever, respiratory problems—I don't know what is going on, he didn't go to school for two days, they have him on a pump."

There is Kellie Tabb, who recently had her right lung removed because of cancer and suffers from heart palpitations—a symptom of chloroprene inhalation according to the International Programme on Chemical Safety.

There is Mary Hampton, who has lost five family members to cancer.

There is Yvonne Perkins, who says, "I can't even tell you how many people I've seen die."

There is Robert Taylor, whose mother died from a rare bone cancer, whose brother and a nephew both died from lung cancer, whose daughter has a rare immune disease and heart palpitations, whose wife of 54 years is a breast cancer survivor.

And then there's Geraldine Watkins, an elderly lady who lives on the fence-line of the plant. "I know I'm gonna be dead soon," she says. "My time is almost up, but I have grandchildren, and four great-grandchildren, and they're constantly sick. It's important they have decent air. Let's give them a break, let's give them a fighting chance."

The meeting, which lasts over two hours, is tense and fiery and frustrating but it is democracy, it is human beings who have been told they have no power and can do nothing coming together to create power and do something. "We need to be able to strike back!" says Taylor.

Night falls—we drive to the coast. "I am committed to keeping our air and water clean," President Trump tweeted on Earth Day, "but always remember that economic growth enhances environmental protection. Jobs matter!" The fear of local politicians, time and again, both Subra and the General say, is that if these plants leave these communities—even though residents in communities like Reserve rarely work in the plants—the people will become even poorer, even worse off than before. One can only imagine the zilch level of concern for a compound like chloroprene by President Trump, who had at his side when he signed an executive order in February stipulating the roll-back of government regulations the chief executive of Dow Chemical—"Andrew, I would like to thank you for . . . the fantastic job you've done," Trump told Dow chief Andrew Liveris, then handed him his signing pen to keep as a souvenir. Meanwhile the people in St. James Parish, home to the new Yuhuang Chemical methanol plant, were recently interviewed by a local TV reporter. "We can't even come outside and breathe," said one. "They are killing us," said another.

If you want to tell us that to have plastics in hospitals and gas in your Subaru and neoprene scuba suits poor people in Louisiana will need to get cancer and lose their lungs and raise sick children, then fine, give us an honest calculation, tell us how many people will be killed, how many years shaved off these children's lives. But don't tell us there is no other way, don't darken our horizons from the start and try to convince us that a society that rocketed human beings through the black hell of space and landed them on the moon cannot run its vehicles on a new fuel and make materials without chemicals whose production maims and kills people.

And do not even think of using the word climate change, because it is not about that, it is about running a toxic open-air chemistry experiment next to human beings, and their backyards and schools and churches. Do not pretend that this moment is the zenith of human expertise and imagination. Do not tell us not to dream. Do not silence people like Lieutenant General Russel Honore and Wilma Subra and Robert Taylor and Geraldine Watkins, who simply wants her great-grandchildren to be able to breathe. This column will be a space for dreams, and ideas that may seem too grand to be anything but. And it will be a space to call out the non-dreamers, to bring them in front of the court of the children of the future.

We're at the coast now, a perfect spot for a final drink in the sand. The sky dims, goes lavender, purple, black, and one by one lights twinkle on the horizon, oil rigs, dotting the Gulf, lighting the night, some of the roughly 4,000 production rigs and drilling platforms located off the coast of Louisiana. And beneath the waves are more than 27,000 abandoned oil and gas wells, many of which are leaking. This is Louisiana, America, 2017. But it doesn't have to be. All matters are merely a matter of vision.

JACK E. DAVIS

The Gulf: The Making of an American Sea (2017)

> Jack Davis's Pulitzer Prize–winning book is a biography of the Gulf, orienting
> the reader immediately to the nonhuman narrative, the life of this ocean ba-
> sin. Davis chronologically leads the reader through the birth and life of this
> body of water, exploring its botanical, animal, geologic, oceanic, and human
> history and the intersections between them. In this excerpt, Davis narrates the
> intersection between flora like the manchineel tree's impact on history—its
> poison might have killed the infamous colonist Ponce de León—and the long-
> leaf pine, which allowed Spanish conquistadors to construct rafts to replace
> their lost fleet. Davis's narrative history shows how the colonization of the
> New World was fundamentally premised on extraction of natural resources,
> a mentality that has lingered in American culture. However, *The Gulf* is, in the
> end, an optimistic story, that the place will continue to exist and flourish, with
> or without us.
>
> Davis is a professor of environmental history at the University of Florida.
> He has published numerous books including the first comprehensive biog-
> raphy of Marjory Stoneman Douglas, whose writing is also included in this
> anthology.

The manchineel tree grows across the tropics, often sharing space with
mangroves. About the same size as the mangrove, with wriggling exposed
roots, the manchineel probably got to Gulf shores from Central America
after its seeded fruit bobbed along the loop current. The tree has flawless
green leaves, a sweet-scented blossom, and a cute, palm-sized apple-like
fruit—an appearance that belies its lethality. The Spanish named it man-
zanilla de la muerte, "little apple of death."

When Ponce de Leon returned with colonists on a second voyage to
south Florida in 1521, a Calusa defender using a hand-carved projectile
thrower, called an atlatl, hit him in the thigh with a dart. The thwarted
settlers fled, carrying away their semi-lucid leader. The tip of the dart was
almost certainly laced with the manchineel's poison. Ponce de Leon was
dead within days of retreating to Cuba. Centuries later, the American poet

William Carlos Williams wryly observed that the Calusa had "let out his fountain."[1]

Thousands of natives lived on the Gulf coast at the time, with strong defenses and effective communication networks that reached great distances across land and water. Seafaring people, they did not live in primitive isolation, as the Spanish assumed. Their world reached beyond horizons. Indeed, they knew of the Spanish before the Spanish knew of them. They were aware of the enslaving and killing of Indians in the Bahamas, Hispaniola, and Cuba. Shipwrecks, too, so common in the age, gave away the presence of others. Flotsam had been washing onto Indian shores around the Gulf since the early days of European exploration, and the "gear of foreign dead men," to quote T. S. Eliot, sometimes included dead men themselves, their faces oddly covered with hair and their bodies weighted with clothing. On occasion, a live one crawled onto the beach, revealing even more about the foreigners. The first time Ponce de Leon met the Calusa, whom he knew nothing about, a native greeted his expedition with Spanish words.[2]

That the conquistador returned eight years later, when he succumbed to the apple of his would-be Eden, would not have surprised Gulf Indians. Nor would they have been surprised when, seven years after there came another, Panfilo de Narvaez. The conquistadors were known to be relentless, as well as ruthless, and Narvaez was as cold-blooded as any. Historians have described him as an Olympian brute—a "hollow-voiced bully," as one put it—burdened by a vindictive streak to settle a score with Hernan Cortes, no sweet lamb himself. A Castilian by birth, wreathed in a red beard, Narvaez was a major player in the conquests of Jamaica and Cuba. Cortes had been part of the Cuba campaign too. He and Narvaez served under Diego Velazquez de Cuellar, who prosecuted the conquest before becoming governor and the husbander of thirty thousand swine.[3]

In addition to fostering his massive drove, Velazquez's island was fertile ground for profitable cash crops—such as cassava (called yucca in Cuba)—but worthless without a healthy labor source. Much of the indigenous supply had been lost to either foreign pathogens or the brutality of enslavers. Following two mostly unsuccessful slaving raids to Yucatan, Velazquez dispatched Cortes on a third in late 1518. It turned out to be a mistake. Once Cortes gained Aztec gold and silver, he showed no inclination to return and share the bounty with Velazquez, who had funded the expedition. After a year, the governor appointed Narvaez to bring Cortes back. One of Cortes's swordsmen, Bernal Diaz, later remembered Narvaez as a "mad dog [out] to destroy us all." But Cortes proved the shrewder of the two. As he did with the Aztecs, he did with his Castilian rival: he defeated Narvaez's larger force with a smaller one. Narvaez lost an eye but was spared his life. He spent nearly four years imprisoned on the Veracruz Gulf coast—the first permanent European settlement in North America—before his wife secured his release.[4]

Freedom was merely an opportunity to deal with unfinished business. Narvaez sailed to Spain to petition for a royal charter to compete with Cortes. Charles V was generous. He granted Ponce de Leon's old territory and more: the Florida peninsula up to the modern northern border, west twenty-five hundred miles to the Pacific, and down into Mexico, abutting the contested domain where Narvaez had wasted in chains. Two-thirds of the Gulf shoreline fell under his authority, a coast barely touched by white men. Aside from monarchs, no individual had ever possessed so much waterfront. Narvaez walked away with a satchel full of titles too: governor, captain-general, chief law enforcer, superintendent of fortresses, and adelantado (civilian authority). His return to the Gulf was to be self-funded. But, presumably, there would be payoffs (gold, silver, and slaves) and the opportunity to settle accounts with Cortes—the kinds of motives that might impair a leader's judgment. There was the investment in lives too. Some six hundred soldiers, sailors, and colonists wagered on his venture. It was a bad bet.

Historians have long said that Narvaez was not only the most ruthless, but the "most unfortunate of the conquistadors." Risk sailed with every transoceanic trek; a safe passage was epic, so dangerous was each. Narvaez's fleet of five ships made its Atlantic crossing in the summer of 1527 without mishap. But misfortune could be epic too, and once he was in the New World, bad luck latched onto his expedition like a leech and slowly sucked the life out of it. A rare November hurricane took two ships, sixty men, and twenty horses. Narvaez replaced the vessels while in Cuba, where he also hired a pilot, Diego Muerlo, who claimed the expertise required to navigate the unfamiliar Gulf. Four days on the job, he ran the fleet up onto hidden shoals on Cuba's southern coast, where the boats rocked on grounded keels for a fortnight. Then a storm, typically the mariner's worst enemy, blew up from the south, fattened the water, and set them free. Proceeding to refreshment and supplies in Havana, they yawed and pitched through another storm, then a second, and a third.[5]

After regrouping in Havana, the hexed Spaniards were finally ready to depart for Mexico. Finding one's way around the New World still depended

on instruments of ancient-Greek vintage: the magnetic compass to determine direction, and the astrolabe to measure latitude, although impre-
cisely before the development of the sextant two centuries later. Charts of
the day were unreliable, often misplacing landmarks and giving incorrect
distances between them. Mariners had to wait until later in the century
for the chip log, which calculated sailing speed, and until the eighteenth
century for the chronometer, which determined longitude, east-west positioning. No less important than the limited technology a pilot had at his
disposal was an ability at dead reckoning, which is to say, guesswork based
on the speed of the ship—gauged by bubbles passing on the water's surface—and the direction of prevailing currents, still a mystery in the Gulf.

When the fleet left Cuba, something went terribly wrong. The pilot
Muerlo would have set his compass for a westerly course toward his destination at Rio de las Palmas, 125 miles south of the Rio Grande, and then
watched the bubbles on the water to track his whereabouts and progress.
After an unknown number of days at sea, however, the crew sighted land,
not at Rio de las Palmas, but nine-hundred-plus miles on the other side of
the Gulf near Tampa Bay—not due west of Havana, but due north.

Muerlo and the other pilots insisted they had gotten the fleet to Mexico—even though the sun set behind the sea rather than the land—and
that Rio de las Palmas lay ten to fifteen leagues up the coast. How the little
flotilla ended up so far off course remains a mystery. Some historians believe yet another storm cursed Narvaez; others say the ships got caught in
the Gulf Stream and loop currents. Either theory is plausible.

What is certain is that critical questions demanded Narvaez's immediate attention. Should the lost Spaniards try to find the Rio de las Palmas?
If so, by foot or by boat? How would the natives respond to them? Did the
natives have gold or know where it could be found? Did they have food?

Replenishments were the first priority of the passenger-colonists.
They were a fair picture of Spanish society—artisans, merchants, lawyers,
physicians, hidalgos, and friars. All were Christians, save for some of the
slaves, duty bound to follow their lord and Narvaez, soldier of Christ, and
among them were surely the qualities of discipline, endurance, faith, and
charity. But increasingly, doubt, if also fear and regret, characterized their
mood, and ominously, none among the hungry lot was familiar with estuarine abundance.

It would be to their peril that they never took full measure of the life
below the water's surface, beginning with Tampa Bay. Estuaries are the
bustling urban centers of oceans—cities that never sleep—and Tampa

Bay is the Big Apple of the Gulf's east coast. Fish are like the hordes at a market or souk. Nothing on the land above an insect resembles their density. Throughout Gulf sea grass beds, up to two hundred fish species engage in an unending contest of hide-and-seek with shrimp, crabs, and smaller fish, and they freely take at the beds of oysters, clams, and scallops. Sharks, rays, bottlenose dolphins, otters, and more than two dozen species of birds lengthen the food chain to the uppermost links below humans.

The best guess of scientists is that many millennia back, Tampa Bay was a freshwater drainage basin that took shape when sections of the region's limestone substructure collapsed. Swelling Gulf water began sluicing into the basin perhaps six thousand years ago, encouraging the tenancy of marine flora and fauna that exists today. Four rivers draining twenty-two hundred square miles infused the estuary with bracing freshwater, changing its biology ever so slightly between cycles of drought and seasonal upwellings. Some areas stayed more turbid or clear, and more salty or fresh, than others, and the shoreline supported mostly mangroves and salt marshes.

The Spanish early on called Tampa Bay Bahia Honda, "deep bay." Although its twelve-foot average depth was fine for the Narvaez fleet, the bay was later unsuitable for large-draft vessels without dredged channels. Perhaps a more fitting name would have been Bahia Muchos. Sprawling across four hundred square miles, Tampa Bay is a bay of bays (Terra Ceia, Boca Ciega, Hillsborough, Old Tampa, Little Cockroach, Miguel, Mobbly, Double Branch, East, McKay, and Joe) and of bayous (Coffee Pot, Cabbagehead, Boat, Mullet Key, Clam, Cooper, Little, Big, Emerson, Cambar, Champlain, Critical, Custer, Tillette, and Williams). Although estuaries are constantly changing, today's Tampa Bay is a fair outline of the one Narvaez mistook for Mexican waters.

Most of the historical details about his expedition come from Alvar Nunez Cabeza de Vaca, a survivor who set down events in a report to the Crown. Historians regard Cabeza de Vaca as a reliable eyewitness, short of his overlooking Narvaez's harsh treatment of natives. Chroniclers later learned of the conquistador's deeds from other sources, including stories passed down from those who endured his savagery.

Cabeza de Vaca, the orphan of a hidalgo of southern Spain and a New World virgin, had signed on with Narvaez in Spain as the expedition's royal treasurer. Today, a monument to Cabeza de Vaca resides in Hermann

Park in Houston. The patina bust on top, which seems a fair rendition, has him in ringleted beard, fluted shirt sleeves, morion (the classic conquistador helmet), and a chest-puffing breastplate, with a stare more inquisitive than stalwart. The state recognizes him as the patron saint of the Texas Surgical Society (he excised a projectile point lodged in an Indian's chest), first European merchant of Texas (he coordinated trade among Indian groups), first ethnologist (he recorded descriptions of hunter-gatherer societies), and first historian (he chronicled his time on the coast)—activities that followed the demise of the Narvaez expedition.

Cabeza de Vaca also made note of indigenous plants and animals. New World nature for the Spaniards was on one level fascinating, and on another, repellent. Absent from his observations was evident exuberance for the verdant wild. Nature was less likely to get the attention of a conquistador when it was unthreatening than when it was menacing—a notable hindrance to conquest. Cabeza de Vaca described the Gulf coast as a "land so strange and so bad and so totally lacking in resources either for staying or leaving." Yet, at minimum, 350,000 Gulf-side natives thrived on that land, most of them beside an estuary.[6]

Upon arrival at Tampa Bay, the expedition mounted to colonize, explore, gain wealth, and take revenge soon began unfolding into a hellish saga that would drag on for eight years and expose Narvaez's cruel nature and flawed leadership. It also revealed how two cultures, native and European, can take the same environment and turn it into different things: friend of one and adversary of another.

From the native view around Tampa Bay, the five anchored ships swinging with the tides were a loathsome sight. The natives were probably the sun-worshipping Tocobaga, who tattooed their bodies with snakes and birds and geometric shapes. They neither attacked nor opened their arms to the sea-weary and lost Spanish.

To conquistadors, no wild coast was more dangerous than that populated by Indios, as they called the inhabitants of the "new founde lands." From the Spanish perspective, which primed that of other Europeans, the natives lacked the ambitions and accomplishments of Western civilization. God had created them, yet they had not accepted His grace and instead worshipped, as one Dominican friar wrote, "their natural lords." A reality in interactions between Gulf natives and Europeans that historians rarely account for is that the natives' relationship with nature, as much as spiritual practices, reinforced European images of Indian inferiority and the righteousness of conquest. People who had failed to exploit their surrounding abundance for commercial purposes were artless and lazy, in the judgment of the Spaniards, who therefore felt justified in taking the God-given gifts of nature and enslaving heathens to aid their quest. It seemed the Indios lived simply—half-naked and impoverished—as idle subordinates to nature, and in failing to dominate it, they had become as wild as it. They were savages born of a savage land. For a time, they could be useful to the Spanish as guides, slaves, and providers of food. Otherwise, like thorny underbrush, the Spanish wanted them cleared out of the way.[7]

When the expedition made contact with the Tocobaga, Narvaez expected them to hand over food to his heavily manned enterprise and to guide him to gold or silver. Gripped by ambitions of wealth and power, he could not accept that deposits of neither existed around the Gulf outside Mexico. Patience was not one of his virtues either. According to an early source, during a quarrel with the Tocobaga he lopped off the nose of a cacique and loosed mauling war dogs on his mother. Eager to rid themselves of this bearded tyrant, the Tocobaga pointed north and assured Narvaez that what he desired could be found in a place called Apalachee. Narvaez sent his ships to search the coast for Rio de las Palmas, the intended destination, while he marched overland toward the fantasy of wealth, leading three hundred men, forty malnourished horses, and an uncertain number of friars, who, no matter their plight, were to Christianize the natives. The plan was to rendezvous at some point with the fleet, though no one was clear about when or where. Narvaez was decisive at crucial moments, but not always right in his decision.

For two-hundred-plus miles, Narvaez's party followed native pathways. It also laid down fresh European footprints through cypress swamps and hardwood and pine woodlands, axmen opening the way. By the time they lumbered into Apalachee, near present-day Tallahassee in north Florida, every man and horse was in a weakened state, and they found neither riches nor respite. The Tocobaga had deceived the Spaniards. Warned of the approaching conquistadors, the peoples of Apalachee had vacated their villages, and from the camouflage of woods and swamp they discharged random bursts of cane arrows tipped by fish bones, crab claws, or chert, hitting Spanish targets time and again.

Food and escape quickly replaced the quest for gold and silver as the expedition's main objective. The Spaniards withdrew to Apalachee Bay on the coast, where they prayed for a rendezvous with the ships. None occurred.

The stranded Spaniards resolved to rescue themselves. By now, they had figured out they were on the wrong side of the Gulf. Their best option, they decided, was to build log rafts to take them to Spanish territory in Mexico—easier to imagine than to do. No one within this rough cross section of Spanish society seems to have had skills in shipbuilding, yet the desperate endeavor became a high point in an expedition in need of intelligent direction.

The men, now numbering 250 or so, worked together to build seaworthy craft—an undertaking inspired by the area's endowments. The shore was thick with tall, straight pines. In centuries to come, many would be extracted with mechanical ease for the paper pulp industry. But with no tools for sawing or chopping, the Spaniards improvised a bellows from horsehide to melt down spurs, armor, swords, cutlasses—any metal in their possession. They forged makeshift axes, which felled roughly 150 mature pines, thirty per raft. Each would have to carry four tons of human and material cargo. Ultimately, the rafts were crude but eminently sturdy—models of resourcefulness in the use of imported and local materials. Cypress wood made paddles. Sails were a patchwork of stitched-together clothing. To seal gaps between the logs, the novice shipwrights fashioned a mixture of stripped palmetto leaves and pine pitch.

They also had Apalachee Bay at their disposal, which sits at the top of the Big Bend, a two-hundred-mile coastal estuarine region between Tarpon Springs in the south and Ocklocknee Bay (pronounced "ohCLAHK-nee") in the north, including the Homosassa basin that in 1904 would delight Winslow Homer with the best fishing he knew. The water of the Big Bend is shallow and almost pool-like, making conditions right for the expanse of tidal marshes, cordgrass, and needlerush. The gentle water, combined with the sunlit shallows, encourages the growth of sea grasses, primarily turtle and manatee grass, which sprawl out to a twelve-hundred-square-mile underwater prairie. In the warmer months, manatees come up from the south to graze. Some people call these large mammals sea cows; Columbus allegedly mistook them for mermaids. Eighty-five percent of the eastern Gulf's fish spend part of their lives foraging in Big Bend grass, where scallops, shrimp, crabs, sea horses, and sea stars hide from predators. For ages, this estuarine environment has fed people.

But it did not feed the Spaniards. There was plenty to be had in the late-summer months when they were on the bay. Oysters were ubiquitous, their beds feasting grounds for black drum, sheepshead, and blue crabs. The raft building overlapped with the last month of the stone-crab spawning season, when the meaty-clawed crustaceans migrate into shallow water, and the beginning of redfish spawning, the only time the monastic species gather in schools. The self-taught raft builders seemed to have little aptitude for learning how to harvest seafood. To survive, they slaughtered a horse every other day, consuming the last just before pushing off on their log vessels on September 22—just about when throngs of mullet would have been coming to inshore water until winter spawning. Underway, the rafts carried a store of commandeered Indian corn, which was rationed at a handful per man per day.

The wind and longshore current drove the Spaniards in the desired direction, west. The tenuous fleet initially stayed between the shore and barrier islands, careful to avoid oyster beds. Indigenous people valued oyster beds as a year-round food source; the Spaniards could see them as little more than serrated shoals threatening to rip apart their hard-won vessels, which quickly swelled with the hunger of the passengers. They resorted to custom and raided Indian settlements on their route, a danger of another sort. The confiscated food, Cabeza de Vaca wrote, was a "great help for the necessity in which we found ourselves." They could hardly disparage the diet of the various oyster and mullet fishers from whom they stole. "All the Indians we had seen are a people wonderfully built, very lean and of great strength and agility." From a "distance they appear to be giants."[8]

Leaving the protection of the inland waterway, the raftsmen drifted into bad weather. Rough seas loosened the lashings around the logs, but they held, a testament to the craftsmanship of novices. The men fared less well. Freshwater and food remained in constant shortage—"our bones could easily be counted"—and natives often attacked when the vulnerable flotilla made land for food stores. Nor'easter season replaced hurricane season, and chilling winds and the opaque winter sea routinely battered the rafts. Narvaez declared every man for himself, following a maritime protocol of last resort for occasions when acting as a group jeopardizes individual survival. Cabeza de Vaca believed instead that his commander had turned cowardly.[9]

Soon after, on a frigid November night, the surf breaking "loudly in the dark," waves tossed the rafts one by one onto the beach. The Spaniards were in Texas, strewn between Galveston and Corpus Christi. Natives ambushed the raft that washed ashore at the southernmost point. Those aboard had survived the harrowing sea journey, only to meet death at its conclusion. To spare himself the same, Narvaez exercised the privilege of rank and took two men to spend the night in the presumed security of his raft anchored offshore. At some point, the wind came up and carried the sleeping party out to sea and their demise.[10]

Narvaez's bad luck and ego had left behind Cabeza de Vaca and some forty survivors, staring wearily into a new ordeal on land. Many crouched on the beach naked, having lost everything since Apalachee. Winter on the upper Gulf, the raw north wind a constant, was not a season that engendered a spirit of providential salvation. Exposure was only one concern. The barrier islands were the restless winter residence of migratory hunter-gatherers. Utterly defenseless, knowing nothing about their haven from the cold sea, the survivors resigned themselves to the mercy of the natives.

Cabeza de Vaca later named the island Malhado, "Island of Misfortune," something of a misnomer, since the island's natives saved him. They took him and the others as slaves, yet gave them food, shelter, and their lives. They also left unharmed five who decided to fend for themselves for fear of falling to human sacrifice or cannibalism. It turned out they had no one to fear but themselves. Out of either ignorance or apprehension, they forfeited the goodness of the estuary and met a terrible fate. They "ate each other up," wrote Cabeza de Vaca, "until only one of them survived." The Christians committed the very unthinkable act they regarded as custom in a savage land. Stories of aboriginal cannibalism were fodder for European chroniclers eager for sensational tales of the New World. No lesser figures than archaeologists of latter-day American universities refused to let the myth die. One historian, writing in 1959, called Texas's Indian shores the "cannibal coast." Yet no one's field studies ever uncovered unimpeachable evidence of the practice, ritualistic or culinary. To the contrary, Cabeza de Vaca reported that the natives were appalled by the desperate appetite of the cannibalizing strangers.[11]

The Spaniards were marooned on the island province of the Karankawa. Although Cabeza de Vaca's report contains not a single ill word about his captors, history would treat the Karankawa as bloodthirsty terrorists. For centuries, whites trembled at the thought of being shipwrecked on the Texas coast, so allegedly quick were the natives to torture, slay, and eat outsiders. No nostalgic statements accompanied the passing of the last Karankawa sometime around 1830.

A hundred years later, Texas's coastal natives were still remembered coldly in stories of old-timers. They also became a subject of scholarly interest when Edwin Booth Sayles, a founder of the Texas Archeological and

Paleontological Society, completed a preliminary survey of the state's aboriginal past, while accompanied by his Jack Russell mix named Happy.
Many researchers followed, reconstructing the aboriginal culture one
spear point, shell mound, and dig site at a time. Like the Calusa, the
Karankawa were forceful and dominant. For centuries after European
contact, they fiercely defended their territory and way of life against multiple aggressors coming at them by land and sea—the Spanish, French,
Mexicans, and Americans. To stereotype the native defenders as "hostile"
(a descriptive that Anglo-American society still today reserves for indigenous peoples), says Texas archaeologist Robert Ricklis, condemns them
for behavior exhibited most profoundly by the invading aggressors.[12]

Ricklis is among the latest researchers in the line descending from Sayles. The Karankawa, he maintains, were not a mere tattered group of scav-
engers randomly scratching out a survival. That image is no more accurate
than their reputation for bellicosity and cannibalism. Succeeding from ancestors who had arrived on the coast eight to ten millennia earlier, they
were a people of physical and societal integrity endowed with a traditional
knowledge of the earth. Accepting nature as the sacred force of human
life, society, and culture set up fateful distinctions between aborigine and
European.

Differences might begin with something as seemingly irrelevant as native mosquito repellent, commonly a confection of alligator fat and shark
oil, with a pungency that failed to convince European visitors of native
humanity. Said one student of the Texas coast, "You might be able to smell
a Karankawa before you see him." They decorated their bodies with tat-
toos and favored necklaces of conch shells, coyote teeth, and carved bison-
bone danglers, which, unlike their Calusa counterparts on the other side
of the Gulf, reflected their semi-nomadic existence. They quit the islands
in spring, vacating their encampments of hide-covered oval huts to escape
the mosquitoes and irritating midges, and continued to gather oysters and
clams on inland waters before following white-tailed deer and bison across
grazing territory until fall, when the natives returned to their island
places. On the coast, where the harvest was dependable, they ate more
heartily.[13]

The Karankawa were physically impressive like other Gulf coast natives,
and better fed than peoples of the interior. "All witnesses from earlier and
later epochs are unanimous," commented a nineteenth-century ethnologist, "that their men were very tall, magnificently formed, strongly built
and approaching perfection in their bodily proportions." Ricklis writes

that the "possibility that physical stature resulted in part from dietary factors rather than strictly from a culturally maintained gene pool must be kept in mind."[14]

The 367-mile Texas coastline of bays, back bays, bayous, tidal passes, and sounds that the Karankawa controlled is an arcing series of estuaries, luxuriant and supple. Many took shape after aboriginal settlement on the Gulf and had a prior life in another form, like estuaries everywhere. Chesapeake Bay and Narragansett Bay were once river valleys that flooded during glacial melts. Some estuaries, like Tampa Bay, began as lake bottoms. Other systems are located on what was once solid land before collapsing during tectonic or volcanic unrest. San Francisco Bay came from the former. Puget Sound has estuaries of this origin too. It also has fjord-type estuaries that were once deep-walled valleys cut by glaciers before ice-cold water filled them. The Texas coast is modestly low-lying and riven with no bold valleys or fjords. It has, instead, flooded river deltas, including Galveston, Matagorda, and Corpus Christi Bays. They converge with a lagoon breed of estuaries, formed as sand piled up off the coast into barrier islands.

The largest estuarine lagoon in Texas is Laguna Madre. On a map, it appears as a narrow blue line between Padre Island and the mainland. The three-thousand-year-old mother lagoon runs from Corpus Christi Bay in the north to the Rio Grande delta in the south, 115 miles (the same distance from Cuba to Key West). A second half, Lower Laguna Madre, separated from the Upper Laguna Madre by tidal flats and the border between the US and Mexico, extends the same distance along the shore in the state of Tamaulipas. This is where Narvaez's ill-fated fleet was supposed to make landfall after leaving Cuba.

Back on Upper Laguna Madre at the middle is Baffin Bay, named for its distant Arctic cousin. Like Corpus Christi Bay, Baffin joins a drowned-river-delta estuary with Laguna Madre's arterial lagoon estuary. The absence of substantial fresh river water, combined with the lagoon's shallow depth and slow flush rate, has made it one of the saltiest bays or lagoons in the world—saltier than the Gulf. Too salty, as it happens, for oysters, a historically important comestible on the Texas coast. Still, three-quarters of the state's sea grass meadows range across sixty-five percent of the lagoon, and along with sprawling tidal flats and cul-de-sacs of black mangroves, they give vegetative residency to crabs, fish—mullet, skipjack, sea trout, redfish, and more—and young brown shrimp and pink shrimp, all of which are major contributors to Texas's contemporary commercial fishery.

Over seventy percent, roughly one million, of North America's redhead ducks winter on Laguna Madre—an embarrassment of riches that sportsmen discovered in the early nineteenth century.

Most of the raft-wrecked Spaniards were beached north of Laguna Madre on island shores adjacent to Galveston Bay or one of its minor water bodies—Christmas, West, or Drum Bay. A confusion of sub-bays are cordoned behind the islands of Galveston, Follet's, and San Luis, where historians believe Cabeza de Vaca landed. Galveston Bay is the largest bay on the US Gulf coast, two hundred square miles more expansive than Tampa Bay. It is part of the Trinity-San Jacinto Estuary, the amplest estuary in Texas, the seventh largest and among the most bountiful in the nation, with a trifling seven-foot average depth. Thirty-three thousand square miles shed freshwater to it via overland runoff and the Trinity and San Jacinto Rivers, supplying enriching sediment and a brackish mix. When the Spaniards landed there, the bay was alive with oysters, not to mention shrimp, crabs, and fish, black drum and redfish in particular.

During their increasingly despairing journey across from Apalachee Bay, some of the wan refugees had fumbled with harvesting shellfish. In Texas, the survivors learned how to forage in an estuarine environment from their captors, who expected the Spanish to gather food for all. A century and a half later, when the French expedition of Robert de La Salle was marooned at Matagorda Bay, a hundred miles down the coast from the Spanish landing, its members were grateful for the estuary as a source of protein. The "water was agitating and boiling with fish darting from one side to the other . . . and we made an enormous catch," expedition member Henri Joutel noted in his journal. "This type of catch was made often and contributed much to our subsistence."[15]

One conspicuous yet furtive source of carbohydrates for the natives, comparable with corn and rice, was the cattails that colonized the wetlands. Cabeza de Vaca ate Indian bread made from the starchy pulp pounded and then scraped with clamshells from cattail root mass. During the mainland months, he dug up assorted edible roots and cut prickly pear cactus, and he joined in the fall gathering of pecans at wild groves along the Guadalupe River valley, a festival-like harvest that drew bands of natives from great distances. The Indians also hunted white-tailed deer, a staple of the woodlands and riparian corridors around the Gulf, as well as bison. The Narvaez refugees were likely the first Europeans to taste bison flesh, and Cabeza de Vaca imagined a future in which European cattle would graze on the amber grassland that supported North America's largest beast. Bison accounted for a sizable portion of aboriginal meat consumption, according to Ricklis's research, but not as sizable as the "estuarine aquatic fauna." Not one of the Spaniards was apparently envisioning an empire of commercial fishing.[16]

Despite his salvation, Cabeza de Vaca remained malnourished much of the time. For years, he was passed as slave from one family to another, finding himself in the position the Spanish readily imposed on indigenous peoples of conquered lands. Still, Cabeza de Vaca was constantly plotting escape. Finally, he and two Spaniards and one enslaved Moroccan who had belonged to another expedition member slipped away in an attempt to reunite with their countrymen in Mexico. Walking fragments of the Narvaez quest, they groped inland across sun-scalded land and northward through the stiff range of the Sierra Madre Occidental. It was the final link in an extraordinary journey. On the coast, they had acquired a reputation for healing the sick. Word traveled the indigenous networks of communication, and at villages and encampments on their route, their services were demanded in return for continued passage. Usually, a prayer and sign of the cross over the ill secured the four safety and food. By mid-1535, they had reached north-central Mexico and began moving southwest on ancient trade routes over the Sierra Madre Oriental and down through the Sonoran Desert toward the sunset.

Nearly eight years after being tossed up on a frigid Texas beach, four ghostlike survivors, the only known of Narvaez's original overland party—emaciated, sun bruised, clad in skins, three unrecognizable Christians and a foreign slave—reached their countrymen at San Miguel de Culiacan near the Pacific coast.

NOTES

1. William Carlos Williams, *In the American Grain* (New Directions, 1925), 44.

2. T. S. Eliot, "The Dry Savages," in *T.S. Eliot: Poetry, Plays and Prose* (Atlantic, 2008), 141.

3. Marjory Stoneman Douglas, *Florida: The Long Frontier* (Harper & Row, 1967), 51.

4. Bernal Diaz del Castillo, *The Memoirs of the Conquistador Bernal Diaz del Castillo*, vol. 1, trans. John Ingram Lockhart (J. Hatchard Lockhart, 1844), 302–28.

5. Samuel Eliot Morison and Henry Steele Commager, *The Growth of the American Republic* (Oxford University Press, 1962), 33.

6. *The Account: Álvar Nuñez Cabeza de Vaca's Relación*, trans. Martin A. Favata and José B. Fernández (Arte Público Press, 1962), 46.

7. Robert F. Berkhofer, *The White Man's Indian: Images of the American Indians from Columbus to Present* (Vintage, 1979), 5, 11.

8. Andre Reséndez, *A Land So Strange: The Epic Journey of Cabeza de Vaca* (Basic Books, 2009), 104, 121; *Account: Álvar Nuñez Cabeza de Vaca's Relación*, 23.

9. *Álvar Nuñez Cabeza de Vaca's Relación*, 56.

10. Ibid.

11. Ibid.; Edward W. Kilman, *Cannibal Coast* (Naylor, 1959).

12. Robert A. Ricklis, *The Karankawa Indians of Texas: An Ecological Study of Cultural Tradition and Change* (University of Texas Press, 1996).

13. C. Herndon Williams, *Texas Gulf Coast Stories* (History Press, 2010), 13.

14. Albert S. Gatschet, *The Karankawa Indians: The Coast People of Texas* (Peabody Museum of American Archeology and Ethnology, 1891), 56; Ricklis, *Karankawa Indians of Texas,* 10, 109–10.

15. William C. Foster, ed., *The La Salle Expedition to Texas: The Journal of Henri Joutel 1684–1687* (Texas State Historical Association, 1998), 99.

16. Ricklis, *Karankawa Indians of Texas,* 61.

SOURCES AND CREDITS

Barnett, Cynthia. Excerpt from *Mirage: Florida and the Vanishing Water of the Eastern U.S.* Reprinted with permission from University of Michigan Press, 2007; permission conveyed through Copyright Clearance Center, Inc.

Barry, John. Excerpt from *Rising Tide: The Great Mississippi Flood of 1927 and How It Changed America.* Reprinted with permission of Simon & Schuster, Inc. and ICM Partners. Copyright © 1997 by John M. Barry. All rights reserved.

Bullard, Robert. Excerpt from *Dumping in Dixie: Race, Class, And Environmental Quality.* Westview Press Inc., 1990. Republished with permission of Taylor and Francis Group; permission conveyed through Copyright Clearance Center, Inc.

Corthell, E. L. Excerpt from "The Delta of the Mississippi River," *The National Geographic Magazine,* vol. 8, no. 12, Dec. 1897.

Crone, Moira. Excerpt from *The Not Yet.* University of New Orleans Press, 2012. Reprinted by permission of Moira Crone and University of New Orleans Press.

Davis, Jack E. Excerpt from *The Gulf: The Making of an American Sea.* W. W. Norton & Co., 2017. Copyright © 2017 by Jack E. Davis. Used by permission of Liveright Publishing Corporation.

Douglas, Marjory Stoneman. Excerpt from *The Everglades: River of Grass,* 3rd ed. Rowman & Littlefield, 1997. Used by permission of Rowman & Littlefield Publishing Group. All rights reserved.

Faulkner, William. Excerpt from "Old Man," from *The Wild Palms.* Random House, 1939. Copyright © 1939 and renewed 1967 by Mrs. William Faulkner and Mrs. Paul D. Summers. Used by permission of Random House, an imprint and division of Penguin Random House LLC. All rights reserved. Published by Chatto & Windus. Reprinted by permission of The Random House Group Limited. Copyright © 1940.

Field, Martha. "Last Island," *New Orleans Daily Picayune,* July 29, 1888, Orig. pub. *Catharine Cole: Voyages around Louisiana,* eds. Joan B. McLaughlin and Jack McLaughlin. University of Mississippi Press, 2006. Reprinted with permission from University of Mississippi Press.

Florida Tribe of Eastern Creek Indians, Excerpt from "Petition for Recognition of the Florida Tribe of Eastern Creek Indians." 1978. Reprinted with permission of the Tribal Council of the Muscogee Nation of Florida. This is dedicated on behalf of the people of the Florida Tribe of Florida Tribe of Eastern Creek Indians, Muscogee Nation of Florida, our past leaders, and the ancestors who continue to watch over us and walk with us through our sovereign struggle.

Frankland, Peggy. Excerpt from *Women Pioneers of the Environmental Movement*. University of Mississippi Press, 2013. Reprinted with permission from University of Mississippi Press.

Galbraith, Kate, and Asher Price. Excerpt from *The Great Texas Wind Rush: How George Bush, Ann Richards, and a Bunch of Tinkerers Helped the Oil and Gas State Win the Race to Wind Power*. University of Texas Press, 2013. Reprinted by permission of University of Texas Press.

Gessner, David. Excerpt from *Tarball Chronicles: A Journey Beyond the Oiled Pelican and Into the Heart of the Gulf Oil Spill*. Milkweed Editions, 2011. Reprinted with permission by David Gessner and Scovil Galen Ghosh Literary Agency, Inc.

González, Jovita. "El Cenizo," "The Mocking Bird," and "The Guadalupana Vine," from *Texas and Southwestern Lore*, ed. J. Frank Dobie, (Publications of the Texas Folklore Society Vol. 6). Southern Methodist University Press, 1927; reprint 2000 University of North Texas Press.

Grunewald, Michael. Excerpt from *The Swamp: The Everglades, Florida, and the Politics of Paradise*. Simon & Schuster, 2006. Reprinted with the permission of Simon & Schuster, Inc. All rights reserved. Copyright © 2007 by Michael Grunwald. Used by permission of The Wylie Agency.

Harjo, Joy. "New Orleans," from *She Had Some Horses*. Copyright © 1983 by Joy Harjo. Used by permission of W. W. Norton & Company, Inc.

Harris, Eddy. Excerpt from *Mississippi Solo*. Nick Lyons Books, 1st edition, 1988. Reprinted by permission of SLL/Sterling Lord Literistic, Inc.

Hearn, Lafcadio. Excerpt from "Chita: A Memory of Last Island," *Harper's New Monthly Magazine*, 1888, orig. pub.

Hochschild, Arlie. Excerpt from *Strangers in Their Own Land: Anger and Mourning on the American Right*. The New Press, 2016. Copyright © 2016 by Arlie Russell Hochschild. Reprinted by permission of The New Press, http://www.thenewpress.com.

Houck, Oliver A. Excerpt from *Down on the Batture*. Reprinted with permission from University Press of Mississippi, 2010. Pp. 35-40.

Hurston, Zora Neale. Excerpt from "Their Eyes Were Watching God" Copyright 1937 by Zora Neale Hurston; Copyright renewed 1965 by John C. Hurston. First published in Great Britain by Virago, an imprint of Little, Brown Book Group. Reprinted by permission of the Proprietor. / Chapter 18 (pp. 154–167), from Their Eyes Were Watching God, by Zora Neale Hurston. Reprinted by permission of HarperCollins Publishers.

Juhasz, Antonia. Excerpt from "Thirty Million Gallons Under the Sea: Following the Trail of BP's Oil in the Gulf of Mexico," *Harper's Magazine*, June 2015. Copyright

Harper's Magazine. All Rights Reserved. Reproduced from the June issue by special permission.

Lerner, Stephen D. Excerpt from *Diamond: A Struggle for Environmental Justice in Louisiana's Chemical Corridor*, Massachusetts Institute of Technology Press, 2004, pp. 1–5. Reprinted with permission of The MIT Press.

Marshall, Bob. Excerpt from "Gulf of Mexico Oil Spill Is Just the Latest Blow for Delacroix," *The Times-Picayune*, August 1, 2010. Republished with permission by NOLA Media Group and Bancroft Media.

Marshall, Bob, Brian Jacobs, and Al Shaw. Excerpt from "Losing Ground." Published in collaboration between *The Lens* and *ProPublica,* Aug. 28, 2014. Reprinted with permission from *The Lens* and *ProPublica*.

McPhee, John. "Atchafalaya," *The Control of Nature*. Copyright © 1989 John McPhee. Reprinted with permission from Farrar, Straus, and Giroux.

Mizelle, Richard M., Jr. Excerpt from *Backwater Blues: The Mississippi Flood of 1927 in the African American Imagination*. University of Minnesota, 2014. Copyright 2014 by the Regents of the University of Minnesota. Reprinted with permission from University of Minnesota Press.

Muir, John. Excerpt from *A Thousand-Mile Walk to the Gulf.* Houghton Mifflin, 1916.

Neufeld, Josh. "Illustrations," from *A.D.: New Orleans after the Deluge*. Copyright © 2009 by Josh Neufeld. Used by permission of Pantheon Books, an imprint of the Knopf Doubleday Publishing Group, a division of Penguin Random House LLC. All rights reserved.

Nobel, Justin. "The Louisiana Environmental Apocalypse Road Trip." *Longreads*, June 2017. Reprinted by permission of the author, Justin Nobel.

Orlean, Susan. "A Green Hell" from *The Orchid Thief*. Copyright © 1998 by Susan Orlean. Used by permission of Random House, an imprint and division of Penguin Random House LLC. All rights reserved (US) / Published by William Heinemann. Reprinted with permission by the Random House Group Ltd. Copyright 1999 (UK).

Rawlings, Marjorie Kinnan. Excerpt from *The Yearling*. Copyright © 1938 by Marjorie Kinnan Rawlings; copyright renewed (c) 1966 by Norton Baskin. Reprinted with permission of Atheneum Books for Young Readers, an imprint of Simon & Schuster Children's Division. All rights reserved (US). *The Yearling* by Marjorie Kinnan Rawlings. Copyright © 1938 by Marjorie Kinnan Rawlings, renewed © 1966 by Norton Baskin. Used by permission of Brandt & Hochman Literary Agents, Inc. All rights reserved (UK).

Rosengarten, Theodore. Excerpt from *All God's Dangers* by Theodore Rosengarten. Copyright © 1974 by Theodore Rosengarten and the Estate of Ned Cobb. Used by permission of Alfred A. Knopf, an imprint of the Knopf Doubleday Publishing Group, a division of Penguin Random House LLC. All rights reserved.

Tidwell, Mike. Excerpt from *Bayou Farewell: The Rich Life and Tragic Death of Louisiana's Cajun Coast*. Copyright © 2003 by Mike Tidwell. Used by permission of Pantheon Books, an imprint of the Knopf Doubleday Publishing Group, a division of Penguin Random House LLC. All rights reserved.

Trethewey, Natasha. "Liturgies." From *Beyond Katrina*. Reprinted with permission by University of Georgia Press, 2010.

Satija, Neena, Kiah Collier, Al Shaw, Jeff Larson, and Ryan Murphy. "Hell or High Water." Reprinted with permission from *The Texas Tribune*, *Reveal*, and *ProPublica*, March 3, 2016.

Stouff, Roger. "Back End of the Canal." Originally published in *The St. Mary & Franklin Banner-Tribune*, August 27, 2004. Reprinted with permission from the author.

Ward, Jesmyn. *Salvage the Bones*. Bloomsbury Publishing, 2011. Copyright Jesmyn Ward. Reprinted with permission of Bloomsbury Publishing, Inc.

Wilson, Diane. Excerpt from *An Unreasonable Woman: A True Story of Shrimpers, Politicos, Polluters, and the Fight for Seadrift, Texas*. Copyright 2005 by Diane Wilson, used with permission from Chelsea Green Publishing, http://www.chelseagreen.com.

Wilson, Edward O. Excerpt from *Half-Earth: Our Planet's Fight for Life*. Copyright © 2016 by Edward O. Wilson. Used by permission of Liveright Publishing Corporation.

APPENDIX 1

Collected Texts in Thematic Order

Environmental Justice and Activism

John Muir, *A Thousand-Mile Walk to the Gulf* (1916)

Marjory Stoneman Douglas, *The Everglades: River of Grass* (1947)

Theodore Rosengarten, *All God's Dangers* (1974)

Florida Tribe of Eastern Creek Indians, "Petition for Recognition" (1978)

Joy Harjo, "New Orleans," *She Had Some Horses* (1983)

Robert Bullard, *Dumping in Dixie: Race, Class, and Environmental Quality* (1990)

Roger Emilie Stouff, "The Back End of the Canal" (2003)

Steve Lerner, *Diamond: A Struggle for Environmental Justice in Louisiana's Chemical Corridor* (2005)

Diane Wilson, *An Unreasonable Woman: A True Story of Shrimpers, Politicos, Polluters, and the Fight for Seadrift, Texas* (2005)

Peggy Frankland, *Women Pioneers of the Louisiana Environmental Movement* (2013)

Weather Systems

Catherine Cole, "Last Island," *New Orleans Daily Picayune* (1888)

Lafcadio Hearn, *Chita: A Memory of Last Island* (1889)

Zora Neale Hurston, *Their Eyes Were Watching God* (1937)

Eddy Harris, *Mississippi Solo* (1988)

Josh Neufeld, *A.D.: New Orleans After the Deluge* (2010)

Natasha Trethewey, *Beyond Katrina: A Meditation on the Mississippi Gulf Coast* (2010)

Jesmyn Ward, *Salvage the Bones* (2011)

Kate Galbraith and Asher Price, *The Great Texas Wind Rush: How George Bush, Ann Richards, and a Bunch of Tinkerers Helped the Oil and Gas State Win the Race to Wind Power* (2013)

Neena Satija, Kiah Collier, Al Shaw, Jeff Larson, and Ryan Murphy, "Hell and High Water," *The Texas Tribune, Reveal, ProPublica* (2016)

Controlling and Polluting Ecologies

E. L. Corthell, "The Delta of the Mississippi River" (1897)

John McPhee, "Atchafalaya," *The Control of Nature* (1989)

John Barry, *Rising Tide: The Great Mississippi Flood of 1927 and How It Changed America* (1997)

David Gessner, *The Tarball Chronicles: A Journey Beyond the Oiled Pelican and Into the Heart of the Gulf Oil Spill* (2011)

Bob Marshall, Brian Jacobs, and Al Shaw, "Losing Ground" *The Lens, ProPublica* (2015)

Antonia Juhasz, "Thirty Million Gallons Under the Sea" *Harper's Magazine* (2015)

Arlie Hochschild, *Strangers in Their Own Land: Anger and Mourning on the American Right* (2016)

Justin Nobel, "The Louisiana Environmental Apocalypse Road Trip," *Longreads* (2017)

Inundations

William Faulkner, "Old Man," *The Wild Palms* (1939)

Mike Tidwell, *Bayou Farewell: The Rich Life and Tragic Death of Louisiana's Cajun Coast* (2003)

Bob Marshall, "A Paradise Lost," *The Times Picayune* (2010)

Moira Crone, *The Not Yet* (2012)

Richard M. Mizelle Jr., *Backwater Blues: The Mississippi Flood of 1927 in the African American Imagination* (2014)

Animal and Plant Entanglements

Jovita González, "El Cenizo," "The Mocking Bird," and "The Guadalupana Vine," *Texas and Southwestern Lore* (1927)

Marjorie Kinnan Rawlings, *The Yearling* (1938)

Susan Orlean, *The Orchid Thief: A True Story of Beauty and Obsession* (1998)

Michael Grunewald, *The Swamp: The Everglades, Florida, and the Politics of Paradise* (2007)

Cynthia Barnett, *Mirage: Florida and the Vanishing Water of the Eastern U.S.* (2008)

Oliver Houck, *Down on the Batture* (2010)

Edward O. Wilson, *Half-Earth: Our Planet's Fight for Life* (2016)

Jack E. Davis, *The Gulf: The Making of an American Sea* (2017)

APPENDIX 2

A Very Limited List of Additional Suggested Reading

Gulf Coast Books

Walter Anderson. *The Horn Island Logs*. U of Mississippi P, 1981.

Cynthia Barnett. *Rain: A Natural and Cultural History*. Broadway, 2016.

Shane K. Bernard. *Teche: A History of Louisiana's Most Famous Bayou*. U P of Mississippi, 2016.

Eric D. Bookhardt. *Geopsychic Wonders of New Orleans*. Contemporary Art Center, 1977.

Charles Bowden. *Killing the Hidden Waters*. U of Texas P, 1977.

Sarah Broom. *The Yellow House*. Grove, 2019.

Robert D. Bullard and Beverly Wright. *Race, Place, and Environmental Justice after Hurricane Katrina*. Westview, 2009.

David M. Burley. *Losing Ground: Identity and Land Loss in Coastal Louisiana*. U P of Mississippi, 2009.

Rachel Carson. *The Edge of the Sea*. Houghton, Mifflin, 1955.

———. *The Sea Around Us*. Oxford U P, 1951.

———. *Under the Sea Wind: A Naturalist's Picture of Ocean Life*. Simon & Schuster, 1941.

Craig Colton. *An Unnatural Metropolis: Wresting New Orleans from Nature*. LSU P, 2005.

Jack E. Davis. *An Everglades Providence*. U of Georgia P, 2009.

Dave Eggers. *Zeitoun*. Vintage, 2010.

William Faulkner. "The Bear," *Go Down, Moses*. Penguin Random House, 1942.

Gail Fishman. *Journeys through Paradise*. U P of Florida, 2000.

LeAnne Howe. *Shell Shaker*. Aunt Lute, 2001.

Rowan Jacobsen. *Shadows on the Gulf: A Journey through Our Last Great Wetland*. Bloomsbury USA, 2011.

Gloria Jahoda. *River of the Golden Ibis*. U P of Florida, 2000.

Antonia Juhasz. *Black Tide*. John Wiley & Sons, 2011.

Eben Kirksley. *The Multispecies Salon*. Duke U P, 2014.

Yusef Komunyakaa. *Dien Cai Dau*. Wesleyan U P, 1988.

Erik Larson. *Isaac's Storm: A Man, a Time, and the Deadliest Hurricane in History*. Vintage, 2000.

Peter Matthiessen. *Killing Mr. Watson*. Vintage, 1990.

Janet McAdams, Geary Hobson, and Kathryn Walkiewicz. *The People Who Stayed: Southeastern Indian Writing after Removal*. U of Oklahoma P, 2010.

John McQuaid and Mark Schleifstein. *Path of Destruction: The Devastation of New Orleans and the Coming Age of Superstorms*. Little, Brown, 2006.

Christopher Rieger. *Clear Cutting Eden: Ecology and the Pastoral in Southern Literature*. U of Alabama P, 2009.

Ellen Griffith Spears. *Baptized in PCBs: Race, Pollution, and Justice in an All-American Town*. U of North Carolina P, 2016.

Natasha Trethewey. *Native Guard*. Houghton, Mifflin. 2006.

Zackary Vernon. *Ecocriticism and the Future of Southern Studies*. LSU Press, 2020.

Other Environmental Writing

Edward Abbey. *Desert Solitaire*. McGraw-Hill, 1968.

Margaret Atwood. *Oryx and Crake*. McClelland and Stewart, 2003.

Mary Hunter Austin. *The Land of Little Rain*. Houghton, Mifflin, 1903.

Wendell Berry. *The World-Ending Fire: The Essential Wendell Berry*. Counterpoint, 2019.

Octavia Butler. *Parable of the Sower*. Four Walls Eight Windows, 1993.

Rachel Carson. *Silent Spring*. Houghton, Mifflin, 1962.

Willa Cather. *O Pioneers!*. Houghton, Mifflin, 1913.

Annie Dillard. *Pilgrim at Tinker Creek*. Harper's Magazine Press, 1975.

Jill Ker Conway. *The Road to Coorain*. Vintage, 1990.

Susan Fenimore Cooper. *Rural Hours*. U of Georgia P, 1998.

Camille T. Dungy. *Black Nature: Four Centuries of African American Nature Poetry*. U of Georgia P, 2009.

Amitov Ghosh. *The Hungry Tide*. Mariner, 2005.

Nadine Gordimer. *The Conservationist*. Penguin, 1983.

Linda Hogan. *Solar Storms*. Scribner, 1994.

Robin Wall Kimmerer. *Braiding Sweetgrass: Indigenous Wisdom, Scientific Knowledge, and the Teachings of Plants*. Milkweed, 2013.

Elizabeth Kolbert. *Field Notes from a Catastrophe: Man, Nature, and Climate Change*. Bloomsbury USA, 2016.

———. *The Sixth Extinction: An Unnatural History*. Henry Holt, 2014.

Aldo Leopold. *A Sand County Almanac*. Oxford U P, 1949.

Barry Lopez. *Arctic Dreams*. Bantam, 1996.

Peter Matthiessen. *The Snow Leopard*. Penguin, 1978.

Michael McCarthy. *The Moth Snowstorm: Nature and Joy*. New York Review Books, 2016.

Bill McKibben, ed. *American Earth: Environmental Writing since Thoreau*. Library of America, 2008.

———. *The End of Nature*. Penguin Random House. 1989.

Richard Powers. *The Overstory*. Norton, 2018.

Janisse Ray. *Ecology of a Cracker Childhood*. Milkweed, 1999.

Elizabeth Rush. *Rising: Dispatches from the New American Shore*. Milkweed, 2018.

Nicole Seymour. *Bad Environmentalism: Irony and Irreverence in the Ecological Age*. U of Minnesota P, 2018.

Leslie Silko. *Ceremony*. Penguin, 1977.

Indra Singha. *Animal's People*. Simon & Schuster, 2007.

Rebecca Solnit. *A Paradise Built in Hell: The Extraordinary Communities That Arise in Disaster*. Penguin, 2009.

John Steinbeck. *The Grapes of Wrath*. Viking, 1939.

Henry David Thoreau. *Walden*. Ticknor and Fields, 1854.

Melissa Tuckey. *Ghost Fishing: An Eco-Justice Poetry Anthology*. U of Georgia P, 2018.

Walt Whitman. *Leaves of Grass*. Self-published, 1855.

Terry Tempest Williams. *Refuge: An Unnatural History of Family and Place*. Vintage, 1992.

Ecocriticism

Joni Adamson. *American Indian Literature, Environmental Justice, and Ecocriticism*. U of Arizona P, 2001.

Stacy Alaimo. *Exposed: Environmental Politics and Pleasures in Posthuman Times*. U of Minnesota P, 2016.

Lawrence Buell. *The Environmental Imagination*. Harvard U P, 1995.

Greg Garrard. *Ecocriticism*. Routledge, 2011.

Amitav Ghosh. *The Great Derangement: Climate Change and the Unthinkable*. U of Chicago P, 2016.

Cheryll Glotfelty and Harold Fromm. *The Ecocriticism Reader: Landmarks in Literary Ecology*. U of Georgia P, 1996.

Donna J. Haraway. *Staying with the Trouble: Making Kin in the Chthulucene*. Duke U P, 2016.

Ursula K. Heise. *Imagining Extinction: The Cultural Meanings of Endangered Species*. U of Chicago P, 2016.

Eduardo Kohn. *How Forests Think: Toward an Anthropology beyond the Human*. U of California P, 2013.

Bruno Latour. *Down to Earth: Politics in the New Climate Regime*. Polity, 2018.

Stephanie Lemenager. *Living Oil: Petroleum Culture in The American Century*. Oxford Studies in American Literary History, 2014.

Timothy Morton. *Dark Ecology: For a Logic of Future Coexistence*. Columbia U P, 2016.

Rob Nixon. *Slow Violence and the Environmentalism of the Poor*. Harvard U P, 2011.

Adam Trexler. *Anthropocene Fictions: The Novel in the Time of Climate Change*. U of Virginia P, 2015.

Anna Lowenhaupt Tsing. *The Mushroom at the End of the World: On the Possibility of Life in Capitalist Ruins*. Princeton U P, 2015.

Kathryn Yusoff. *A Billion Black Anthropocenes or None*. U of Minnesota P, 2018.

INDEX OF AUTHORS

INDEX OF CONCEPTS

INDEX OF PLACES

INDEX OF TITLES

Tori Bush is a writer, teacher, and PhD candidate in the English Department at LSU. She previously edited *Unheard Voices: Poetry and Prose by Women Writers in the Orleans Parish Justice Center*. She has had writing published in *Art in America*, *64 Parishes*, and other journals. She received a Monroe Fellowship in 2018 for this book. Bush lives in New Orleans with her husband and dogs.

Richard Goodman is associate professor of creative nonfiction writing at the University of New Orleans. He is the author of several books, including *French Dirt: The Story of a Garden in the South of France*, *The Bicycle Diaries: One New Yorker's Journey Through 9-11*, and *The Soul of Creative Writing*. He has written essays for national media such as the *New York Times* and *Vanity Fair*. In collaboration with New Orleans NPR affiliate WWNO, Goodman created Storyville, a program showcasing original work about New Orleans written by University of New Orleans MFA students.